Education for Struggle

The American Labor Colleges of the 1920s and 1930s

Labor and Social Change,
A SERIES EDITED BY

PAULA RAYMAN and CARMEN SIRIANNI

EDUCATION FOR

STRUGGLE

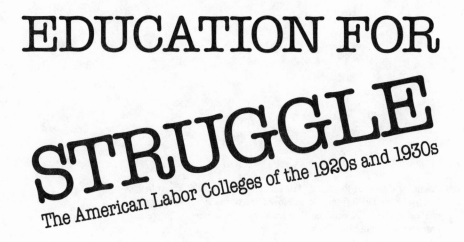

The American Labor Colleges of the 1920s and 1930s

Richard J. Altenbaugh

Temple University Press
Philadelphia

Temple University Press, Philadelphia 19122
Copyright © 1990 by Temple University. All rights reserved
Published 1990
Printed in the United States of America

The paper used in this publication meets the minimum requirements of American National Standard for Information Sciences—Permanence of Paper for Printed Library Materials, ANSI Z39.48-1984

Library of Congress Cataloging-in-Publication Data

Altenbaugh, Richard J.
    Education for struggle : the American labor colleges of the 1920s and 1930s / Richard J. Altenbaugh.
        p.   cm. — (Labor and social change)
    Includes bibliographical references and index.
    ISBN 0-87722-680-6 (alk. paper)
    1. Working class—Education (Higher)—United States.   2. Labor movement—United States.   I. Title.   II. Series.
LC5051.A69   1990
370.19—dc20

                                                    89-34815
                                                        CIP

To Ian and Colin,
so that they may never
forget that their grandparents
were working people

Contents

Acknowledgments

THIS BOOK represents more than a scholarly endeavor; it symbolizes a piece of my personal, professional, and intellectual being. And, as with life, it has been a bittersweet experience. Since 1982, when I embarked on writing this book, Marianne and I have given birth to two wonderful children, Ian and Colin, and acquired another member of the family, Buffy. Children's laughter and a dog's barking have filled our lives, but added chaos to our household, interfering with this work. Ian sat on my lap while I typed and Colin slept in my arms as I attempted to read some additional books and articles, working frantically to meet the publisher's deadline. Yet I would not have traded this existence for anything. Through it all, Marianne remained steadfast in her support of me and the publication of this study. She delayed countless meals for me, arranging the family's schedule around my work periods. Her strength buoyed me through difficult times, her patience encouraged me as I spent precious household money to buy books or pay for photocopying, and her love represented the single most important thing to me. If not for my loving family, this book would not have been written.

Work on the manuscript also accompanied me as I roamed, like an academic nomad, from one institution to another, often delaying my writing. Still, Don Martin and Rolland G. Paulston, at the University of Pittsburgh, nurtured the dissertation and urged me to revive it after a two-year dormancy. Jane Flanders read it several times, providing vital stylistic comments. Edward Berman, at the University of Louisville, never questioned its scholarly worth. I am most grateful to those colleagues and friends in the department of history at Northern Illinois University who provided me with the intellectual environment to complete the manuscript. In particular, J. Carroll Moody patiently read the entire manuscript twice, offering sensitive criticisms. How-

ix

ever, while I may be the parent of this study, Bruce Nelson most certainly is its uncle. I finally found someone whose passion for history matched my own. We spent hours talking on the phone, watching Bears' games at his apartment, or sitting on the floor of my apartment until the early morning hours, discussing, reading, and critiquing our mutual projects. This intellectual process continued as we played baseball during the summers; often digressing to debate the virtues of Adirondack and Louisville Slugger bats. Regional biases, eastern versus midwestern, clouded these latter, more serious, disputations. I also want to thank the students in my graduate seminar on workers' education. Their tireless challenges clarified my thinking. Finally, the congeniality and typing skills of Cheryl Fuller eased the book's composition.

Others have offered long-distance support. My personal discussions in 1982 and 1989 with Jonathan Bloom about Brookwood influenced my thinking about the school. I look forward to his dissertation on the college. My study also seemed to reach full circle with James Barrett's final reading of it. We had been acquaintances as graduate students at Pitt, where the study originated. Finally, I owe an intellectual debt to David Montgomery, whose fertile mind and stimulating work shaped my intellect. I also appreciated his occasional encouraging notes from afar.

I am indebted to archives, archivists, and funding agencies. I mined documents and collections at the New York City Public Library and Tamiment Institute, among other sources scattered throughout Minnesota and Arkansas. Rudolph Vecoli, at the Immigration History Research Center at the University of Minnesota proved hospitable. Nevertheless, this study could not have been completed without the invaluable services and gracious attitudes of George Tselos, Dione Miles, Warner Pflug, and Philip Mason at the Archives of Labor and Urban Affairs, Wayne State University. The National Endowment for the Humanities and the Kaiser Foundation supplied vital funding for research trips.

The people at Temple University Press have been extremely helpful. The initial readers, Paula Rayman and David Roediger, offered positive comments and constructive critiques. Michael Ames expedited the review stage, enthusiastically ushered it through the approval process, and consoled me through the revisions. His staff proved accessible, kind, and professional.

5-98

I only hope that this book reflects all of the love, friendship, and support that nurtured it.

In closing, I hope that this study does more than fill a gap in social and educational history. It does not presume to be the last word. Rather, it is intended to stimulate further research, provoke scholarly debate, and spark other interpretations that elaborate, support, or refute it.

Education for Struggle

The American Labor Colleges of the 1920s and 1930s

Introduction

The Communists have not invented the intervention of society in education; they do but seek to alter the character of that intervention, and to rescue education from the influence of the ruling class.
> —Karl Marx,
> *The Communist Manifesto* (1848)

THIS IS not a story of a sweeping or cataclysmic event involving the famous or powerful. Rather, it is a history of a modest but profound and ambitious attempt by ordinary working people to conceive and support their own educational institutions.

The concept of workers' education, as well as the actual term, originated in Europe, where it was used to describe a widespread movement to educate those who traditionally had been denied more than rudimentary schooling. Workers' education in the United States, however, assumed distinctly American characteristics, growing out of the political and economic struggles of American workers during the early twentieth century. Workers saw education as political. And the American labor college movement of the 1920s and 1930s functioned as an educational experience removed from the aegis of conventional or formal schools, colleges, and universities. During its heyday, it served an important role in social-class formation in the United States. This study examines how the labor colleges fit into the broader workers' education movement, explores the origins and theoretical bases of the colleges, outlines their programmatic characteristics, reviews the backgrounds of teachers and students, analyzes the schools' conflicts, and sketches the careers of some labor college "graduates."

Three labor colleges—Work People's, Brookwood, and Commonwealth—were selected because of their longevity, notoriety, and geographical diversity. Brookwood Labor College, the bastion of labor pro-

3

gressivism, was founded in 1921 in Katonah, New York, and claimed the distinction of being the first residential, coeducational labor college in the nation. However, this claim was somewhat unjustified, since there was an earlier one, Work People's College, which had originated in 1903 in Duluth, Minnesota. It had evolved from a Finnish folk high school to a full-fledged workers' school that served Finnish socialists and later operated as the education center for the Industrial Workers of the World (IWW), or Wobblies, achieving the greatest longevity of all of the labor colleges. Commonwealth College, situated near Mena, Arkansas, in 1925, quickly became known as the "Brookwood of the Southwest" and principally attracted Socialists and labor progressives. Because of their notoriety, rich archives have been preserved for each of these schools. Collectively, these three schools accounted for more than sixty years of workers' education during the early 1900s.

This investigation argues that such workers' schools operated as an integral part of the dialectic. In sharp contrast to the cultural and economic reproduction functions of the formal education system, the labor colleges served liberating rather than adjustive outcomes, addressing the cognitive domain of human agency. They upheld working-class culture and provided adult worker–students with the knowledge and skills necessary to serve the labor movement. The schools also avoided traditional, authoritarian teaching methods and relied heavily on progressive, democratic pedagogy. While these colleges trained labor organizers and activists, many of whom worked to restructure the labor movement during the 1930s, a new social order, as they envisioned it, never became a reality; repression and sectarianism took their toll on the schools. The labor colleges generated only a limited amount of change, normative, structural, or behavioral, but their existence and flourishing for a time are significant. Small workers' colleges appeared incongruous in a country which boasted a national public school system as well as hundreds of colleges and universities. Yet many workers perceived a need for such schools and, with left and liberal intellectual backing, created them and supported them for many years.

A way of understanding the social and educational goals and practices of the labor colleges lies in Antonio Gramsci's analysis of hegemony and social change. Although the schools did not consciously model themselves after Gramsci, their function could be described in terms of his war-of-position strategy. Gramsci elaborates Karl Marx and Friedrich Engels's concept of hegemony, that is, "the ideological predominance of bourgeois values and norms over the subordinate classes."[1] Bourgeois society is maintained through "cultural organizations" such as schools and churches; besides these there exist other agents of hegemony, including "newspapers, reviews, and books, private scholastic institutions, whether linked with the State school or as cultural institutions like Popular Universities."[2] Bourgeois hegemony is pervasive and, at times, subtle. It results in the " 'spontaneous' consent given by the great masses of the population to the direction imprinted on the social life by the fundamental ruling class, a consent which comes into existence 'historically' from the 'prestige' . . . accruing to the ruling class from its position and its function in the world of production." However, this does not preclude the use of force, "the apparatus of State coercion, which 'legally' ensures the discipline of those groups which do not 'consent' either actively or passively."[3]

Therefore, the maintenance of hegemony assumes different strategies and forms, and is a never-ending process. George Lipsitz puts this experience in cruder, but clearer, terms:

> It is almost as if the ideological dogcatchers have to be sent out every morning to round up the ideological strays, only to be confronted by a new group of loose mutts the next day. Under these conditions, dominant groups can ill afford to assume their own society is wholly pacified, although of course it is in their interest to have others think all opposition has been successfully precluded or contained.[4]

Education plays a significant role in hegemony. Martin Carnoy points out that "state schooling [is] class structured, part of the ideological apparatus of the bourgeois State and a contributor to bourgeois hegemony."[5] Schooling functions in an elusive way, not necessarily engaging in overt indoctrination. Rather, as T. J. Jackson Lears asserts, it implicitly denies social-class or group conflict, presenting "a picture of competitive strivers within a benevolent nation–state." Formal schooling also produces intellectuals who rationalize the existing ideology and provide technical expertise for the capitalist mode of production. The school system further gives the impression of facilitating upward mobility, which is necessary in legitimating bourgeois society. And when workers fail to experience social mobility, they blame themselves, not society. Why? Because they have "internalized a class struggle in their own minds," Lears adds, "punishing themselves for their failure to acquire the culture's badges of ability even as they recognize that those badges are often a sham."[6] Finally, schooling is class divided despite its democratic pretense, differentiating the children of the subordinate class from those of the bourgeoisie. This represents an important function in the maintenance of class-based power relations.[7]

Education is also necessary for "every cultural movement which aims to replace" the existing hegemony, and is manifested in the "war of position." This involves the "idea of surrounding the State apparatus with a counter-hegemony, a hegemony created by mass organization of the working class and by developing working-class institutions and culture."[8] The basis of this strategy is not to organize for a frontal attack on the State but, as Carnoy asserts, "to establish working-class organizations as the foundation of a new culture—the norms and values of a new, proletarian society." It is this proletarian hegemony that will confront bourgeois hegemony in a "war of position —of trenches moving back and forth in an ideological struggle over the consciousness of the working class—until the new superstructure . . . surrounds the old, including the State apparatus."[9]

But state schooling cannot cultivate proletarian hegemony. Just as Gramsci proposes to surround the bourgeois State with working-class hegemony, he likewise sees the formal schools as encircled by an educational process guided by revolutionary principles. Carnoy summarizes that process:

> The key to a Gramscian educational strategy, then, is the creation of counter-hegemony *outside* the state schools, and the use of this counter-hegemony to develop organic intellectuals, to mobilize disillusioned bourgeois intellectuals and those traditional working-class intellectuals who have become separated from their class origins, and to contribute to resistance by working-class youth to the use of schools as centers of maintaining and extending bourgeois dominance.[10]

The organic intellectual represents a critical variable in the creation of counter-hegemony, and it is here that we see the educational process unfold. Gramsci defines intellectuals by reference to their commitment and social function, rather than specific intellectual skills or interests. Harold Entwistle explains both the intellectual and economic roles of the organic intellectual:

> As organic, intellectual activity can be socio-political, related primarily to articulation of the economic, social and political dilemmas and interests of a particular class: in this case, where intellectualism is exercised in relation to the socio-political superstructure, a working-class organic intellectual would be the product of liberal or humanistic education, probably exercising leadership as a shop steward, union official, political organizer or propagandist. [11]

The social change process hinges, Entwistle adds, on the fact "that organic intellectuals should be generated from within the working class itself, from amongst the ranks of manual workers and not simply through the conversion of sympathetic intellectuals from other social classes."

Organic intellectuals are needed because, although intellectual skills are independent of the existing hegemony, traditional intellectuals are not tied directly to the working class. First, while they may swear allegiance to the workers' cause, they are "not linked with the people" and do "not emerge from the people," but represent an "expression of the traditional intermediary classes." [12] Second, because of this identification problem, the traditional intellectual will abandon the workers and return to the fold during a crisis. Third, these volunteers, who supposedly commit themselves to the service of the working class, are often welcomed reluctantly; workers appear ambivalent about traditional intellectuals because of their bourgeois roots.

Nevertheless, organic intellectuals are formed only in alliance with traditional intellectuals, who have the requisite knowledge and cognitive skills. But the danger implicit in such a relationship is the cooptation of the former by the latter. This can be prevented, however. The cultivation of organic intellectuals involves keeping them close to the workplace. As Entwistle explains the process: "Being organic, intellectuals would not only originate in the working class, but they would also be in constant conversation with its members." [13] This avoids a paternalistic relationship, of course.

This interaction also represents an extension of the educational process inherent in producing counter-hegemony. The dialectic between intellectuals and workers serves as the basis of praxis, the uniting of theory with practice. And this "essentially educational enterprise," as Entwistle terms it, is relegated to the adult realm. Such political education is rooted in the workplace:

> Workers [have] to be educated with reference both to the technical aspects of work and to its political and cultural implications. Political activity is not a chronological outcome of political education. The two are concurrent, an engagement with theoretical knowledge whilst engaged in productive work and grappling with the political and social predicaments generated by economic activity.[14]

Organic intellectuals should not only have knowledge of the broader political context and be able to organize and lead workers, but they should be attuned to the technical aspects of the production process. These bureaucratic and economic skills are necessary for them to be able to direct workers to take control of the factories and efficiently administer the productive process. As Entwistle explicates it,

> This underlies Gramsci's notion that counter-hegemonic activity must be educational and not simply an attempt at forcible replacement of the capitalist class. Expropriation of the means of production without understanding the relations of production and the administrative and fiscal skills required to organize production in complex industrial enterprises would produce what we now call lame industrial ducks, [as Gramsci puts it] not "the capacity to put into operation and direct the process of production of economic goods."[15]

Following Gramsci's argument, the historical role of the labor colleges becomes clear: They were institutions clearly formulated to serve a counter-hegemonic function, promote proletarian culture, and train a working-class cadre.

The founders and supporters of the labor colleges believed that the education of workers in a full-time residential setting, with a curriculum dominated by the social sciences, best prepared them for service in the labor movement. Their goal was to train a cadre, that is, activists, propagandists, and leaders who could organize workers and sharpen their awareness of the potential for a society controlled by workers. This educational experience represented an important development in social and educational history. It illustrates how working-class radicals created and supported their own educational institutions in their struggle to alter American society.

Still, this study of three labor colleges not only represents a history of working people and their struggles, but also illuminates the history of the noncommunist left during the early decades of this century. The labor colleges identified with the political tenets of the noncommunist left and sought to expand the labor movement based on these beliefs. This ideological distinction served as a fundamental characteristic, given the political complexities of the period. For, as Len De Caux, a former Brookwood student, recalls, "A number of Brookwood students leaned to this body of beliefs and were politely classified as of 'the left.' In their turn, they called those aiding their current campaigns 'progressive'; and those opposing, 'rightwing' or 'reactionary.'" American Federation of Labor (AFL) officials likewise maintained this dichotomous view of the world—albeit conversely and with a vengence: "The 'right' or more conservative were less finicky about definitions. They called all who criticized them from the left—particularly in union elections—'lousy communists' or 'communist stooges'." [16] De Caux's comments could be generalized to the other labor colleges as well. More importantly, his observations reveal the source of serious opposition to Brookwood in particular.

Another, but certainly related, theme of this investigation is that the fragmentation of the political left likewise doomed the schools. Disputes between Socialists, Wobblies, and Communists destroyed any notion of a united political front. The left was too distracted with internecine battles to provide sustained moral and financial backing for the labor colleges. Similarly, internal political feuds among leftists at the labor colleges disrupted the schools and, in some cases, sapped their strength and vitality.

I further emphasize that these labor colleges early on sealed their own fate. Their founders rejected any notion of institutional ties in order to remain politically unfettered. But this penchant for independence, more than any other single factor, brought about their ultimate downfall. The workers' education ventures that fostered and maintained institutional affiliations—that is, union- and university-sponsored workers' education—endured because of their financial links to institutions. Although institutional dependency implied political alignments, it also guaranteed, in most cases, the ongoing existence of the workers' education enterprise. When the founders of the labor colleges chose institutional autonomy as a means of assuring their academic and political freedom, they sacrificed the schools' economic security and financial stability. Thus, political freedom presupposed financial uncertainty.

Finally, in one sense, this book is addressed to two audiences who seldom talk to each other. Labor historians should be taking a closer look at the relationship between the working class and education, and educational historians should be focusing on working-class attitudes towards education and the various institutional manifestations of these perspectives. In another sense, this history fits into the more recent trends in labor and educational historiography. David Montgomery points to a move, among labor historians, away from the narrative of traditional trade-union history and towards a new social history that examines working people and their role in the workplace, probes the complexities of social consciousness, and studies the impact of various economic and political activities and struggles of American workers.[17] Simultaneously, Lawrence Cremin has urged educational historians to move beyond the conventional analysis of schools and colleges. He broadly defines education "as the deliberate, systematic, and sustained effort to transmit, evoke, or acquire knowledge, values, skills, or sensibilities, as well as any learning that results from the effort, direct or indirect, intended or unintended."[18] Cremin's perspective on education goes beyond actual schooling to encompass the didactic role of the workplace, the family, and religion, and of reading and learning received through other channels. He also considers the immediate impact of current affairs—contemporary political, economic, social, and military events.

Herbert G. Gutman's work attempts to synthesize the two somewhat disparate fields of labor history and educational history. He appeals to educational historians to transcend the exclusive study of institutional history by studying nonelite populations—among them working men and women—and to explore such untouched themes as "working-class self-activity and its relationship to class development and formation."[19] Self-activity, for Gutman, represents a metaphor for self-organized working-class behavior of all sorts. Like Gutman, Rolland G. Paulston argues for the study of "nonformal education" in social movements. Paulston's work delineates a theoretical framework to ascertain the social and economic conditions, ideological bases, programmatic character, and contributions of social movement education. He defines such education as structured, systematic, nonschool learning directed at a fairly distinct target population over a relatively short period. "It is, in sum, education that does not advance to a higher level of the hierarchical school system."[20]

My own study runs counter to the prevailing literature in educational history regarding the education of working people. This literature can usually be divided into two interpretive frameworks: The first views the public schools in more positive terms, while the second sees the schools in a somewhat critical light. In the former case, the formal educational system, although not totally devoid of conflict, is placed in a consensus framework; that is, proponents of this view argue that the working class embraced—at times, enthusiastically—the public schools' mission of literacy training, the value of social mobility, and the expansion of democracy. This history of the labor colleges challenges that interpretation, because many working people did, in fact, reject the formal school system. Further, I dispute the second, critical approach, the mechanistic, reproductive theory that asserts that all aspects of schooling function to impose—albeit sometimes subtly—the existing social relationships in order to produce a docile and pliant work force. In either historical interpretation, working people are too often portrayed as accommodating or acquiescent; they were not. History, as E. P. Thompson and David Montgomery assert, is human agency—a cultural approach to the history of class relations. Or, as Mari Jo Buhle and Paul Buhle explain it, Thompson saw social class as a "cultural, more than an economic, category and class consciousness as a collective expression not necessarily encompassed by such institutions as trade unions or political parties."[21]

There exists a more recent, and more vital and useful, interpretive framework that critically examines the interaction between the working class and public education. William J. Reese maintains a conflict perspective in analyzing workers' efforts to fashion the schools. He generally sees education as "contested terrain" during the Progressive era: "Efficiency versus democracy, freedom versus control, respect for labor versus power for the capitalist: these were the many conflicts that citizens confronted on the shopfloor as well as in the local neighborhood school."[22] David J. Hogan similarly traces the conflict over educational policy in Chicago during the early twentieth century. Hogan reminds us that education is inherently political as he analyzes how both capital and labor took a vital interest in what happened in the city's schools, pitting various business groups against the Chicago Federation of Labor and the Chicago Teachers' Federation. He specifically points to workers' efforts to fight progressive reformers and their goal of transforming "childhood, the family, and schooling into adjuncts of the market economy."[23] Hence, working people often attempted to shape public education according to their own needs and interests.

Yet, for all of their strengths, these studies are fixated on the public schools. The concept of education should not be relegated solely to public schooling; besides, worker resistance assumed other guises. What is too often overlooked, as James R. Barrett points out, is the role "unions, radical political parties, and individual workmates play in the education, acculturation, and socialization of immigrant workers and their children." These experiences, he continues, "are important to the discussion of class formation because they direct us to alternative ideas and values beyond those of employers and public schools."[24] This leads to investigations, like Kenneth Teitelbaum's, that reveal the extent of worker dissatisfaction with the public schools and focus on how this became manifested through radical education efforts. Teitelbaum concentrates on socialist weekend schools for children, between 1900 and 1920, that attempted "to counteract the individualistic, competitive, nationalistic, militaristic, and anti-working-class themes that seemed to be prevalent in contemporary public schools and other social institutions."[25] Thus, when working-class efforts to refashion the schools failed, they sometimes created their own alternative institutions.

Montgomery gives us fresh insight into this process of "deliberate human agency" as well as its historiographic significance. As he explicates it: "Class consciousness was more than the unmediated product of daily experience. It was also a project." Working-class activists and liberal intellectuals, "who had linked their aspirations to the workers' movement," persisted in their efforts to cultivate worker solidarity, despite the marshaling of overwhelming state power against them. They relied upon a rich assortment of educational techniques, including the "spoken and printed work, strikes, meetings, reading circles, military drill, dances, athletic and singing clubs, and cooperative stores." Further, as Montgomery points out, these activists and their efforts have been largely ignored: "Both 'history from the bottom up' and the common fixation on great leaders have obscured the decisive role of those whom twentieth-century syndicalists have called the 'militant minority': the men and women who endeavored to mold their workmates and neighbors into a self-aware and purposeful working class."[26] Although Montgomery addresses this concern in a brilliant manner, a fundamental question remains: Where did this "militant minority" come from? That issue leads us to an investigation of workers' education, one means of producing these organic intellectuals.

A literature treating workers' education is beginning to emerge, but it is modest and a significant gap still exists. Barbara Mayer Wertheimer has compiled a comprehensive, practical guide to a variety of current workers' education programs for women. An historical overview is included, but it is too brief.[27] A fine anthology by Joyce L. Kornbluh and Mary Frederickson relies on a historical focus and stresses union and university programs for women workers. However, the foremost independent workers' schools, the American labor colleges, have been largely overlooked.[28] Scattered articles on Work People's College, Brookwood, and Commonwealth, along with a personal account of Commonwealth, have appeared, yet no comprehensive analysis exists that thoroughly compares and contrasts the schools' educational and social goals and programs, as well as their outcomes, within the context of the labor movement.[29]

This study is organized in four parts. The first chapter examines the context from which the labor colleges emerged. It presents the workers' education movement in three categories: union-sponsored education, university experiments, and independent bodies. Union efforts are briefly described through an example, the International Ladies' Garment Workers' Union (ILGWU); a university-sponsored experiment at the University of Wisconsin School for Workers will illustrate the role of higher education in the workers' education movement. Part II, comprising Chapters 2 through 4, is devoted to an intensive study of the social and educational goals and practices of the labor colleges, or independent workers' schools. Chapter 2 treats the motives for founding the labor colleges: socialist dissatisfaction with the nation's public school system and its hegemonic role, their discontent with the status quo policies of the AFL, and in general the influence of early twentieth-century radicalism and middle-class liberalism. The writings and backgrounds of some of the important figures in the founding and support of Work People's College, Brookwood Labor College, and Commonwealth College are scrutinized in this section in order to show how their experiences and viewpoints influenced the social and educational goals of the labor colleges. Chapter 3 examines the educational programs of the colleges, including their curricula, reading lists, nonacademic and off-campus activities, and extension courses to demonstrate how strongly the program conformed to the schools' social and educational goals. The diverse backgrounds of the teachers and students, and the ways in which the labor college environment strove to cultivate egalitarianism and cooperation, are illustrated in Chapter 4.

Part III analyzes how the labor colleges' objectives and practices provoked sharp reactions from trade unionists and employers and generated endless debates among radicals. This incessant conflict and struggle sapped the schools' energies and eroded their bases of support. Chapter 5 depicts many of the schools' day-to-day troubles, focusing on external confrontations. Internal political disputes are the focus of Chapter 6. Chapter 7 analyzes the reasons for the closings of the schools, stressing state repression and sectarianism. In Part IV, the impact the labor colleges had on the American labor movement is shown to be part of their educational legacy. The activities and careers of some labor college graduates are described in the final chapter.

The history of working-class education is fluid and complex. This work emphasizes that the labor colleges did not remain static during their existence. Instead, they evolved, like living organisms, according to the changing needs and demands of the American working class and the labor movement. The schools sprouted when workers needed assistance in their early struggles and in their attempt to formulate a viable labor movement and generate social change. They grew and flourished when workers sought to expand the labor movement. They dwindled and died after the movement had grown and matured. But this organic metaphor alone does not adequately summarize the historical experience of the labor colleges. Just as they were affected by political and social developments within the labor movement, the colleges likewise brought about change by training numerous labor leaders, writers, and organizers, and by directly or indirectly raising the consciousness of many American workers. This often resulted in positive gains for the labor movement, but it also sometimes sparked negative reactions from conservative social forces as well as from more radical groups within the movement. In short, while the labor colleges were on the one hand praised by Socialists and liberals for their progressive contributions to the labor movement, they were on the other hand cursed by angry AFL bureaucrats, conservative politicians, and frustrated employers for their radical activities; at the same time they were being ridiculed by dogmatic Communists for their bourgeois tendencies. To tell the story of their fluctuating fortunes is the purpose of this book.

Hopefully, its educational lessons will not be relegated to the past. The present crisis in the political economy requires the construction of a new social structure of accumulation. To meet this need, the "New Right" has effected a paternalistic state mechanism at best and a hostile one at worst that has eroded the "gains achieved by working-class groups" and dismantled environmental laws, health and safety regulations, income maintenance programs, and the general welfare state. The crucial question remains: Can its opposition put forward a coherent alternative plan? Without subscribing to a cyclical historical perspective, the defensive posture of labor appears reminiscent of that movement during the 1920s. As David Gordon, Richard Edwards, and Michael Reich assert, "To put the matter more directly, in order for the present crisis to be resolved in a way favorable to the working class, the Left must advance a plan for the construction of a new social structure of accumulation. . . . This kind of opportunity for restructuring comes only once a generation."[30] Can education assist in the revitalization and reformulation of the labor movement as it once did?

Part I

A Context for the Labor Colleges

1

Workers' Education

> When labor strikes, it says to its master: I shall no longer work at
> your command. When it votes for a party of its own, it says: I shall
> no longer vote at your command. When it creates its own classes and
> colleges, it says: I shall no longer think at your command. Labor's
> challenge to education is the most fundamental of the three.
> —Henry de Man,
> *New Republic* (1921)

WHY DID many workers seemingly reject the formal education system—public, private, and parochial schools at the elementary and
secondary level, as well as colleges and universities—to pursue their
own educational alternatives? Part of the explanation is obvious: Many
were simply unable to sacrifice the time and wages necessary to attend
high school. Economic conditions determined who attended school.
Low wages forced working-class families, in order to subsist, to withdraw their children from the public schools. In 1900, some two million
children below the age of sixteen worked, and 26 percent of cotton
textile workers in 1907 were less than sixteen years old. Helen Todd, a
factory inspector, reported in her 1909 survey of Chicago factory children that they worked because of economic necessity: "A great part of
child labor comes from the premature death or disability of the father
through industrial accident or disease, or the unemployment of the
father through being engaged in an industry which occupies its people
only a portion of the year at low wages." School offered long-term in-
tangible rewards while work guaranteed immediate monetary gains.
In 1916, a government study of the conditions of child and women

wage earners determined the value of that trade-off. The study encompassed the cotton, glass, and silk industries and reported that working children aged fourteen and fifteen provided for 18.3 percent of the average family income, a crucial margin.[1] A college education became even more unattainable to those without secondary preparation. Even for adult workers who had finished high school, it appeared unlikely that they would have the money or time to attend college.

Working-class leaders and liberal educators provided an ideological rationale for the need for workers' education, arguing that the formal educational system reflected and perpetuated bourgeois society. Although the Gramscian concept of cultural hegemony had not yet been formulated, Alexander Fichlander, director of the ILGWU's Workers' University (founded in 1917), made this point in 1921: "[Workers] feel that they cannot obtain in non-workers' educational institutions correct information on subjects affecting their own interests. They feel that they are frequently deceived and are furnished with interpretations of life which are intended to keep them *docile* and *submissive*. They feel that the truth will be told to them only by those of their own choosing, whose outlook on life is their outlook on life, whose sympathies are their sympathies, whose interests are their interests."[2]

This reasoning appeared to have some historical justification. In many ways, the public schools facilitated the shift in cultural and social patterns of time, work, and discipline engendered by industrial capitalism. Preindustrial society, according to E. P. Thompson, measured time and work by natural cycles, but factory work, "with the time-keeper, the informers, and the fines," required different work habits. Dominated by the exigencies of time and profit, preindustrial work attitudes were considered inefficient and wasteful. Thompson, as well as Herbert G. Gutman, asserts that schools served an important role in spreading the new industrial values. "Once within the school gates," Thompson explains, "the child entered the new universe of disciplined time."[3] Just as time regulated the workplace, it too dominated the school routine. Bells began the school day, divided it into distinct periods of study, and ended the school day for the students. The schools not only taught students to be punctual and regular, but trained them to be industrious, frugal, and orderly as well.

Many early manufacturers recognized the key role schools could play in transmitting the attitudes necessary for an efficient industrial workplace. And as originally cast in Massachusetts, the pioneer in state-financed education, the schools too often were seen as socialization mechanisms. Horace Mann, serving as the first secretary of education in that state, set the tone in his "Report for 1841," stressing the "utilitarian use of education." In compiling his report, Mann conducted interviews and corresponded "with many of the most practical, sagacious, and intelligent businessmen . . . who for many years have had large numbers of persons in their employment." Mann's concerns focused on social rather than intellectual matters; that is, he wanted to know if educated workers tended to be docile, obedient, clean, temperate, frugal, religious, productive, and punctual. The letters that Mann received from manufacturers and contractors, which he included in the text of the report, confirmed his preconceptions. Further, a Lowell, Massachusetts, manufacturer replied that educated workers were less "troublesome," or radical. Consequently, Mann assumed that he had proven, beyond a doubt, the "superiority, in productive power, of the educated over the uneducated laborer."[4] Mann's views achieved an immediate and profound impact, as Maris A. Vinovskis points out: "The 'Report' was hailed throughout the nation and abroad as evidence of the importance of further school reforms. The New York Legislature ordered 18,000 copies to be printed."[5] Thus education became popular among many employers solely for its "economic value." There appeared little doubt that the schools usually served capital's interests, not labor's.

Public school teachers often employed harsh methods in order to instill the "right" habits and attitudes in working-class children. This became clear in Todd's survey: "Of some 800 children questioned, 269 gave as their one reason for preferring a factory to a school, that they were not hit there." One child described his school experiences to Todd: "They hits ye if ye don't learn, and they hits ye if ye whisper, and they hits ye if ye have string in yer pocket, and they hits ye if yer seat squeaks, and they hits ye if yer scrape yer feet, and they hits ye if ye don't stan' up in time, and they hits ye if yer late, and they hits ye if ye forget the page."[6] Ironically, at times school discipline seemed to be far more oppressive than factory work. "Nothing that a factory sets them to do," Todd related, "is so hard as learning."

In sum, the American public school reproduced and legitimated the existing social system. Supported by manufacturers and promoted by schoolmen, the schools rarely served the poor. As Michael Katz summarizes it, the elite "wished to preserve the distribution of power and resources that existed, permitting just enough social mobility . . . to assure social peace." Public education therefore served bourgeois hegemony. Relying on a Gramscian framework, Katz adds that "the popular acceptance of public education represented ideological hegemony: the unselfconscious and willing acceptance of a direction imposed on social life by the dominant fundamental group."[7]

Some working-class leaders recognized this dilemma. Writing in 1896, Eugene V. Debs saw the formal education system, particularly higher education, as at best "not equipped to solve labor problems," and at worst "arrogantly hostile to labor."[8] In a similar vein, Victor Berger, writing in 1915, argued against the public schools falling under the sole influence of the capitalists, making the "schools into 'efficient,' card-catalogued, time clocked, well bossed factories for the manufacture of standardized wage slaves."[9]

Some workers attempted to rectify this situation. As William J. Reese points out, Berger supported efforts to democratize the schools because he, like others, saw education as a "decidedly political enterprise." Hence, in a few cases, radicals, like Berger, attempted to generate change within the public schools by backing the election of radical candidates to serve on school boards, but these efforts proved to be sporadic and generally disappointing.[10] Frustrated and alienated by their failure to make an impact on mainstream education, many radical labor leaders and liberal critics articulated the need for an alternative educational experience controlled by workers for workers. Unlike formal and public education, its supporters claimed, workers' education would contribute to an enlarged and militant labor movement. As an integral part of a social-class movement, workers' education was to function, according to Richard W. Hogue, as "labor's newest weapon in the defense of its rights and the support of its progress."[11]

Educational efforts sponsored by American workers and their organizations represented a long tradition. The origins of these educational activities have been traced to the colonial apprenticeship system. While this system emphasized "mechanical arts," it also included a smattering of general education. The tradition finally produced mechanics' institutes, which originated in Great Britain and quickly spread to the United States, peaking during the 1830s. The institutes attempted to teach master craftsmen, journeymen, and apprentices, through guest lecturers, the scientific principles behind their vocations. In addition to popularizing science, they taught the values of hard work and social mobility. The institutes maintained reading rooms and libraries. From the outset, the Franklin Institute of Philadelphia, established in 1824, represented the best of the American mechanics' institutes. Distinguished by a varied and active program of teaching, research, and publication, it hired a permanent faculty, scheduled regular classes, and maintained an impressive neoclassical hall. As Bruce Sinclair asserts: "While the pattern for its structure apparently came from mechanics' institutes in Great Britain, the Philadelphia organization embodied ideals already in the American character." [12] Lyceums combined instruction and amusement for a low fee, provided newspapers, musical entertainment, gymnastics, and dancing, and offered to teach reading, writing, grammar, sewing, and knitting.

Short-lived and infrequent, these educational endeavors may be best characterized as informal education. More importantly, they maintained an apolitical approach. Mechanics' institutes, lyceums, apprentices' libraries, and other such associations shared similar goals, serving individualistic rather than social ends. Although under artisan control, these efforts generally avoided social-class distinctions, stressing self-improvement in the rising democracy. This was not surprising given the ambiguous composition of workingmen's organizations. The term "working man" was taken in its literal sense, and the term "workingmen's association" had broad connotations. A member of a workingmen's organization did not necessarily have to belong to a laboring, sweat-of-the-brow class. Workingmen's associations during the early 1800s included merchants, manufacturers, gentlemen, tailors, teachers, carpenters, smiths, masons, painters, farmers, and many others who simply listed no occupation. Men of wealth as well as the propertyless belonged to these organizations. Nor did workingmen dominate them. "The unusual nature of this early labor movement," Edward Pessen states, "is best illustrated in the fact that among its leaders were men who employed the labor of others." [13]

Education assumed a more political role with the advent of national trade unions and the emergence of a more class-conscious working class. William Sylvis, of the National Labor Union (NLU), urged workers to found and control their own reading rooms and libraries. The efforts of Uriah Stephens and Terence V. Powderly in the Knights of Labor likewise raised education to a political level. Education, along with secrecy and cooperation, was to play a critical, but vague, role in uniting workers in a general mass organization. Further, Bruce C. Nelson describes how the class-conscious membership of various radi-

cal associations in Chicago during the 1870s and 1880s "actively created, maintained, and expanded a vital, militant, and socialist culture
inside the city's working class." [14] They relied principally on informal
activities, such as singing societies, theater groups, socialist and anarchist Sunday schools, dances, picnics, and parades and processions.
Still, while more political, these educational efforts by workers maintained ambiguous goals—at least for the NLU and the Knights—and
remained largely informal and loosely structured.

Nevertheless, such preinstitutional educational activities revealed
a nascent pedagogy. In Chicago, both the clubs and the radical press
promoted the cause, served didactic roles, and fostered solidarity.
Socialist and anarchist clubs traced their roots to the pre–Civil War
period. A club functioned as lyceum, library, schoolhouse, benefit
society, and social center. It grew out of the traditions of the mechanics' institutes and the Arbeiter-Verein.

Promoting republicanism and artisan culture, the Arbeiter-Verein
became the German immigrant equivalent of the mechanics' institute.
But the Arbeiter-Verein represented a more politicized version, cultivating class consciousness. The Chicago radical press, beginning in
the 1850s, predated the organized socialist movement with several
socialist and anarchist weeklies. By 1886, such prominent newspapers
as the *Alarm* and the *Arbeiter–Zeitung* contained lively social commen-
tary, demonstration and strike reports, union proceedings, readers'
correspondence, reprints from other socialist publications, and educational articles on revolutionary theory. The radical press also sponsored publishing organizations such as the Socialist Publishing Society, which, founded in 1874, was the oldest and most emulated of such
organizations, distributing tens of thousands of books, pamphlets,
and circulars in the early 1880s. [15]

Structured, class-conscious workers' education—both the entity
and the term—originated in Europe. However, it was the British
workers' education movement that had the most significant impact,
both in goals and structure, on the United States. In 1899, Walter
Vrooman and Charles Beard, two Americans, started Ruskin College, for working-class students, at Oxford. It aimed to equip students
for effective service in the British labor movement. However, within
months, militant students sympathetic to syndicalism and the IWW
formed the Plebs League. These students recognized class struggle
as inevitable and wanted an even more radical approach to workers'
education. They formally seceded from Ruskin in 1909 and created the

Central Labour College (CLC), moving it to London in 1911. The Plebs League spread the concept of CLC workers' education to the provinces and organized classes, in association with trade unionists and socialists, that met on evenings and Sundays. This represented a highly political educational activity, stressing working-class unity and solidarity in action enlightened by a solid grounding in the social sciences. In 1921, these local branches—called "labour colleges"—were recognized nationally as the National Council of Labour Colleges (NCLC). The NCLC claimed autonomy as its key characteristic. Its independence from any state agency or university made it markedly different from the earlier Workers' Education Association (WEA), founded in 1903 by a small group of trade unionists. The WEA served broad goals, emphasizing education for individual growth and enrichment. The Association furthered its objectives through its close relationship with the university community and other mainstream educational bodies. In particular, the WEA maintained tutorials at Oxford that attracted many white-collar students.[16] Both the class-conscious approach of the labour colleges and the self-improvement emphasis of the WEA had American counterparts.

Although U.S. workers' schools and colleges had appeared early in this century, the intensification of socialist ideas and working-class activism during and after the war stimulated their growth. As de Man described the phenomenon in 1921, "Amidst the industrial and political turmoil that expresses the gradual awakening of the American labor movement to a broader sense of social responsibility, there is one symptom of changed behavior that is less conspicuous, but more fundamental perhaps than any other. This is the creation, in a number of cities, of a network of educational institutions by the labor movement, for the purposes of the labor movement." By the 1920s, some three hundred workers' educational activities were undertaken by a variety of organizations, with some ten thousand worker–students in attendance. Dagmar Schultz analyzes the development incisively:

> Workers' education is inherently political. It speaks to the special interests of an economic class and/or the groupings and organizations within it. The class whose concerns it addresses is crucial and indispensable in determining the political nature of a given society. Workers' education is potentially one instrument through which this political nature may be given direction. Whether or not this potential is realized and what forms it takes depends on the

agents in workers' education, on its clientele, and on the historical setting in which they find themselves. [17]

Diverse groups and agencies created these workers' education classes and schools, and their social and educational purposes and programs reflected these differences.

Feminism played a key role in the workers' education movement. Women's colleges and schools spearheaded the workers' education movement in the United States. The National Women's Trade Union League (NWTUL), founded by a group of trade unionists and liberal middle-class women in 1903, provided financial support, publicity, and staff assistance for organizing women workers as well as lobbying for legislation that would regulate their hours, wages, and working conditions. Education emerged by 1913 as the League's dominant focus at both the national and local levels. The NWTUL established the Chicago-based Training School for Women Organizers in 1914, which represented the first full-time national labor program in the country and the first adult leadership program for women workers. Because of the limited financial resources of the school, the NWTUL national executive board maintained stiff admission requirements. Guided by recommendations from members of local leagues and union officials, the board based its selections on an assessment of the applicants' intellectual abilities, union experience, leadership potential, and seriousness of purpose. The board also took great pains to avoid antagonizing the American Federation of Labor (AFL) and rejected applicants who might have offended Federation officials. Yet the board refused to conform to racist tendencies in the AFL and accepted black female workers. Scholarships covered students' expenses while they were enrolled in college-level courses at Chicago universities, and students were tutored to compensate for their lack of formal education. Course work included labor history, industrial relations, labor legislation, theory and practice of trade agreements, English, public speaking, and parliamentary procedure. Fieldwork involved organizing and administrative activities under the supervision of the NWTUL and of union officers from the Chicago Federation of Labor. Specifically, the women workers were to gain experience in planning, conducting, and publicizing union meetings, recruiting unorganized workers, handling employee grievances, and writing reports and articles for the press.

In its thirteen years of existence, the program trained forty-four women from seventeen trades. Thirty-two of them remained active in the labor movement throughout their lives. The NWTUL later became one of the principal sponsors of the Bryn Mawr Summer School for Workers and the first union to hold an institute at Brookwood Labor College. The New York League, the largest and most active of the NWTUL's chapters, began evening classes in 1922 under the direction of Hilda Worthington Smith of the Bryn Mawr Summer School. Courses included economics, trade union training, English, public speaking, pottery, and dance theatre. In the span of eleven years, the New York League's evening classes trained some sixteen hundred women workers. [18]

The Socialist party sponsored many educational activities as well. An initial educational effort was made to spread socialist ideas through the press, and the most striking aspects of the socialist press before 1920 were its attention to educating the masses about socialism and its emphasis on the common goals of the party. In 1911 alone, the Socialists sent out thirty-seven different leaflets and pamphlets, which amounted to five million pieces of literature. The party also established the Socialist Lyceum Bureau in 1911, which sent speakers to deliver fifteen hundred lectures to some three hundred socialist locals. In 1912, the Socialist party sponsored 323 daily, weekly, and monthly publications in English and in foreign languages. The total circulation of socialist periodicals in 1913 exceeded two million. [19]

J. A. Wayland's publishing house, located in Girard, Kansas, represented "the largest publishing enterprise of American socialism," with the *Appeal to Reason* serving as "the one national weekly newspaper that unified the movement from coast to coast." Wayland printed the first issue in August 1885, and by 1903 it had accumulated a circulation of over two hundred thousand, maintaining a staff of fifty people. At that time, the *Appeal* claimed the fourth largest circulation in the country, and had become "the largest political weekly ever to be published in the United States." [20] Its staff expanded to one hundred by 1908, and its circulation grew to five hundred thousand subscribers in 1912.

The *Appeal*, like the radical press in general, served an educational and exhortative, if not propagandistic, function. Wayland subsidized Upton Sinclair's research for *The Jungle* and serialized it in the paper throughout 1905. The story portrayed the main character's conversion to socialism, "chiefly as the effect of hearing speeches and reading, not of his economic condition, which the novel describes as having turned him into little more than an animal."[21] Sinclair continued to write for the *Appeal* for ten years.

Ironically, the *Appeal* began its decline in 1912, the year of its peak circulation and the Socialist party's best electoral showing. Several political and personal setbacks accounted for the weekly's demise. Its credibility within the socialist movement was jeopardized by its sensationalized coverage of the infamous McNamara trial. In April 1911 James B. and John J. McNamara, both trade unionists, were arrested in Chicago and Indianapolis, respectively, and illegally extradited to Los Angeles to stand trial for the dynamiting of the Los Angeles *Times* building, which resulted in the death of twenty-one employees. Although Clarence Darrow and Job Harriman, among others, served as their attorneys, the McNamara brothers pleaded guilty, during the highly publicized trial, to the bombing as retribution for the viciously antiunion policies of General Harrison Gray Otis, owner of the newspaper. The plea proved embarrassing to the *Appeal*, which had supported their innocence, waged a defense campaign for them, and marshaled much sympathy on their behalf. On the heels of that tragedy, the federal government opened an investigation of the *Appeal*, "an indication of the seriousness with which the government viewed the paper and the threat of the socialist movement."[22] This action was not surprising, however. The weekly had always encountered less than a cooperative attitude from post office officials—particularly after 1906, when Debs had written defiant articles in defense of William "Big Bill" Haywood during the Steunenberg trial. On December 30, 1905, former Idaho Governor Frank Steunenberg was killed by a bomb that exploded as he opened the gate to his home. Harry Orchard confessed to the murder of the antiunion Steunenberg, who had earned his reputation from his unrelenting strikebreaking efforts against the Western Federation of Miners in the Coeur d'Alenes conflict. Orchard also implicated Haywood, who was illegally extradited to Idaho. Darrow successfully defended Haywood, with the jury finding him not guilty.

Finally, Wayland, despondent over his wife's death, committed suicide, sealing the paper's fate. It continued to be published until 1922, but it had become emasculated. The weekly's new editors supported the war effort, thus avoiding further government harassment. Many disgusted Socialists cancelled their subscriptions, and circulation plummeted. In spite of its later campaign to release Debs from federal prison, the *Appeal to Reason* had long ceased to function as a rallying point for the socialist movement.

Charles H. Kerr and Company, of Chicago, operated "the most significant publishing venture of the socialist movement." The company began as a religious press; Kerr's rationale for its radical publishing efforts stemmed from his concern over ideological dominance by the "ruling class." This appeared "natural" in a society which the major institutions, like "the church, the schools, the personal influence of capitalists and their hirelings, and especially books and newspapers, and the law, with its judges and soldiers," were controlled, serving as the "means employed by capitalists to impose false moral ideas." As Allen Ruff argues, "Typical of the vast majority of socialists in that first decade of the century, Kerr placed all his hope for a brighter future in the effectiveness of an informed, class conscious and politicized electorate."[23] Hence, he forged a publishing business not for personal gain, "but for education, recruitment, and advancement of 'the cause,'" producing countless pamphlets, books, and other publications. He subsidized the firm by selling shares at ten dollars each. Because this represented an exorbitant price for many potential working-class investors, Kerr sold the stock on the installment plan, accepting a dollar a month as payment. However, instead of distributing dividends, he extended book discounts to shareholders.

Kerr produced an extensive list of publications that fell into three basic categories. First, he and his associates imported and translated socialist "classics" from Europe, subsidizing and distributing the first English version of Marx's *Capital*. Second, Kerr published Marxian analyses by American authors, introducing, in March 1899, the "little red books"—a monthly series that boasted thirty-five titles and sold over five hundred thousand copies by May 1902. Third, in 1900, Kerr launched a monthly journal, the *International Socialist Review* (*ISR*). While early editions stressed theory, later editions, after 1908 and under Kerr's personal editorship, emphasized action, becoming the national voice for the left wing of the Socialist party in general and the IWW in particular.

Kerr ensured that the *ISR* served workers' education. The publication used a glossy, colorful format that rivaled its commercial counterparts, but emphasized the diffusion of "scientific socialism" and recruited working people for the socialist perspective. It also critiqued the "inadequacies and class nature of mainstream or 'bourgeois' educational institutions." This commitment to workers' education extended beyond the confines of political economy, encompassing discussions of fine art, evolution, botany, zoology, and anthropology. Mary Marcy, a Kerr staff member and regular contributor, wrote articles on prehistoric society. The monthly further included poetry and short stories by Jack London, Carl Sandberg, Ralph Chaplin, and Joe Hill. Other articles addressed utilitarian matters, such as local organizing techniques and effective street speaking and agitation. Militants across the country sent their practical suggestions to share with their comrades. For Ruff, "The *ISR* in such fashion became an invaluable and inexpensive reference guide and instructional manual for the actual daily nuts-and-bolts mechanics for the cause."[24]

Reflecting the socialist position, Kerr's publications opposed U.S. participation in the First World War and supported the Russian Revolution. As a result, the press suffered repression. Citing the Espionage Act as their authority, post office officials refused to process the *ISR* beginning with the June 1917 issue. Charles H. Kerr and Company managed to survive the war, but the *ISR* did not. Kerr visited Kate Richards O'Hare, endorsing her workers' education venture at Commonwealth College, in 1927, just prior to his retirement. His publishing house continued, though saved from oblivion in 1971 largely through the efforts of long-time socialist, IWW activist, and former Work People's College teacher and director Fred W. Thompson.[25]

During the early 1900s, Socialists across America, but especially in its eastern urban areas, organized socialist Sunday schools for school-aged children. Their mission was not to provide the conventional Bible education commonly associated with church schools. Rather, working-class radicals wanted to provide their children with a formal weekend education that lacked the capitalistic biases dominant in the public schools. As William Reese and Kenneth N. Teitelbaum argue, "The Socialist Sunday Schools represented the most obvious, formal, and widespread educational activity for children ever undertaken by American socialists."[26] The earliest schools—albeit sometimes short-lived—existed in San Jose in 1902, and Chicago, Boston, and Omaha by 1903. By 1911, New York City claimed twelve socialist Sunday schools, while Chicago hosted eight in 1919. Their size fluctuated, but Rochester possessed one of the largest and most successful operations. Beginning with thirty students in 1910, the school, stressing brotherhood, solidarity, good citizenship, and the formation of "good Socialists," grew to a size of over two hundred students in 1912 and eventually accommodated between three and four hundred pupils during the next two years.

The Rand School of Social Science—"the pioneer school of Workers' Education in America," as Marius Hansome, an occasional lecturer at the school, phrased it—likewise possessed socialist roots. Conceived by a group of radical immigrant workers, Marxist intellectuals, and middle-class sympathizers, and supported by a generous bequest from Mrs. Carrie Rand, mother-in-law of George D. Herron, the Iowa socialist writer and propagandist, the school opened in 1906 in New York City, hoping to become the intellectual center of the American socialist movement. By the end of its first year, the Rand School, with such noted lecturers as Charles Beard, Lester Frank Ward, and David Starr Jordan, claimed a gross attendance of 6,819 adult worker–students and offered a variety of subjects that followed basic socialist tenets.

The school's curriculum gained further coherence in 1911, when it introduced the first formal "workers' training course" in the country. Its purpose, Hansome recalled, "was to attract serious-minded men and women . . . and to equip them for better service in the political, trade union, and cooperative activities of the labor and socialist movements."[27] The school granted no degrees, and teaching methods varied: Formal lectures became taboo, whereas textbooks, question and answer periods, examinations, and personal tutoring were stressed. Still, the Rand School chronically suffered from irregular attendance. And worse, the school experienced serious political intrusions from both the right and the left following the war. In its efforts to investigate radical activities in the state of New York, the Lusk committee raided the school, confiscated much of its property, and attempted to outlaw it by introducing an ill-fated bill in the state legislature. Further, leftists at the school wrangled with each other over the school's commitment to radical social change. These external and internal political conflicts crippled the school. Yet, by 1926, the school, bolstered by a scholarship fund donated by the American Fund for Public Service (AFPS), reestablished its workers' training course, geared primarily for part-time evening students.

The IWW also recognized the potential of workers' education for cultivating class consciousness and a revolutionary spirit. Wobblies organized propaganda leagues, industrial education clubs, Sunday evening meetings, and open forums; it also sponsored speakers and

printed and distributed pamphlets. The union published six newspapers, with *Solidarity* and the *Industrial Worker* as its most popular
weeklies. Numerous IWW halls contained libraries and reading rooms
as well. Support for organized educational activities was not always
unanimous, however. For some Wobbly leaders, workers were to be
educated through participation in class warfare; that is, by relying
on direct action activities in the workplace. For other Wobblies, the
ideal working-class intellectual studied to serve the interests of the
working class, to lead the revolution, and to rule the future cooperative commonwealth.[28] Yet, on the whole, workers' education activities
sponsored by both the Socialists and the IWW remained haphazard,
loosely structured, and, at best, part-time experiences.

In sum, workers' education in America served several goals. First,
many workers founded their own presses and formulated their own
classes and schools to counter bourgeois hegemony—particularly that
promulgated by the formal educational system. In this regard, workers' education generally functioned as a consciousness-raising experience. A second, and equally radical, goal of many workers' education
experiments was the reorganization of society along socialist lines.
Furthermore, some labor leaders, among them Joseph Schlossberg and
J. B. S. Hardman, educational director of the Amalgamated Clothing
Workers of America (ACWA), spoke specifically of training workers
to "take control of modern industry."[29] These political objectives were
not the schools' sole aspirations.

There existed a third, more immediate and not necessarily political objective, namely, training leaders for the unions. As unions became structured and bureaucratic, many leaders became concerned
with developing what some of them called "our own trained civil service."[30] Socialists and progressives in such unions as the International
Ladies' Garment Workers' Union (ILGWU), the ACWA, the International Association of Machinists (IAM), and the United Mine Workers
(UMW) spearheaded this effort. Leadership training deliberately became institutionalized, and the unions hoped to reap more effective
leadership, at least in the short run. At the same time, as part of structured leadership training as well as to counter the ample resources of
the corporations, many of these same unions formed the Labor Research Bureau for professional research work to match that available
to corporate management. The Rand School, which promoted Marxist
education to prepare workers for the struggle against and the ultimate

overthrow of capitalism, functioned as the prototype for all of this activity. [31]

Workers continued to experiment with a variety of approaches to workers' education throughout the early decades of this century, the most prominent of which were associated with the trade unions, universities, and independent programs initiated by individuals, special interest groups, or political organizations.[32] While institutional affiliation with a union or university usually entailed constraints that often resulted in the gradual depoliticization of the workers' education program, for the most part independent workers' classes and schools, like the labor colleges, consciously avoided restrictive institutional relationships and functioned as highly politicized versions of workers' education. It was precisely for this reason that union- and university-sponsored workers' education outlived the independent labor colleges.

Workers' Education and the Trade Unions

Jewish workers in New York City created an association in 1885 and the United Hebrew Trades (UHT) three years later. The UHT supported and won a bakery workers' strike in 1889 and a shirtmakers' strike in 1890. In both cases, the UHT gave workers intensive courses in the principles and methods of trade unionism and leadership skills. The ILGWU, organized in 1900, consisted of Jewish, Italian, Bohemian, and Polish immigrant male and female workers. Steeped in socialist thought, it pioneered union activities in the field of workers' education when it established an educational program in 1914. The ILGWU convention that year agreed that the educational programs then available to workers were too sporadic and unsystematic to be useful, and decreed that a more structured approach to workers' education be implemented. With that mandate, Benjamin Schlesinger, ILGWU president, made arrangements with the Rand School to accommodate union members. The school offered three courses—"Trade Unionism," "Methods of Labor Organization," and English—twice a week. Only a hundred members of the union enrolled, however; Because of poor attendance, union officials terminated the modest program. [33]

In spite of the International's aborted effort, many New York City garment worker locals organized grass-roots education activities by creating free libraries, planning concerts and lectures, and sponsoring classes in local public school buildings. These archetypical union education efforts were not only based on socialist principles but, according to Alice Kessler-Harris, also served the special needs of women workers. Male leadership and rank-and-file members often expressed reluctant support for female workers. Feelings of displacement and the need for support, therefore, may have generated the drive on the part of women workers of the ILGWU's Local 25, the New York Waist and Dressmakers' Union, to create an educational department under the leadership of Juliet Stuart Poyntz and then introduce the Unity House concept in 1915. Poyntz established Unity House in Pine Hill, New York, to function as a summer vacation house and recreational retreat for union members and their families, as well as a place for informal discussions and forums. She also organized Unity Centers at local public schools, where workers attended shop meetings, union lectures, and courses in English and physical training taught by board-of-education teachers. [34]

Prompted by the activity and success of its locals in 1916, the ILGWU's General Executive Board approved the formation of a five-member Education Committee, appropriated $5,000 for educational work, and dispatched it to instruct the largely immigrant garment workers in the elements of trade unionism and to train leaders for administrative posts. The union was now formally involved in workers' education.

Given its socialist sympathies, the Garment Workers' Union assumed a much broader and more radical view of the objectives of workers' education than did most labor organizations; training for service in the union was thus intertwined with socialist theory. This union, in fact, represented one of the strongest socialist bastions within the AFL; for John Laslett, "The union vigorously supported the postwar revival of the radical movement, upholding, for example, government ownership of the railroads, as well as the idea of union-owned shops and factories in the garment industry as a 'first step towards collective ownership.'" In spite of their ideological differences, the ILGWU and the AFL maintained cordial relations. Actually, Samuel Gompers, AFL president, and Herman Robinson, the Federation's New York organizer, had helped to keep the International going in New York City during the critical years from 1905 to 1908, and the AFL was particularly helpful on a number of occasions. As Laslett adds, "a sense of loyalty toward the AFL was developed, and there were rarely any suggestions that the ILGWU should withdraw from the Federation altogether, such as were sometimes made in other radical trade unions." Although the ILGWU often used its substantial voting power in behalf of radical resolutions, it did not allow its criticisms to become excessive and reckless. Laslett concludes that the ILGWU "delegates to AFL conventions resisted efforts to require them to vote against Gompers and other conservative officers."[35]

This "social unionism," as the ILGWU's philosophy was dubbed, moved beyond the notion of "pure and simple" unionism by addressing not only the economic concerns of workers for high wages and shorter hours, but also their needs for recreation, education, health care, and housing. As Susan Stone Wong observes, "Social unionism tied the building of a union to the creation of a new and better social order." In so doing, its "philosophy reflected both the practical needs and the political ideals of its immigrant constituency and provided the theoretical underpinnings for workers' education in the ILGWU."[36]

Poyntz accepted the part-time position as the union's first educational director and Fannia Cohn, a vice-president of the union, agreed to serve as the organizing secretary of the Educational Department. Poyntz was born in 1886 in Omaha, Nebraska, was raised in a middle-class family, and went east to attend Barnard College. Because of her outstanding academic performance, Poyntz received a fellowship from the General Federation of Women's Clubs to study at Oxford and the London School of Economics. Poyntz joined the Socialist party in 1909, and in addition to teaching at Barnard, worked with the ILGWU and headed the Rand School's Labor Research Department. In 1917, she abandoned the Socialist party for the newly organized Workers' party. The later bitter disputes between the Communists and the Socialists within the ILGWU forced her to resign from the union. In the early 1920s, Poyntz helped to organize the Communist Workers' School in New York City, but she left shortly thereafter in order to become a top party official and candidate.[37]

As director of the ILGWU's Educational Department, Poyntz expanded the number of Unity Centers and established the Workers' University at Washington Irving High School in New York City. The union's 1918 convention endorsed these activities and budgeted $10,000 toward the continuation of the ILGWU's educational work. The Educational Department's course announcement best expressed its goals: "The work of the Educational Department of the ILGWU is based on a conviction that the aims and aspirations of the workers can be realized through their own efforts in the economic and educational fields. While organization gives them power, education gives them the ability to use that power intelligently and effectively."[38] The Educational Department focused its attention on the New York City locals but maintained contact with those in other cities. The ILGWU increased its educational appropriations to $15,000 and $17,000 in 1920 and 1922 respectively. In 1920, the General Executive Board appointed Dr. Alexander Fichlander, a Brooklyn junior high school principal, as director of the Workers' University. Therefore, by late 1918, when Poyntz resigned and was replaced by Dr. Louis Friedland, the basic direction of the ILGWU's educational program had been charted.

Fannia Cohn remained the heart and soul of the ILGWU's educational activities. Born in Minsk, Russia, in 1885, she had been privately educated by her rather prosperous family for a professional career. Drawn by the allure of radical politics, she joined the outlawed Socialist Revolutionary party in 1901. Three years later she emigrated to New York City and began to study pharmacology. In 1905, she abandoned her studies, dedicated her life to the labor movement, and entered the garment workshops. "For Cohn," Wong argues, "socialism was a basic creed, an article of faith. Unlike Poytnz, however, she eschewed both doctrine and formal party affiliations. As a result, she was able to work with both Socialists and Communists within the ILGWU."[39] This ability was to prove valuable in the volatile ideological climate of the ILGWU during the 1920s. By 1909, Cohn had been elected to the executive board of Local 41, and in 1914 she departed for Chicago to enroll in the NWTUL's training school. In August 1915, she headed the first successful strike of Chicago's dress and white goods workers. She gained instant recognition for her prowess as an organizer and, in 1916, became the first woman vice-president of the ILGWU. A year later she was appointed organizing secretary of the Education Committee.

With a financed, well-organized program, the ILGWU Educational Department emphasized a three-part plan between 1918 and 1924. The Unity Centers served as the backbone of the educational system and provided basic courses in English, which were popular among the predominantly immigrant members. They also arranged lectures in psychology, literature, American history, trade unionism, music appreciation, health, and physical education, and sponsored dances, concerts, and plays. With generally small classes, teachers used a discussion format that emphasized problem-solving skills. The Evening

School Department of the New York City Board of Education supplied the teachers—about forty during the 1922–23 school year—and public school facilities free of charge. The union also invited guest lecturers. In 1922, some thirty-one hundred students attended the eight Unity Centers located in their neighborhoods throughout the New York metropolitan area.

The Workers' University provided opportunities for more advanced and systematic study for union members. The social sciences dominated the curriculum, with four of the main courses under these headings: "Foundations of Modern Capitalism," "Social and Political History of the United States," "Trade Union Policies and Tactics," and "Tendencies in Modern Literature." The ILGWU Educational Department in this case relied upon professional teachers and lecturers. No more than 350 students could attend during any single term, and students could not enroll in courses unless they had prior experience in a workers' education program, preferably a Unity Center. As with the centers, unionists attended the Workers' University without charge, and most completed the course of study.

The ILGWU also developed an Extension Division between 1922 and 1924 that sought to provide educational programs for workers unable to attend regularly scheduled classes. These activities included concerts, forums, and plays in various neighborhoods, and museum excursions. Lectures given in the immigrant workers' native tongue often followed local business meetings. During strikes, organized workers, as well as unorganized workers, were welcome at the lectures given by the union. Finally, with the help of the Extension Division, many locals created libraries. [40]

The educational activities of the ILGWU stirred the interest of other unions. Delegates at the AFL's 1918 convention discussed the successful work of the Garment Workers' Union. The Federation's Executive Council appointed a committee to investigate the ILGWU's educational system as well as other workers' education efforts. At the following convention, the committee praised the International's educational work but declined to make an endorsement. Instead, the committee recommended that workers, through their unions, attempt to adapt the public school system to their needs by securing representation on school boards, gaining wider access to school facilities for adult education classes, and lobbying for the implementation of classes on subjects that specifically benefited the cause of trade unionism: for example, industrial legislation, the history of industry, and the trade union movement. If these efforts should fail, the committee continued, then local labor bodies should organize their own educational activities "with as much cooperation from the public schools as may be obtained." [41]

Although the AFL leadership appeared reluctant to encourage their members to abandon the existing school system, many labor educators, labor leaders, and radicals thought differently and called for a forum for the exchange of ideas about workers' education. On April 2, 1921, the First National Conference on Workers' Education was held in New York City. Cohn presided; Gompers did not attend, but he sent his blessings. The participants discussed the various educational activities sponsored by their unions, comparing enrollment figures, the characteristics of students and teachers, pedagogies, texts, and their ideas about the goals of workers' education in general.

More importantly, these delegates recognized the need for a national organization to facilitate workers' education activities, and the Workers' Education Bureau (WEB), a direct imitation of its British predecessor, the WEA, was the product of the conference. The bureau did no teaching, but rather served as a clearinghouse for information and publicity, maintaining lists of qualified teachers, preparing and publishing syllabi and textbooks, reviewing curricula, and suggesting experiments with different teaching methods. The WEB, in short, supplemented the diverse educational activities of workers' classes and schools sponsored by unions and universities as well as by independent bodies. In addition, early organizers and supporters of the bureau hoped that it would become a link between the conservative trade unionists and the socialist progressives. Membership in the WEB included national and international labor unions, state labor federations, city central labor unions, local labor unions, cooperative associations, and labor education enterprises. Members also included teachers, organizers, educators, and other interested individuals and groups. James H. Maurer, a founder and supporter of Brookwood Labor College, served as chairman of the WEB, and Spencer Miller, Jr., became secretary–treasurer. The executive committee consisted of John Brophy, of the UMW and Brookwood; J. B. S. Hardman, educational director for the ACWA; and Fannia Cohn. Alexander Fichlander, Arthur Gleason, and Thomas Kennedy, among other labor progressives interested in workers' education, made up the advisory committee. [42]

In addition to the pioneering efforts of the ILGWU's educational program, the union's Educational Department exerted a leadership role in the burgeoning workers' education movement. In 1921, with the launching of the WEB, Brookwood Labor College, and the Bryn Mawr Summer School for Women Workers in Industry, the workers' education movement appeared to be assuming a central role in the labor movement. Cohn and the bureau's other organizers hoped it could become the movement's centerpiece. Cohn also saw to it that the International provided Brookwood with students and scholarships as well as moral and political support. She was less sanguine about the Bryn Mawr experiment. Her experiences at the NWTUL Training School had created doubts about the summer school concept for women workers. More significantly, she resented the middle- and upper-class women who ran these purported workers' education programs: as Wong argues, "Cohn's attendance at the NWTUL's school reinforced her belief that workers' education would succeed only when provided by trade unionists for trade unionists."[43] Cohn thus declined to serve on the organizing committee for the Bryn Mawr Summer School, but the ILGWU's Educational Department did supply scholarships to send union members to both the Bryn Mawr and the Barnard summer schools.

At the 1922 AFL convention, the Executive Council acknowledged the growth of workers' education and noted its potential significance for strengthening the cause of organized labor: "Workers' education is the very basis of a permanent and responsible workers' organization; it must be coordinated with the labor movement and therefore should be regarded as an integral part of the trade union itself."[44] Federation leaders began to realize that workers' education was gaining an important position and following in the labor movement, and that it also represented a potential threat. It would be wise to work with this new force, not against it. With the sanction and approval of the Federation's Executive Council, the Educational Committee entered into a "cooperative relationship" with the WEB in order to further promote workers' education in the trade-union movement while the Federation leadership sought an even "closer affiliation" with the bureau. After first negotiating to have only unionists on the WEB executive committee, the AFL and its national unions then gradually captured control of the bureau. By 1927, the AFL had so twisted WEB policy that it avoided questions of trade-union policy and functioned strictly as an educational and research organization. "Had the American Federation of Labor not gained control of the Workers' Education Bureau," James O.

Morris speculates, "that organization might have become a center of progressive labor opposition to the AFL."[45] Federation leaders knew that they had a great deal at stake in their emasculation of the WEB.

In addition to the damage inflicted by their cooptation by the AFL, union-sponsored workers' education programs were hurt by declining trade union membership and the proliferation of internecine political feuds. Moreover, public opinion had already turned hostile to both socialism and the labor movement. In 1920, union membership numbered 5 million; by 1923 this total had dropped to 3.6 million. Although this downward trend had slackened somewhat by 1927, the decline continued, and by 1930 only 2.9 million workers claimed union membership. Put another way, union membership in 1930 amounted to a paltry 10.2 percent of the more than thirty million nonagricultural employees counted in the census, a marked drop from 19.4 percent in 1920. More importantly, union organization remained concentrated in a handful of industries, namely, construction, coal, railroads, printing, clothing, street railways, water transportation, and music. This left large segments of the manufacturing sector, including such important industries as steel, automobiles, electrical equipment, rubber, cement, textiles, chemicals, and food, virtually devoid of unionization. This "paralysis of the labor movement," as Irving Bernstein labels it, resulted from the open-shop campaigns of the early twenties, strike-breaking tactics, scientific management, mechanization, industry shutdowns, and a lethargic and conservative AFL that refused to organize unskilled industrial workers. Dwindling membership rolls, of course, directly affected union-sponsored classes by reducing the potential pool from which students were drawn.[46]

Internal political disputes throughout the 1920s posed a greater threat and ultimately altered the fundamental aims of union education, particularly among the garment workers. Fierce political conflicts, initiated by Communist members, undermined financial stability and sapped union strength. The ILGWU, as a result, had little energy to divert to long-term schemes for educating workers; it was too distracted by the very struggle for existence.

The ILGWU emerged from the reactionary excesses of the war years with a renewed zeal for social change, sparked both by its own tradition of radicalism, which had germinated in the sweatshop and immigrant ghetto, and by the promise of the Russian Revolution. Still, this renascent radicalism represented a double-edged sword because the union also now found itself irreconcilably divided, like other radical trade unions, over the actual tactics and policies of the Communists. This division grew out of the much larger 1919 Socialist–Communist split. Laslett summarizes the source of turmoil within the Garment Workers' Union:

> A number of its more recently arrived members had joined either the Russian or one of the other eastern European language federations in the Socialist Party, and for these members, as well as for many of the older radical stalwarts on the union's left, the Communist Party became the legitimate representative of the Russian Revolution, whatever tactics it undertook. For the more moderate members of the union, however, the Communists' surreptitious efforts at "boring from within" the labor movement, and the accusations which they made against the ILGWU leadership of corruption, antidemocratic methods, and class collaboration, particularly in an organization so well known for its progressive and democratic policies, were utterly repugnant.

These differences produced an upheaval within the International, which, given the sizeable communist faction in the union, "was more serious," Laslett adds, "than it was in almost any other American trade union."[47]

Although insurgency within the ILGWU had occurred as early as 1917, the first organized opposition erupted in the fall of 1919 when Local 25, the New York Waist and Dressmakers, introduced the idea of the "shop delegate system." Numbering twenty-five thousand in 1918 and one of the most radical locals in the International, Local 25 promoted the notion that the shop floor should become the basis of union organization and worker control as well as the place to express rank-and-file grievances. Shop workers were to elect two delegates who were to form the governing body of the local unions. This assembly of shop delegates was to possess legislative and executive powers and was to elect a general executive and a standing committee. After the establishment of the Trade Union Education League (TUEL) in 1920, the Communists exploited the shop delegate cause in order to secure power in the ILGWU as a whole, using Local 25 as their foothold.

Lenin, vis-à-vis the Third International (Comintern), declared that it was the official policy of the Communist party, and the first stage of the revolution, to penetrate existing workers' organizations, that is, to bore from within. William Z. Foster led the American campaign by organizing the TUEL, eventually affiliating with the Red International of Labor Unions and the Communist party in 1921. The TUEL was not a union, nor did it issue charters or collect dues; its sole function was to coordinate Communist party penetration of the American labor movement in general and the AFL in particular. It made inroads among the machinists, carpenters, mine workers, Pullman porters, and seamen; yet the main thrust of the TUEL drive centered on the needle trades, whose workers were concentrated in New York City and consisted largely of southern and eastern European immigrants, many already with radical sympathies.

The International's General Executive Board swiftly countered the shop delegate movement. President Schlesinger, with the blessing of the union's 1920 convention, divided Local 25, the source of the Communist revolt, into two separate locals in order to eradicate the local and concomitantly to squelch the shop delegate concept. Ironically, the unpopularity of this decision only fueled Communist agitation within the ILGWU. Moreover, because the New York Dressmakers' Union, now Local 22, drew its membership from an expanding sector of the garment industry, it soon became the largest local of the ILGWU. To the dismay of the International's leadership, Communist influence, through the shop delegate movement, continued to grow, not only in Locals 22 and 25, but also in Locals 2 and 9 in New York City. The shop delegate plan also appealed to officers in local unions who, for pragmatic reasons, believed that the new idea might rekindle interest in unionism among the somewhat disaffected membership and stir renewed interest in the union's meetings and daily routine.[48]

The political tumult within the ILGWU gained momentum and assumed the guise of a civil war. Under the leadership of Morris Sigman, who replaced the ailing Schlesinger in February 1923, and David Dubinsky, a leading figure in the union, the administration fought desperately to retain control of the union. Sigman attempted to purge the union of Communists by outlawing the shop delegate cause, ordering the dissolution of the TUEL cells, suspending nineteen members of Local 22's executive board, and reorganizing locals in Philadelphia and Boston, among other cities, to offset the Communist-dominated locals in New York City. Sigman also mandated that candidates in the forthcoming union elections sign anti-Communist oaths. These tactics backfired, however. The Communists gleefully complied with Sigman's directive and proceeded to win elections in New York Locals 2, 9, and 22, which comprised the mass of workers in the cloak and dress industries and thus the heart of the union. Nevertheless, Communist delegates were refused seats at the 1924 ILGWU convention because of their membership in the TUEL.

The TUEL remained undaunted and succeeded in capturing the New York Joint Board the following year. At the stormy Philadelphia convention in late 1925, Sigman won a close victory as union president. This was due solely to the support provided by locals outside of New York City, the Italian locals in the city, and Dubinsky's skilled cutters in Local 10. The final showdown occurred when, in July 1926, the Communist leaders in the New York Cloakmakers Joint Board, under orders from the Communist party, ordered a hopeless, and ultimately disastrous, strike against the coat and suit manufacturers. The twenty-eight-week strike not only ended in failure, but in the collapse of Communist leadership; in its wake, the International's leadership suspended or disbanded Communist locals.

The political strife left the union devastated and debt-ridden: The 1926 strike alone cost the ILGWU over $3 million. In 1920, ILGWU membership had numbered 105,400, but by 1929 it had dropped to 32,300. Banker Herbert H. Lehman had to loan the garment workers' union $25,000, interest free, in order to sustain it in 1928.[49] Still, as Laslett concludes, "The remarkable thing was . . . that despite its postwar preoccupation with combating the communists—as well as the open-shop campaigns of the employers, which was pursued just as vigorously in the garment industry as it was elsewhere—the ILGWU did not lose its interest in the Socialist party or socialism."[50]

Joseph Stalin reorganized the Comintern in 1928 and shortly thereafter replaced the TUEL with the Trade Union Unity League (TUUL). Openly revolutionary, the TUUL attempted to organize unskilled and semiskilled industrial workers largely ignored by the AFL. The Communists, in short, intended to destroy the Federation by spawning new unions, that is, through dual unionism. AFL leaders responded in kind. As Bernstein emphasizes, "At a time when few Americans took domestic communism seriously, the Federation executives fought it bitterly, and that struggle was to leave an enduring mark on their thought."[51] Union interest in workers' education, as a result, generally waned. As we shall see in Chapter 6, Brookwood Labor College in particular was to feel the full brunt of this policy.

In spite of Cohn's efforts to keep the ILGWU educational department above that fray, the ILGWU's educational efforts suffered in every way. Because of Cohn's neutrality, both sides viewed her with suspicion and, consequently, in 1925 she lost her bid for a fifth term as an ILGWU vice-president. She still continued to serve as the department's executive secretary, but lacked the clout the vice-presidency had conferred. Further, the nearly bankrupt union had little money for books, supplies, or teachers, or for Cohn's meager salary. With diminishing resources, she struggled to continue the irregular educational activities of the union, staging the occasional musical or play, arranging for concerts and lectures, and teaching the few classes that the Educational Department sponsored. Finally, and more fundamentally, Cohn deliberately purged politics from the union's educational program to preserve it.

As the ILGWU's socialist leaders emerged victorious from the factional struggles of the 1920s, they cast a jaundiced eye toward any workers' education that reflected, even in the slightest manner, the political utopianism that they had come to associate with their Communist rivals. The union's educational efforts now skirted social issues and focused on entertainment, as courses in political economy were replaced by trips to museums and Broadway shows. Lacking sustained support from the International, Cohn turned outside the union for help. As Wong points out, "The Brookwood staff—notably A. J. Muste, Helen G. Norton, and David J. Saposs—provided teachers, educational material, and moral support whenever possible."[52]

Thus, because of ideological conflicts in the 1920s, many union leaders preferred that workers' education should avoid political matters, especially political issues that deviated from established union policy. Since union educational efforts were institutionally dependent upon the sponsoring union, their educational policies and programs could be easily manipulated to reflect the political perspective of the parent union. The unfettered exploration of ideas became taboo. This depoliticized education evolved into the mere training of union bureaucrats who would, in turn, unquestionably implement the objectives of the union.[53]

Practical problems also plagued union-sponsored workers' education. In many cases, classes lacked structure and pedagogy. Few qualified personnel existed to formulate programs and to instruct classes. Professional teachers simply did not have the proper training or background for workers' education. Buildings, equipment, libraries, and books were likewise in short supply. The garment union, for example, began to encounter difficulties obtaining classrooms from the New York City School Board because workers' education connoted social-class education. Many school board members saw this as a revolutionary activity and often refused requests by the union to use public school classrooms. Textbooks, moreover, appeared to be too abstract and academic for the worker–students. Students, furthermore, irregularly attended the part-time courses. Fatigue, union activities, lack of ability, and leisure all interfered with classes.

By the early thirties, union-affiliated workers' education appeared weak and, in some cases, such as with the ACWA, nonexistent. The Great Depression exacerbated that situation. Declining union revenue and a generally defensive posture made workers' education expendable. Within this context, the idea—so strong only a few years earlier —that workers' education functioned to serve and to promote the labor movement became passé. Union education, conceived in 1920 as an integral part of unionism, not as cloistered study but as a form of union action, was by 1930 perceived as a peripheral luxury that could only be indulged in during periods of unusual prosperity.

New Deal legislation, however, legitimized unionization and ushered in an era favorable to workers' education. A spurt in union membership and revenue revived interest in workers' education. By 1934, union-sponsored education for garment workers resumed a vigorous and important role in ILGWU activities and became an established part of the union's institutional structure. Cohn remained as executive secretary of the ILGWU's Educational Department, while Mark Starr, active in the British and American workers' education movements and a former faculty member at Brookwood Labor College, became the department's director in 1934.

More significant, perhaps, was the ongoing transformation in social thought underlying union-sponsored workers' education. This change had begun during the late twenties because of union leadership mistrust of the political nature of workers' education. In earlier decades, workers' classes and schools had strived for a fully reconstructed social order, which often was envisioned as a worker-controlled, cooperative commonwealth. By the mid-thirties, such dreams had faded. The basic objectives of labor education had become utilitarian, focusing on sustaining the trade-union movement; leadership training and the need for membership loyalty became paramount. Prolabor legislation profoundly influenced the shift in the social and educational aims of union education. As Robert Schaefer writes, "The labor movement generally preferred to exploit the potential created by a friendly government rather than dissipating its energies in clamoring for the eradication of capitalist society."[54] New unions, such as those of the auto workers, rubber workers, and steel workers, likewise established educational departments to assist them in their organizing efforts. This transition in educational policy reflected the growing concern over solidifying the internal structure of unions. It also showed that workers' education no longer nurtured critical thinking among the rank-and-file towards democratic ideals.

The ILGWU clearly illustrated that political transformation. The union expanded its educational program during the 1930s and emphasized three levels of activities. The first included recreation, entertainment, lectures on union history, cultural events such as art exhibits and concerts, radio plays, and other similar apolitical functions with little or no intention of helping workers comprehend complex social and economic problems. The second comprised courses in parliamentary law, public speaking, English, labor journalism, labor and social history, economic geography, and current events. The third provided advanced training for those members who aspired to union office. By the 1940s, the political and intellectual scope of the ILGWU educational program further narrowed when the union reduced its choices to trade-union methods and history, parliamentary law, public speaking, labor problems, and current events. Labor history gradually evolved into a narrative of the history of the ILGWU rather than a full survey of the history of the labor movement. This tended to promote parochialism and undermine class consciousness. Studies of such broad areas as the social history of the United States and economic geography were replaced with courses in social hygiene, cooking, and foreign languages. This benign educational program, to be sure, reflected the ideological shift of the International. As Schaefer explains, "There can be no long-continued deliberate cleavage between what is taught and the policies of those who control the teachers."[55] Nevertheless, in 1937–38, the program claimed more than twenty-two thousand students in 620 classes and groups in fifty-eight cities.

College- and University-Sponsored Workers' Education

THE BRYN MAWR SUMMER SCHOOL FOR WOMEN WORKERS

Many colleges and universities also established workers' education programs. The model of the Bryn Mawr Summer School for Women

Workers prompted the initiation of a series of summer residential programs for women workers. The University of California created an extension service in 1921; shortly thereafter, Syracuse, Harvard, MIT, Tufts, Amherst, and the Universities of Cincinnati and Oklahoma offered similar programs. Workers' education ventures sponsored by colleges and universities tended to emphasize cultural subjects and remained basically uncommitted, as far as social philosophy and attitudes were concerned, to social-class consciousness.

In 1919, M. Carey Thomas, president of Bryn Mawr College and an ardent supporter of higher education for women, proposed that education for working women might bring about a more harmonious society. Yet she remained vague about how this would occur. Rita Heller stresses that this concept was firmly rooted in the Jeffersonian belief that a vital democracy requires an educated electorate: "Thomas's dynamic feminism caused her to extend this progressive vision to laboring women; she was convinced that they, too, could benefit from exposure to the liberal humanist heritage. At its outset, the school strove primarily to enhance individual capacity."[56] During the summer of 1921, Bryn Mawr, located near Philadelphia, created the first residential school in workers' education and named it the Bryn Mawr Summer School for Women Workers in Industry. Hilda Smith, dean of undergraduate students and a trained social worker who had been active in the suffrage movement, served as director.[57]

An administrative committee consisting of female workers in industry, college representatives, and members of the Bryn Mawr Alumnae Association perceived the school's mission as one of offering "young women of character and ability a fuller special education and an opportunity to study liberal subjects, in order that they may widen their influence in the industrial world, help in the coming social reconstruction, and increase the happiness and usefulness of their lives." The committee believed that institutions of higher learning could play a unique role in workers' education by furnishing students with opportunities for "systematic intellectual work through courses of study pursued for a number of consecutive weeks in academic surroundings of beauty, under the same favorable conditions of complete freedom from economic anxiety and domestic care which college students enjoy."[58] Reflecting a middle-class "missionary" attitude towards workers and their social and economic plight, this statement implied that genteel academia could provide the worker–student with an environment of intellectual stimulation and freedom lacking in her everyday life. The college campus would function as a temporary haven, or escape—"in academic surroundings of beauty"—for the workers from their drab world. [59]

The committee established rigid admission standards. Students had to have at least three years of wage-earning experience, two in industry. The committee considered only women who worked with the tools of their trade. This stipulation clearly excluded supervisors, forewomen, saleswomen, clerical workers, and teachers. The committee preferred that applicants be between twenty and thirty-five years of age and possess at least a sixth-grade education—preferably with some subsequent study as well—and be able to read and write in English.

The first session ran from June 15 to August 10, 1921, and included some seventy women who had each received $200 scholarships from Bryn Mawr alumnae and "public-spirited men and women." Most students came from the needle trades and textile mills, and had been recruited by, or from, the industrial clubs of the Young Women's Christian Association (YWCA), the NWTUL, and garment unions in eastern cities. The Bryn Mawr Summer School offered courses in three basic areas of study. The "industrial group" consisted of courses in economics, labor, and "subjects of special interest to industrial workers"; the "social group" contained literature, history, government, law, and psychology courses; and the "cultural group" included a course in art, "the story of pictures," and architecture. Students could also participate in physical hygiene, recreation, swimming, dancing, and walking. The "working girl students" resided in the regular dormitories and had access to all of the college's facilities during their stay.

Bryn Mawr's apolitical course of study mirrored the nebulous goals of the school's educational program for women workers. Indeed, it typified the general attitude of colleges and universities, almost exclusively elite institutions, towards workers' education. In the end, institutions of higher education, despite their self-proclaimed liberalism, did not create an environment of intellectual and political freedom for working-class students. Universities rarely, if ever, gave workers an equal share in the direction of their education programs; at best, workers and their unions served in an advisory capacity. Using the University of Wisconsin School for Women Workers in Industry as a case study, Dagmar Schultz argues that the workers' school

experienced over time a growing accommodation to and cooptation by the University. . . . To the extent that this is so, it may be argued that the program had become more sensitive to the changing needs of the *sponsors* than those of its *clients*. . . . This process resulted in the School's political orientation becoming increasingly conservative in response to the growing conservatism of the University. [60]

Schultz's basic premise, that university-sponsored workers' education was politically coopted, is significant and deserves further examination.

THE UNIVERSITY OF WISCONSIN
SCHOOL FOR WOMEN WORKERS

Impressed with the Bryn Mawr experience, the board of the Madison YWCA organized a school for workers at the University of Wisconsin in 1923. The YWCA's Industrial Department, staffed by middle-class college graduates, had worked in close conjunction with the labor movement since 1904, organizing conferences, recruiting and financing students for residential schools for women workers, and offering summer programs. The Madison YWCA, a particularly active chapter, had already organized evening discussions on labor problems for college students and working women. The proposed university school was to foster the cultural growth of the individual and a deeper sense of the beauty of life; it was, that is, devoid of social-class considerations. The organizers did not eschew social reform, but they perceived it as a by-product of the individual educational experience. [61]

Not surprisingly, many of the early students saw the school as a means of social mobility for themselves. The university consented to accommodate the working women during the summer months, and with scholarships from the YWCA, eight Madison women attended the first session of the Wisconsin School for Women Workers in Industry in 1924. The majority were factory workers between eighteen and twenty-five years of age with diverse educational backgrounds. The university, however, did not bother to establish separate classes for the worker–students. Although many were not adequately prepared for college work, they were required to enroll in regular university courses in English literature, economics, and physical education. To make matters worse, instructors refused to adapt their teaching to the worker–students and simply employed their customary lecture method.

The School for Workers lacked both secure backing and a clear sense of direction during its early years. The commitment of the local

YWCA to educating working women was not shared by the university administration. Since business interests dominated the university's board of regents, the Workers' School received only piecemeal moral and financial support, operated without a full-time director, and suffered from a shortage of teachers. Further, labor groups, such as the Wisconsin Federation of Labor (WFL), viewed the school with suspicion because the university controlled the selection of teachers and courses. More importantly, manufacturers and employers served on the advisory and scholarship committees and thereby played a crucial role in formulating the school's policies during the early years. This situation profoundly affected the content of the courses and the pedagogy; that is, the views of both labor and management were presented in the classroom. The academic atmosphere of the university, which had political neutrality as one of its basic claims, certainly reinforced this "balanced" approach.

By the late twenties and early thirties, the Wisconsin Workers' School had gained support from the university and had cultivated closer ties with organized labor. University president Glenn Frank favored the school and met regularly with the advisory committee. Alice Shoemaker—who had received her Ph.D. in history from Wisconsin, served as industrial secretary of the YWCA, and taught at the Bryn Mawr Summer School for Women Workers—became executive secretary. Shoemaker promoted the school among labor groups and replaced faculty members who failed to express a strong prolabor orientation.

The WFL showed serious interest in the school only when it became coeducational. Unions had little interest in raising funds to be diverted, ostensibly, to sending nonunion women workers to the school; first, because few women were members of unions, and second, because organized labor in Wisconsin had traditionally emphasized the need for trained male leadership. While all forty-one students were female in 1925, with only four claiming union affiliation, the school was coeducational by 1932. Fifteen male and twenty-one female students, ten of whom were union members, attended that year. The school continued to solicit employers' interest and support, but this began to wane with the increased involvement of organized labor in the school.

Shoemaker assumed the school's directorship in 1934 and continued her efforts to expand the role of organized labor in formulating school policies and programs. The WFL responded favorably to Shoemaker's overtures because its own labor colleges and classes had disintegrated with the onset of the Depression. Three labor representatives, at the request of university president Glenn Frank, met periodically with the school's committee and served in an advisory capacity. Because of its prolabor leanings, employer backing as well as middle-class support for the school continued to dwindle. Consequently, the school became more dependent upon the unions for financial support. During the 1932–33 school year, the school received 23 percent of its funds from business and professional groups, 74 percent from scholarship committees (chiefly middle class), and 3 percent from labor organizations and individuals. A significant shift had occurred by the 1935–36 school year. The business and scholarship portions had decreased to 14 and 49 percent, respectively, while labor's share had increased to 37 percent. In response to the needs of local labor groups, Shoemaker attempted to expand the school's educational work by initiating a labor institute for the summer session and organizing radio programs between 1931 and 1937.[62]

The School for Workers began to evolve a more class-conscious ideology and program. Although course titles remained largely unchanged, both content and teaching methods reflected the transition from a predominantly cultural approach to wholly industrial concerns. By 1935, Marx, Engels, Lenin, and Trotsky appeared on the reading lists; Shoemaker, moreover, sought instructors who had previous experience in teaching workers and who were committed to the workers' movement. In 1932, Shoemaker hired Arthur W. Calhoun, who had taught at Brookwood Labor College, and Lucien Koch, who had been director of Commonwealth College. The increased activism of the students in the labor movement further reflected the ideological shift of the school.

The financial and political constraints of college- and university-sponsored workers' education became evident when Shoemaker recommended that the School for Workers become a regular department of the university in order to qualify for a year-round budget. The university regents refused that request and slashed the school's budget by one-third. Attempts by the Wisconsin Federation of Labor to enlarge the program and expand its control of school policies met with a similar fate. A fear of labor domination over the school, as well as the increasingly radical, political orientation of the educational program, appeared to be the motives behind the regents' action.

Shoemaker and organized labor continued their efforts to broaden the program, but they did not succeed until May 1937, when a sympathetic, liberal state legislature formally recognized the School for Workers. With a curriculum moving towards a class-conscious perspective now funded by the state and with aid from the Works Progress Administration (WPA), the school embarked upon a year-round statewide program between 1937 and 1939. During the 1937–38 school year, the first year in which state funds were used, over fifty-three hundred students registered for the eighty-three classes run in thirty-five cities and the twenty-one rural classes set up in eight counties. Twenty-five teachers were employed in the urban program and about thirty-five in the rural program by the following year.

According to Dagmar Schultz, the appointment of the politically moderate Ernest Schwarztrauber by the university to replace Shoemaker in 1937 marked the beginning of the school's formal integration into the university and its subsequent accommodation to university policies. Because of the school's expanding and popular educational program and its increased dependence upon the state and university administrations for its fiscal and bureaucratic needs, university administrators found that they had no further need for a female director. The WFL, dominated by male leadership, likewise favored a male director, particularly one with a more moderate political perspective than Shoemaker's, to head the expanded work of the school. It appeared that as long as the School for Workers remained a fledgling and struggling educational program for working women, the university and organized labor tolerated Shoemaker as director. But when the state legislature legitimated and subsidized the school, male leadership became necessary. Not surprisingly, classes for women workers began to disappear after 1937.

This same attitude applied to black workers. During the 1920s, the School for Workers arranged interracial housing and promoted friendly feelings among black and white worker–students. Later, in the 1930s, studies in race relations were an integral part of the school's curriculum. Hilton Hanna, the only black member of the school's staff, taught courses in parliamentary procedure, consumer problems, black history, and poetry by Langston Hughes. After Schwarztrauber became director, Hanna's teaching responsibilities lessened, and the program deemphasized the role of the industrial black worker.

The issue of control over the school's program erupted once more between the university and the WFL in 1937. Schwarztrauber insisted that labor only serve in an advisory fashion, while organized labor demanded equal authority. The broader conflict between the AFL and the Congress of Industrial Organizations (CIO) exacerbated the situation. The Wisconsin CIO wanted the School for Workers to cater to its needs rather than those of the WFL. The school responded by offering a compromise program, but the CIO objected, and as a result, the university asserted its complete domination over the school's policies and programs in order to avoid future disputes.

Conservative attacks on the School for Workers in 1938 further narrowed its scope and program. The school had overstepped its bounds by engaging in activities that questioned the status quo and the forces from which the university drew its financial strength. Employers accused the school of teaching communist propaganda, and suspicious public school board members—like their earlier counterparts in New York City—refused to allow the school to use school facilities for its statewide extension program. Other antilabor groups pounced on the school's teacher training center at Camp Douglas. The university hierarchy, led by conservative president Clarence Dykstra, disassociated itself from that center. This episode clearly illustrated the university's reluctance to support the school when its political views differed from those of university administrators. In 1939, the Republican administration of Governor Julius P. Heil, in keeping with its general antilabor and antifarmer stance, discontinued state funds for the school's statewide work. The board of regents, however, permitted the school to continue its six-week resident summer program. The School for Workers was forced to operate during the 1940 school year with a budget equivalent to its 1929 level. It is clear, as Schultz argues, that workers' education at a state university could only flourish and expand as long as it functioned within a political framework acceptable to industry and business. Such a relationship, of course, often contradicted the best interests of the workers.

Now under the full auspices of the university, the School for Workers completed its political transition from quasi class consciousness to class collaboration. The university administration placed the school in the Extension Department in order to formally integrate it into the university structure. The school's staff persuaded employers to supply scholarships, a policy that had been abandoned during the early thirties. In 1944, the school even engaged several employers as guest speakers. In this manner, the school's program moved closer to the employer's viewpoint and endeavored to train labor statesmen who would responsibly and intelligently negotiate with employers, rather than training labor activists who favored radical social change. The school also emphasized practical courses, such as collective bargaining, the handling of grievances, and the study of a particular industry, as more conservative labor leaders preferred. The emphasis on utilitarianism, to be sure, created a workers' education program that served an increasingly bureaucratized labor movement. One- and two-week institutes, first introduced in the late thirties, gained popularity with many unions and by 1943 replaced the six-week sessions. Union leaders selected the students—many of whom already occupied responsible positions in their unions—who would attend the school. The segregation of workers from different industries and unions contributed to the erosion of worker solidarity and a unifying class consciousness.

The School for Workers continued its move to the political right throughout the 1950s and 1960s. With the retirement of Schwarztrauber in 1950, the university administration appointed directors who were even more conservative: Edwin Young in 1950 and Robert Ozanne in 1952. They reflected the cold war atmosphere and McCarthyism by fighting communism and cooperated with the State and Labor departments by training foreign trade unionists, particularly from Third World countries. The school further cultivated its ties to management and continued its emphasis on skill training designed to prepare labor bureaucrats. [63]

In general, institutional dependency and concomitant controls often limited the growth and scope of workers' education programs, because the sponsoring institutions often identified with and supported the status quo. As a result, institutionally affiliated workers' education activities could not sustain radical goals and programs— or even liberal ones, for that matter—because of the constant threat of political suppression, or financial abjuration, or both. Moreover, union- and university-sponsored educational programs evolved a parochial perspective by deemphasizing the experiences of the working class and concentrating instead on the narrow histories of individual unions, or by employing segregation tactics that discouraged an awareness of the solidarity of the working class. Finally, the universities provided residential, full-time education, which was better than the part-time classes offered by the unions—but only during the summer months. Workers were denied regular, full-time, residential educational experiences during the academic year through union- or university-supported programs alike. Certainly, union and university efforts in workers' education did not adequately train workers for service in the labor movement; the independent labor colleges would.

Part II

Social and Educational Goals and Practices

2

A Culture in Overalls and Workmarked Hands

> A school or educational system is always in the last analysis a child
> or instrument of some social group. . . . Brookwood, all similar enter-
> prises, are the children and the instruments of a militant labor progres-
> sivism.
>
> —A. J. Muste, *Labor Age* (1929)

INDEPENDENT WORKERS' schools did not have to contend with the
institutional constraints that manipulated and often restricted educational content in union-affiliated and university-associated colleges.
Because they were not tied to large established organizations with
strong connections to conservative or mainstream social interests, the
independent schools could pursue more radical policies, try more
innovative pedagogical techniques, and attract more committed students. Founded and supported by radical workers, labor leaders, and
intellectual liberals who sympathized with the cause of working-class
education, they saw a reconstructed social order as their mission and
they prepared worker-students theoretically and practically for service in the labor movement. That service was to be a struggle for
social change, for enhancing the economic and political power of the
organized workers, and for a new society. The schools' teachers were
dissatisfied with the business-oriented union leadership of the AFL
and criticized it vigorously and tirelessly. Moreover, the schools demonstrated their commitment to a democratic and cooperative society
through their daily routine and administration. Students, faculty, and

administrators shared responsibilities as well as an equal voice, and alumni were involved in the schools' affairs long after their departure. Reflecting the schools' independent status, funding came through individual donations and trade-union scholarships. Perhaps Dagmar Schultz best articulates the essence of the independent workers' education movement: "Free of restrictions which special trade union policies and university administrators placed on workers' education programs, several of the independent schools represented the militant conscience of the labor movement."[1]

It is not easy to define or classify the many independent labor colleges that thrived during the early decades of the twentieth century. "The term labor college is used indiscriminately," Marius Hansome observed in 1931. "It is high-sounding and agreeable to the megalomania for which we Americans are notorious. It is used to describe schools with a two-year residential course as well as evening study classes, lecture series, etc."[2] The differences between the trade-union colleges and the independent labor colleges illustrate Hansome's point. Colleges founded and supported by the trade unions existed in New York, Boston, Philadelphia, Baltimore, Rochester, Pittsburgh, Cleveland, Chicago, Milwaukee, Seattle, San Francisco, and Los Angeles. They generally offered part-time, evening educational programs.[3] In contrast, the independent labor colleges, including the three institutions selected for detailed examination here—Work People's College, Brookwood Labor College, and Commonwealth College—avoided institutional restrictions and maintained far more radical goals than their trade-union counterparts. Independent labor colleges usually provided long-term, structured educational programs that reflected their ideology. Full-time devotion by the worker–students to their academic work also required that the labor colleges function as residential centers. Finally, the labor colleges sought and obtained financial support from a variety of sources to ensure their political autonomy.

Work People's College

Although the labor colleges possessed similar social and educational goals and programs, they had diverse origins. Work People's College, in Duluth, Minnesota, began in 1903 as an immigrant Finnish "folk" high school dedicated to preserving the Lutheran religion and Finnish language and evolved into a labor college that served the Finnish working-class movement for several decades.

The Finns, one of the smaller immigrant groups in American society, made an unusually important contribution to American labor history. Finnish immigrants had settled along the Delaware River as early as the colonial period, but Finnish emigration to the United States remained low until the Russian army began to draft Finns in 1900. While only 3,500 Finns emigrated to America in 1898, over 23,000 did so in 1902. They brought their socialist convictions with them. Socialism appeared to be particularly strong among the Finns who settled in the Pacific Northwest, in the Duluth–Superior district on the Minnesota–Wisconsin state line, along the upper peninsula of Michigan, and in Massachusetts. By 1905, Finns constituted 39.8 percent —the largest proportion—of the foreign-born groups in the Mesabi Iron Range, located in northern Minnesota. Russian suppression of the 1905 general strike in Finland, a protest against Russian rule, and the 1906 Viapori rebellion caused a second wave of Finnish radicals to escape to the United States. This group represented the "new left" in European socialism that was skeptical about gradual social reform through the electoral process. According to Carl Ross, "They brought to America and into the Finnish American socialist movement a conviction that only some form of workers' revolutionary action, and not socialist politics alone, could establish socialism."[4] The Finnish migration, as Peter Kivisto asserts, is best seen as a dialectic in which immigrants, to the extent they were able, constructed a meaningful social reality out of the old and the new. Thus, they brought a radical spirit with them, and this found new forms in the United States.[5] Leo Laukki and Yrjo Sirola, pursued by the czarist police because of their activities in the Viapori uprising and general strike, respectively, were among the militant Finns who became involved in American radical movements and in workers' education.

The interaction of the Finnish peasant culture with American industrial society further intensified the Finns' socialist beliefs and their economic and political activities. Instead of the worldly paradise they had been led to believe they would find in the New World, Finnish miners encountered squalid living and working conditions in Michigan, Minnesota, and Montana. They also encountered ethnic discrimination. Like other immigrant miners, Finnish iron miners earned an annual income of $716 for their families, while non-Finnish households in the western Great Lakes mining region averaged $990 per year. Most families of immigrant miners in the copper and iron industries had to accommodate boarders to supplement their meager incomes. As a result, foreign-born miners generally lived in over-crowded, poorly ventilated, and unsanitary tarred paper shacks, log huts, and the cheap company barracks and cottages that often graced the pit sides. These miners also suffered from unsafe job conditions. During 1905 and 1906, the death rate on the Mesabi Range was about 7.5 workers per thousand employed. Between 1905 and 1907, 277 workers were killed in Saint Louis County, Minnesota, alone. Discrimination exacerbated the problems of southern and eastern European and Finnish immigrant miners because they were condemned to drudge as manual laborers throughout their working lives, while advancement went to the few native-born American laborers as well as to the Cornishmen and Scandinavians. Since few Finnish children enrolled in the public schools, opportunities for advancement became even more problematic. Finally, Finnish miners found themselves wholly lacking in trade-union representation because they were excluded from the craft-oriented AFL.[6]

On July 19, 1907, Finnish miners struck against U.S. Steel's mining division, the Mesabi's largest employer. The Western Federation of Miners, which had split from the AFL at that time, provided considerable organizational leadership; Finnish Socialists played active roles in the strike and volunteered their meeting halls as strike headquarters, supplied numerous pickets, including women and children, and furnished many strike leaders. The mining company reacted by importing strikebreakers and hiring private police to guard them. After two bitter months, the strike ended in a defeat for the miners; worse yet, Finnish miners became the target of retribution by the mining company. The company blacklisted Finnish miners regardless of their political affiliation. Finns made up about 18 percent of the company's work force before the strike, but only accounted for 8 percent after the strike. Indeed, the lessons learned in the "school of Morgan and Rockefeller," as the Finnish socialists jokingly called American capitalism, proved to be difficult.[7]

Finnish radicalism also found expression in political activities. Finns formed the pioneer foreign-language socialist federation, the Finnish Socialist Federation, in 1904. The Federation affiliated with the Socialist Party of America in 1907; other immigrant groups soon followed the Finnish model. In 1917 the foreign-language federations accounted for 41 percent of the Socialist party's total membership of 80,126, with the Finnish Socialist Federation being the largest and most powerful affiliate organization. In 1912, Finnish Socialists claimed 255 locals with 11,535 members, four newspapers, seventy-six meeting halls, eighty libraries, a combined organizational income of $184,123.83, and the Work People's College, with 123 students. [8]

The origins of that Work People's College can be traced to September 15, 1903, when authorities of the Finnish Evangelical Lutheran church opened a folk high school in Minneapolis. Created to train ministers, the school sought to preserve Finnish culture and nationalism by teaching religion and language to adult students. Yet only eight students enrolled, and it closed after twelve days. Undaunted, clergymen moved the school to Duluth in late 1903, purchased a three-story building near Spirit Lake, and incorporated as the Finnish People's College and Theological Seminary on January 5, 1904. Liberal clergy invited secularized Finns to participate in the folk school venture, and Finnish Socialists responded enthusiastically, purchasing blocks of the school's stock at a dollar a share. That had long been a typical way for Finns, particularly radical Finns, to subsidize publishing and cooperative enterprises. Socialists also registered at the school and soon represented the majority of the students. They saw no viable alternative, as the only other institution that could teach Finnish immigrants was Suomi College and Theological Seminary. But Socialists hardly found themselves welcomed there because the school was elitist and symbolized the repressive old order of Finland. [9]

Nevertheless, the Finnish People's College and Theological Seminary faced an uncertain future. A board of directors consisting of lay members and church officials controlled the school's secular aspects, while the clergy alone supervised its seminary. The school's dual nature soon produced insurmountable problems. The clerics, who grew increasingly antisocialist, and the socialist lay members, who were anticlerical, vied for control of the school. The socialist students, most in their late twenties and well past conventional student age, chafed under religious restrictions and resented courses imposed upon them by church officials. Prayers were mandatory, while discussions of social class issues were forbidden. Students led a strike to protest the "oppressive" nature of the school in the fall of 1904. This action spelled disaster for the school, since all but two students carried out their threat to leave it. As Douglas J. Ollila reports, this incident erupted after a required prayer meeting when a student rebel named Juvenius announced, "Now let's have a waltz." [10] The Reverend E. W. Saranen, who had served as director, resigned as a result of the incident.

Religious conflict and anemic enrollment forced the board of directors to reconsider closing the school. Alex Halonen, a socialist board member, raised additional funds for the school by selling membership certificates to Finnish Socialist locals. In this manner, Socialists obtained a majority of the stock and moved to assert their dominance over the board of directors. As Guss Aakula, a former student and teacher, recalled, their effort was to "organize the school as a people's institute . . . to teach the subjects most important to the people, that is the workers." [11] The school failed to open during the fall of 1905 because it lacked a qualified director, but beginning on February 1, 1906, the school held sporadic and short-lived classes for some half-dozen students.

Socialists consolidated their control of the school in 1907, reshaped its educational and social goals, and renamed it Work People's College. The board of directors hired K. L. Haataja, a Socialist, as director and also as an instructor. Leo Laukki, and later Yrjo Sirola, joined the teaching staff as well. Reino Salo, one of the founders of the Finnish Socialist Federation, from Cloquet, Minnesota, was elected secretary and business manager. New life had been breathed into the moribund institution. Sixty-four students attended classes that fall semester, nearly all of them Socialists. [12]

While many immigrant groups saw education as a means of preserving the past, the Finnish-American left treated education as dynamic, orienting itself to changing the future. More than 98 percent of the Finns arriving between 1899 and 1907 were literate, in marked contrast to most of their immigrant counterparts. This was due principally to church mandates in Finland. And Finnish immigrants, compulsive in their thirst for knowledge and information, maintained an extremely high subscription rate to newspapers and periodicals. Finnish Socialists were especially active in cultural and propagandistic endeavors. As Ollila illustrates:

The Finnish Socialist Federation understood itself as an agency for education, and Federation locals sponsored lectures, debating societies, cultural forums, drama and music. Nearly every labor temple boasted of a "discussion room" where the weightier matters of Marxian dialectic and its application to the American scene were endlessly debated. Socialist children attended their own Sunday and summer schools where they memorized A. B. Makela's primer which included a "Socialist Child's Ten Commandments" and didactic narratives about greedy capitalists who exploited the impoverished proletariat. [13]

Through these efforts, the Finnish radical community hoped to develop its own cadre—including editors, teachers, and agitators—who would serve the cause, and Work People's College was designed specifically to train these functionaries in preparation for the advent of the socialist commonwealth. [14]

Socialist Finns created their own educational programs to accomplish these goals because, Halonen notes, they perceived the American system of public education to be training children to reject "the enthusiasm and social aims of their socialistic parents." [15] Contempt for the public schools was expressed in one unidentified Socialist's comments at the 1909 convention of the Finnish Socialist Federation:

> We know very well that immigrants, particularly Finnish immigrants, already in the second and third generation, under the influence of environment, become conservatively minded and scorn their own nationality, language, and class. They become Finn-Yanks whose only interests in life are dancing, fine clothes, chewing gum and American street manner. [16]

Radical Finns believed that public schools taught their children conformity and hedonistic materialism, serving bourgeois hegemony. Work People's College, in contrast, sought to preserve Finnish culture, promote literacy, and instill socialist ideals.

In 1914, the Finnish Socialist Federation experienced the same internal political upheaval and organizational fragmentation as the American Socialist Party had endured in 1912. The events that precipitated the crisis engulfed Work People's College. Actually, the situation had been deteriorating for some time. Many radical Finns, Halonen insists, realized the meaning of industrial struggle as early as the founding meeting of the Finnish Socialist Federation: "To win political machinery for a social revolution was still a theoretical question, but to win a strike was a practical problem." [17]

As far back as at the 1909 convention of the Finnish Federation, in the wake of the ill-fated 1907 Mesabi Iron Range strike, debate centered on political action versus economic action, and the chief topic debated at that convention was the IWW. Proponents of the new union argued that modern industrial conditions demanded an industrial union; direct economic action, through the "one big" strike, represented the only effective way for workers to solve their problems. Other means were doomed to failure or simply took too long. On the one hand, craft unions like those in the AFL were wholly ineffective, they charged, because they often compromised with management. Conventional political action, on the other hand, was time-consuming and fruitless, not only because politics was a tool of the capitalist classes, but also because many workers, particularly immigrant workers, were disenfranchised. Although the 1909 convention voted not to recognize the IWW, this turmoil inevitably entangled Work People's College. Under the leadership of Laukki, who assumed the directorship in 1908, the school moved steadily leftward and concomitantly condemned the political action ideology of the eastern bloc of Finnish Socialists. [18]

The issues of industrial unionism and the increased radicalism of Work People's College arose again at the 1912 convention of the Finnish Socialist Federation. Some Socialists, impressed with the IWW's success in the Lawrence, Massachusetts, textile strike of 1912, argued for a more tolerant view of the union. However, the removal of Big Bill Haywood, a popular IWW leader, from the National Executive Committee of the Socialist party only served to aggravate the situation. The schism between the proponents of socialist political action and the supporters of the IWW's direct economic action appeared to be widening. To make matters worse, factionalism had reached serious proportions at the Finnish labor college. Many loyal socialist delegates were incensed by teacher and student criticisms of the Socialist party's parliamentarian policies. The Finnish Socialist Federation assessed its members fifty cents—and occasionally a dollar—to help subsidize the school, yet the school produced students who opposed socialist goals. One delegate vented his anger and sense of betrayal: "Yesterday I talked with one former student [who] had attended the college for two years and said that the party platform may go to hell! That's the result of the teaching at the college." [19] The convention, nonetheless, voted to continue its annual contribution of $11,000 to the school in the hope that its teachings would conform to party precepts.

Differences between socialist hard-liners and industrial unionists had become irreconcilable by 1914. Many branches of the Finnish Socialist Federation were fragmented over the question of tactics. The eastern district of the Federation voted to remain loyal to the party and condemned the IWW, while the central district aligned itself with the

IWW and severed its connection with the Socialist party. The Finnish Socialist Federation Convention, held in Chicago, witnessed a hopeless split between those who favored political action and those for who favored direct action. As a result, the Finnish Socialist Federation began its organizational decline. With 17,316 members in May 1913, membership in the organization never exceeded 11,000 after 1914. According to Arne Halonen, an uncompromising, dogmatic spirit among the Finnish radicals represented the apparent reason for the dissolution: "To keep up Marxian principles in their purity, was more important than unity in an organization which had done much to awaken the Finnish workers to socialistic thought."[20]

A 1914 pamphlet, "The Controversy Within the Finnish Socialist Organization of United States, Its Issues and Reasons," served as a polemic against the Wobbly insurrection. In it, angry Finnish Socialists pointed to the "Workers' College" as the "seat of 'radicalism' " for the IWW movement among the Finns. An investigation of the school by an official delegation from the Finnish Socialist Federation received a cool reception. Laukki, the college's principal, "and his Board of Directors," the pamphlet reported, "treated the committee very indifferently and insolently and presented terms and conditions, which made any investigation impossible. Thus the committee was compelled to return home without having accomplished anything." The outraged Socialists promptly withdrew their financial support and smugly predicted that "the persistent insubmission of the will of the majority of the Finnish organization on the part of the Radicals [sic] has now jeopardized even the existence of the College, as it is very doubtful, how the College with its heavy debts and mortgages can continue its existence after the withdrawal of a yearly subsidy of more than 6,000 dollars."[21] Their prediction proved a bit faulty.

Despite the loss of support from the Finnish Socialist Federation, Work People's College continued to survive with the aid of more radical Finns and the IWW. The IWW formally acknowledged Work People's College as its official school in 1921 and became the largest single stockholder, controlling 300 shares. Several years before this, however, radical Finns sympathetic to the IWW, like their socialist predecessors, had secured a majority of the college's stock and voted to officially adopt the union's doctrine. Furthermore, under the tutelage of Laukki and Sirola, the school had continued its leftward political shift towards industrial unionism. Laukki at times echoed union policy and suggested that sabotage was sometimes necessary in order to effect a successful industrial revolution. According to John Wiita, a former student and teacher, Sirola espoused a less doctrinaire position: "While [Sirola] accepted the industrial form of unionism in preference to craft unionism and even recognized the IWW . . . as a pioneer for industrial unionism, he never accepted IWW's syndicalist theories or methods, destruction of property or the means of production, or any form of sabotage."[22]

Wobbly support for educational efforts like Work People's College was not surprising given the union's experiences with the public schools. Elizabeth Gurley Flynn, one of the most notorious Wobblies, recalled the antistrike activities of the Lawrence public schools during the IWW-led 1912 textile strike: "The efforts of the . . . schools were directed to driving a wedge between the school children and their striking parents. Often children in such towns became ashamed of their foreign-born, foreign-speaking parents, their old-country ways, their accents, their foreign newspapers, and even their strike and mass picketing. . . . Some of the teachers called the strikers lazy, said they should go back to work or 'back where they came from.' "[23] Flynn and Haywood attempted to counteract school propaganda in Lawrence by conducting "children's meetings" of their own. Haywood also noted that the public schools performed the very same antiunion role during the ill-fated Paterson, New Jersey, silk workers' strike of 1913, again led by the IWW. The strikers' children, as Haywood recalled in his autobiography, resorted to "a school strike because the teachers had called the striking silk workers and their organizers 'anarchists and good-for-nothing foreigners.' "[24] Thus, Haywood purchased stock in Work People's College and proclaimed, "The IWW had much reason to be proud of its school, which has graduated many efficient organizers."[25]

The announcement of courses for the 1923–24 school year delineated the school's revolutionary orientation and adherence to IWW tenets:

This school recognizes the existence of class struggle in society, and its courses of study have been prepared so that industrially organized workers, both men and women, dissatisfied with conditions under our capitalist system, can more efficiently carry on an organized class struggle for the attainment of industrial demands, and realistically of a new social order.[26]

Work People's College served, first, to create "a revolutionary working class" in order to generate radical social change, and second, to prepare workers to govern the new social order. "In the future," T. Kekkonen wrote in an advertisement for the school in 1924, "working class education is more important in view of the necessary revolutionary change that is expected to take place in the control in the means of production and distribution." Therefore, Work People's College did not educate workers "to rise out of" their social class, but trained them "to become a more powerful factor in the class struggle." [27] The social and educational goals of Work People's College entailed a rejection of bourgeois ideology propagated by the formal school system. By teaching English to Finnish working-class immigrants and imbuing them with socialist and later IWW doctrine, the founders and proponents of the school hoped that its students, as labor activists, would help to realize the political aspirations of the radical labor movement.

The year between the Lawrence and Paterson strikes represented the high-water mark for the IWW. Following the Paterson defeat, the union declined in the East—where it had achieved its most dramatic gains—because of internal disintegration and the disaffection of its socialist and anarchist allies. In 1915 and 1916, the IWW thrived in the West and Midwest, taking advantage of the expansion of lumber and agricultural production spurred by the European war. However, as soon as the United States entered the conflict, the government no longer tolerated interference in the production process and directed the massive repression of the union. Still, industrial unionism, notably membership in the IWW, remained strong among the upper midwestern Finns well into the 1920s. In spite of an unsuccessful three-month strike led by the IWW in the Mesabi Range in 1916, the union and its ideology continued to maintain a foothold in the region. The 1919 nationwide government purge of the union likewise did not abate its influence in the West and Midwest, especially in the lumber camps of Washington and in the farming areas of North Dakota and Montana during harvest time. Throughout the spring and summer of 1923, the IWW resorted to strike actions to gain the release of "class war prisoners" incarcerated in federal prisons. While Wobblies debated among themselves over the relative success or failure of the strike strategy, the union received wide support, particularly from the American Civil Liberties Union (ACLU) and from various liberals, for its amnesty campaign. By the end of the year, all of the federally held IWW prisoners had been released. The IWW exerted some influence among lumber, general construction, maritime, and migrant workers through the early twenties, but the mechanization of the agricultural and construction industries and the concomitant elimination of masses of unskilled workers during the mid- and late twenties sounded the death knell for the IWW in those industries. Yet, as late as 1927, the IWW led the Colorado miners' strike with its usual flair for publicity and color. [28]

Brookwood Labor College

Brookwood, located near Katonah, New York, experienced a far less turbulent beginning than Work People's College. It was founded in 1921 as a result of a remarkable conference of idealistic labor leaders and intellectuals who believed that the workers' cause and the goal of a new society could best be advanced through education.

Shortly after the First World War, William and Helen Fincke, both pacifists, opened a progressive school for working-class children in a Westchester County, New York, mansion that strongly resembled Mount Vernon. William W. Fincke, the son of a coal operator and graduate of Yale, brought strong ideological and spiritual convictions to the project. He had become a pacifist after working at a base hospital during the war, and had served as pastor of the Presbyterian Labor Temple in New York City. Added to his religious and political commitments was an active involvement in the labor movement; in 1919 he was arrested in Duquesne, Pennsylvania, for his participation in the Great Steel Strike.

The Finckes' strong convictions had an impact on their school. They attempted to combine labor education with peace studies in order to instill in their students social awareness and a respect for peace and brotherhood. They expressed their devotion to democratic principles by making the school democratic almost to a fault. Eight or ten committees, known in the Quaker tradition as "delegations," governed the Brookwood School, and new committee chairs were elected every month. Relying heavily on John Dewey's philosophy of progressive education, the Finckes set about training workers who, upon reaching adulthood, would play an important role in bringing about social and political reforms within their own particular labor organization as well as in the industrial sector of American society as a whole.

Although filled to capacity in its second year, the Brookwood School was a financial drain on its founders. Moreover, their concern about contemporary social conditions, specifically the plight of the exploited working class, brought the Finckes closer to a labor perspective. In 1921 they decided to change the institution from a preparatory school to a college for adult workers; to this end, they invited the backing of the labor movement. Appealing to their labor contacts, largely from New York City, they called a historic conference of labor leaders, leading Socialists, educators, and radicals to discuss the prospect of founding "the first workers' college in America."[29]

The participants at the conference, which convened on March 31, 1921 in Katonah, predicated the need for a labor college on four assumptions:

First—That a new social order is needed and is coming—in fact, that is already on the way.

Second—That education will not only hasten its coming, but will reduce to a minimum and perhaps do away entirely with a resort to violent methods.

Third—That the workers are the ones who will usher in the new social order.

Fourth—That there is immediate need for a workers' college with a broad curriculum, located amid healthy country surroundings, where the student can completely apply themselves to the task at hand.[30]

Released to the *New York Times*, this declaration echoed a strong socialist influence. More importantly, as with Work People's College, the founders of Brookwood Labor College emphasized that education could play a significant role in social change.

The political and labor backgrounds of the conferees attested to the meeting's radical character. Self-styled labor progressives opposed the conservative AFL leadership and some of their reactionary policies. They attacked the exclusive craft unionism of the Federation and proposed that industrial workers should be included as well, and attempted to reform the AFL by boring from within. As Morris points out, "These people, many of them representatives of left-wing philosophies (especially socialism), came to express their reform sentiment through such workers' education enterprises as the Workers' Education Bureau and Brookwood Labor College and also through the Labor Publication Society, which published *Labor Age*, and the Conference for Progressive Labor Action." David Montgomery adds that "they pinned their hopes on workers' education to train cadre for future union efforts and to prepare organized workers to assume active roles in the management of their own industries." This was significant, since it signaled the "transformation of the meaning of 'workers' control" in these circles from an immediate collective seizure of power in the factory to training, as educator Horace Kallen put it, to enter 'into the tasks and problems of management.' " [31] (This group is also discussed in Chapters 3 and 5.)

Many struggling unions, particularly those in steel, textile, clothing, and mining, expressed interest in the project. William Z. Foster and John Fitzpatrick had played important roles in the Great Steel Strike of 1919 and were invited, but Foster declined because of prior commitments. Charles Kutz, chairman of the International Association of Machinists of the Pennsylvania Railroad, and Abraham Lefkowitz, of the American Federation of Teachers (AFT), participated in the conference. The ACWA sent its secretary, Joseph Schlossberg, while John Brophy, as president of District No. 2, represented the UMW. Not surprisingly, the ILGWU's Fannia Cohn, a strong proponent of workers' education, also joined in the proceedings along with Rose Schneiderman, head of the New York Women's Trade Union League. Although Debs could not attend the conference—he was still in prison—he later sent his "good wishes" in support of the educational venture. A. J. Muste, executive secretary of the Amalgamated Textile Workers (ATW), played an especially vital role in the school's development and growth.

Muste did not possess the rough-and-tumble labor background one would expect of the director of the country's foremost labor college. Rather, he gradually developed a militant social and educational perspective. Born in Holland in 1885, Muste came to the United States with his humble immigrant family in 1891, settling in Grand Rapids, Michigan. After graduating from Hope College, Muste taught in Iowa for a year before enrolling at the New Brunswick Theological Seminary, in New Jersey, in 1906. He concurrently attended philosophy classes at New York University and Columbia University, where he came into contact with many leading intellectuals, among them William James and John Dewey, "who later became a devoted friend." After his graduation and ordination in 1909, Muste married and accepted a position as a minister for the affluent Fort Washington Collegiate Church in New York's Washington Heights section. The Collegiate Church was the oldest church in the city, dating back to the original Dutch colony of New Amsterdam. As Muste recalled, "One advantage of the location was that it was only a few blocks north of where the Yankee ballpark was then located. Another was that Union Theological Seminary was close enough . . . to take some courses there."[32]

Muste had been profoundly influenced by proponents of the social gospel. Protestant clergymen, disturbed by the social-class cleavages of American society, offered their own answers embodied in what came to be known as the social gospel. These religious critics argued that an immoral society was incompatible with the ideals of moral human beings. The salvation of society replaced the redemption of an individual soul as the principal religious goal. Although the majority of social gospel adherents were moderates, some saw society recast in the form of a Christian socialist commonwealth, thereby offering individuals an opportunity to lead moral lives. These teachers and their notions of social reform, in Muste's own words, "opened a new approach to the study of religion and new historical vistas, eventually forcing an 'agonizing re-appraisal' of the beliefs in which I had been reared."[33] His first encounter with Norman Thomas, then a young Presbyterian minister, took place in a graduate seminar. In 1912, Muste graduated magna cum laude with a bachelor of divinity degree.

In spite of his orthodox religious background and training, Muste's social and political orientation continued to shift toward theological liberalism. He voted for Debs, the Socialist candidate, in the 1912 presidential election, and resigned his ministerial post in 1914 to accept a similar position at the less conservative Central Congregation Church in Newtonville, Massachusetts, a Boston suburb. Here he began his studies of the Christian mystics as well as of pacifism. Muste vacillated on the war between 1916 and 1917, but eventually embraced pacifism and stunned the congregation with his antiwar stand. His relationship with that congregation further deteriorated because of his antiwar activities, and he was asked to resign in 1918. Muste moved to Providence, Rhode Island, and began to attend meetings of the Providence Society of Friends. Soon hired as a minister, he taught a Bible class at the Quaker school, helped to form adult education groups, and maintained a reading room in the meeting house basement. Muste had absorbed the social action philosophy of the Society of Friends, his spiritual home for the rest of his life. Muste also maintained a working relationship with antiwar activists in Boston. His acquaintance with Roger N. Baldwin dates from this period. Baldwin, in 1917, assisted by Muste's Union classmate, Norman Thomas, founded the National Civil Liberties Bureau, the precursor to the ACLU. Muste returned to Boston as a Quaker minister in the fall of 1918, but alarmed even the Friends with his increasingly radical ideas. His plunge into labor activism ended his career as a Quaker minister.

Muste played an important role in the 1919 Lawrence, Massachusetts, textile strike. Like the 1912 mass strike, the strike seven years later entailed a walkout, on February 3, 1919, of some thirty thousand immigrant weavers who protested the threat of wage cuts and the chronically poor job conditions. The IWW, which had provided the organizational leadership for the protracted 1912 strike, was weak and ineffective in the East because of its defeat in the 1913 Paterson, New Jersey, silk workers' strike, internecine warfare, and government suppression during and after the war. The AFL affiliate, the United Textile Workers, denounced the walkout as part of a revolutionary movement. Although the workers lacked organizational support, they remained undaunted.

Muste had traveled to Lawrence to study mill conditions and to observe the strike first hand. He was invited by the workers to sit in on the early strike committee meetings. Because of his education and social contacts, he was urged by the strikers to accept the position of executive head so that they could achieve more favorable press coverage. They also thought he would be able to facilitate more efficient communications among the strikers and participate in strategic planning. Muste soon learned the price of labor activism when he was beaten and jailed for picketing. He was subsequently released and acquitted of the charges but continued to face threats of labor spies and further encounters with the police. Although often provoked by the police and the mill owners, the strikers remained largely nonviolent, due to a large extent to the Muste's pacifist counseling. In April, the workers organized the ATW, a union independent of the AFL, and received assistance from the ACWA.

By May, both strikers and mill owners were exhausted. The owners capitulated, and the workers won all of their demands. Muste was elected general secretary of the ATW in October and assumed the editorship of the *New Textile Worker*, the union's official organ. Muste advocated that ATW members not be satisfied with shorter hours and higher wages alone; rather, they should strike for a "future reorganization of the system of production." Reflecting his militancy and foreshadowing his involvement with Brookwood Labor College, Muste promoted worker cooperatives in Lawrence and workers' education in Passaic, New Jersey.

In October 1921, at the age of thirty-six, Muste resigned his union post and accepted William Fincke's plea that he serve as director of Brookwood Labor College. Weary of the incessant conflicts that plagued his official post in the ATW and in dire need of a more reflective mode of life, Muste saw the Brookwood position as ideal: "I had never intended to become a labor official. I believed that my background, training, and so-called talents were such as to enable me to be much more useful in a workers' education venture than in the textile union post." [34]

Many of Brookwood's founders and early labor supporters were socialists. As Muste recalled, "All had something of a socialist background and could be classified as socialists with a small 's.'" They were neither intellectuals nor theorists, but all had come out of the ranks of the workers and were most concerned with organizing workers in order "to carry on the day-to-day struggle for improved working conditions, shorter hours, better wages, and status in the mill, mine, or schoolroom." In short, they were "practical" and "down to earth," and as Muste recalled, they "indulged in the habit of broadcasting this fact to all and sundry." They criticized the AFL's narrow craft unionism and claimed "that the workers would never solve their basic problems unless they strove for a radical reorganization of society, and that such a reorganization was possible." Their interest in workers' education, particularly in a resident labor college, stemmed in part from their own lack of formal education, which, they felt, handicapped their union activities and personal intellectual lives. "The younger strike leaders and trade unionists to whom the older leaders looked to back them up in local unions and on shop or pit committees—children of working-class families—had for the most part been compelled to go to work on graduation from eighth grade, if not before." [35]

James H. Maurer, socialist president of the Pennsylvania Federation of Labor, typified this group of labor leaders. Born and raised in the Reading–Pottstown area of eastern Pennsylvania, Maurer was a lifelong labor radical. He joined the Knights of Labor as an apprentice machinist in 1880, on his sixteenth birthday, and shortly thereafter became Worthy Foreman, or vice-president, and organized Iron

Workers' Assembly No. 7975. Later he opened his own machine shop, but local businessmen, who opposed his support of the Populist party, ruined the business venture.

After similar short-lived attempts as a newspaper publisher and cigar store owner, Maurer and his brother organized a socialist local in 1899 in Hamburg, Pennsylvania. Employers blacklisted Maurer for his radical activities. Nevertheless, he formally joined the Socialist party in 1901 and became a member of the State Executive Committee in 1903. A year later he began his long service on the party's National Executive Committee. In 1910, Maurer became the first Socialist elected to the Pennsylvania General Assembly; he was reelected in 1914. A rank-and-file movement also elected him president of the Pennsylvania Federation of Labor in 1912, a post he held until 1928. As a Socialist, Maurer opposed America's participation in the First World War, and with Morris Hillquit and Meyer London, met with President Woodrow Wilson to express this view. The Pennsylvania Federation of Labor voted to oppose the war, incurring Gompers's wrath. Maurer's political and labor activities during the 1920s were highlighted by his 1927 election, along with other Socialists, to the Reading, Pennsylvania, city council, his nomination as the Socialist party's vice-presidential candidate with Norman Thomas in 1928 and 1932, and, finally, his active support of and participation in the workers' education movement as chairman of the Workers' Education Bureau and president of the Brookwood board of directors. The AFPS asked him to survey the workers' education movement in 1923, and among those he recommended for financial support were Work People's College, Brookwood, and Commonwealth College. [36]

Maurer's support for workers' education stemmed from his strong opinions about public education in the United States. Because of his irregular attendance, he rated his own public school education as marginal and generally viewed the public school system as a "penal institution." More importantly, for Maurer, the formal schools propagated antilabor attitudes:

Workingmen's children return from school with accounts of indictments of the labor movement made by their teachers or by propagandists who have been allowed to address the pupils. Horrible stories have been told about the Bolsheviki, and in the next breath the suggestion has been made that the American labor unions are filled with such people. Children have been led to feel that their own fathers, as active unionists, have been made the dupes of treasonable conspirators.

Because the public schools shunned prolabor perspectives, academic freedom was a sham. Maurer continued,

> From all parts of the country come hundreds of authentic reports of restrictions put upon professors and teachers who would discuss labor problems freely. But what else can we expect? The boards of education and the boards of trustees of the colleges and the universities are composed almost entirely of influential business and professional men who have a deep-seated fear and hatred of anything that can be construed as encouragement to the labor movement. They are extremely conservative, if not reactionary, on all social and economic questions.

Formal education, in Maurer's opinion, taught passive acceptance and conformity to a bourgeois value system:

> The individuality of the student is suppressed. The attempt is made to mold all minds by the same pattern and independence, originality, and self-reliance are discouraged. Our children are being trained like dogs and ponies, not developed as individuals. Such methods, together with the vicious propaganda on social and economic questions to which the children are subjected, produce just the results that the conservative and reactionary elements of the country want, namely, uniformity of thought and conduct, no originality or self-reliance except for money-making schemes, a worshipful attitude toward those who have wealth and power, intolerance for anything that the business element condemns, and ignorance of the great social and economic forces that are shaping the destinies of all of us. [37]

The public high schools permitted the creation of junior chambers of commerce, but ignored working-class problems. As Maurer saw it, the formal education system could not function to liberate the workers; this would be labor's task.

Unionists at the 1921 Katonah conference that founded Brookwood supported the notion of a resident labor college because they felt that workers should be imbued with socialist theory and trained to participate in social change. Maurer best expressed this point, in 1927, in a speech delivered to the Fifth Annual Convention of the Workers' Education Bureau: "The underlying purpose of workers' education is the desire for a better social order, the desire of workers for a richer and fuller life, individually and collectively. . . . Labor education aims at the ultimate liberation of the working masses." Maurer emphasized that in order to maintain radical goals, workers' education classes and schools had to avoid affiliation with any capitalist institution, including the use of public school facilities. In Pennsylvania, he pointed out, school boards generally balked at requests to use public school facilities for workers' education because they feared a "bolshevik point of view." Put simply, radical workers' classes and schools had to be independent. Only then, Maurer argued, could labor problems and solutions be discussed freely and critically:

> In its broadest sense, workers' education cannot limit itself to conducting classes or to preparing reports on books, but must embrace every phase of culture and study every part of our social structure. No dogma, whether originating among the employing class or in some labor or radical group, must be held sacred. Instead we must seek light and understanding everywhere in order that the individual may determine for himself or herself proper guidance and the ways of truth.

For Maurer, this concept of workers' education served a broader social movement. "Labor education is part of the labor movement and is necessary for its existence because the labor movement is the essential force in the remodeling of the social structure."[38]

To accomplish this objective, the labor participants at the Katonah conference insisted that potential union leaders and activists be equipped with the skills necessary to organize and perpetuate a union. Yet they emphatically avoided creating a school to train labor bureaucrats. By so doing, Brookwood's labor proponents maintained theoretical as well as practical goals for the curriculum.

Other groups attended the Katonah meeting as well. Like working-class radicals, some middle-class liberals supported the establishment of alternative forms of education for workers during the early 1900s. As Schultz has characterized this phenomenon, "Workers' education . . . until the 1940's often attracted intellectuals who subscribed to a left liberal or left analysis of society and who felt that the working class should be instrumental in bringing about changes in the social order and that workers' education was one means by which to give workers the knowledge and skills to carry out such changes."[39] Brookwood's founding meeting included social scientists following in the path of John R. Commons and progressive educators in the mold of John Dewey. Roger Baldwin, AFPS director and a founder of the newly organized ACLU, attended the Katonah meeting. Other participants, such as Arthur Gleason, who had recently returned from a five-year stint in London as a reporter for the *New York Tribune*, brought the European experience of workers' education with them.[40]

Thus, distinct perceptions of social and educational change influenced and supported the creation of some of the labor colleges during the early decades of the twentieth century. Working-class radicals, on the one hand, articulated the need for fundamental social change and recognized that workers' education, as an integral part of the labor movement, could contribute to the change process. Liberals, on the other hand, espoused social reform and argued that educational reform, possibly in the guise of workers' education, could ameliorate social problems.

The early links between Brookwood and the Workers' Education Bureau were indeed close. The Katonah conference adjourned after two days so that several of the participants could attend the founding meeting of the WEB in New York City. In fact, many of the same union officials selected as labor advisors for Brookwood were also elected to the WEB's executive committee.

An announcement released to the *New York Times* outlined the social and educational goals of Brookwood Labor College. First, Brookwood would challenge "the prevailing system of higher education in the United States which is dominated by men who benefit by special privilege." Because of capitalist domination, the American education system failed to serve the needs of the "laboring class." Second, unlike institutions in the formal education system, Brookwood intended to serve the interests of workers and the labor movement. The official statement proclaimed:

> It was decided to unite with the labor union movement a force
> of education that will serve American labor with trained, respon-
> sible, liberally educated men and women from the ranks of the
> workers. . . . The college will closely cooperate with the national
> and international labor groups, also with the various local colleges

and schools that send to it working men and women who show promise as to need further education in order to best serve the labor movement and through it society. [41]

Brookwood's founders further claimed that the school would represent the first resident workers' college in the nation; they inexplicably overlooked Duluth's Work People's College and its many years of service in the workers' education movement.

The founding committee further enumerated Brookwood's goals in another statement that appeared in the *New York Times* during the summer of 1921. Because Brookwood stood for "a new and better social order," the school maintained "social values rather than pecuniary ones." Hence, Brookwood endeavored to produce labor activists and leaders who would serve as "economists, statisticians, journalists, writers and teachers, as well as organizers, workers and speakers for the labor and farm movements." Brookwood's working-class students were expected to use their training to solve labor problems. The school eschewed the conventional goals of social mobility and personal advancement, so prominent in the formal educational system. Brookwood served as a professional school, the statement continued, "to educate workers to work in the workers' movements and frankly aims not to educate workers out of their class." [42]

Throughout the years, Brookwood's *Bulletin and Announcement of Courses* expressed similar, if less cogent, statements of the school's purposes. The 1932–33 bulletin provides an example:

> Brookwood thinks of itself as part of the labor movement of America and the world. Brookwood thinks of the labor movement both as a practical instrument by which workers achieve higher wages, shorter hours, and better conditions of work, and as a great social force having as its ultimate goal the good life for all men in a social order free from exploitation and based upon control by the workers. Our chief concern in this connection has been to discover means for increasing the power of the working class and its organizations, for the achievement of its immediate and ultimate goals. [43]

Having successfully transferred Brookwood's leadership to the labor movement, the Finckes agreed to donate their forty-two-acre estate to the resident labor college. Leaving Muste on his own to

shape the new educational venture, they left Brookwood to establish the Manumit School, a progressive labor school for working-class
children, in nearby Dutchess County, New York. Muste's next task
was to secure a faculty. He persuaded labor historian David J. Saposs
and sociologist Arthur W. Calhoun to join the faculty; Sarah Cleghorn, a carryover from the Finckes' preparatory school, became an
English instructor, but was replaced at midyear by Josephine "Polly"
Colby, an AFT organizer. A variety of short-term teachers and visiting lecturers completed the faculty, and a dietitian, a superintendent
of buildings and grounds, and secretarial employees rounded out the
staff. In September 1921 Brookwood opened for classes with great
optimism against the backdrop of the Russian Revolution, which for
many radicals and progressives became the harbinger of dramatic and
positive social change everywhere.[44] Evelyn Preston, a major benefactor of Brookwood, later recalled the heady atmosphere: "Workers'
education seemed an important adjunct to the efficient and successful
assumption of power by the workers themselves."[45]

Commonwealth College

Commonwealth College, which opened in 1923 in the unlikely
location of western Louisiana and later moved to Mena, Arkansas, was
often called the "Brookwood of the Southwest." Among the school's
founders were William E. Zeuch and Kate Richards O'Hare—the "first
lady of American socialism"—who held a lifelong commitment to
socialist education.

Born in 1876 to a Kansas farm family, Kate Richards moved to
Kansas City when a severe drought forced her father to seek work as
a machinist. Kate attended elementary school there and later a normal
school, for teacher training, in Nebraska. She briefly taught school
and worked as a bookkeeper, but at the age of seventeen she made the
decision—remarkable for a young woman in the 1890s—to become
a machinist's apprentice and joined the IAM. A speech by the legendary Mother Jones at a cigar makers' hall sparked Kate's interest in
socialism, and in 1901 she enrolled at the newly opened International
School of Social Economy, a training school for Socialist party workers
in Girard, Kansas. There she met and married Frank P. O'Hare in a
ceremony held at J. A. Wayland's home. As newlyweds they toured
the Midwest and East making speeches and writing for the socialist
cause. They returned to Kansas City and eventually settled in Okla-

homa, where they raised four children. Family responsibilities did not keep Kate O'Hare from activism. She traveled throughout the Southwest speaking at the popular summer encampments that were reminiscent of the religious and Populist camp meetings of former days. As Philip S. Foner and Sally M. Miller write, "Throngs of five thousand and more would gather for a week or two under the broiling southwestern sun to hear O'Hare, Gene Debs, Mother Jones, and others, to sing socialist songs set to gospel and other familiar melodies, and to attend economic and historical 'educationals.' " [46]

By 1910, Kate Richards O'Hare had earned a national reputation as a spellbinding speaker second only to Debs in popularity on the Socialist platform. Between 1911 and 1917, she served on the Women's National Committee and the National Executive Committee of the Socialist party, edited the *National Rip-Saw*, ran for the House and the Senate, sought the party's vice-presidential nomination, and presided as chairwoman of the War and Militarism Committee at the highly significant Saint Louis Emergency Convention in April 1917. O'Hare was also elected international secretary of the Socialist party in 1912 and became the only American woman to hold that post in the Second International. During the First World War, the government prosecuted O'Hare, like Debs and other radical leaders, under the Espionage Act for her antiwar speeches. She served fourteen months of a five-year sentence at the Missouri State Penitentiary.

O'Hare held complex and often contradictory notions of socialism. On the one hand, she adopted a reformist view of socialism closer to the Berger-Hillquit wing of the Socialist party than to the more radical Debsian wing. Thus, Neil Basen points out, "No force or violence was required to promote the millennium, and even compensation to expropriated capitalists to ensure a peaceful transition was conceivable." [47] On the other hand, O'Hare, like Debs, endorsed industrial unionism and condemned the pure and simple unionism of the AFL as well as Gompers's class collaboration with the National Civic Federation (NCF). Unlike Debs, however, O'Hare held the IWW in low regard and in 1912 supported the Socialist party's censure of the union's revolutionary platform of sabotage and direct economic action. O'Hare argued, like Berger and Hillquit, that the AFL could gradually be converted to socialism through aggressive tactics of "boring from within." Moreover, she actively opposed sexism within the party and advocated women's rights. Paradoxically, she also maintained racist ideas. Before the war, she saw the goal of a cooperative commonwealth as having two distinct social realities. Yet, by the 1920s, because of her association with black prisoners at the Missouri State Penitentiary, O'Hare's racial attitudes had softened and eventually evolved to advocate complete economic and social equality for blacks. In Basen's words, "Militant in tone and temperament, moderate in theory and tactics, and 'American as apple pie,' she was a pragmatic, conciliatory, constructive, and centrist socialist who courageously devoted twenty years of her life to building a viable, democratic mass movement."[48]

O'Hare's experience as a social activist contrasted sharply with William Zeuch's academic background. Born in Iowa in 1891, Zeuch attended Lenox College from 1911 to 1915, taught school for a brief period, then earned a master's degree in sociology at Clark University. After serving in the armed forces, Zeuch worked as a high school principal in Iowa before entering the Cornell graduate school in 1919. Zeuch eventually completed his doctorate at the University of Wisconsin in 1922, where he served as a research assistant to John R. Commons. Zeuch taught at Wisconsin and the University of Illinois until he left in the summer of 1923 to become Commonwealth College's first director.

Zeuch became involved with the new college through his association with Kate and Frank O'Hare. The concept of Commonwealth originated in 1917 when Zeuch and Kate O'Hare met with other planners to discuss the problems at Ruskin College, a Christian Socialist school in Tampa, Florida. For ideological reasons, that school had disintegrated after the United States' entrance into World War I, and the conferees decided not to attempt to reopen the school until after the war. However, O'Hare, who had just spent two years at Ruskin, and Zeuch agreed that there was a need for a resident workers' college that offered cultural enrichment and technical training for young workers and farmers from socialist, trade-union, and cooperative movements. The political repression of the left during the war, which resulted in the arrest and imprisonment of many socialist, anarchist, and IWW leaders, had further created a need for new leaders to revitalize the left. As Zeuch recalled ten years later, "Over a period of several months, Mrs. O'Hare and I studied Ruskin, talked over our own educational ideas, and decided to work together to establish a school for workers. The war cut into our plans. . . . When the war orgy was over we took up our plans again. For a period of six years, all told, we searched for an opportunity to launch our experiment."[49]

Their idea for a labor school found an unexpected ally. Early in

1923, the O'Hares had moved the publication of their periodical, the *American Vanguard*—previously the *National Rip-Saw*, suppressed by the government during the war—to the Newllano Cooperative Colony in western Louisiana. Patterned after nineteenth-century utopian experiments, that colony functioned as a model cooperative society and was the brainchild of Job Harriman, a prominent Socialist and Clarence Darrow's legal associate during the notorious McNamara brothers case. Harriman had joined a Nationalist Club in the early 1890s, one of 158 such groups which attempted to achieve Edward Bellamy's vision of a fully cooperative state. While he embraced Marxism, Harriman was convinced that socialism could only be spread through practical economic activity, not politics. His vision took form in May 1914 as the Llano Cooperative Colony, in Antelope Valley, north of Los Angeles, which by 1917 claimed eight hundred colonists. Organizational problems and water shortages, however, forced the colony to move to Vernon Parish, Louisiana, that same year, where it was renamed Newllano. Internal dissension, poor leadership, and insolvency reduced Newllano's membership from 200 to 65 colonists within a year. Under the leadership of George Pickett, a longtime colonist and manager of Llano's educational system, the colony had partially recovered between 1920 and 1922. Eventually it became one of the largest and most successful cooperative colonies in America, with 600 colonists and 20,000 acres, containing factories, presses, and sawmills. The colonists welcomed the O'Hares and hoped that their presence and publishing operation would enhance the colony. The *Vanguard*, it was proposed, would be published in the colony print shop, under the O'Hares' management, for one year. After that time, the paper would be transferred to the colony in exchange for membership for the O'Hares.

Yet Kate O'Hare's concerns were still focused on establishing a resident labor college for workers; she found Newllano an ideal location for the college and contacted Zeuch. Together they made plans to open the school, believing that it had to remain independent of any institutional or factional constraints. The colonists generally expressed enthusiasm for the idea and voted to donate forty acres for a campus. Ironically, that land was mortgaged, but the colonists decided not to inform the O'Hares. Thus, if buildings were erected, they would be owned neither by the college nor by the colony—a "slimy" state of affairs, as one observer noted later. O'Hare, Zeuch, and A. James McDonald, selected by Pickett as the colony's representative, formed an unincorporated trusteeship, the Commonwealth College Association. The *Vanguard* ran glowing double-paged announcements that attracted a large number of applicants. The students, in return for twenty-four hours of work a week for the colony, were to receive the same food and housing as the colonists. At McDonald's suggestion, enrollment was limited to fifty students, because the colony's primitive equipment could not furnish enough work.

As one of the school's founders and as its first director, Zeuch voiced its goals at the opening ceremony on September 30, 1923: "Here any worker may acquire education by earning while he is here, lack of money barring no one. Commonwealth . . . is experimental and in a laboratory way trying to work out a better system of economic and social relationships." The school offered a three-year course of study taught by O'Hare, Zeuch, Harriman, Howard Buck, and F. M. Goodhue, among others. O'Hare also served as field director, McDonald as financial director, and Howard Z. Brown as executive secretary. The curriculum had a definite socialistic flavoring; "Proletarian Literature," for example, was among the courses offered. [50]

Despite that strong start, the overcrowded students suffered from poor housing and a monotonous diet of sweet potatoes, rice, and syrup. Worse yet, the colony's physical conditions were less than ideal, with poor sanitation, stable waste, open toilets, and drains full of vegetation and rubbish. Typhoid struck in 1923, and Kate O'Hare fell victim, recovering only after a brush with death. Local authorities intervened and ordered the colony to clean up immediately. Because colony officials refused to provide the money for a centralized college building, college trustees were forced to apply to the American Fund for Public Service for a grant.

The AFPS encapsulated much of the history of the American left during the 1920s. Charles Garland, Harvard graduate, pacifist, son of a Wall Street banker, and anything but an ideologue, reluctantly accepted his father's inheritance of one million dollars in 1920 but immediately decided to distribute it among friends for worthy, radical causes. Roger Baldwin, of the ACLU, quickly established an organizational structure, consisting of a board of directors, to oversee the dispersal operations. Baldwin consciously organized the agency for, as he stated it, the "radical destruction of the capitalist system" through intellectual and "proletarian power." Gloria Garrett Samson argues that the activities of the AFPS anticipated Gramsci's notion of counter-hegemony: "From the outset, Baldwin envisioned the Fund as a counter-hegemonic force, which would promote the vision of a society radically different from that promoted by bourgeois opinion-makers and myth-promoters, those with a stake in the status quo."[51] In this regard, members of the AFPS board, influenced by Dewey's philosophy, saw education as "extremely important in the quest of a good society," and they viewed workers' education as a vehicle to combat bourgeois influences; or, as Samson states it, "to overcome the dominant ideology and to instill critical self-consciousness in the workers."[52] During its existence, the Fund invested $366,000 in various workers' education operations, and its contributions sustained both Brookwood and Commonwealth through the 1920s. The directors delayed their decision about Commonwealth's initial request for funding pending an investigation of the school and a review of another grant application from Newllano Colony. Unknowingly, the colonists and the "Commoners" had initiated the first of many conflicts that would eventually divide them.

Relations between Newllano and Commonwealth deteriorated further when it became known that the *Vanguard*, which had published fifteen issues at Newllano, had accumulated considerable debts and became a major financial burden. In May 1924, the Newllano board of directors voted to cease publication of the *Vanguard*. Bitter debates raged between the colonists and the college group when Newllano's administration advocated absorbing the college into the colony's own school system. The Commoners felt that such a step would destroy the academic freedom that was essential to Commonwealth's educational purpose. A break between the colony and the college became inevitable: the college would have to go elsewhere.

The Commoners embarked upon an eventful odyssey in their search for a new location. The O'Hares withdrew from the colony during the late summer, and Kate traveled to New York to raise funds for the new school. Meanwhile, a site selection committee, which included Zeuch, scoured Oklahoma, southern Missouri, Tennessee, and Arkansas for a new location. The general requirements of soil, climate, and landscape appeared to be ideally met in Polk County, Arkansas. In December 1924, Dick O'Hare, Kate's eldest son, rented buildings in Mena, which were intended only as a temporary site. A faculty of eight, thirty-five students, and several families soon arrived from Newllano. After setting up a library, auditorium, dining hall, class-rooms, and dormitories, they immediately settled into their routine. A new Commonwealth College Association was created in the spring of

1925, but the school was bankrupt. Zeuch went to New York to expedite an emergency grant from the AFPS, and he visited with Muste at Brookwood to review Commonwealth's dilemma. Muste sent a recommendation to Roger Baldwin on behalf of Commonwealth. Yet Muste's letter of support expressed some doubts about the school, focusing on the ambitious plans for Commonwealth's physical plant, which he felt were too "big" and would consume "a tremendous amount of energy." He further questioned the length of Commonwealth's program, which would take "people out of the labor movement for four years, or in the case of those who take some preparatory work, as much as six or seven years, and then [expect] them to go back and find a place in the [labor] movement."[53]

Still other problems plagued the school. The religious orthodoxy of the rural Mena community soon asserted itself. A student, Willie Seegars, was arrested in March 1925 for unlawful cohabitation; his wife's father had contested their marriage. Seegars's marriage was upheld and he was released. Commoners also aroused fundamentalist ire when some female students unabashedly wore knickers in public. This was too much for Mena residents to bear. They could not help but notice "the proportions and attractiveness of plump calves and otherwise sturdily formed underpinnings."[54] While most students complied with the college's request to cease and desist wearing knickers, two students, with some faculty support, flouted it. Zeuch resolved the dispute when he returned from New York, but only after the two protestors had been restricted to their quarters. The whole matter was soon forgotten.

Fortunately, before any other confrontations occurred, Commoners located a permanent site for the school, an eighty-acre farm eleven miles west of Mena and only four miles from the Oklahoma border. They secured an $800 mortgage but faced the unhappy prospect of insufficient housing on the new "campus." People crowded into the existing farmhouse, which was little more than a shack, and slept on the floor. Others arranged living quarters in the two barns, while some, like Zeuch, pitched old army tents. Commoners immediately embarked on an extensive building program. When Kate O'Hare arrived, she subsidized the construction of her own house, which later became the guest house. Zeuch resumed his duties as director while O'Hare continued to serve as field secretary and teach classes.

However, the local, largely Baptist community regarded Commonwealth with suspicion and remained aloof. They believed the institution to be a Roman Catholic organization in disguise. When they discovered the true nature of the school, they appeared greatly relieved and became very friendly. Many of the college's neighbors even attended the opening ceremony on October 1, 1925, and heard O'Hare proclaim: "Commonwealth College was founded to help meet the great need of the labor movement for its own institutions of higher learning."[55]

Commonwealth continued to experience a smooth transition. In November, the AFPS sent Clinton Golden to inspect the new school and submit a progress report. He left campus impressed. Based on his recommendation, the Fund gave the college $35,000 to buy 240 additional acres, purchase a truck, machinery, and tools, and pay debts. The Fund did not supply the subsidy in a lump sum, but made the same arrangement with Commonwealth as it did with Brookwood, that is, it allotted the money over time.

The ideological background of Commonwealth's founders certainly shaped the school's early social and educational purposes. Indeed, Kate O'Hare's perception of workers' education reflected her socialist background. In addition to political action and an expanded labor movement, she saw an important role for education in attaining the cooperative commonwealth. At the inaugural ceremonies for Commonwealth in 1923 (at Newllano), O'Hare had explicated the need for workers' education separate from the mainstream. For O'Hare, the entire formal education system served the needs of the "owning classes," who presided over the public school boards and ultimately determined what was taught. "Under the domination of the ruling class," O'Hare argued, echoing Maurer, "our public school system has developed into an efficient method of molding and shaping the growing generation to the ideals most useful to the exploiters of labor." O'Hare pointed to the privately endowed institutions of higher learning that were reserved exclusively for the privileged classes and wholly excluded workers. Even the state universities and the colleges of agriculture and mechanics were created to train managers and technicians for industry. Commonwealth College, in contrast, was conceived "by the workers, for the workers, with a cultural ideal harmonious with productive life." Ultimately, Commonwealth would help workers overthrow capitalism and create a new society, a society that would retain the best of bourgeois life.

Commonwealth comes into being to build a culture in overalls and workmarked hands; a culture whose ideal is a working class fit to

inherit and hold the earth and the fulness thereof. But because it is
to be a working-class culture is no reason that it should be coarse
and uncouth. Boorishness is not strength, and true refinement
and gentleness are not weakness. . . . We shall take from the old
college all that is fine and useful and beautiful and make it our
own. We shall claim all the best of literature, music, art, and the
thoughtful consideration for others that are the foundations and
ornaments of manhood and womanhood.[56]

Zeuch likewise envisioned workers' education committed to social
change:

Workers' education . . . is not for the individual aggrandizement
of the worker; it is no economic or social ladder. . . . The intelligent, progressive young workers of today desire an education that
will give them insight into the dynamics of social change so as to
enable them more to foster and promote their group interests and
along with such interests the general welfare of society.[57]

In order for a resident labor college to maintain a commitment to social
change, it had to remain autonomous. Zeuch appeared to emphasize
this latter point. Moreover, only a nondogmatic educational program
guaranteed a democratic and scientific approach to finding practical
solutions to pressing social and economic problems. As long as Zeuch
remained as director of Commonwealth, "academic objectivity" appeared to be more than pretentious rhetoric—albeit not without creating some tension among the teachers and students. However, this
"objective scientific attitude," as Zeuch termed it, did not preclude a
critical examination of social problems and the labor movement. Independent labor colleges served the labor movement as "the center of
intellectual ferment to leaven a dynamic labor movement."

Commonwealth's stated goals conformed to these notions. As
Zeuch turned the first sod at the new site, he recited, "We will here
build an institution that will mark an epoch in the history of education
for workers—and thereby prepare for service directed to the enlight-
enment of the masses and the reconstruction of society—and with this
hope we face the future with confidence." Commonwealth opposed
the prevailing ideology of the formal educational system. "Established
education," by educating the elite, functioned to maintain the status
quo; it served individual interests, that is, individual social mobility
rather than social reform. For Commonwealth, however, "social re-

vision" remained axiomatic. The school's existence was "based upon a sense of social responsibility and a refusal to unthinkingly accept things as they are." As the *Commonwealth College Fortnightly* expressed it, Commonwealth's "object is to serve all the organizations and promote all the activities that aim at the improvement of the life and conditions of the productive workers. It seeks to help young workers fit themselves for intelligent, constructive services to their class."[58] Thus, Commonwealth did not symbolize a utopian society like the Newllano Colony but prepared workers to further the political and economic aims of the American labor movement through collective action. Raymond and Charlotte Koch, former students and later teachers and administrators at the school, cogently summarized Commonwealth's mission: "We were never interested in becoming a haven of escape from the evils of capitalism. One of our premises was that the entire structure of society would have to be reformed and transformed to eliminate the disorders of an unplanned, competitive society."[59]

In summary, the social and educational purpose of all three of the labor colleges—the preparation of labor leaders and activists to organize and lead workers in radical social change activity—reflected the tenets of the radical labor movement in general and the experiences and ideological backgrounds of their founders and supporters in particular. However, although Work People's College, Brookwood Labor College, and Commonwealth College evinced similar goals, minor differences did exist. While Brookwood and Commonwealth remained institutionally autonomous, Work People's College maintained its ties with the Socialist party—indirectly through the Finnish Socialist Federation—and the IWW. Yet this affiliation failed to inhibit the transition in the school's perspective from a socialist political action perspective to the IWW's direct action view. Hence, the college's institutional associations appeared to be loose and in no way infringed upon its political autonomy and critical attitude. This represented an important distinction, as the teachers and students chose to remain loyal to industrial unionism; they never appeared to be captives of the union.

In an article published in the *Commonwealth College Fortnightly* in 1926, Arthur Calhoun, an instructor and director of studies at Brookwood, noted an apparent dissimilarity between Brookwood and Commonwealth.

One [school] is to provide a general, all round, education, dominated by the scientific spirit and governed by the belief that the labor movement may be best served by the broadest sort of scientific culture. The other is to offer a narrower, more professional training, shaped and limited by close consideration of what will presumably be utilitarian for active members of the labor movement. The former tendency is embodied in Commonwealth, the latter in Brookwood. [60]

Calhoun drew attention to the academism of Commonwealth and contrasted it to the functionalism of Brookwood. Yet this did not represent a fundamental difference, because both schools served the same basic purpose; that is, they strove to prepare leaders for a new social order. Calhoun expanded on this point: "Commonwealth may have more disinterested ideals of pure science in the objective sense; but we at Brookwood have faith in the class-consciousness of Commonwealth and in its pragmatic soundness. It will not worship a fetich of pseudo-science; on the contrary it will have only one goal—the emancipation of the working class." Brookwood, moreover, maintained intellectual standards not unlike Commonwealth's. As Calhoun pointed out: "We are not interested [at Brookwood] in buncombe, clap-trap, and short cuts, but . . . we aim to ground our work in a sound knowledge of reality, and to be scientific in the double sense of knowing what is what and of presenting it in such a way that it will grip those that have had no opportunity to find out for themselves."

In their efforts to provide an educational alternative to the formal school system, the labor colleges endeavored to train working-class activists and leaders to serve the labor movement and to transform bourgeois society into the cooperative commonwealth. This commitment to social change, more than any other characteristic, distinguished the labor-college education from union- and university-sponsored workers' education. The labor colleges equipped worker–students, through a full-time residential educational program, with the intellectual and practical skills necessary to organize and lead workers to a new social order.

3

Knowledge Is Power

Sound knowledge must precede successful action.
— *Work People's College Bulletin* (1923)

Action based on knowledge is power.
— Fannia Cohn, *Brookwood Labor
College Fifteenth Anniversary
Review* (1936)

LUCIEN KOCH, a teacher and later a director at Commonwealth College, once summarized the school's purpose as "educating leaders for a new society." In so doing, he succinctly delineated the general social and educational aspirations of the labor colleges. And the schools formulated educational programs that pursued these ideals. He believed that existing colleges and universities were incapable of providing effective workers' education because they were dominated by a bourgeois mentality that resulted in binding endowments by special interest groups or constraining legislative appropriations. Koch also attacked exclusive fraternity and sorority systems, excessive emphasis on varsity sports, and compulsory religious services. The founders of the labor colleges believed that without this bourgeois "claptrap" their students would not be distracted from their basic goal of education for social change, and accordingly fashioned an educational program that specifically served the needs and interests of workers. [1]

The labor colleges relied upon an ideological-confrontational educational program that emphasized social-class conflict and working-class solidarity. They achieved this through a variety of courses stressing content and social issues, and pedagogical techniques combining classroom interaction with militant off-campus activities. First, the formal curriculum provided rudimentary learning skills for workers with limited educational backgrounds. Second, every aspect of the formal curriculum sought to imbue the worker–student with class consciousness. The social sciences dominated the curriculum and concentrated on areas pertinent to the students' backgrounds and needs, while activities such as labor drama and fieldwork stressed class conflict. Third, informational courses enabled students to acquire the intellectual skills necessary to analyze their society and determine the roots of working-class problems. Fourth, "tool" courses emphasized the practical means by which to ameliorate working-class conditions. Helen G. Norton, a Brookwood instructor, concisely outlined these points:

> They're coming, in the first place, for knowledge . . . knowledge about their own unions, about the history of the labor movement in this and other countries. . . .
> Then they're coming to learn how to use facts after they have them—how to express their ideals so the crowd will get them and be moved to *action* by them; how to put ideas into print so people will read and understand them. They're coming to learn how people act under given conditions and why, and all the other things that psychology can teach about handling groups and individuals.

The labor college curriculum prepared students to serve the labor movement as active organizers and leaders instead of as union bureaucrats; in Norton's words, the schools expected them to return "to the union—to the bench, to the mine face, to the local as business agents, or to pass on some of this knowledge in workers' education classes."[2] Fifth, informal on-campus and off-campus activities ensured that students unable to attend the full-time residential program could participate in workers' education. For the labor colleges in general and for Brookwood in particular after 1927, the formal and informal curricula often functioned as forums in which the staid policies of the AFL were attacked. These criticisms, to be sure, did not escape the attention of the Federation hierarchy.

Formal courses fell into two broad categories: informational (or background) courses and tool (or instrumental) courses. According to the *Brookwood Review*, the school's monthly publication, background courses gave "students a working knowledge of economics and social factors," while tool courses enabled students "to acquire and impart ideas effectively."[3] The former immersed students in abstract economic and social concepts and were therefore academically oriented, and the latter conveyed utilitarian skills. Typical background courses were labor history and economics; journalism, public speaking, and social psychology acted as tool courses.

The Brookwood Curriculum

Brookwood's curriculum had matured, for the most part, by 1925, and throughout most of its existence offered one- and two-year programs of study. Brookwood's one-year program was geared for "industrial workers with some trade union experience but also for workers from unorganized industries and centers who may have little or no trade union experience." Background courses included "History of the American Labor Movement" and "Trade Union Organization Work." One of the primary reasons that radicals like Maurer distrusted the public school system was that it either ignored the history of labor or distorted it, thereby instilling antilabor attitudes in working-class children. The labor colleges attempted to counter what Maurer saw as the bourgeois hegemony propagated by the public schools by purposefully promoting a favorable attitude toward the labor movement. Moreover, courses like "American Labor History," "Foreign Labor History," "Modern Industry," and "Basic Industries" awakened workers to the realization that they were not alone in their struggle. Their objective was to foster worker solidarity.[4]

David Saposs's "Trade Union Organization Work," a comprehensive course, first surveyed the labor movement and then concentrated on how the movement functioned and how it was organized and financed. The course also dealt with political action, economic strikes, collective bargaining, and employers' associations. Concerning the latter, Saposs equated welfare capitalism with what he termed "industrial feudalism" and relied heavily upon case studies to reinforce his points. Concluding his discussion of "organizing campaigns as educational ferment," Saposs emphasized to his students that organizing and strike campaigns acted as learning experiences:

Agitation must be supplemented by education so as to create a permanent interest in the labor movement and in social problems.

It makes no difference whether the situation turns out favorably or unfavorably, intelligent handling and effective follow-up work with extensive and intensive education will bring results. On the other hand, it is a mistake to cease activity and abandon contact with the workers involved, for then the effort made during the critical periods is lost.[5]

In Saposs's view, consciousness-raising superseded the actual outcome of the strike because the workers' most difficult struggle was long-term. In "Trade Union Organization Work," students read Saposs's *Left Wing Unionism* as well as works by John R. Commons and William Z. Foster, among others. In *Left Wing Unionism*, Saposs discussed "the policies and tactics arising from the dual struggle of the radicals, on the one hand [with] the conservatives and on the other among themselves." Two strategies—boring from within and dual unionism, or setting up rival organizations—grew out of socialist and anarchist activities of the nineteenth century. After establishing a theoretical and tactical framework, Saposs utilized case studies to review the boring-from-within plans of the Socialists and the communist TUEL as well as the dual unionism of the IWW in their efforts either to alter the policies of the AFL or to topple the Federation completely. Saposs likewise analyzed the internecine battles among various radical groups.[6] From the course and the readings, the student gained considerable insight into the sophisticated means of radical political warfare that had been developed in the American labor movement.

"Advanced Economics," another Brookwood course, relied on a Marxist interpretation of contemporary history and compared American capitalist society with Soviet society. It focused on natural resources and wealth, transportation systems, women's activities and opportunities, ethnic groups, forms of government, economic systems, and education. The objective of "Advanced Economics" was to expose students to an alternative social system. It opened with a thorough grounding in Marxism and the *Communist Manifesto*, then pedantically compared economic statistics for the United States and the Soviet Union. The suggested reading list, composed by John C. Kennedy, the instructor, consisted of Charles Beard's *Rise of American Civilization* and *American Government and Politics*, J. A. Hobson's *Evolution of Modern Capitalism*, Stuart Chase's *Men and Machines* and *Tragedy and Waste*, Broadus Mitchell's *Rise of the Cotton Mills in the South*, Louis Lorwin's *Labor and Internationalism*, and works by Foster and Commons.

Brookwood's tool courses taught students how to organize and lead workers and how to maintain a union. Verbal communication was recognized as an important organizing skill. Public speaking, taught by Josephine Colby in 1926–27, emphasized resonance and pronunciation. She drilled the students in voice exercises involving vowel sounds, and in poetry readings, developing rhetorical skills. By 1930, still under Colby's tutelage, the public-speaking course had assumed a more technical and political character and gave students practice "in the organization and delivery of speeches dealing with workers' problems." Workers practiced public speaking to become more effective union members, run better union meetings, and attain self-confidence when confronting management. The students practiced Debs's speeches and occasionally participated in debates—most notably the one with students from Vassar College on February 24, 1926, over the question, Should workers take over industry? Thomas Dabney, Charles Maute, and Anna Sasnofsky argued the affirmative against three members of the Vassar Student League for Industrial Democracy, who opposed the proposition. The amicable debate ended in an apparent draw; however, as the *Brookwood Review* reported it, a great deal was learned by both sides: "The Vassar girls were perhaps surprised to find that, even though lacking in polish, labor 'radicals' were reasonable beings after all, and certainly the Brookwood students were surprised to find so much intelligent interest in problems which they were accustomed to regard as the exclusive property of the Labor Movement."[7]

Tool courses taught other practical skills as well. According to the 1932–33 *Brookwood Bulletin and Announcement of Courses*, "Parliamentary Law" instructed students how to organize and run a union meeting efficiently by summarizing the role of each officer and recounting parliamentary procedure. "Trade Union Administration Technique" was more detailed in its scope and involved such facets as the collection of dues, maintenance of records and membership statistics, bookkeeping, and benefit provisions. Union employment procedures were also reviewed, and it was emphasized that qualified unemployed workers were to receive preferential hiring treatment for union positions. "Labor Journalism" trained students in publicity and news correspondence by having them write "labor news, editorials, feature stories, and semi-technical articles for the labor press and general publication." Students learned how to construct posters, print leaflets, and write correspondence for local newspapers, and obtained practical experience by submitting and publishing articles in the *Brookwood Review*, which began its publication during the spring of 1923 under the supervision of Helen Norton, an English teacher. A course in psychology also served the union cause by teaching "effective methods of approaching and organizing workers." Another class examined the theory of workers' education and provided methods of organization. A course entitled "Workers' Political Action" analyzed "the nature of the state and structure of the American political machine," with special attention given to workers' and farmers' political movements. A short course entitled "Cooperation" covered "the history, activities, and technique of consumers' cooperatives." Brookwood usually offered its classes three hours a week during fifteen-week sessions. [8]

A Brookwood student's second year consisted of more advanced work. Those who had completed the first year and a small number of college graduates who wished "to prepare for teaching workers' classes or for other activities in connection with the labor movement" qualified for the second year at Brookwood. By 1927 elective courses included the regular subjects as well as a seminar on labor strategy and courses in government, the techniques of workers' education, and labor organization problems. Individual or group conferences or seminars often replaced regular classroom work. As the bulletin declared, "Even more expressly than previous Brookwood courses, the seminars readied students for returning to activity in the labor movement." [9]

Not all of Brookwood's worker–students were prepared for such an advanced and rigorous program, however. Rudimentary reading and writing classes were established for those with limited education. In 1927, for example, more than 50 percent of Brookwood's students claimed only a grade school education. [10]

The Curriculum of Work People's College

Compared with Brookwood, the educational program at Work People's College appeared to be more loosely structured, but the school did maintain theoretical as well as practical courses of study. The students, for the most part, planned the program themselves and selected their own classes. The social science curriculum included courses in general history, economics, civics, citizenship, sociology, evolutionary biology, labor tactics, and public speaking. In the last course Guss Aakula, a teacher at the school and a former student, pointed out that "correct manners and speech . . . were regarded as important concerning mass function."[11] Books for these courses included classics like Marx's *Capital*, Engels's *Origin of the Family, Private Property, and the State*, and Kautsky's *Erfurt Program*, representing a Marxian orthodoxy. Darwin's *Origin of Species* and *Descent of Man* stressed the concept of evolution, and Hillquit's *History of Socialism in the United States* reflected the ideas of the socialist right wing, pragmatic and opposed to dual unionism. Some students found these readings too difficult and abstract. Since many students balked at what they called "scientific socialism," just as they had previously resisted religion classes forced on them by the clerics, the 1912 stockholder's meeting required that all students had to enroll in at least one course on socialism. However, as Ollila concludes, "the most important learning which took place could be described as 'experiential' in the sense of emotional commitment, comradeship, and a faith that 'the world would soon be ours.'"[12]

Concerned with more practical matters, the Commercial Department of Work People's College offered double-entry American bookkeeping, commercial arithmetic, law, and correspondence. According to John Wiita, these courses were intended to prepare "business managers, bookkeepers, clerks for our [Finnish] newspapers, cooperatives and private businesses. Some [students] even became businessmen."[13] The school also offered geometry, poetry, and other subjects at the students' request.

Work People's College expanded that program in 1910 when the completion of a second building allowed enrollment to increase to 112 students. Teachers were required to work year-round. Theoretical, or abstract, courses continued to dominate the students' time at the school. Students devoted some nine periods a week to history, five to economics, and two to the history of socialism. Finnish, which included composition, was taught six periods a week; English, nine periods; and German, one period. The college offered practical courses such as math, accounting, and public speaking only three to five periods a week. During the 1909–10 school year, when Finns, loyal to the Finnish Socialist Federation and hostile to the IWW, began criticizing the radical orientation of Work People's College, "a so-called 'question of direction' and a 'tactics hour' were added to the educational program."[14] The school's use of William D. Haywood and Frank Bohn's pamphlet, *Industrial Socialism*, further incensed some Socialists. Published by Charles Kerr, it represented the most clearly defined articulation of the political position of the Socialist party's left wing and symbolized the college's drift to industrial unionism.

Throughout its early years—which included an ideological transition from socialism to industrial unionism—Work People's College continued to stress citizenship.[15] Finns continued to dominate the student body, although some Hungarian and Italian students were admitted. The rudiments of mathematics and the basic rules of Finnish grammar had to be taught to worker–students who, although literate, came from poor, rural backgrounds in Finland, which required a minimal amount of formal schooling.[16] Fred W. Thompson, the director at Work People's College during much of its IWW period, recalls that the institution

> was primarily a place to acculturate Finnish immigrants both to the history and language of this country, and to its labor movement. . . . For many, no matter what the course might be called, the main content was the English language—economics, labor history, English, or what[ever]. . . . Arithmetic was an important subject to some, usually with some practical applications . . . how to use the carpenter's square, how to figure one's paycheck, etc. . . . Classes included a couple who had some college [education], and also some who had got past grade seven or its equivalent in some other country. We managed to make all get something out of it.[17]

That assimilation process did not contradict the school's basic social and educational tenets. As Peter Kivisto points out, "When socialist leaders urged the rank-and-file to Americanize (i.e., to learn English and apply for citizenship), it was not in order to assimilate the values and role expectations of the dominant culture, but to provide the bases for forging class solidarity."[18] Since the Socialist party relied on the ballot box, suffrage represented the obvious purpose of citizenship.

The formal curriculum of Work People's College reflected little fundamental ideological change after its official affiliation with the IWW in 1921. The school required only one course, the "Essentials of the Labor Movement," which exposed students to the basics of economics, sociology, and labor history.[19] The Scientific Department offered courses in history, sociology, economics, geography, biology, and arithmetic. The college offered a history of the labor movement in the United States with, among other texts, Commons's *History of Labor in the United States* which pioneered the institutional approach, and the IWW's *Historical Catechism of American Unionism*. The reading list for the "Materialistic Conception of History" recommended that students read standard works like Engels's *Origin of the Family, Pri-*

vate Property, and the State, and Marx's *Eighteenth Brumaire, Civil War in France*, and *Revolution and Counter Revolution*. A course called "Motives of Social Activity" used Ward's *Dynamic Sociology*. Industrial geography equipped "revolutionists with a knowledge of the physical basis of industry, and the strategic points for attack on the capitalist system." Economics texts, in addition to U.S. documents, census reports, trade journals, and market reports, included *Economic Interpretation of the Job*, an IWW publication; *Student's Marx*, by Edward Aveling, Marx's son-in-law; *Capital*, by Marx; and *Theoretical Systems of Karl Marx*, by Boudin—a Kerr publication recognized "as the one major contribution to the corpus of Marxian thought produced by an American author during the period of the Second International."[20]

While the Scientific Department emphasized theoretical issues, the Department of Labor Propaganda and Organization taught practical skills. Public speaking, debating, reporting and editing, delegates' work, bookkeeping, and a course called "IWW Structure, Methods, Present Policies and Position" fell into this category. The description for the public-speaking class, as outlined in the 1923 "Announcement of Courses," clearly illustrated its utilitarian nature: "Students to prepare lectures on subjects of propaganda value. Lecture to be given to class *as if to an audience of workers*. Class and instructor will criticize material, arrangement and delivery."[21] The best articles written for the reporting and editing class often found their way into IWW publications. "Delegates' Work" taught students the finer points of union bureaucracy, while the bookkeeping courses covered practical financial skills. The English Department maintained a militant demeanor by demanding that students read "radical literature." Finally, the program included a short course on the questions asked of candidates for naturalization.[22]

The Commonwealth College Curriculum

During its early years, Commonwealth College, like Work People's College, had no clear-cut academic program; students usually enrolled in courses according to their needs and interests. Like Brookwood and Work People's College, Commonwealth stressed background and tool courses. Economics, English, history and government, law, mathematics, music, psychology, sociology, stenography, and modern languages represented the main subjects, offered three hours a week each during fifteen-week semesters. Social psychology students read

Dewey's *Human Nature and Conduct*, and in history they studied H. G. Wells's *Outline of History*. Meanwhile, reflecting the approach pioneered by John Commons at Wisconsin, labor history remained subsumed under economics. [23]

Beginning in 1928, Commonwealth's educational program evolved to a more structured and elaborate level. The school added an orientation year composed of "tutorial work based on the needs of the individual adult student," followed by three years of course work. An expanded formal curriculum included elementary journalism during the first year; labor economics, a course on imperialism, and labor journalism in the second year; and courses in modern drama and co-operation during the third year.[24] Commonwealth, moreover, dropped the semester system in favor of a quarterly plan, including a summer session, both to accommodate students with seasonal jobs and to use the school's educational facilities year-round. [25]

In 1930, Commoners further refined the school's educational program when they organized it into four major areas of study:

(1) workers' education, for those who wish to prepare themselves for teaching in labor schools; (2) labor-economics, for those who want to fit themselves as labor organizers; (3) labor-journalism, for those who aim to work in the labor-journalism field; and (4) labor law, for those who wish to enter the field as labor lawyers. [26]

Each area required three years of study of three quarters each. The first year for each category was similar and required courses in writing, economics, history, and public speaking. More specialized study dominated the second and third years. For instance, students interested in labor journalism usually studied editing, feature writing, and the labor press. Students, in addition, wrote and printed the *Commonwealth College Fortnightly*, the student newspaper. [27]

Zeuch's departure from Commonwealth in 1931 signaled a fundamental transformation in the school's educational style and emphasis. His predominantly academic background had given it a somewhat objective, scientific aura. After Zeuch left, however, the program assumed a more distinctly radical character. The *Fortnightly*, in 1933, recalled the profound ideological and programmatic shift: "In the fall of 1931, the school clarified its position with relation to the labor movement, openly accepted a class-conscious program, and since that time has placed a greater emphasis on the problems which the depression has brought out in strong relief."[28] Reflecting this political transition, a course in Marxian theory, described as "a reading course in the philosophy and economic theories of the founder of Socialism," appeared as an integral part of the formal curriculum. By 1932, that addition had grown into two comprehensive courses, "Marxism I" and "Marxism II," which examined *Capital*; the revisionist's view of Marxism; the Marxist critics (Boehm-Bawerk, Tugan-Baranowsky, John Bates Clark, and Thorstein Veblen); municipal and state socialism versus Marxism; and "the limits of Marxism as applied to the economic programs of the Socialists of Austria, Germany, England, and the Scandinavian countries, and the Communists of Russia." "American Labor History" investigated the rise of labor from about 1890 to 1920, including the growth of the AFL, "the Socialist Trades and Labor Alliance, the Industrial Workers of the World, the early labor parties, the rise of the Socialist party, the development of syndicalist and anarchist movements, etc." Social psychology now scrutinized Sigmund Freud, Alfred Adler, and William Terman, among others, and was conceived, of course, "to help students interpret the problems they meet and to function more effectively in a workers' world." Finally, Commonwealth condensed the orientation year into a quarter.[29]

Drama in the Labor Colleges

Proletarian drama represented a unique component and an integral part of the social activist environment of the labor colleges. The plays sought to arouse the social consciousness of the audiences as well as that of the participants. This use of drama illustrates how workers enlisted art forms to aid them in their struggles.

The labor college version of drama traced its roots to a long tradition of socially conscious drama. This does not imply that theater workers and audiences consciously built upon the dramatic and theatrical traditions of those who preceded them. Indeed, there exists much evidence to the contrary suggesting that the roots of working-class theater had to be constantly rediscovered. German Socialists first introduced amateur theatrical activities in New York City in 1877, and the movement soon spread to other large cities, including Cincinnati, Louisville, Saint Louis, and Chicago. Performances by local socialist theater groups became a popular feature of mass political meetings or festivals, such as those commemorating the Paris Commune or New Year's—the latter of which might be termed "anti-Christmas" gatherings. Workers' theaters aimed at serving both entertaining and didactic functions, with emphasis on the latter objective, as Carol J. Poore reveals: "These groups hoped to spread fundamental ideas of socialism in an entertaining way, to offer models for action and images of a better future, and thereby reach an audience which would be less receptive to political lectures, which perhaps did not read the socialist press, and which would be difficult to approach in other ways."[30] Individual Socialists or members of workers' dramatic groups wrote plays that had the desired agitational effect. Through thoughtful casting and staging, the plays' directors sought community participation, with women acting in major parts.

Socially conscious theater achieved notoriety in 1915 with the creation of the Provincetown Players and gained momentum during the 1920s with the emergence of the Workers Drama League in 1926 and the New Playwrights' Theatre in 1927. The 1929 crash and the Depression generated even more radical efforts to dramatize the struggles of the working class. Plays began to assume social reform themes, extolling liberty, encouraging rebellion, denouncing social injustice, fascism, and war. Radical plays were produced in New York City by Artef (1927–37, 1939, 1941), the Theatre Collective (1933–36), the Theatre Union (1933–37), the Actors' Repertory Theatre (1934–37), and, on a national basis, by the Federal Theatre (1935–39), a WPA-backed experiment. The New Theatre League, formed in 1935, previously known as the League of Worker Theatres, represented the culmination of this theatrical activity when some three to four hundred theaters across the country affiliated with it.

A more immediate inspiration for the dramatic tradition that flowered in the labor colleges was the theater of agitation and propaganda that originated in the Soviet Union about 1920 and was later adopted by workers' movements in Germany. In the United States, this and other forms of proletarian drama stemmed from workers' organizations and the workers themselves, a Sovietization of the radical American theater tradition. In a 1934 article, "Theatre Is a Weapon," Mordecai Gorelik, a set designer for many of the radical theater groups, articulated the position of the movement at the time: "The cultural leadership of the working class has definitely passed out of the hands of sympathetic intellectuals into those of the revolutionary workers themselves to whom it is a truism that the class war exists in the cultural field as in any other."[31] Drama, an art form, became a means of organizing workers and fomenting social change.

Several theater companies, including the Workers' Laboratory Theatre, Artef, and to a certain extent the Theatre Union, turned to "agitprop," the theatre of agitation and propaganda. Gorelik described its basic properties: they were "portable productions whose actors brought their settings and costumes to union meetings, strike headquarters, street corners, parks, or workers' social affairs. Their repertory, one-act pieces, for the most part, consisted almost entirely of political satires in which the capitalist in a silk hat was the inevitable villain and the worker in overalls the shining hero."[32] Somewhat elementary in its approach, agitprop served a didactic purpose by emphasizing a social-class theme and appealing to social activism. According to Malcolm Goldstein, "Some of the earlier agitprop skits were realistic but crude, but more were a blend of chanted dialogue and mass-movement in which the actors, performing in unison, symbolized the working-class solidarity necessary for the overthrow of the bosses."[33] Agitprop dispensed with the complexities of human character and, instead, concentrated on recognizable symbols. "In this way," Jay Williams asserts, agitprop "resembled the expressionist theatre out of which it had grown and which tended to concern itself with types rather than individuals."[34] Agitprop drama came to have a significant influence on the dramatic efforts of the labor colleges.

At Brookwood, drama was experimentally introduced in the fall of 1925 as a manifestation of the "increasing interest of the trade union movement in popularizing and dramatizing labor's problems and achievements through such agencies as motion pictures, pageantry, and dramas."[35] Brookwood at first lacked the facilities to rehearse and stage plays, but students and teachers remedied that situation in 1932 by converting an old barn. At Commonwealth, drama began as an informal endeavor that grew out of Sunday evening programs devoted to singing, dancing, and plays. Early dramatic efforts did not appear to emphasize social themes, but they were performed solely for entertainment. According to the *Fortnightly*, modern drama became a formal part of the curriculum during the 1927–28 school year. The course description noted its purposes and content as "a study of drama from the standpoint of its psychological and social import. The plays used will be selected from Strindberg, Ibsen, Shaw, O'Neill, and other contemporary playwrights."[36] Commoners staged their first quasi-social drama during the Christmas celebration of 1927 at the school for farm neighbors and their children. The holiday pageantry included a tableau portraying "the trials and tribulations of the masses." The *Fortnightly* recorded the event in melodramatic tones:

> The shifting scenes of the tableau depict modern working-class problems in a biblical setting. A cotton farmer is dispossessed because he cannot pay his taxes; a negro is lynched because of an alleged assault upon a white woman; strikers are starved into submission; workers become machines. As Capital lashes Labor behold! a new star appears in the sky. The Glad Evangel is born to make men free. [37]

Commoners often staged their plays in the Commons, "with its stage at one end of the dining space with a few simple flats, a cyclorama and two baby spots." Labor drama at Work People's College, unlike that at Brookwood and Commonwealth, never became a part of the formal curriculum, but operated as an extracurricular activity. [38]

Performing and writing plays with social and political themes played an important role in the labor colleges, and for A. J. Muste served several purposes at Brookwood:

> It may be a means of self expression, making the Labor Movement more vital to the workers themselves; it may interpret the Labor Movement for the public in more sympathetic and appealing terms than abstract reasoning can do; it may be a means of entertainment, particularly in isolated regions where the pool room and blind tiger [a speakeasy] are the only means of diversion. [39]

Commonwealth College saw a similar role for drama as part of the learning experience, and by 1932 labor drama, art, and literature had been integrated into the school's curriculum. These courses aimed to train potential organizers how to use drama, art, and literature to appeal to exploited laborers and convince them of the hopelessness of their current situation and the necessity of forming militant labor unions if they hoped to better their lot. In addition to consciousness raising, propaganda, and recreation, the workers' play gave worker–students at the labor colleges some practical background in play production and selection, acting, coaching, costume design, and occasionally playwriting. In 1927, Jesse Slaughter, a Brookwood student, argued "that labor drama created by workers and expressing the true working-class spirit is of tremendous significance and value to Labor, and that it can be easily, effectively, and successfully done by students who have had practical experience in all various phases of labor dramatics."[40] Thus, labor drama within the labor college setting functioned as a multidimensional "educational tool."[41]

Why did the students and teachers at the labor colleges reject standard drama? Rosa Knutti, an instructor at Work People's College, offered one explanation. While Knutti praised the best among contemporary playwrights, such as Shaw, Ibsen, Gorky, and O'Neill, she stressed the critical function of art. The theater had to be more than entertainment; "as propaganda, it provides something to think about." Most plays relied upon what she termed the "bourgeois formula," which romanticized working-class life by portraying a harmonious, albeit at times strained, relationship between labor and capital. Moreover, it often stressed "that if the poor are poor it is the fault of their stubbornness of laziness, or etc. [sic], and the rich, though they be rich and masters of workers' destinations, are still good-hearted and are well supplied with the milk of human kindness." Worst of all, the bourgeois formula acted as "subtle propaganda in the name of art." Knutti saw the need for workers' drama that exposed the drab existence and the harsh realities of working-class life.[42] Proletarian drama at the labor colleges consciously avoided that bourgeois formula and endeavored to supply workers with thought-provoking entertainment framed in class conflict terms. Or, as Muste summarized it: "There is material for drama in the experiences and thoughts and emotions of workingmen and women that other people do not know and that the workers themselves do not really appreciate because they are too close to it."[43] As a result, the themes of labor drama reflected working-class culture and problems, emphasizing class struggle, unionization, solidarity, dangerous job conditions, and the evils of sexism and racism.

The Brookwood Players produced their first plays under Polly Colby's direction before the annual WEB conference in Boston in April 1925. The school hired Hazel MacKaye specifically for "pageantry work" for the 1925–26 school year. From December 12 to 13, 1925, Brookwooders performed three one-act dramas at the school. They performed them again at the Labor Temple in New York City on March 5, 1986. David Pinsky's *A Dollar* satirized money and status by depicting a wandering and indigent acting company that finds a dollar bill lying in a country road. The players worship that dollar:

We must contemplate the dollar with a religious reverence. . . .
A dollar is spread out before us—a real dollar in the midst of our
circle, and everything within us draws irresistably. . . . Remember you are before the Ruler, before the Almighty. On your knees
before him and pray. On your knees.

Since wealth, of course, is synonymous with power, a member
of the troupe, who plays the Villain, grabs the dollar and declares
himself the ruler. A scuffle (that is, a revolution) over its possession
ensues until the players agree to divide the dollar equally among themselves. The theme of social-class conflict as a means of attaining an
equitable distribution of wealth is made clear when one of the actors
challenges the Villain with these words: "Let there be blood. . . . You
are to give the dollar up to all of us. At the first opportunity we will
get change and divide it into equal parts." Although simplistic and
bordering on the comedic, the play taught a profound lesson. The
other plays included *Peggy*, by Harold Williamson, which portrayed
the tragic lives and struggles of poor white southern farmers, and
The People, by Susan Glaspell, which illustrated the trials and tribulations of an impoverished radical magazine that attempted to raise the
social awareness of workers and ultimately to spark the "social revolution." The twelve-member cast of *The People* mirrored the diverse
student body at Brookwood—English, Jewish, Italian, Finnish, Slav,
and black—and included workers from numerous trades, especially
the New York City needle trades and textiles, plumbing, and mining.
Schoolteachers were also included.[44]
    Because of a dearth of suitable plays as well as prohibitive royalty
fees, labor college students and teachers began to compose many of
their own one-act "social dramas." One Brookwood student, Bessie
(Bonchi) Friedman, a Russian immigrant and a member of New York
Local 248 of the Amalgamated Clothing Workers, wrote a play entitled *The Miners—A Drama of the Non-Union Coal Fields of West Virginia*. Twenty-five students presented that play in February 1926 before Brookwood's annual National Workers' Education Conference. As
Helen Norton reported it in *Labor Age*, Brookwood's unofficial organ:

There was the real stuff of life in that play—the loyalty of workers
to their union; the sacrifice not only of self but what is infinitely
harder, of one's family; resentfulness of workers who have no

alternative but violence against the schemes of the capitalist boss; mob action that is well intentioned but dangerous unless held steady by clear-sighted leaders—these things were as the author of the play had seen them. [45]

That the play embraced Brookwood's objectives is not lost in this passage. *Risen from the Ranks, Or From Office Boy to President*, written by Harold Coy, a Commoner, attacked the "Horatio Alger myth" and the "Hoover Depression." At Work People's College, students wrote dramas in the playwriting class and created "labor skits that the school and other labor groups [could] use." Students did not write "anything more pretentious than the one-act play." [46]

Because of Brookwood's close proximity to New York City, the school's labor dramas tended to treat themes most relevant to urban industrial workers. *The Tailor Shop*, a one-act musical written, arranged, and choreographed by Brookwood students, dramatized the power and the benefits gained by garment workers through unionization. [47] That play, with an all-female cast, opens in a garment shop with "The Song of the Workers":

> In the sweat shop days, we'd dare not to play
> But we'd slave from dawn to dark
> For the eight-hour day which our union gained
> Makes us ready for a lark,
> Still we get too tired if we work eight hours
> Without pause for rest and play
> But if you watch us here and now
> To join work and play we will show you how.

Individual workers, such as the Cutter, the Needle-Hand, and the Button-Sewer, sing various songs that relate to their work. The Machine-Operator sings the following lyrics praising the union:

> Now I can see how they built it
> And planned all for me.
> I never knew what a worker goes through,
> There's nothing the union can't do.
>
> Union I swear by you.
> You've made my dreams come true.

Since I began first to sew,
You made things better I know.
I didn't join right away,
I waited till I was swayed.
I don't know any way I can ever repay—
Union I swear by you!

The entrance song of the Boss is, not surprisingly, "Get Back to Work" and is followed by "The Owner of a Union Shop," set to music adapted from "My Gallant Crew," from Gilbert and Sullivan's *H. M. S. Pinafore*. In the song, the Boss laments his loss of absolute control over the workers because of the union: "I used to work my girls twelve hours. / Till the union made you stop." The play ends with the workers ridiculing the Boss and his aping of the bourgeoisie. While unorganized workers who saw this play easily recognized the strength and self-assurance that workers can derive from a union, they might have identified an implicit feminist theme as well. Female workers comprised a significant portion of the work force in the garment industry. Accordingly, the cast of *The Tailor Shop* consisted of female garment workers who were organized and were consequently treated better; although subtle, the message for these industrial workers was evident.

While the themes of Brookwood's plays appealed to urban industrial workers, Commoners based the ideas for their dramas on the plight of rural agricultural workers, particularly in Arkansas. Commoners presented *Can You Hear Their Voices?* in February 1932 to some three hundred local farmers. Written in 1931 by Hallie Flannagan, a Vassar instructor, and Margaret Ellen Clifford, a teaching assistant, the play followed the agitprop genre. The Experimental Theatre at Vassar College first produced the drama, and it was subsequently adopted by Artef and numerous other worker and college groups; indeed, a representative from the New Theatre League introduced the play to Commoners. The drama, based on factual material, unfolds with a group of southern tenant farmers facing a drought and certain starvation. Ignorant and uneducated, they know little about politics or the workers' struggle, but they become politicized when they are denied bank credit and government relief. In desperation, they turn to the Red Cross for help—which they regard as "charity"—but are refused because of bureaucratic red tape. The plot culminates with the angry farmers and their starving families storming the Red Cross station, attacking its local chairman and taking the food they need. This agitprop drama illustrated the process of radicalization and the results of farmer solidarity, and became a decided hit among the school's "farm neighbors, who had no difficulty understanding what it said about drought, hunger, and lack of credit."[48]

The solution of farmers' problems through collective action, as expected, communicated an important theme. *Get Goin' George*, written and produced in 1938 by the students and staff at Commonwealth for the Arkansas Farmers' Union, depicted the dilemma of George Thompson, a poor farmer who faces certain foreclosure. Because of the efforts of the Farmers' Union, George retains his farm by refinancing the mortgage, and at a lower interest rate than before. The key phrase of the play appears in scene 3, when Mr. Gray, the organizer for the Farmers' Union, states: "When the farmers learn to organize, their problems will be a lot easier for them." In this case, the farmers are organized, and it is this solidarity that eventually saves George's farm.[49] As in *The Tailor Shop*, the benefits of collective action were made clear to the audience.

Commonwealth students also used drama to attack racism, a major impediment to unionization in the South. *We Are Not Alone*, a one-act "Commonwealth Labor Play," written by students of the Labor Drama class in 1938, dramatized the case of "Bubbles" Clayton and Jim Caruthers, otherwise known as the "Blytheville Boys," who had been sentenced to death. The play takes place in the death cell of Tucker Farm, Arkansas, where Clayton and Caruthers, both black workers, await their execution. The injustice of racism and of the concomitant racist judicial system pervades the play. The drama ends with an appeal to unions, churches, and "every mass organization" to send protest letters to the governor and the attorney general of Arkansas and to send donations to the president of the local office of the Little Rock NAACP.[50]

In July 1932, Commoners presented *What Price Coal?* on campus and later staged it for groups of miners. Some four years earlier, Brookwood students had performed the same play at Katonah to raise donations for striking miners and their families in Pennsylvania and Colorado. Written in 1926 by Tom Tippett—later a Brookwood instructor and member of the Theatre Union's executive board—and miners from Sub-District No. 5 in Illinois, that play was "dedicated to the twenty-five hundred coal miners . . . needlessly killed in coal mines of America every year" and illustrated work hazards faced by coal miners. The plot unfolds in the kitchen of a miner's home in the Illinois coal fields as Jack, a coal miner, prepares to leave for the mine. Before he departs, he asks Mary, a housekeeper and his mother's companion, for an answer to the previous evening's marriage proposal. Although the affection between them is apparent, Mary coyly makes him wait until he returns from the mine that evening for her rather obvious reply. Job conditions in the mine are revealed through their discussion about his lunch pail:

Jack: Have you put the lid on tight?
Mary: Sure I put the lid on tight. Why?
Jack: The rats ate most of my dinner yesterday. They got the lid off some way. But rats in a mine have to have food too. I guess they were as hungry as I was.

After Jack leaves, his mother, Ellen, tells Mary about the tragic death of her husband in a mine explosion. She has a premonition that her son will suffer a similar fate. Yet, Ellen says, miners and their families grow hardened to death and injury because it represents an almost daily experience.

We're used to it here. Men are always being killed in coal mines. And there is hardly a day goes by that some of them don't get hurt. And some of the ones that are only hurt would be better off dead. They go about the rest of their lives crippled or blind . . . just a burden to themselves and everybody else.

To make matters worse, in the play, as in life, the miners cannot escape the town to find another job elsewhere because of their indebtedness to the company store. The alarm bell sounds at the mine, signaling a mine explosion, and Jack's corpse is carried into the house. The final line of the play is: "What a price to pay for coal!"[51]

Work People's College also produced and sponsored plays with proletarian themes. One such play, fraught with conflict, was *The Power of One Big Union*, prepared by the school's drama department. The play depicts how both employed and unemployed workers join efforts to fight "the bosses," the military, and the craft unions. The school also sponsored plays written elsewhere. *Shades of Passaic*, first performed before an audience of fifteen hundred striking textile workers and their families at Newbauer's Hall in Passaic, was originally written by two Brookwood students, Bonchi Friedman and Stanley

Guest, and performed by Brookwooders. Unlike Commonwealth, which supplied its "labor skits" free of charge, Work People's College charged rental fees and royalties, ranging from a few cents to ten dollars, in order to generate year-round revenue for the school. During the 1920s, Work People's College rented many plays from Finland, but by 1935 the value of the college's inventory of dramas had reached $635.40. These included some two hundred plays in both Finnish and English. A variety of individuals and workers' clubs rented the plays.

These dramatic efforts also had their ludicrous side and many rough edges. Fred Thompson humorously and candidly recalls

> a group of students serenading me with their renditions of Karl Marx's observations on the historical tendencies of capitalist accumulation preceded by a very prolonged "Ooh" and to the tune of the "Irish Washerwoman Jig." "Ooh, the primitive accumulation of capital resolves itself into the following factors. . . ." These kids weren't all nonsense though. They took the same chapter and developed a short skit out of it about poor Mr. Peel from Manchester landing with goods and servants at Swan River, Australia, to be deserted by his hands for, though he had brought everything else needed to establish capitalist relations there, he had not brought the economic compulsions to make them work for him. Plays put on by those students, some more or less developed by them, and circulated around the country, may have been a fairly effective activity. It did help keep the school going. [52]

Thus, more immediate and pragmatic exigencies, such as the need for a little income, sometimes superseded the political imperatives of the school.

The schools' drama groups often took their shows on the road. In the spring of 1933, a troupe from Work People's College was organized to tour the Finnish communities in northern Minnesota and Upper Michigan. It visited twenty communities in Minnesota, and fourteen in Michigan. All of the net proceeds were given to the school. Tour groups usually received free food and lodging from their local sponsors.

The Brookwood Players also went on tour, performing for workers' education teachers and workers in the New York area. A play written by a second year student, Edith Kowski, entitled *An Open-Shop Summer*, was presented at Columbia University for the League for

Industrial Democracy (LID) in December 1927. They too covered thousands of miles in performing their plays. In the spring of 1932, Brookwood students embarked on a nine-day, 800-mile tour to perform *Mill Shadows*, written by Tom Tippett. The play was based on the violent 1929 textile workers' strike in Marion, North Carolina. Some twenty-eight hundred people "enthusiastically received" the play in Hartford, Philadelphia, Allentown, Baltimore, Washington, D.C., and New Brunswick. For Tippett, *Mill Shadows* "amply demonstrated the propaganda value of labor drama rooted in the American scene." [53]

Brookwooders eventually incorporated labor drama into the traveling chautauqua program sponsored by the school. The chautauquas consisted of plays, songs, skits, and other educational entertainment reminiscent of the old socialist summer encampments in the Southwest. As the *Brookwood Review* characterized it:

> With complete unanimity our worker audiences agreed that a labor movement which moves must have its drama and its marching songs. It must appeal to the heart as well as the head; to the emotions as well as the intellect. All of the sugar-coated movies have not permanently hypnotized the workers so that they cannot recognize and welcome real labor culture. Economics with tears and history with footlights in place of footnotes can be successfully taught by this new method of mass education, and to the thousands that would never think of enrolling in formal classes. Our plays held the mirror of social struggle in the United States . . . up to the workers; they recognized themselves and took new heart for the struggle. [54]

In 1934, twenty-three members of Brookwood's student body formed three different companies and toured fifty-three cities, covering some forty-three hundred miles, and performed before as many as 14,500 workers. During April and May 1935, Brookwooders appeared as often as ninety times before a total audience of twenty thousand people. The sponsors included locals of nineteen industrial unions, thirteen central labor unions, six organizations of unemployed laborers, six workers' education groups, seventeen locals of the Socialist party, and twelve miscellaneous or liberal associations. Yet Brookwooders found themselves less than welcome in a few towns. In some instances, local vigilantes closed the hall just hours before the show was scheduled to begin. [55]

Brookwooders also assisted the New Theatre League by supplying a bus for transportation, representing a joint effort by the New Theatre League, Brookwood, and the Executive Council of the United Textile Workers, a CIO union at this time. The league toured for six weeks throughout industrial New England with Albert Bein's *Let Freedom Ring*, a drama about Carolina hillfolk turned mill workers. The group staged the play thirty-three times before approximately twenty-two thousand workers, many of whom were on strike. The cooperative effort that provided the theatre company with a bus was as significant as the message of the play, as the *New Theatre* reported in 1936:

> If an awareness of the mutual aid which theatre and labor can give each other is growing among the unions, the same may be said of the theatre. Much good work has already been done by the New Theatre League, the Theatre Union, and the touring companies sent out by Brookwood Labor College, towards building a theatre based on trade union support. The *Let Freedom Ring* tour proved that the possibility of enlisting this support is available wherever labor is organized. When touring companies go out with the endorsement of an International, the various locals cooperate by rallying not only their membership, but the rest of the community as well, to its support.
>
> A strong social theatre can only become a reality when the theatre recognizes the need of cooperation with organized labor and achieves that cooperation, and when labor realizes the powerful ally it has in the theatre and utilizes it effectively. [56]

Indeed, Brookwooders realized the educational value of labor drama and exploited it.

In contrast to Brookwood, whose audiences tended to be factory laborers, the Commonwealth players usually performed their plays for farmers or agricultural workers. Rural audiences in Arkansas and Oklahoma applauded *Until the Mortgage Is Due*, by William Cunningham, a Commoner, which satirized the agricultural crisis precipitated by the Great Depression. However, much of the meaning of the school's theatrical efforts was lost on its predominantly fundamentalist audiences. The successful Broadway play *1931*, by Claire and Paul Sifton, was a case in point. First produced by the Group Theatre at the Mansfield Theatre in New York City, the play illustrated the experiences of Adam, a proud warehouse worker. The drama unfolds

as Adam is fired from his job because of a minor scuffle with the foreman. Adam appears confident at first, but begins to realize that his
situation may be hopeless. Adam obviously symbolizes the millions of
unemployed workers during the Depression. As the play progresses,
he is forced to postpone his marriage plans; he fruitlessly searches
the want ads for a job, falls victim to corrupt labor agents, loses his
apartment, panhandles on the streets, and finally, in desperation, attempts to mug an "elegantly dressed" gentleman. Adam's earlier ebul-
lience is gradually eroded, until he is reduced to begging for food at
a soup kitchen and is faced with the realization that his fiancée has
become a prostitute because she too has lost her job. The play ends
when Adam regains his dignity by joining the vanguard of a worker's
revolution. Yet the real message of the drama, which ridiculed the
subjection of hungry people, before they were fed, to the soul-saving
ritual of a Salvation-Army-like minister, was lost on the religiously
conservative, rural audience. To the Commoners' utter dismay, this
scene did not evoke the usual hisses from the audience; rather, the
audience solemnly responded with a chorus of Amens! Commoners
quickly learned that it was often counterproductive to mock any kind
of religious expression with fundamentalist audiences. [57]

Proletarian plays avoided escapism and maintained a didactic mission, reminding workers of their relationship to the world of work.[58]
In this sense, labor skits provided entertainment as well as operating
as instruments of agitation and propaganda. The power of collective
action, as evinced in the labor drama, ameliorated the social and economic problems of workers and farmers. The lessons to be learned by
industrial and agricultural workers from this educational experience
were quite clear. Labor college students, moreover, were expected
to take their theatrical skills back to their unions and communities
in order to share their talents with working people. Helen Norton,
writing in 1926, perhaps best summarized this point:

[The students] are keeping in mind at Brookwood that labor plays
will be most popular and effective not where there are fine theatres and professional actors and expensive scenery, but among
local unions and groups of workers where the Woodman's hall or a
church will be used; where red calico curtains will be pushed back
and forth on baling wire; where coal oil lamps or at best, acety-
lene, will light the stage; where costumes will come, not from a
theatrical house, but out of old trunks; and where tired workers

and sleepy children will have to rehearse at night—which means they must have plays easy to memorize and give. The workers' story thus can be made more attractive.[59]

By 1932, the *Fortnightly* recorded that former students were organizing workers' theaters in Chicago and in the East. Another Commoner, Harry Lessin, left the school and went into acting with the Blue Blouses, a workers' theater in Chicago, and eventually joined the Workers' Laboratory Theatre in New York. Countless Finnish plays were written in the United States and Canada as a direct result of the activities of the Drama Department at Work People's College.[60]

Field Work

Field work represented another unique educational activity in the labor college curriculum. Field work, like labor drama, emphasized social action, and it supplemented background courses by blending practical experience with abstract concepts. Brookwood's *Twelfth Anniversary Review* considered these activities "not as interruptions of school work but as genuine education, and students and teachers alike bring wiser judgement and a keener sense of reality to their classes in consequence." Furthermore, by attempting "to provide practical suggestions to students returning to labor activity," field preparation equipped students with some of the skills and experience necessary to organize and to lead workers.[61] Finally, field work not only functioned to relate theoretical principles to practical situations and to expose students to actual confrontations between labor and capital, but also promoted labor solidarity through the assistance supplied by labor college students and teachers.

According to the *Brookwood Bulletin*, a course called "Preparation for Field Work" involved the "analysis of strike situations and organizing campaigns; . . . making social surveys of localities; soap-boxing tactics; publicity methods; problems of cooperation among different labor groups."[62] Commonwealth similarly required field work, but did not set aside a special preparatory course; rather, the school subsumed field activities under other course work. Thus abstract material in background courses, such as sociology, became more meaningful when students could relate this to practical knowledge gained from tool courses, such as participation in strikes and other field experiences. Work People's College, in contrast, did not sponsor field activities. It only approximated them through "a miniature IWW headquarters with all its various branches and offices formed at the school."[63]

As the course description indicated, field preparation covered a variety of activities. In 1926, when the Brotherhood of Railway and Steamship Clerks, Freight Handlers, Express and Station Employees struck in Brooklyn, Israel Mufson and Joe Kunz, both Brookwood students and members of the Brotherhood, took a leave of absence from the school and participated in the strike. After the strike was settled, they promptly returned to their studies at Brookwood. Similarly, five Brookwood students and members of the ILGWU reported to their union on the eve of its New York City strike in 1926. A student who belonged to the Bookkeepers', Stenographers', and Accountants' Union accompanied them and helped with the union's clerical work during the strike. In addition, Brookwooders often supplied money, food, and clothes to striking workers. In 1926, A. J. Muste and Anna Kula, a student, organized an emergency committee for strike relief during the textile strike in Passaic. Muste and Kula raised large sums of money, distributed pamphlets, and campaigned for greater economic justice and civil rights for workers. The Brookwood Committee for Miners' Relief collected and sent $1,250 and 2,800 pounds of clothes to striking miners in 1927. Brookwooders solicited part of the donations by staging the play *What Price Coal?* before various sympathetic groups.

Field activities often provided opportunities for Brookwooders not only to criticize the established labor movement, but also to participate in reform movements within the labor movement. In 1926, several students and instructors joined John Brophy's "save-the-union" movement in order to attempt to wrest leadership of the UMW, an AFL affiliate, from John L. Lewis. While the Lewis-led UMW was experiencing contract setbacks, a decline in membership, and a loss of revenue, Brophy campaigned for aggressive organizing in nonunion coal fields, nationalization of the coal mines, and the creation of a labor party. Lewis redbaited Brophy during the union's presidential campaign and secured a victory in the election by a wide margin—a triumph Brophy and his supporters later claimed was stolen at the ballot box. More important, the AFL hierarchy took note of the Brookwood-led instruction which had, in this instance, aligned itself with the Communists. Brookwooders likewise used the Sacco–Vanzetti case as a vehicle to excoriate the lethargic AFL. In 1920, as an outgrowth of the Red Scare, Bartolomeo Vanzetti and Nicola Sacco, admitted anarchists, were indicted and convicted of murder, largely on circumstantial evidence. Outraged liberals waged a vigorous campaign, submitting appeal after appeal, but to no avail. Two carloads of Brookwooders drove to Boston on August 23, 1927, the night of the infamous execution, and stood in silent protest outside the Charlestown, Massachusetts, prison at midnight. Muste insisted that the tragedy could have been averted if labor organizations had actively and effectively protested. [64]

One of Brookwood's principal involvements in organizing and strike campaigns, however, occurred in the violent and protracted 1929 Marion textile strike, where Muste, a Brookwood instructor Tom Tippett, and several students and graduates, including Jess Slaughter, Karl Lore, and William Ross, offered assistance. Tippett played a key role in assisting the textile workers in their organizing and strike efforts. Brookwooders collected and distributed 300 pounds of clothing for the strikers and were also present in Marion when six strikers, who had been killed by the local police for picketing, were buried. With no other clergyman present, Muste recited the following prayer at one graveside: "We consecrate this worker's body and give it back to the earth from which it came. He has fought a good fight in a noble cause. He will rest in peace." [65] The strikers had lost.

As an eyewitness to the entire strike and to the strikers' innermost councils, Tippett recorded his account of the walkout in *When Southern Labor Stirs*. The book, besides having an educational purpose, served as a polemic against the AFL. First, for Tippett, the occasion offered a unique opportunity to conduct an extensive survey of southern textile workers' working and living conditions.

> More and more as labor problems are taught in colleges from a practical rather than a theoretical angle and as workers' education endeavors to deal realistically with the workers' own problems does there seem to be a distinct need to trace the actual conduct of significant industrial struggles from beginning to end and to try to analyze the background of these struggles, assessing the losses and gains incurred and evaluating the philosophy that guided their program.

Thus, as a pedagogical tool the Marion strike represented "a typical case to show the origin, conduct, and final settlement of a southern industrial struggle and also to indicate what becomes of workers after a strike is over." [66]

Second, Tippett used the study to attack the AFL. He argued that since the First World War, Federation policies had become increasingly conservative because its leaders, like Gompers, his successor, William Green, as well as Matthew Woll, decided that they did not want to jeopardize the large expansion in membership gained during the war. That increase was threatened by the open-shop drive inaugurated by employers intent on destroying the organized labor movement. Rather than aggressively confronting that menace, AFL leaders chose to collaborate with employers. As Tippett wrote:

> The American Federation of Labor is now attempting to bury its old militant policy and to substitute therefore what it calls union-management cooperation, which tends to reduce strikes or any other form of conflict with employers of labor. This program consists chiefly of convincing the boss that a trade union is an essential part of modern industry which brings assets rather than liabilities to the manufacturing group.

Taken to its fullest, Tippett's analysis is revealing. He more than implies that the compliant, if not naive, union management policy of the AFL was as much to blame for the dire conditions of the southern textile workers as the exploitive policies of the mill owners. The United Textile Workers, the AFL affiliate, "subscribes to the union-management cooperation policy of the American Federation of Labor and is emphasizing that kind of unionism in the South. It does not want strikes, it did not go into trouble zone until after the walkouts of 1929 occurred." And Tippett expressed the ultimate irony: the mill owners refused to tolerate even this brand of unionism: "Four southern governors proved perfectly willing to use the militia to crush the United Textile Workers in spite of the extraordinary efforts of the American Federation of Labor to prove its conservatism and harmlessness."[67]

At Commonwealth, Zeuch preferred that the school remain aloof from field activities, but when he dissociated himself from the school, Commoners became heavily involved in field work and experienced even more harrowing adventures than their Brookwood counterparts. In April 1932, five Commonwealth teachers and students visited the Kentucky coal fields "to inspect the strike area, distribute food and clothing and to make speeches on the Bill of Rights, copies of which they brought along." The Commonwealth contingent, however, received less-than-hospitable treatment from the strike's opponents. The *Fortnightly* reported: "At Pineville, they were seized and turned over to an armed mob, . . . [which] took them through the county and finally flogged them at an isolated spot near the state line."[68] While investigating still another strike in the coalfields of southern Illinois the following August, the *Fortnightly* reported, a teacher and two students were arrested, held incommunicado, threatened, and finally "escorted" out of town. Further, in accordance with its policy to extend its educational program to black workers, Commonwealth sponsored a one-week session, in May 1938, at the Morning Star Baptist Church, a black church located in Little Rock, Arkansas. The instructor, Winifred Chappell, supplied the following assessment: "No book assignments were made, but the students were asked to answer . . . questions on the basis of their own experience, especially questions pertaining to working and living conditions of Negroes and discrimination based on race."[69] Consciousness-raising based on the workers' own experiences served as a consistent element in the labor college curriculum—a truly provocative activity in racist Arkansas.

Informal Programs

In addition to the formal curriculum, the labor colleges offered many and varied informal educational programs and activities. Running summer sessions, publishing handbooks and reading lists, and supplying correspondence and extension courses served several purposes. Many of these programs enabled workers and farmers with limited time and finances to participate in workers' education. In these cases, the labor colleges adapted to the needs of the worker–students. Further, these informal exercises demonstrated the flexible and diverse pedagogy used by the schools to achieve their goals. The schools exposed workers to critical social and labor issues through correspondence and extension courses; recruited potential union members by accommodating younger students and workers during summer sessions; strengthened specific unions by creating special programs for them; and attempted to raise the consciousness of workers and farmers by printing and distributing labor-oriented literature and reading lists. Finally, these educational activities illustrated the aggressive nature of the labor colleges in their efforts to educate, organize, and lead workers in the cause of social change.

Work People's College, Brookwood, and Commonwealth conducted summer sessions for workers who could not attend as full-time students during the regular school year. Work People's College, in particular, sponsored a number of activities geared towards adolescents. The college's regular students published, in 1932, the short-lived *Work People's College Bulletin* for young people: "The idea is this—to give young folk the important information that the public schools do not and cannot give them." Work People's College held its first summer session for Finnish youth in 1929. Over 130 second-generation Finnish boys and girls between the ages of twelve and eighteen attended that first session. Students were mainly from Minnesota, Michigan, and Wisconsin, but some came from as far away as California. The course cost three dollars a week, or twelve dollars for the entire four-week course. The junior summer school attempted to organize young Wobblies by acquainting them with radical literature and poems and the IWW Preamble. Other subjects included Finnish language, parliamentary procedure, labor history, industrial unionism, economics, and public speaking. Classes were held in the morning, leaving afternoons free for study, softball, swimming, or trips into downtown Duluth. [70]

Fred Thompson, writing in the *One Big Union Monthly* in 1937, described in detail the economics course taught to twelve-year-old students at Work People's College that summer.

> In general discussion they have reached the inevitable conclusion that if we can produce so much more than we used to, and do not live more than a couple of times as well, it must be that the working class is gypped of a good part of what it is now able to produce. Then comes the question when and where is the working class gypped? Is it because they are paid too little, or is it perhaps because they are charged too much when they go to buy?

The teacher then led the students through a didactic lesson about the price of candy. From this concrete example, Thompson continues, "these twelve-year-old economists conclude that the gypping of the working class must be perpetrated by the time the worker gets his pay check, that 'exploitation occurs predominantly at the point of production.'" The students next grappled with chronic unemployment, which assumed more the guise of a mathematics problem than a theoretical dilemma. Curiously enough, in 1938, the *One Big Union Monthly*, published by the IWW, devoted an entire issue to Work People's College. The editor's page closed with the following oppressively dogmatic statement: "The labor movement of America needs more schools such as Work People's College where workers learn how to become better fighters in the class war."[71] Ironically, this endorsement came on the heels of Brookwood's demise.

A parallel experiment in "vacation and education" was first initiated on a small scale at Brookwood in 1924, sponsored by the National Women's Trade Union League and planned by Fannia Cohn and Rose Schneiderman, among others. Classes met during the morning and evening hours, with the afternoons reserved for recreation. Brookwood tailored its programs, called "institutes," either to the particular needs of a certain category of workers or to a more general audience. General Labor Institutes were not devoted to a specific industry, union, or problem. They covered broad labor problems, focusing— especially in 1927 and 1928—on organizing nonunion workers, creating industrial unions, and training union organizers. Because of the summer school's early success, Brookwood set aside the first three weeks in August 1925 to accommodate approximately one hundred railroad, clerical, and textile workers, motion picture operators, carpenters, teachers, cap makers, machinists, and miners—among others —from the Midwest, the East, and Canada. About 50 percent of those who attended were union officials; the remainder were rank-and-file workers. The first week was devoted to a Railroad Labor Institute, exclusively for railway workers. During the second and third weeks, a General Labor Institute was open to members of all trades and organizations. In 1926, the Railroad, Textile, and Giant Power Institutes were provided as a service to AFL union officials, giving Brookwooders the opportunity to court union sympathy for the school's larger social and educational goals.[72]

After trying summer recreation and youth camps, Commonwealth College inaugurated a ten-week summer session in 1929 offering economics, labor journalism, social psychology, American history, mathematics, effective writing, and public speaking. It never gave up the recreational goal, however. In 1933, the *Fortnightly* advertised Commonwealth's summer program as casually educational: "For those who wish to attend them, there will be interesting lectures and discussions. . . . But those who prefer to spend their time in repose under a pine or oak or splashing in the swimming creek are welcome to exercise that option."[73]

Brookwood and Commonwealth also furnished inexpensive pamphlets to workers in order to assist them in their organizing and strike activities. Both schools published labor song booklets. The *Brookwood Song Book*, compiled by Brookwooders, represented still another way to use art to inspire workers to organize and struggle for their social and economic goals. Edward J. Falkowski, a Brookwood student and later an instructor at Commonwealth, wrote several songs. One of them, "Onward Brother," was sung to the tune of Beethoven's "Hymn of Joy," from the Ninth Symphony:

> Onward Brothers, march still onward,
> Side by Side to carry on.
> Though the night be dark and hopeless,
> We are coming toward the Dawn.
> Women, children, slave upon us,
> Hard the toil and grim the strife,
> But our souls still sing within us,
> Dreaming of a better life. [74]

Strike Relief, another Brookwood publication, gave its readers a comprehensive guide to fundraising and soliciting other forms of aid during a strike. The pamphlet covered such topics as raising relief through donations from labor organizations, liberals, philanthropists, and the community; obtaining and distributing food, clothing, and medical care; and providing housing for the strikers. It likewise delineated how to maintain relief records and how to organize a relief staff. [75]

Commonwealth printed a number of similar handbooks during its early years. In compliance with the school's ideology, these handbooks contended that employers maintained their domination through the exercise of economic and political power over workers, as well as through control of the press. To help farmers and workers counteract antiunion propaganda, Commonwealth issued a pamphlet designed to teach strikers how to distribute publications of their own. Through "clear-cut, simple explanations," the *Handbook of Mimeograph Technique* stated, "the most unlettered farmer, the least skilled worker and the smallest union treasury can afford excellent quality and quantity reproduction of influential and educational material, without which no organization can succeed." [76] In addition to describing the rudiments of typewriting, the handbook went on to explain, in didactic fashion, the general mimeograph process and included print, production, layout, mimeoscopes, letter spacing and guides, and shading—all techniques that could prove to be essential during a propaganda campaign.

Work People's College and Brookwood also offered correspondence courses. Beginning in 1912, Work People's College supplied courses in Finnish, English, and arithmetic. According to Guss Aakula, "Thousands of correspondence courses were printed in the English language."[77] Brookwood implemented a series of correspondence lessons through its labor pamphlets and through articles that appeared in *Labor Age*. The labor pamphlets, which functioned as an educational tool, also attempted to compensate for the paucity of prolabor literature. David Saposs, editor of the pamphlets, explained:

> These Brookwood Labor Pamphlets are designed to present the important ideas and facts about the labor movement in a clear and simple manner in terms of the workers' experience. However, since they include material rarely found in the usual books on labor they should also prove valuable to non-workers and students. . . . Brookwood, as a school for progressive labor education, aiming to make education available not only to workers who come within its walls but to workers everywhere, has keenly felt the responsibility of providing readable literature for workers on social and economic questions.[78]

The titles of the pamphlets, such as *What a Union Did for the Coal Miners* and *Important Union Methods*, illustrated their teaching function. *Our Labor Movement Today*, by Katherine H. Pollak, detailed the southern textile strikes of 1929–30 and criticized the conservative, no-strike policy of the AFL and its affiliate, the UTW, in the southern textile struggles. The pedagogical uses for the pamphlets were clear from "Questions for Thought and Discussion" and "A Few Reading Suggestions," included at the end of the pamphlet.

In fact, Pollak's main function at Brookwood was to produce such workers' education materials. Ironically, she had served as a participant on the Vassar team during the 1926 Brookwood–Vassar debate, later joining the Brookwood instructional staff. Born in 1905 in Yonkers, New York, and raised in an affluent Jewish family, Pollak attended Vassar but, as she remembers, was sensitive to "social changes which obviously were needed." She ultimately saw her political outlook evolve to that of a "militant socialist." After graduation in 1926, she started tutoring at the New York Women's Trade Union League, where she soon discovered the rewards of workers' education: "I found that the students wanted to learn and I didn't have the problem of having wiggly students in front of me who were not interested in learning. And I also liked the fact that when teaching workers, I found I was learning too, because they had experiences which they talked about." Pollak then moved on to the Bryn Mawr Summer School, serving as a tutor during the summers of 1927, 1928, and 1929, eventually becoming an economics teacher in 1929. She accomplished all of this while attending graduate school, majoring in economics, at Columbia University. Through her workers' education experiences, she discovered a dire need for educational and teaching resources for workers' classes and schools, and turned to Brookwood to fill this void. It was no surprise that she chose Brookwood, Pollak asserts, because "Brookwood Labor College had already been a place I had gone to because it was a center of so much workers' education activity and progressive ideas." In her recollections of Brookwood, Pollak expresses the school's social and educational mission, as well as its ideological position, more clearly perhaps than anyone:

> To understand Brookwood's role you have to view it in the background of the labor movement in the '20's, and the decline it was going through as the result of the anti-union attitudes of employers, the whole paternalistic approach. . . . Brookwood overlapped to some extent with some of the progressives in the unions and in the Socialist party. . . . So it wasn't a clear cut separate group but it was less labelled than the Socialist party. And it did in its early years have the objective of not being sectarian, of wanting to bring together people of various groups.[79]

The brookwood labor pamphlets, which she developed, readily reflected this view.

The school published numerous instructive articles, such as "American Labor in the War and Post-War Period" and "A Consideration of the Wage Problem," in "Brookwood's Pages," a section set aside in *Labor Age*. From 1913 to 1933, the publication served as the organ of labor progressives who opposed the dominant AFL strategy of that period, which emphasized union–management cooperation and promoted organized craft unionism as "respectable" and "patriotic." It originated as the *Intercollegiate Socialist* in 1913 and appeared briefly as the *Socialist Review* from 1919 until 1921. As Herbert Gutman writes, "Over its entire life, the magazine bore witness and gave testimony to the collapse of the pre-1920 Socialist movement, the growing conservatism of trade unionists such as Samuel Gompers, William Green, Matthew Woll, and John Frey, the despair and isolation of their radical critics, and finally to the breakdown of the new capitalism itself between 1929 and 1933."[80]

The Labor Publication Society (LPS), which was founded at the same time as Brookwood and which sponsored *Labor Age*, included progressives, Socialists, and radicals on its board of directors, among them Harry Laidler, Louis Budenz, Elizabeth Gurley Flynn, Stuart Chase, and A. J. Muste. James Maurer served as president of the society, Joseph Schlossberg, ACWA's president, and Thomas Kennedy, UMW's secretary-treasurer, functioned as vice-presidents. This group —including the leaders of fifteen state AFL affiliates and twelve national unions—favored more aggressive labor policies, including amalgamation and industrial unionism. They were instrumental in creating, in addition to the LPS and *Labor Age*, in 1921, the Workers' Education Bureau, Brookwood Labor College, and, finally, after a severe conflict with the national AFL leadership, the Conference for Progressive Labor Action (CPLA) in 1929. After 1926, tensions deepened between the labor progressives and AFL leadership. The increased conservatism of Green, Woll, and Frey clashed with the volatility of Muste, Budenz, and Laidler. The radicalism of the latter group questioned official AFL policies, favored organization of the mass-production industries, and urged attention to groups, including women and blacks, overlooked by the craft unions.[81]

Brookwood, alone among the labor colleges, created an extension program, supervised in its early years by Tom Tippett. He had previously organized a workers' education program in southern Illinois and taught "regular weekly classes in a circuit of eight mining towns and coal camps," and appeared to be the natural choice as director of Brookwood's extension work. The Extension Department supplied speakers and educational assistance to "trade unions, labor colleges and classes, cooperative societies, Y.W.C.A., industrial clubs, discussion groups and other groups and individuals." Several faculty members conducted regular courses as well as serving as advisers for the Educational Department of the New York Central Trades and Labor Council. Faculty also taught summer courses at the ILGWU Unity House and the Textile Workers' Institute in New England. In 1926, the Brookwood faculty taught courses to members of the ILGWU at the Washington Irving High School in New York City every Saturday morning for ten weeks. This particular program accommodated some seventy-five students. Tippett also organized extension courses in Philadelphia, Harrisburg, Lancaster, and York, Pennsylvania; Newark and Paterson, New Jersey; Durham and Greensboro, North Carolina; and Baltimore, Maryland. Perhaps the most glamorous component of the school's extension program was the "Brookwood Hour." Brookwood faculty and guest speakers appeared on this educational radio program broadcast on New York's WEVD on Thursday evenings. The AFPS supported the school's extension efforts with a $1,000 contribution in February 1928. Brookwooders viewed extension work as a means to counter antilabor education and propaganda as well as to recruit students. [82]

Commonwealth, like Brookwood, instituted its own unique educational activities. In late 1934, Commoners put together a museum depicting the decline of capitalism. The "advance advertisement" proclaimed: "We are building up a complete record of the collapse of capitalism while it is still in process and the records of the collapse are at hand to preserve and classify. We do this in the knowledge that it will not only help hasten the day but become a permanent archive of research and educational amusement to the ever-growing class conscious." Commonwealth's Museum of Social Change was modeled after the Soviet Revolutionary Museum and emphasized the impending fall of capitalism through "the increasing extravagance of the wealthy", intellectual and ethical breakdown, increased concentration of wealth, and growth of militarism and fascism. Among the display items were a depression plow drawn by human power, homemade shoes soled with inner tubing, "tear-gas bombs and bloody lynch ropes, and depression clothes made of old sacking." [83] Commonwealth's librarian and students also assembled, printed, and distributed, upon request, reading lists pertinent to labor problems. "A List of Recent References on a Farmer-Labor Party" recommended works by the Communist party, Dewey, Lenin, Muste, and Reinhold Niebuhr, among others. Other lists included "Fascism: A Guide to Reading," "Significant Articles in the Labor Press," and "Recent Federal Government Publications Useful for Workers' Courses." [84]

The labor colleges' educational programs represented comprehensive attempts to counter the bourgeois values propagated by the public educational system, train a labor cadre, and usher in a new social order. In so doing, the labor colleges emphasized the social progress of the working class rather than the social mobility of the individual. And the unique combination of background and tool courses, supplemented with proletarian art forms and informal activities, were intended to serve working-class struggles. As a result, working-class life, as depicted in songs and dramas, was elevated to an art form; in the meantime, working-class children, during summer sessions, were prepared for future activity in the labor movement. Finally, social-class conflict permeated every facet of the curriculum and was especially manifested in field work.

In addition to their educational programs, the processes of education at the labor colleges were likewise formulated to fulfill the schools' social and educational objectives, as we shall see.

4

Teachers and Students

> No college professor to stalk around in cap and gown to give the impression that he knows a lot, but men who have had many years' experience as wage slaves.
>
> —Work People's College Bulletin
> (1923)

THE RADICAL social and educational goals and programs of the labor colleges did not alone ensure that students would become labor activists imbued with the ideal of a new and more egalitarian society. What also must be taken into consideration is the process of education at the labor colleges. This entailed more than mere pedagogy; for this process must include an examination of personality and interaction among teachers and students.

Traditional authoritarian pedagogy involves rote learning: lecturing by the instructor followed by testing to evaluate student retention. This approach is anathema to radicals. Gramsci's arguments reject such "encyclopedic knowledge," which causes students to become "mere receptacles to be stuffed full of empirical data and a mass of unconnected raw facts, which have to be filed in the brain as in the columns of a dictionary, enabling their owner to respond to the various stimuli from the outside world." According to Paulo Freire, a more recent radical education theorist, this approach constitutes a "banking" concept of schooling. In this context, education operates merely as a depositing procedure; that is, the students serve as depositories. The teacher, the depositor, is held in high regard as the omniscient source of information, while students are perceived as totally ignorant, bringing no worthwhile experiences with them into the classroom.[1]

129

Such attitudes were incompatible with the labor colleges' fundamental tenets because they relegated the worker–students to a passive role. Traditional tests, competitive grades, and perfunctory diplomas reinforced this hierarchical approach to schooling, which, in turn, acted to reproduce the division of labor that the labor colleges sought to combat. In a sense, teacher–student relationships in the classroom reflected a political microcosm. The more completely students accepted the passive and subservient role imposed upon them in a traditional classroom, the more they would adapt to a stratified, capitalist society instead of functioning as active agents for social change. Traditional pedagogy, therefore, served as a form of oppression.

The radical founders and supporters of the labor colleges, influenced and supported by progressive educators, saw education as playing a role in social change. They thought that pedagogy should involve students as active participants, encourage inquiry, and emphasize praxis. As part of the dialectic, such pedagogy was to become a liberating experience, both intellectually and socially, rather than an exercise in domination. The labor college classroom emphasized active participation in learning by its worker–students, which meant that they not only came to the college equipped with a set of past experiences, but also continued to gain practical experience during their training. Paternalistic teacher–student relationships were thus avoided. The absence of tests, grades, and diplomas similarly encouraged a sharing of knowledge among the students as well as with workers in general, rather than a monopolization of it.

Personal relationships became another component of the educational process at the labor colleges. How were students selected? What were their acknowledged reasons for attending the labor colleges? As with traditional classroom pedagogy, a competitive, or elitist, selection policy would have contradicted the labor colleges' egalitarian nature. In order to promote solidarity, all workers—regardless of gender, race, religion, political affiliation, trade, and educational background—had to have access to the labor colleges. The colleges also discouraged self-interested reasons for attending. Although motivation for academic achievement is an elusive variable, the colleges avoided the social mobility mentality so prevalent in the formal school system—the pursuit of college degree as an entrée into the middle class. The self-interested student was not the ideal labor college worker–student. The schools preferred students who would return to the workplace.

Because the labor colleges required competent instruction in both background and tool courses, very different kinds of faculty were employed. Some teachers were qualified primarily by academic training; others had practical experience in the labor movement. While many held academic degrees, others brought an activist background into the classroom. Thus, while academically prepared instructors would have been hard-put to relate strike tactics to the students, on the other side, lifetime working-class and social activists would have found it difficult to explicate sophisticated sociological and economic theories underlying the workers' cause. The labor colleges therefore tapped the services of both types of teachers.

The classroom routine at Brookwood ranged from highly sophisticated exchanges of insights into the psychology, sociology, and politics of labor organizing to rudimentary exercises in speaking and writing. For many students at Work People's College and Brookwood, English had to be taught as a foreign language. As a result, teaching methods were traditional or innovative, depending on the subject matter and the abilities of the students. [2]

Extra-classroom interaction, not only between students and teachers, but also among students themselves, played an important part in the educational process at the labor colleges. If instructors were to remain aloof from their students, they would have merely replaced social-class differences with an intellectual—even authoritarian—caste system. Similarly, student organizations, such as fraternities and sororities, with exclusive and clique-like features would have undermined group solidarity. Thus teacher–student relations should be addressed, as well as relationships among students themselves, both in and out of the classroom, at these workers' colleges.

Classroom Methods

An authoritarian relationship between students and teachers, standard in virtually all schools and colleges of the period, was consciously avoided at the labor colleges. Teachers often maintained an informal demeanor, and students addressed them by their first names. Not every student adapted to such casual behavior. As Helen Norton, a Brookwood teacher, recalls: "We had to argue the case with the rather older students who didn't think it was quite polite and had to be rather urged to call the faculty by their first names." [3] Students and teachers participated on an equal basis in many extracurricular activities, such as wrestling, swimming, biking, tennis, ice skating, horseshoes, and working at chores. At Brookwood, Muste was able to indulge his passion for baseball, earning a reputation for "wild heaves from first base." The lack of social and educational distinctions contributed to a feeling of community and conformed to the schools' ultimate social ideal. Raymond and Charlotte Koch write about Commonwealth:

> We were . . . united by rejection of the kind of competition stressed in other colleges and universities. We might vie to reach the top of a mountain trail, or to do a good day's work, or to innovate a way of doing a chore more quickly, more easily, more efficiently. We played volleyball, but there was an unwritten law that everybody could play. A team was whoever showed up—boys, girls, young, old, even handicapped. We played hard, and to win, but I can't remember records of who scored or which side won. [4]

The ideology of the labor colleges and the backgrounds of the students dictated the classroom pedagogy. The colleges tried to eschew the competitive mentality that dominated the formal school system— not to mention the society at large. This noncompetitive principle encompassed all facets of the educational experience—namely, grades, tests, and diplomas. Instead of assigning letter grades, Commonwealth teachers wrote a detailed evaluation of each student's progress in a course of study. To avoid the hierarchical nature of conventional schooling and to nurture a cooperative attitude that reflected the hope for an egalitarian, noncompetitive society, the labor colleges gave no grades and tests and did not award diplomas. This indifference to the usual forms of recognition was also consistent with the schools' preference that their students should not use their educational experience merely for personal advancement. As Muste put it, it was Brookwood's intention to leave its graduates "in a situation where the only ways in which their schooling . . . would tell would be in the actual work they did in unions." [5] Hence, it was Brookwood's avowed claim, as it was for the other labor colleges, to see to it that students applied their knowledge through activism, rather than using it merely to advance their private lot.

Students and teachers appeared to be intensely motivated. Class meetings were held in various indoor facilities and, at Brookwood and Commonwealth, outdoor areas across the grounds. At Brookwood, even the basement of the main building was used as a classroom. Discussions and debates that exceeded the prescribed class time continued at the dinner table, in the fields (at Commonwealth), or around the stone fireplaces of the instructors' cottages during the evening hours. Although attendance at Commonwealth was wholly voluntary, teachers dismissed those who seemed to have neglected "suggested" readings, while students could discharge instructors who failed to teach them anything of any value. Such a technique assured that both teachers and students worked conscientiously. The teachers had to keep the students; to accomplish this, they had to educate to the students' satisfaction, and the students were not the least bit shy about challenging a lecturer's position based on their own work experience. This often exasperated guest lecturers trained in the authoritarian, academic manner. Professor Anton Friedrich, a former Brookings Institute economist, spent a hapless 1926–27 school year at Brookwood thoroughly boring students with his pedantic style and was especially overwhelmed by the students' objections to his discussion of the coal industry. Edward J. Falkowski, a student on leave from his work as a coal miner in Pennsylvania, wrote in his diary about Friedrich's dull manner: "We yawned as he played around his subject, stalling for time. No salt to his meat. No tang to his ale. No bubbles in his palaver. Hackneyed facts and shoddy ideas. Miraculously inept." [6] At the end of the year, Friedrich fled Brookwood for the sedate, academic environment of New York University.

Fred Thompson, principal of Work People's College, gives us an even clearer picture of the pedagogy employed at the labor colleges. Students were not to be passive learners; teachers were to dictate neither the learning process nor content. He recalls:

In general, you had a schedule of classes. But, I would say that the overall purpose was to get people doing things that led them to hunt up information; have people put on skits, have them practice soapboxing. I tried to get it so they were doing and I was the instigator, rather than the lecturer. I found that one of the best ways to get people actually to use their noodle and find something else was to get them into teams for a debate. We would debate all kinds of subjects. Topics would come up, somebody would say, "Let's debate this thing." In general, while we had classes that were named various subjects, I would say that as far as I was concerned, the whole thrust of the thing was to get people interested in finding something else and then getting on their hind legs and talking about it. I'll admit that every once in a while I would find that it was degrading into lectures, because the easiest way [is] you tell it to them and put some things on the blackboard. But I found that was the poorest way that you could devise to transmit information, a very poor way.[7]

Since their experiences provided "much case material for a critical study of society," students assumed active roles in the labor college classroom. This was necessary, Muste argued, because the

trade unionists that come to our workers' classes and colleges have a background. They are emotionally mature. *They have had years of experience in the hard school of industry*. The problem of teaching them is a very different one from the problem of teaching boys and girls in high schools or colleges. Very crudely, one might say that in the main the boys and girls in the colleges have nothing to say but know how to say it, because of their training in organization of thought and expression in the lower schools. On the other hand, the members of our trade union classes have much to say, a rich experience, but they do not know how to say it.[8]

As a result, labor colleges exposed students to classroom situations that encouraged them to articulate their experiences, to raise their level of social consciousness, and to give them practice in speaking before groups. Small classes certainly facilitated this approach. Classes at Commonwealth, for example, seldom exceeded twelve students. Tucker P. Smith, who replaced Muste as Brookwood's director in 1933, described the classroom routine:

The students' lack of familiarity with books, their lack of experience in getting information from books is overcome in part by dividing the class into research committees, with the good readers distributed among the committees. Reading, research, organizing and reporting material, and public speaking are thus combined, under student cooperation, with the specific subject, be it economics, history, or basic industries. There is always animated discussion of committee reports, with convincing student protests against poorly prepared statements which waste the time of the class.[9]

Lively discussions and heated debates characterized the labor college pedagogy. While many classes included lectures, like Brookwood's

"History of Civilization" course, teachers tapped student experiences through reports and discussions. Edward Falkowski recorded his experiences as a student in an English class at Brookwood:

> In Polly Colby's class this morning I spoke on the "Relationship of Brookwooders to the Labor Movement". . . . "We are not here so much to absorb theories as to take them apart and see what is in them. We mustn't think the world is waiting for us to bring salvation to them." The talk went very well, provoking comment hot and cold. . . . The rest of the day I was being buttonholed by those who disagreed with me. [10]

At Commonwealth, mock trials were designed to bring laboratory practice into the law class, lifting class work above theory. Of course, mock trials also prepared students for the judicial rigors that they were sure to encounter as labor activists. Students occasionally gained teaching experience when the regular instructor became ill, or when, as an experiment, the teacher turned the class over to one of them. [11]

Although the students possessed extensive work experience, they usually lacked formal schooling. Instructors adapted their teaching methods to their students' educational backgrounds by painstakingly reviewing lessons and devoting time to students to ensure that they comprehended the material. Clifford Ellis, a teacher at Work People's College, captured the intense, yet cooperative, spirit of the labor college classroom:

> We opened with the reading in class of Mary E. Marcy's "Shop Talks on Economics." Its words are simple. Its lessons are direct. They reflect the daily experience of the workers. The students read back a paragraph at a time. From the blackboard the instructor followed step by step, turning now and then to the board to illustrate in graphic outline some cogent lesson of the text. The students were earnest and attentive. They did not laugh when some reader stumbled over an unfamiliar word. They were there to help, not to ridicule. [12]

Marcy's pamphlet initially appeared in the *International Socialist Review* in 1911 and soon became a classic primer in Marxian economics, attempting "to say," she hoped, "in the language of working men and women, the things Marx says in his own books." [13]

Students

Full-time enrollment always remained modest at the schools. Work People's College, because of its longevity, experienced the most fluctuations. As pointed out earlier, it accommodated only eight students its first year, gradually climbing to an annual average of 133 between 1910 and 1915; most of these were male. For example, during the 1910–11 school year, the college claimed 112 students, with 15 females. Because of the rupture between Finnish Socialists and industrial unionists, attendance fell dramatically to about 38 in 1915–16. By the 1920s, enrollment varied from 40 to 70 students a year, but in the 1930s this dipped to the thirties, with only 30 students in the school's last year. Brookwood and Commonwealth usually hosted 40 to 50 students each year. Nevertheless, over the years, the labor colleges prepared an impressive number of working-class cadre. Brookwood, with the least, claimed 600 to 800, while Work People's College, with the most, easily doubled this figure with an estimated 1,600 to 2,000. This excludes, of course, all of the students exposed to the labor colleges' field programs, summer institutes, and extension work. [14]

Labor college students were older and more experienced than the typical college student. Their ages ranged from nineteen to fifty with most in their twenties: yet they lacked extensive formal schooling. At Work People's College, one-third had never been to school at all, and few had advanced beyond grammer school. Brookwood's students, in comparison, possessed a more diverse cultural and educational background. Of the forty-two students who attended Brookwood in 1927, only four had no public education; slightly more than half had attended grammar school; and fifteen had acquired some high school experience. Twenty-five of these students had previously participated in some other form of workers' education. As Muste characterized them:

They ranged culturally from people who were orthodox and devout church members from isolated and backward villages to extremely sophisticated people who read Marx and the great Russian novelists; who attended Provincetown Playhouse in New York and saw the O'Neill plays before they came to Broadway; saved pennies to get standing-room admission to the Metropolitan Opera House; and went to avant garde dances in Greenwich Village on weekends. [15]

Commonwealth appeared to host the most formally educated group of students, since a few even claimed some college or university background.

Political zeal more than compensated for educational deficiencies. Many students were active in or sympathetic to the Socialist, Communist, and Proletarian parties, or to the anarchist movement. Such intensity, even dogmatism, seemed extreme, in the opinion of Brookwood's Sarah Cleghorn. Instead of the "warm, mellow climate" she had enjoyed as a teacher at the Finckes' Brookwood School, she was distressed by the "Labor Puritans" who enrolled in the newly converted labor college. She looked forward to teaching "mature men and women, with experience in life, ardent for the Labor movement"; yet "these Labor-conscious workers, these demanders of 'the good life for all'" were excessively intense and serious of purpose. "They wanted literary feeling, personal expression, not for life in general, but for the Labor movement alone."[16] Cleghorn was basically correct in her description of Brookwood students—indeed, such singlemindedness of purpose was consistent with the college's announced objectives. The college sought to avoid scholarly remoteness from actual experience and to pursue practical solutions to working-class problems.

Admission requirements differed somewhat among the schools, but all characteristically maintained minimum restrictions. At Work People's College, all applicants had to be wage earners. As its announcement of courses for 1923–24 congenially related:

> Those desiring to become students at Work People's College
> should write . . . and tell the manager what courses they are interested in, what preparation for the studies they have had, if any,
> how long they have been in the movement, what offices they have
> held, if any, and how long they will probably be able to remain at
> the college. This is information useful to the instructors in planning their lessons and arranging courses.[17]

Perhaps Marius Hansome best captured the school's attitude toward rigid entrance requirements: "The school sets no barrier such as an entrance test, for the school believes that 'the man or woman least able to pass an entrance examination is the one most in need of education.'"[18]

Brookwood required three references, "at least two of whom must be persons in responsible positions in the labor movement, who are able to vouch for [the student's] loyalty to organized labor." Ironically, some students attended Brookwood because, as Mark Starr humorously recalls, "their chieftains sent them . . . as at least temporary relief from a pain in the neck . . . somebody who was talking too much in the union ranks!"[19] Like Work People's College, Brookwood did not specify that students take entrance examinations or have preparatory schooling for admission, but the college did give preference to applicants who had worked in industry and held membership in a labor union for at least one year. Brookwood's executive board screened all of the applicants.

Commonwealth College required a written application. This document appeared to be traditional in the sense of asking questions about educational background, work history, travel experiences, and parents' occupations, but deviated from the standard by asking about membership in a trade union, fraternal association, or farmer organization. The application further required a fifty-word essay covering student background in the labor movement and how the students planned to use their labor college education. If students lacked secondary schooling, they were required to enroll in Commonwealth's preparatory department before being admitted. Otherwise, the labor colleges appeared to measure applicants against one basic criterion: they were to be students who seemed "to have a social purpose, and who wish[ed] to prepare themselves for service to their fellow workers."[20]

The labor colleges fostered worker solidarity by admitting students from different occupations, geographical regions, and ethnic and racial backgrounds. All applicants, of course, had to be wage earners, but they did not necessarily have to be unionized. Covering the entire agricultural and industrial spectrum, they included farmers, sheepherders, cowboys, sailors, cooks, carpenters, cab drivers, and auto, glass, steel, and migrant workers. Students from all sections of the country and all parts of the world found their way to the labor colleges; as the *Commonwealth College Fortnightly* recorded in 1926, "many students 'hitch-hike' a thousand miles or more to and from the school." In other cases, students endured the severe hardships and risks of boxcar transit to reach the schools. One student, unable to afford railway fare, rode most of the trip from Saskatoon, Saskatchewan, to Duluth on the outside of a train, exposed to icy blasts of wind. "Such is the thirst," declared Clifford Ellis, "for education among workers."[21]

Brookwood's early students tended to be older, bona fide trade unionists who came predominantly from major urban areas. Bonchi

Friedman, a member of Brookwood's first class of twenty students, was a twenty-three-year-old garment worker from New York City who had previously attended the Bryn Mawr Summer School for Women Workers. John Gancz, thirty-two, was a machinist from Rhode Island with prior workers' education experience at the Rand School. Because of more aggressive recruitment, later students tended to be younger, less urbanized, and not quite as steeped in the trade-union movement as the original group. Lawrence Hogan, a strike leader in the ill-fated Marion strike, had been indicted for insurrection. While appealing his case, he enrolled at Brookwood in December 1929, three weeks after the Marion massacre. He returned to Marion during early March 1930 and began to revive union interest among the textile workers as well as creating study classes for them. Hogan's activities ceased when the court rejected his appeal, and he had to serve his sentence on a chain gang. During Brookwood's final years, the student composition changed yet again. Lawrence Rogin, a Brookwood teacher, delineates the differences between Brookwood's earlier and later students:

There were these worker intellectuals that had educated themselves because, coming from Europe, they came from a tradition in which education wasn't open. They had to educate themselves if they were going to be educated. In addition, they were revolutionary. An educational system was establishment. So, they weren't about to be taken in by it. So, there were these centers [like Brookwood]. Now, when I was at Brookwood, it was a later period. We were getting the people who were identified in the organization as good prospects for union staff. [22]

Edward Falkowski, another Brookwood student, personified much of what the labor colleges hoped to accomplish. Born in 1901 in Shenandoah, Pennsylvania, Falkowski started to work in the anthracite mines at age fifteen. Later, he drifted into odd jobs in Ohio and New York City, but eventually returned to the Shenandoah mines until he was accepted at Brookwood in 1926. He attended until 1928, after which he traveled to Europe and the Soviet Union. During that odyssey, Falkowski labored in German mines, visited Poland, and worked as a miner in the Donbas coal mines in the Soviet Union and as a reporter and city editor for the *Moscow News*. Returning to the United States in 1938, Falkowski became an instructor in labor history at Commonwealth College. After completing a teaching stint, he moved to Toledo, Ohio, and continued his work as a free-lance writer until he was drafted for the Second World War.[23] While at Brookwood and Commonwealth, Falkowski kept copious and articulate notes about his experiences, which provide invaluable insights into life at the schools.

Len De Caux, a former Brookwood student, remembered the school in distinctly romantic terms:

> Brookwood was beautiful—if not beyond compare, certainly by compare. To the miner, Brookwood was green, clean, all above ground—no coaldust, no cricks in the back. To the machinist, Brookwood was greaseless days far from the grinding roar of metal against metal. To makers of suits, dresses, hats, Brookwood was fairytale country to which they were wand-wafted from the square, treeless hills, the trash-strewn cement valleys of Manhattan or Chicago. To those who had known poverty, Brookwood offered ease, security, the fresh-air pleasures of the well-to-do.
> . . . Spiritually, Brookwood was a labor movement in microcosm —without bureaucrats or racketeers—with emphasis on youth, aspirations, ideals. [24]

Located in the predominantly agricultural upper Midwest, Work People's College tended to attract seasonal workers. The more pragmatic and studious saw the school as convenient wintering quarters. This was the case with C. Mauritz Erkkila. He came from a Finnish working-class family that held "the working man and his struggle for survival" in high regard. Erkkila attended Work People's College during the winter sessions of 1933–34 and 1934–35 in order to learn why the country was experiencing a serious economic breakdown. [25]

Commonwealth boasted a cosmopolitan group of students during the 1920s that included, among others, Frank Bird, a farmer and commercial teacher from Morrilton, Arkansas, Fred Hocevar, a union carpenter from Chicago, and Adolph Sloch, a machinist's apprentice from Altoona, Pennsylvania. [26]

The labor colleges also invited foreign students, who attended Brookwood and Commonwealth in particular to learn about the American labor movement. In 1922, Brookwooders welcomed Charles Moore, a postal clerk from England, as their first exchange student from a foreign workers' education center. Later, Brookwooders accommodated Swedish students, while Commoners hosted Cubans. Occasionally, the schools boarded whole families. Both August Daniels-son, a member of the United Brotherhood of Carpenters and Joiners, and Otti Danielsson, his wife and a member of the International Fur Workers Union, enrolled at Commonwealth during the 1926–27 school year.[27] Even Work People's College began to lose some of its ethnic, parochial character by the late 1920s, causing Fred Thompson to re-mark: "Each year the activities of the school are being conducted more and more in English, due not only to the increased interest of English speaking students but also to the changes among the Finnish people who started the school and who still own the majority of the stock in it."[28]

Nevertheless, the labor colleges, like their traditional counterparts, generally attracted the majority of their students from the local geo-graphic region. Sulo Peltola, who attended Work People's College in 1932–33, was born and raised in the Iron Range in northern Minne-sota. When he was three years old, his father, a radical Finn and avid supporter of Work People's College, participated in the ill-fated miners' strike of 1916 and was summarily blacklisted by the iron ore companies. Peltola could only afford to attend Work People's College through a unique fund-raising technique. A stipend program was held in the Finn halls throughout the area. Two- or four-month stipends were issued by the school, and tickets were sold as either raffle tickets for donations to the school or as admission tickets to social events, where drawings were held. Winners could use the stipends, sell them to someone else, or give them away to friends; Peltola received his from a friend. With his father unemployed and the country in the throes of the Great Depression, this was a rare opportunity that Peltola could not afford to pass up.[29]

While Work People's College catered primarily to the local Finns, Brookwood and Commonwealth admitted students from a variety of ethnic and racial groups. Some of the more provincial students at first balked at this ethnic mixture. At Brookwood,

a miner from the Middle West, looking over his fellow students for the first time, asked, "What are these Jewish girls doing here? There ain't no Jews in the labor movement." The needle trades unions were completely unknown to him and he was even more surprised when the girls not only outshone him on labor theory —of which, in truth, he had very little—but even in discussions of labor tactics on which he considered himself an authority. The

girls, too, soon had to revise their opinion of the miner and ac-
knowledge that lack of sophistication did not betoken hopeless
ignorance.[30]

Commonwealth welcomed immigrants from Austria, Germany,
and Sweden, among other countries. Ida Mindlin, a Russian immigrant who labored in New York's garment industry, enrolled at Commonwealth to extend her education. Oscar Easton, a Swede who had
settled in Massachusetts, wanted to perfect his English for union committee work and other organizational activities.

Labor college students and teachers attacked racism. Brookwooders, in particular, openly criticized the AFL for its segregationist policies and drew attention to the problems of black workers through a
number of conferences with noted black leaders. Brookwooders sponsored an early summer institute in May, 1927 entitled "The Negro
in Industry and the Labor Movement." David Saposs organized the
meeting and invited participants from the National Association for
the Advancement of Colored People (NAACP), the National Urban
League, the Pullman Car Porters, and the Atlanta School of Social
Work. With A. Philip Randolph in attendance as a speaker, the weekend institute clearly served as a forum for black workers to express
their dissatisfaction with the AFL's racist policies and call for integration of the union's locals. With W. E. B. DuBois serving as chair,
Brookwood sponsored another black workers' education conference
in December 1930, which adopted a statement protesting the AFL's
policy of segregated locals.

Brookwood strengthened that commitment by admitting black
student–workers. This process began as early as 1925 with NAACP
scholarship support. Floria Pinkney, a Brooklyn dressmaker, was sent
to Brookwood by the local branch of the YWCA's Industrial League
and later served on the staff of the ILGWU. Lee B. Stanley, Muste's
secretary from 1923 to 1925, recounted how one white student reacted
to Pinkney's presence on the Brookwood campus: "We also had a student from the Railroad Brotherhood from the South who up to that
time had never lived or eaten with a Negro, made a big fuss about
it and declared he wasn't going to. He was told that he either *did* or
he could leave. He stayed and became very friendly with [her]. That
taught him a lesson."[31]

Commonwealth, in contrast, faced insurmountable obstacles in
heavily segregated Arkansas. "To racist vigilantes in the area," Raymond and Charlotte Koch recall, "the social, political, and economic

exclusion of blacks was Scripture." Unable to invite black workers to campus because of local white opposition, Commonwealth compensated by sending students and teachers to help organize black sharecroppers. Commoners became involved in the integrated Southern Tenant Farmers' Union (STFU) during the 1930s and provided scholarships to STFU members to attend the school. Planters in the Arkansas Delta, angered by Commonwealth's assistance to the tenant farmers, often vented their frustration by beating and arresting Commonwealth's organizers.

Lucien Koch, then director of Commonwealth College, and two students, Atley Delaney, a member of the Young People's Socialist League from Boston, and Robert Reed, a member of the Young Communist League from Texas, incurred the planters' wrath. While Delaney attended an organizing meeting at Marked Tree, Arkansas, Koch and Reed went to another assembly at a black church in Gilmore, ten miles to the east. Shortly after the meeting began, the crowd of forty to fifty black sharecroppers was dispersed by four white men with guns. Reed recalls the terror he felt:

> They started clubbing Lucien, and covered me with guns. They were drunk. . . . At least one of them was a deputy sheriff. . . . They slugged us around pretty bad, with threats of killing us. Those guns were boring into us, and could have gone off any minute. They had a rope with them . . . tied in a hangman's knot. . . . They took us to the county seat . . . [but] they didn't put us in jail. They took us downstairs to the washroom, and told us to clean up. . . . Then they took us into the office of the county judge. . . . They wanted to know our background, where we came from, and why we were in their county, and what were white men doing involved in dealing with blacks, though they didn't call them that. [32]

After several more threats, Koch and Reed were driven to the county line and deposited unceremoniously onto the pavement. The lesson was over.

Teachers

Labor college faculty brought a wide variety of work experiences and educational backgrounds with them to their classrooms. Still, teachers at Brookwood and Commonwealth, with few exceptions, appeared to be more formally educated than their counterparts at Work People's College. By 1932, seven of the nine faculty members at Brookwood had graduated from an institution of higher learning, with many claiming some graduate experience. "All the faculty were really committed," Brookwood instructor Katherine Pollak asserts. "They were there because they believed in it. Nobody went into this because it was a good way to make money." During one school year, Commonwealth's full-time faculty included two with doctorates, one bachelor of arts, and one with a master of science degree. John E. Kirkpatrick, who taught a course in government, had graduated from Harvard and had served on the faculties of Washburn College, the University of Michigan, and Olivet College. [33]

WORK PEOPLE'S COLLEGE

The teachers at Work People's College, like its students, came from the ranks of labor. "The instructors here," the school's bulletin proclaimed in 1923, "are drawn from among the wage workers in industry. No college professor to stalk around in cap and gown to give the impression that he knows a lot, but men who have had many years' experience as wage slaves." During the school's industrial union period, the teachers joined the ranks of workers in the IWW. They assumed routine teaching responsibilities, such as recording student attendance, checking assignments, correcting students' work promptly, and attending meetings of the teachers' council. The council met regularly with the principal to organize student schedules, order books, and make suggestions to the board of directors regarding the purchase of teaching equipment and the implementation of curriculum changes. [34]

Yrjo Sirola's teaching career at Work People's College spanned the socialist and IWW periods. Before he fled Finland as a victim of Russian political purges, Sirola had been an important member of the Social Democratic party of Finland. He had also worked on the editorial staff of *Kansan Lehti* (People's Journal) in the large industrial city of Tampere, Finland, on the editorial staff of the Helsinki *Työmies* (the Worker), and as general secretary of the Finnish Social Democratic party and as a member of the *Eduskunta* (parliament). Sirola became dean of the faculty at Work People's College in 1910, remained in that post for four years, and quickly earned a reputation as a taskmaster in the classroom. John Wiita recounts Sirola's teaching approach: "The important aspect of Sirola's teaching was that he was conscious that

Työvöen Opisto [Work People's College] was a Finnish Socialist Federation institute and his program and method of teaching was not only to teach theories of social sciences but to try to help students to apply what they had learned in their practical work for the benefit of labor organizations." Sirola's political evolution paralleled the school's; he "drifted from a . . . social democratic centrist position towards a more leftist, revolutionary position, which was a general trend in many European social democratic parties," writes Wiita, "and also among the American socialists and in our Finnish Socialist Federation and the Työvöen Opisto student body." With the approval of the board of directors, Sirola created an instructor's training program from the school's own students. He eventually returned to Finland, became a Communist, and moved to the Soviet Union to take an important post in the Bolshevik party. Sirola became dean of the Finnish section of the Lenin School in 1930 and died in Moscow in 1937.

Leo Laukki, like Sirola, fled the Russian purges in Finland. At Work People's College, students acknowledged Laukki as a "spiritual giant" and "encyclopedia," and he earned a reputation as an orator, electrifying students and audiences with his wealth of knowledge and brilliant delivery. However, as Wiita recalls, "once when Laukki spoke at the Finnish socialist hall in Duluth, after orating six hours, he took a pause, saying 'and secondly' and continued his speech several more hours."[35]

Other teachers included Wiita himself, who had come to Work People's College as a student in 1909. He ultimately became a member of the board of directors, served as secretary of the college, taught as an assistant instructor, rose to managing director of the correspondence school, and in 1915 assumed the post of faculty dean. He severed his connections with the school when the IWW gained control of it. Archie Brown likewise entered Work People's College as a student and later accepted a teaching position.[36]

Fred Thompson, remembered fondly by his former students, possessed a tremendous grasp of his subject matter, demonstrated a subtle and engaging wit, and became the college's best-known director. Thompson was born in Saint John, New Brunswick, in 1900, and according to his recollections, became a radical in 1913 after reading *The Wealth of Nations* by Adam Smith. He wryly recalls, "I would say my radicalism came far more from Adam Smith than it did from Karl Marx." Smith's book had sparked Thompson's interest in economics. He proceeded to study, on his own, the writings of the nineteenth-century utopian socialists and soon joined the Socialist party, eventually becoming secretary of his local. A construction worker, he labored on tunnels, irrigation ditches, dams, quarries, and railroad tracks.

Thompson first became active in the IWW in Alberta, Canada, in 1919, moved to Vancouver, then sought work, in 1922, across the border in Washington. He describes that experience and its political implications:

> We always boxcared from one job to another, never paid any fare. I had heard of the Wobblies; . . . weird stories, that they were a bunch of nuts trying to change the world by burning haystacks and stuff like that. I found a tremendous difference between this myth and the reality. They were a very serious bunch of men with understanding: even if we do win our immediate demands, the boss and I will still have a fight. Let's run the works for our own good, so we won't have to fight any more. They had this notion: someday . . . But, right now, let's clean up these camps, let's raise the wages.

He was arrested, on criminal charges, for IWW organizing activities in California. As he remembers: "I went in on the anniversary of the Russian Revolution, November 7, 1923, and came out on March 7, 1927." Thompson had read advertisements about Work People's College in various IWW newspapers and periodicals:

> I figured I could probably get myself a good place to put in a winter. I wanted to study something. I was interested in what they're doing up there. So, from time to time, I sent some money up there, to be sure not to spend it. That wasn't an unusual thing. People coming there to school, if they were wandering around working, they would put money on deposit up there, if they had some, because otherwise they were very likely to have the snowflakes come down and no money in your pocket.

He arrived at the school to discover that a teacher was needed for a course in Marxist economics, and he was recruited. Again, he recalls:

> Even as a kid, I got over to Halifax, from my hometown, and put in a winter there. But as soon as the Labor party there found out that I had actually read all through the whole first volume of *Capi-*

tal, the only man they knew who had read Smith . . . [I taught] a
class in economics every Sunday. So, it wasn't altogether new to
me to have something like that happen to me. [37]

Thompson eventually became principal of Work People's College, and
served as editor of the *Industrial Worker* for several decades.

BROOKWOOD TEACHERS

Brookwood's early instructors, in addition to Muste of course, included Arthur W. Calhoun and David J. Saposs, among others. Calhoun was born in Dayton, Pennsylvania, in 1885, the son of a physi-
cian. He graduated from the University of Pittsburgh in 1906 and
taught literature, history, and Latin at a number of high schools and
small colleges. Along with Saposs, he studied for his master's degree
in 1913 at Wisconsin, then went to Clark University in Worcester, Massachusetts, and began the preparation for the publication of his doc-
toral thesis, "The Social History of the American Family." It proved to
be a pioneering treatise in the field, later published in three volumes.

Despite his reputation as a superb teacher and successful author,
Calhoun lost many positions because of his radical opinions and pacifism and his refusal to sign loyalty oaths. Calhoun forfeited his teaching position at Clark in 1918 because of his vocal opposition to the First
World War. Between 1918 and 1923, he taught at four different institutions of higher education as well as a Florida junior high school, in
none of them for more than a year. During the 1920–21 academic year,
Calhoun taught at the Rand School, where he first met Muste. They
developed an instant rapport, since they were, in many ways, alike.
They were the same age, had suffered the same fates for their pacifist
views, and shared similar dreams of expanding the labor movement.
Calhoun and his wife, Mildred, joined the Brookwood instructional
staff in 1923. He taught economics and sociology; she taught English.

Calhoun's interest in workers' education predated his tenure at
Brookwood. In addition to his experience at the Rand School, Calhoun was well acquainted with William Zeuch, one of the founders
of Commonwealth College. Zeuch had been one of Calhoun's undergraduate students at Lenox College, in Iowa, during the 1912–13 academic year, and later was a graduate student at Clark University. Their
relationship eventually blossomed into a long-term correspondence
and friendship. In November 1917, Zeuch wrote Calhoun about his
plans to visit Ruskin College, in Florida, to see if he could "find some

sort of work to do there during the winter." Zeuch went to Ruskin because he had been fired from a teaching position at Indiana University, where he had written a letter to a newspaper "protesting against its German-baiting policy." It was at Ruskin, of course, that Zeuch first met Kate Richards O'Hare, and they formulated the idea for a new workers' school. Later, in 1923, Zeuch wrote to Calhoun from Newllano Colony, inviting him to teach at Commonwealth College. Calhoun found the projected school to be "too proletarian, too pioneering, and too radical," and declined the offer.[38] Nevertheless, in March 1923, Zeuch again corresponded with Calhoun in order to consult with him about Commonwealth's proposed curriculum.

David Saposs, like Muste, was the son of immigrants. His parents were Russian Jews who had settled in Milwaukee, Wisconsin, a city steeped in the socialist tradition. Born there in 1886, Saposs worked in a brewery and as a newsboy, and was a night court stenographer in Madison while he attended the University of Wisconsin. He became an associate of John R. Commons and contributed to his ten-volume *Documentary History of American Industrial Society* and his two-volume *History of Labor in the United States*, both of which have become classics. Saposs gained extensive teaching experience at Wisconsin, the University of Toledo, the Rand School, and in the ILGWU's workers' education classes, and he served as educational director for the ACWA. He also participated in the 1919 steel strike as an active observer and reporter. Thus, he brought a theoretical and practical background to his labor history and labor problems courses at Brookwood. Saposs and his wife, Bertha Tigay Saposs, a University of Chicago–educated social worker, joined Brookwood's faculty in 1922 and stayed for eleven years.[39]

The Brookwood staff also included Sarah Cleghorn, Josephine Colby, Clinton Golden, Helen Norton, Mark Starr and Lawrence Rogin. Cleghorn, a liberal pacifist who described herself as a "New England spinster," had attended Burr and Burton Seminary, a private school for farm children in Manchester, Vermont. Responding to an advertisement in the *Nation*, she applied for a teaching position at the Finckes' Brookwood School; supported by Norman Thomas, Cleghorn breezed through a friendly interview and joined the preparatory school's staff. When the school became a labor college in 1921, she remained as an English instructor but soon became disillusioned with the students. After a brief sojourn in New York City as a writer for a publication called the *World Tomorrow*, Cleghorn rejoined the Finckes at their new location, the Manumit School, in Pawling, New York.[40]

Josephine "Polly" Colby resigned her position as a California high school teacher in order to devote more time to union activities. She served for two years as an organizer and publicity agent for the newly formed AFT and rose to become vice-president in 1920. Colby replaced Cleghorn and quickly earned a reputation as an excellent English teacher, particularly at the elementary level, where many of the adult students found themselves. Edward Falkowski, a student in her English class, praised her teaching abilities in his diary:

Polly is a consummate artist; facile, sure-mannered, tactful—she surprises us afresh with her charming manner of teaching at each session. She personalizes English; she is approachable—does not surround herself with a tough rind of erudition, does not impress with her vast learning. Gently she imparts her knowledge. So softly we almost breathe in the lesson of the morning, and leave the class feeling reinvigorated and wiser. [41]

Falkowski's affectionate account of Colby contrasted sharply with the dreary picture he painted of economist Anton Friedrich's "miraculously inept" style.

Clinton Golden, born in 1884 and raised in Pottsville, Pennsylvania, brought extensive union experience with him to Brookwood. His father died when he was nine, forcing him to quit school at eleven in sixth grade in order to go to work in the ore mines. He served a three-year apprenticeship as a machinist and was employed as a locomotive fireman and engineman from 1904 to 1916. He assumed several important positions in the Brotherhood of Locomotive Firemen and Enginemen, participating on the grievance committee and as a wage negotiator. Golden affiliated with the Socialist party in 1911, received his political education from the socialist press, and campaigned for Debs in 1912. He joined the IAM in 1917, was elected district representative for Philadelphia two years later, and played an active role in the strike of the William Cramp Ship and Engine Building Company. Realizing the value of education, he organized a public-speaking course and helped to establish the Philadelphia Labor College. As an early and enthusiastic supporter of Brookwood, Golden encouraged his union members to attend the school; workers needed, in his words, "expert knowledge as a weapon in their struggle for justice. By developing and controlling our own institutions of learning, for the men and women of our movement, we will educate the workers into the service of their fellow workers rather than away from the labor movement, as is so often the case when the ambitious unionist enters the average university." Golden joined the AFPS board of directors in 1924, following a brief stint as the ACWA's general organizer, and became Brookwood's field representative as well. This produced a conflict of interests which the Fund's board quickly resolved, allowing him to retain the two positions and paying for both of them. Thus Golden toured the country recruiting students for Brookwood and investigating workers' education enterprises for the AFPS. This resulted in recommendations amounting to some $250,000 in appropriations to develop workers' education activities. Beginning in 1926, he worked exclusively for Brookwood, adding "business manager" to his other titles. The college assumed his full salary. [42]

Twenty-eight-year-old Helen Norton became Brookwood's youngest instructor in 1925. She was the daughter of a Kansas machinist and had worked in the offices of the Santa Fe Railroad and as a schoolteacher before she entered Kansas State Agricultural College in Manhatten, Kansas, in 1921. After working her way through college, Norton read about a labor journalism position at Brookwood and applied. She interviewed with Golden, who was at Denver Labor College on business, and was hired for the position.

Mark Starr played a significant role in the British and American workers' education movements over a period of seventy years. Born near the Shoscombe, Somerset, coal field in 1894, Starr quit school in 1907 to work as a builder's mortar boy. A year later he entered the coal mines, working at night carrying powder to miners. Soon Starr was promoted to carting boy, whose function was to squeeze into the mines where horses could not be used. With a chain around his neck, and often drenched by mine water, he pulled a sled or a wagon. "The harness they gave to young fellows made me a socialist," Starr recalled; he joined the Independent Labour party. In 1913, he moved to the South Wales coal mines where, as he recounts it, the "seams were wider then, I didn't have to wear the gus and crook, I could stay upright in working." Starr won a miner's essay scholarship to the Central Labour College in London. Attending classes and encountering such works as Marx's *Capital*, he became further radicalized. According to his recollections, "I had been reared a Methodist. I found these ideas not competent to explain the problems that I met in [sic] everyday." Starr's workers' education experience was interrupted by the First World War. He registered as a conscientious objector and was permitted to return to the mines rather than serve in the armed forces, but was arrested in 1917 and imprisoned. After his release in 1919, his union allowed him to complete his labor college studies.

Beginning in 1921, Starr completely devoted himself to workers' education. He wrote books and pamphlets to be used in British workers' classes, taught for the Plebs League, and eventually became a divisional organizer for the National Council of Labour Colleges. The Plebs League, unlike its counterpart, the Workers' Education Association, which received a government subsidy, drew its financial support from the unions. That distinction was crucial for Starr: "True independence means that the workers' education movement must finance itself." Likewise, the social and educational goals and program of the Plebs League appeared to be strikingly similar to that of the American labor colleges. In Britain, Starr recalls:

> We wanted education for a new social order. . . . [To] teach people all the personal necessities to make good union officers. But teach them the history of the labour movement. Teach them the economics, how they are exploited. Teach them the dangers of imperialism. Teach them public speaking as tool courses. We divided the course into tool courses and aim courses. You can see why writing and speaking, public speaking, particularly, would be a tool course in order to get over the ideas that you have received.

As Starr saw it, a formal British education did not benefit workers; rather, "we were critical of orthodox education, seeing it as an attempt to inflict bourgeois culture, nationalistic and pseudo-patriotic ideas on the working class. . . . We thought that the main purpose of the official education system was to make robots for the current system." Shortly after a trip to the Soviet Union in 1926, Starr accepted an offer from Muste to teach about the British labor movement at Brookwood. Starr taught at the school from 1928 until 1935, when he left, with his wife, Helen Norton, out of disillusionment with Tucker Smith—Muste's replacement—to become the educational director of the ILGWU. [43]

Lawrence Rogin arrived at Brookwood in 1935, after a major split among faculty and students over affiliation with the Conference for Progressive Labor Action, which resulted in the abrupt departure of Muste and several students and teachers (as we shall see in Chapter 6). Rogin, who had taught at Reading Labor College, went to Brookwood to teach labor journalism and labor drama and to assist in the school's chautauqua program. According to his recollections, his family had "moved around a lot" in New York and New Jersey. Rogin saw himself as an "independent radical" in high school, supporting the Robert La Follette campaign, and completed his graduate work, except for his dissertation, at Columbia University. Because of Muste's defection and the financial strain of the Depression, union and private contributions to the school dwindled. Thus, Rogin witnessed lean years at Brookwood: "We never really drew a salary. What you got out of it was a very nice house with furniture in it; you got food; you got other things. If you could do other work, that was encouraged. That meant that medical bills which could be met for people who had children, all that kind of thing. The two years I was there, I taught night school for City College of New York. What cash we had came from that." In spite of the fiscal crunch, the faculty maintained the school's educational mission. Still, Rogin earned the dubious distinction of remaining at Brookwood until the bitter end: "I was the last faculty member to leave the place, just after Labor Day in 1937." [44]

COMMONWEALTH COLLEGE TEACHERS

Of course, not all of the teachers possessed college or university degrees. Covington Hall, born in 1871, the son of a southern Presbyterian minister, reared in a tiny Louisiana town and a member of the United Sons of Confederate Veterans, possessed a distinctly patrician ancestry. But he also served the IWW as a poet, songwriter, and essayist; from 1909 to 1912, "Swashbuckling" Hall assisted the Louisiana Brotherhood of Timber Workers in its fight against the lumber trust. He became involved as an IWW organizer with Big Bill Haywood during the long and bitter lockout of black and white lumber workers in the Louisiana–Texas timber belt from 1911 to 1912. Later, the Newllano Colony published a volume of his poetry, *Rhymes of A Rebel*. One poem, "The Strike," captures Hall's radicalism:

Say what ye will, ye owls of night;
The strike upholds the cause of right;
The strike compels the judge to pause,
The statesmen to remold the laws.

Say what ye will, the strike is good,
It clears things long misunderstood;
It jolts the social mind awake;
It forces men a stand to take.

Say what ye will, yet without ruth,
The strike drives home the bitter truth;
The strike tears off the mask of things,
To mass the class the issue brings.

Say what ye will, all else above,
The strike is war for bread and love;
For raiment, shelter, freedom all
The human race can justice call.

Hall had followed the O'Hares to Newllano, since he had been contributing columns to the *Vanguard*, but left when they did, drifting to Oklahoma, Chicago, and Florida. Thus, Hall arrived at Commonwealth's new location in late 1925 with nothing more than a radical literary background and a reference from Debs as a "fine Old poet-warrior."

"Cov," as he was affectionately called, took charge of the school's publishing, but seemed restless. In spite of the militant spirit evoked by his poetry, Hall appeared by 1926 to be pessimistic about the prospects of radical social change. He believed that all great revolutions had been largely agrarian, and that the lethargy of the American labor movement during the quiescent twenties offered little hope. His other experiences at Commonwealth proved equally disappointing. He wrote a great deal but published little, and appeared less than enthusiastic about his campus chores. He also taught a few classes, earning a reputation as a competent instructor. Hall became seriously ill during his second year, requiring hospitalization; the school assumed his medical bills. He returned to campus to recover, unable to perform any kind of intellectual or physical work, and departed in 1927. By the late 1930s, Hall had taken up residence at Work People's College. [45]

Perhaps the Koch family best personified the Commonwealth experience, since their tenure at the school encompassed many roles, including that of students, teachers, and administrators, and their association with the college spanned most of its seventeen years. Herman Koch, the son of German immigrants, made several unsuccessful attempts to support his family as a machinist and as a farmer outside of Portland, Oregon. In frustration, he investigated the prospects of moving his family to the Louisiana Newllano Colony. After a brief visit by Herman and his son Lucien, upon seeing the bickering and jealousy among the colony's members, the elder Koch became quickly disillusioned with the communal life. Lucien, however, decided to remain behind at Newllano. When Zeuch and his supporters moved Commonwealth College to Arkansas, an invitation was sent to Herman Koch to consider joining them. The promise of higher education for all eight of the Koch children lured them to sell their farm, pack two Model "T" Fords with their belongings, and drive to Mena to join Lucien at the newly established Commonwealth College. Thus, pragmatic reasons, instead of a zealous commitment to expanding the labor movement and fomenting social change, motivated Herman Koch. The family immediately assumed farming chores, but by 1926 Herman had decided to resume his machinist's trade in Houston, Texas, leaving his family at Commonwealth. He returned to the school the following year in order to pack his family off to Cincinnati. Lucien again decided to remain at Commonwealth, as did his brothers Ernest and Raymond. Ernest somehow managed to continue his education despite the demanding schedule of planting, weeding, and harvesting. Raymond completed his education and eventually became a teacher at Commonwealth. He later married another student, Charlotte Moskowitz, who succeeded Lucien as the school's temporary director.

Lucien Koch's career at Commonwealth proved nothing less than stellar. Born in June 1907, Lucien began working on his family's Oregon farm at an early age and often tackled heavy tasks, such as splitting six cords of wood a day, as a teenager. Lucien earned a reputation as a bright student in grammar school, winning several honors, and attended high school in nearby Oregon City while he worked in a print shop. His trip with his father to Newllano interrupted his high school education, which he quickly resumed at Commonwealth College. Lucien abandoned Newllano with the disaffected Commoners and moved to Arkansas, where his family joined him. During his last two years as a student, Lucien taught a course in elementary economics, and in 1929, after Zeuch made arrangements for him, he attended the University of Wisconsin's School for Workers. At Wisconsin, he served as a part-time instructor in the Department of Economics while he pursued his graduate studies. He returned to Commonwealth in 1921 with his master's degree in labor economics to become, at age twenty-three, the youngest college director in the country. [46]

William Cunningham, a Commonwealth instructor, best summarized teaching at the labor colleges: "The teachers receive no salaries, therefore they are not hoping for increases or fearing reductions. They are not required to frighten adolescents into cultural pursuits or keep them from wickedness and idleness. . . . They are not inquisitors, disciplinarians, wardens, clerks, nor models for the young, therefore they have opportunity to be teachers."[47]

Labor college faculty did more than verbalize their commitment to the labor movement. Teachers at Work People's College joined the IWW, while those at Brookwood and Commonwealth belonged to the AFT. Brookwood's instructors formed Local 189 in 1921, and the Commonwealth faculty organized the first teachers' union in Arkansas, Local 194, in 1926. Officials of the teachers' union, however, delayed Commonwealth's charter out of fear over a potential communist element at the school. Only Muste's steadfast support for Commonwealth assured its union status. Because of the democratic decision-making process at the schools, labor college teachers also played significant roles in determining educational policies. Brookwood's instructors, as we have seen, hosted an annual workers' education conference that attracted labor educators from across the nation who planned curricula and created reading lists for workers' classes and schools. Brookwood eventually assumed the role of a clearinghouse for workers' education materials. At the annual workers' education conference at Brookwood in 1932, representatives from Work People's College and Commonwealth College, among others, attended.

To supplement the faculty, the labor colleges routinely invited guest lecturers to stimulate free and open discussion. Commonwealth accommodated speakers at informal gatherings, such as its Sunday evening lecture series, after-luncheon forums, Friday night seminars, and seminar sessions, while Work People's College made formal arrangements and invited the public—through placards and leaflets—to hear some of its guest lecturers. These included educators, labor officials, writers, and alumni. Most visitors leaned decidedly leftward in their social thought and included occasional Communists. Sumner Schlicter, Norman Ware, A. Philip Randolph, Sinclair Lewis, and Oscar Ameringer represented a few of the more prominent guest speakers who appeared at Brookwood and Commonwealth. John Dewey, visiting the Brookwood campus for a talk, was housed with the Saposs family. Bertha Saposs recalls her guest, revealing a rare personal glimpse of the renowned philosopher. David and Bertha Saposs insisted that Dewey sleep in their bed while they shared a cot. At about two o'clock in the morning, Bertha Saposs reminisces:

> One of my girls was very little, and she called. I got up and took care of her. Professor Dewey's door was open, the light was on, and he was reading. I thought, What hasn't Professor John Dewey read as yet? Assuming it was Greek philosophy, I said, "I'm sorry my child was a disturbance." But he didn't hear me. The next day he went to the conference, and he had a bag. And it was open and there were some books in it. It was the *Red Crime* mystery book! And I thought what hasn't John Dewey read as yet? It was a dime novel!

Not all speakers were enthusiastically welcomed, however. Helen Norton, a Brookwood instructor, cynically recalls a few of the summer visitors who served as guest lecturers as "weekend radicals, who would come out, . . . spend Saturday and Sunday and tell us how Brookwood and the world should be run."[48]

Social Relationships

In 1929, while at Brookwood, Saposs wrote a brief paper, "The Need for a Labor Culture," that revealed his analysis of the existing labor movement. He criticized both American capitalism and trade unions for destroying any semblance of a viable labor movement. Workers needed a dynamic labor movement, Saposs claimed, one "based upon a *labor culture*; that is, a mode of feeling, thinking and acting in terms of the problem of labor, reinforced by the aspiration for a social order in which service instead of profit is the ideal and aspiration of labor." However, at the time, this labor culture did not exist. For culprits, Saposs pointed first to the "viciousness of rampant capitalism" and the "more dangerous paternalistic perversions of welfare capitalism." A second source of labor's malaise lay with the trade-union movement, "pigmy in stature, poor and feeble in spiritual, intellectual and philosophic content." Saposs, in particular, blamed the AFL, "with its business unionism, which deliberately discouraged all working-class organizational activity except unions, and which led workers to immerse themselves in the capitalistic culture." To make matters worse, "the trade union movement [was] apologetically striving to fuse itself with the capitalistic culture." Not only was the AFL strengthening bourgeois hegemony, it was part and parcel of "capitalistic culture" as well. This acted, in turn, to demoralize workers and devastate the labor movement: "The worker in the United States is surrounded with a point of view that is antilabor, or at best nonlabor. . . . This situation holds true of his political party, church, athletic club, fraternal and benefit society, press, theatre and so on." The only solution was for workers to create their own labor culture that could serve as the foundation for an "effective" labor movement.[49] At the labor colleges, this counter-hegemony manifested itself through democratic governance and a communal environment.

Students and teachers maintained significant decision-making roles. "The directors and the student body," *Work People's College Announcement of Courses, 1923–24*, boasted, "administer the affairs of the college making it the most democratic institution known." During its socialist period, the school's student body organized a "comrades' student union" to discuss student problems and published an annual called *Ahjo* ("Forge"). All of the resident students joined that union, which met weekly and handled all student conflicts and discipline problems. Its decisions could be appealed to the school's board, but few students exercised this option. Students and faculty met every Friday evening at the *Toverikunta*. Students continued to remain active in school affairs during the IWW era. They resolved disputes and discipline problems, maintained a student representative on the board of directors, and assembled for a weekly business meeting every Saturday night.

As at Work People's College, students at Brookwood and Commonwealth managed student problems and arranged social functions. At the first meeting of the Brookwood community in 1921, all members of the faculty, administrative group, and student body organized themselves into a voluntary association called the Brookwood Cooperative. Every new Brookwooder automatically became a member of the Cooperative, which had executive power. The faculty and administrators were organized: they had their own officers, held meetings, determined educational policy, and hired teachers. The students likewise had their own officers, supervised student affairs, arranged activities, and exercised advisory power in educational matters. For example, teachers could not be hired without student consent. Although faculty and students largely determined educational policy at Brookwood, other groups were also included in the decision-making pro-

cess. The Labor Cooperating Committee consisted of labor representatives, such as John Fitzpatrick of the Chicago Federation of Labor,
Abraham Lefkowitz of the AFT, Fannia Cohn of the ILGWU, and John
Brophy of the UMW, who had the same status at Brookwood as the
faculty and administrators did and who voted at all community meetings. The Educational Advisory Committee comprised four educators,
usually liberals with university affiliations, who gave advice about
educational matters. Leo Wolman, from the New School for Social
Research, served for several years; other representatives came from
Columbia University and the University of Pennsylvania. In 1925, the
school incorporated and consequently restructured its governing body
into a formalized board of directors. The "labor directors" (the former
Labor Cooperating Committee) possessed ten votes as a bloc. The faculty had five votes, and alumni and students two each; all were elected
by their respective constituencies. Two students, running as avowed
Communists, sparked a heated campaign, eliciting howls of protest
from some of their conservative fellows. Students were allowed to join
the Commonwealth College Association, which owned and controlled
the school. At one point, the association claimed a membership of five
students and five teachers. [50]

Students and teachers even saw their clothing as an important
component of community living. Both males and females wore overalls, denim trousers, shorts, flannel shirts, sandals, workshoes; at
Commonwealth they even went barefoot. Such garb was not intended
to project an antiestablishment image, so prevalent among college
students and teachers during the late 1960s and early 1970s. Instead,
labor college students and teachers simply could not afford to buy any
other clothing. Moreover, they considered themselves members of the
working class and dressed accordingly. Finally, students and teachers,
particularly at Brookwood and Commonwealth, needed this type of
apparel in order to fulfill their strenuous campus work assignments. [51]

The labor colleges made no explicit claims about cultivating a communal environment, but to a great extent they did. Indeed, work was
an important part of the labor college setting. Brookwooders rational-
ized work from a social-class standpoint. The institution refused "to
educate workers out of their class," and the students chose to preserve
working-class life styles; as a result, none were "set apart as exclusively manual workers" at Brookwood. A combination of manual labor
and intellectual work served as the ideal approach to workers' education; or as Brookwood's founding committee stated it, "the importance

and dignity of hand work and head work are both fully appreciated." "All Are Workers at Commonwealth," the title of a *Fortnightly* article, aptly described the sense of solidarity at that school. Since "no social lines" existed at Commonwealth, teachers and students alike worked four hours daily. "Not infrequently," the *Fortnightly* once boasted, "a teacher with several degrees may be observed taking orders from youngsters who happen to be better able to use their hands." Like Brookwood, Commonwealth valued a "close kinship between toil and ideas."

In reality, Brookwood and Commonwealth could not have survived without student and teacher labor. "Commonwealth," the *Fortnightly* recorded in 1926, "must utilize four hours daily labor from its students and teachers efficiently enough to pay all of its bills." Work became a cooperative effort to maintain and expand the schools' facilities and programs. On the other hand, Work People's College —perhaps because of its unique cooperative structure—did not find it necessary to require extensive work activities. Still, students from poor backgrounds could offset tuition and living expenses by working in the dining room, performing janitorial duties, or firing the furnace. In contrast to Work People's College, Brookwood and Commonwealth required that students work at college tasks. As the *Fortnightly* declared: "Room, board and laundry service are furnished by the college to all students in return for four hours of industrial work daily. . . . No student may pay cash for board, room and laundry service."

Students and teachers endured a demanding daily regimen. In 1921, Brookwood's students worked as much as fifty hours a week and studied six. After many of the main buildings had been built or remodeled, Brookwooders had their work hours drastically reduced to ten per week. Classes met six mornings a week from 8:15 A.M. to 12:30 P.M. and also on weekday afternoons. Approximately two hours a day were set aside for various jobs. After the first year, and at the behest of the students, the faculty ceased to take part in the actual physical work at the school. As Helen Norton recalls, these students "were good craft unionists for the most part who thought that, if teachers were going to teach, they shouldn't waste their valuable time washing dishes and peeling potatoes. . . . I don't suppose the faculty fought very hard!" But things changed with the Depression, as Lawrence Rogin remembered it: "Faculty and students, everyone did it. I sure washed enough dishes, and shoveled coal and worked on the road."[52] Commoners, during the early years, devoted twenty-four hours to work each week. By 1930, however, Commoners worked twenty hours and attended classes for fifteen hours. They ate break-fast between 6:30 and 7:00 A.M., attended fifty-minute classes until noon, and after lunch worked at their numerous chores until 5:00 P.M. Classes or discussions occupied the evening hours. [53]

In comparison, students and teachers at Work People's College faced a wholly academic schedule, except that all had to take their turn at "mess duty." Classes began at 8:00 A.M. and ended in the evening. Students usually attended classes twenty hours a week, with evenings occupied by debates or lectures. Yet this strictly academic routine was no less hectic and demanding, as humorously portrayed by one student, Eli Hill, who recorded his daily experiences in a poem that parodied "The Night Before Christmas":

'Twas the minute before seven, when all through the house,
Not a creature was stirring, not even a mouse;
When all of a sudden the cow-bell would clang,
The students would get up with a clatter and bang.

. . .

When the breakfast bell rings, the bunch would stampede
Right through the snow drifts at breath-taking speed;
A few stragglers would come after others had ate,
For they nursed the bad habit of getting up late.

Back to the dormitory, they'd come picking their teeth,
With smiles on their faces, oh, so pleasant and sweet;
In the basement they'd gather like dust on a mop,
And an argument would start between the Wobblies and Co-ops.

. . .

At nine o'clock sharp the class bell would crash,
To classroom B, they'd go in a dash;
The room would be full of hoots and cat-calls,
But the noise was abated by Fellow Worker Hall.

. . .

Next is the period of Charlie Marx,
This is the class where they all have bad marks;
Thompson calls Marx a volume of jokes,
But I think he's screwy, it's nothing but a hoax.

Public speaking is the class that ensues,
An hour of hisses and cat-calls and boos;

The speaker's all flustered and sweatin' like a Turk,
He thought it was fun, but he found that it's work.
    . . .
Some would go back to wrestle with Marx,
While others would be torturing their saxophones and harps;
Industrial Unionism is neither tabooed,
For it's ambitiously studied in room Twenty-two.

With all this commotion being forced to endure,
No wonder my marks in Economics were poor;
When all this racket would slowly subside,
I'd flop into bed at my room-mate's side. [54]

Life at Work People's College was not all academic routine, however. On warm days students swam in the Saint Louis River or walked to the trolley line, three-quarters of a mile away, to ride to downtown Duluth.

Brookwood and Commonwealth endeavored to distribute job assignments on a democratic basis. At Brookwood, the student–faculty education committee elected a "workers' committee," consisting of three students, to assign work that, as far as possible, corresponded to the students' trades. Machinists, electricians, and painters generally plied their own trades. Miners, meanwhile, tended the furnaces or maintained the roads, while garment workers, being female, often washed dishes. When philosopher–writer Scott Nearing visited Brookwood, he sent the workers' committee into a dither by insisting on wiping dishes. Commonwealth, in contrast, appointed a general manager of industrial activities to supervise the work. Since expertise served as the principal criterion for election to this position, students commonly became managers. In 1926, Ernest Koch, while still a students was elected general manager of Commonwealth's industrial activities. Koch claimed experience as a farmer, carpenter, and woodsman and, consequently, was considered "the best man" to direct the school's maintenance activities. As a result, Koch "bossed all of the teachers of Commonwealth College as well as his fellow-students for four hours a day." [55]

Students and teachers performed a variety of tasks at the labor colleges. Although Brookwood's founders located the school on an estate in exclusive Westchester County, the elegant mansion had no central heating; early Brookwooders had to cut and haul wood for the fireplaces. As the *Brookwood Review* reported: "Before the women's dormitory and the faculty cottages were built, there was only room for a small group of students. Roads had to be built and the buildings on the place remodeled to fit them for college use." Other structures had to be built. The red brick women's dormitory was completed in 1925, and a wing was added to the original colonial mansion to house the library. The first floor contained the main hall, with the library on one side and the dining room on the other. The second floor contained offices and two bachelor apartments, and the third floor housed a faculty room. The grounds also included three small cottages, two larger faculty houses, and a stone house, completed in 1926, in which the Saposs family lived. Brookwooders quarried that stone on school property. In 1927, five students and six teachers constructed a six-car garage made of cement block, faced with stone, to protect the school's vehicles from the weather. Brookwooders also erected a twenty-five-foot-high iron water tower, which meant reduced fire insurance premiums as well as cheaper water bills for the school. Students also assumed more mundane tasks, some of which, as Brookwood's *Twelfth Anniversary Review* humorously reminisced, did not always meet with success. "There was a time when students did the cooking too, but when two disciples of Marx were set to peeling potatoes, it sometimes appeared more economical to throw away the potatoes and cook the peelings." Bertha Saposs remembered how an egg, left to be broken into the pot to clear the coffee, was found after breakfast at the bottom of the pot, intact and boiled to a beautiful shade of brown. [56]

The graceful surroundings of Brookwood contrasted with the crude environment of Commonwealth College. Because it was located in rural Arkansas on 320 acres of land containing few habitable buildings, Commonwealth's students and teachers encountered a more formidable work program. The college was also a working farm. Commoners planted a large variety of crops, including potatoes, oats, grapes, apples, strawberries, raspberries, lima beans, tomatoes, melons, lettuce, and carrots. Commonwealth's onions, weighing nearly a pound each, won first prize at a local county fair in 1926. During August and September, Commoners labored day and night to harvest and to can the crops. In 1929, for instance, they canned over 2,000 quarts of peaches, tomatoes, apples, jellies, jams, preserves, and pickles. They also raised cattle and pigs and built fences for them with posts cut and trimmed on campus. Cheese was a special delicacy made by director Zeuch from the dairy's excess milk. Except for 1930, when the region suffered from a long drought, Commoners survived on a varied and inexpensive diet. In some instances, Commonwealth sold some of its surplus yield. Several hundred gallons of sorghum, milled from seven acres of sugar cane, and cotton served as cash crops during the 1920s. [57]

The building efforts of Commoners appear to have been just as impressive as their zeal for farming. They literally created the school. Living conditions during the early years were, at best, primitive. In 1926, Zeuch planned and helped to build most of his frame and stone cottage, which replaced the tent in which he had studied, taught, and slept for more than a year. Eventually, fifteen frame buildings, including dormitories, cottages, cannery and laundry, laboratory, library, commons, barn, guest house, and print shop, were erected by students and teachers laboring together. Commoners also constructed roads, fabricated a stone-lined fruit and vegetable cellar, dug a well, and installed both water and sewage systems. Although conditions remained somewhat spartan, the "college site in the Ouachita Range of the Ozarks was unusually attractive. A mill stream ran at the base of the bluff on which the campus buildings were located and which overlooked the farmland below and the mountains beyond, a constant invitation to hikers." [58]

In 1933, the *Fortnightly* supplied a breakdown of the total hours worked at Commonwealth during the previous year:

Commonwealth teachers taught 4,043 hours during the year. Teachers, students, and maintenance workers worked . . . 2,204 hours in the library, 6,922 hours on the farm, 1,669 hours clearing land, 1,598 hours caring for the stock, 11,336 hours in the kitchen, 2,664 hours canning, 9,603 hours at business management (office work, publicity, bookkeeping, printing, etc.); 5,196 hours cutting, hauling, and distributing wood; 7,407 hours putting up buildings and repairing old buildings; 2,235 hours in the laundry; 2,838 hours at miscellaneous tasks.

Commoners devoted approximately 10 percent of the estimated fifty-eight thousand expended hours to educational pursuits, while work occupied 90 percent of their time. Indeed, work represented an important component. Yet this work did not interfere with the regular classroom responsibilities, because "studies continued as teachers and students plowed a field side by side, prepared a meal together, or split wood." [59]

Still, Edward Falkowski witnessed less harmonious moments at Commonwealth. While serving as an instructor in 1938, he recorded one "production meeting" in which both students and teachers voiced complaints:

> What came out of the meeting was that the school is at present an institution with a highly adolescent student body; that many students, who have come here animated by the best will, look to some "higher" source of discipline—seek a paternalism on campus; and are dissatisfied with the complete freedom that is given the individual. . . . Take for instance the matter on class attendance; there are registrations for classes, but attendance is not obligatory. And pressure of work can always provide an excellent excuse. [60]

The students and teachers debated the issue of conflicting demands of work and study, but never resolved the problem.

Commoners, in addition, ascribed a monetary value to their finished work. The *Fortnightly* reported that Commoners completed 47,715 hours of work during 1932 and estimated, at the very low rate of twenty-five cents an hour, that these hours were worth $14,428.75. Thus Commonwealth was 70 percent self-supporting, with more than two-thirds of the school's upkeep derived from work completed on campus and less than one-third supplied from tuitions and contributions. In 1930, the *Fortnightly* boasted that its expenses, because of the extensive work done by Commoners, amounted to only 10 percent of Brookwood's expenses that year.[61] By 1933, Commonwealth's temporarily solvency was due, to a great extent, to the work performed by its students and teachers.

Residential life at Work People's College contrasted sharply with the more agrarian settings at Brookwood and Commonwealth. Work People's College, at most, possessed two elaborate buildings, which housed dormitory rooms, classrooms, and dining facilities. The second building was completed in 1910 at a cost of $20,000. However, a fire destroyed the old building during the following school year. The shareholders, at the annual meeting, authorized the board of directors to plan the construction of a new building. The new four-story edifice arose during the 1913–14 school year. Guss Aakula describes the facility: "The ground floor of the building was high and wide so coal could be easily driven there. On the second floor was an apartment for the kitchen workers and plenty of space for kitchen, dining room, and rooms for summer festivals. Both buildings were equipped with central heating and hot and cold water." [62] According to the data, none of the students worked on the construction of either building.

Work erased social distinctions and, in turn, engendered a cooperative feeling. Work, furthermore, ensured the very existence of Brookwood and Commonwealth. Without a cooperative effort from students and teachers, these schools would have simply dissolved. Finally, the labor colleges intended to preserve the student–workers' lifestyle. A Brookwooder best summarized the role of work in this latter regard:

> Even if it were possible to run the school without student help it would probably be unwise to do so. Brookwood students are accustomed to working with their hands and a purely academic life would be very uncomfortable for most of them. Moreover, the way a student fits into a cooperative regime, the way he gets on with his co-workers indicate pretty definitely whether he can function successfully in the labor world. And Brookwood had no more use than has Labor at large for the type of pseudo-intellectual who can expound a point of view but can't put it into practice. [63]

Yet, regardless of the heavy emphasis on work, the schools avoided anti-intellectualism. In fact, the labor colleges represented one of the few opportunities for many workers to expand and refine their intellect, acquire and practice organizing skills, and debate and dream about a new social order.

The foremost concern of the labor college community was the expansion of the American labor movement and ultimately the establishment of a cooperative society—that is, one based on a minimum of social distinctions where everyone contributed to the common betterment. In this sense, the labor colleges appeared to be committed to praxis, since they endeavored to educate working-class leaders and activists who would work to expand the labor movement and create a new social order. At Brookwood and Commonwealth, a combination of headwork and handwork functioned as the educational program. As noted, however, Work People's College appeared to adhere to a strictly academic program.

More importantly, the labor colleges refused to function as education factories. The schools rejected competition—so common in the formal school system—and, instead, saw to it that cooperation permeated every facet of the educational setting. Student experiences became an integral part of class lessons; teachers avoided grading students; students and teachers democratically administered the schools; and, at Brookwood and Commonwealth, students and teachers performed work tasks. It was hoped that this communal ideal would encourage the development of fraternal attitudes among workers who belonged to a common union and to a radically new social arrangement. Lawrence Rogin expressed it this way: "What we do is give them a leg up; teach them to get along with people, because you have to live in a community and if you can't live in a community, you can't get along with people, you can't create a union." [64]

This concept of community certainly evolved from socialist ideology, but it also appeared that, on numerous occasions, labor radicals freely borrowed from Dewey's educational theories to blend these ideas into educational practice. The Finckes' Manumit School, for example, symbolized "an alliance of progressive labor and progressive education." It accepted male and female children between the ages of nine and fourteen and, as a residential, progressive school for working-class children, appeared to embody an educational program and environment similar to that of the labor colleges. Muste not surprisingly chaired the school's executive committee. [65] The school's organizers, Muste included, attributed much of the community ideal in workers' education to Dewey. As the official founding statement of Manumit read:

> Of course, the heart and marrow of a school like ours is the community life. The community school is our way of affirming our deep belief in Dewey's maxim that education comes through life. Community life itself is our definition of that freedom and responsibility in which every educational democrat believes. The community life of our school is the socialized incarnation of our belief in industrial democracy. It is our act of faith in the labor movement and in that good life, that rich and noble life for all which the labor movement is going to bring in. [66]

Dewey maintained close ties with Brookwood. David Saposs invited him to the school's first graduation in 1923. Dewey had to decline, but sent his "best wishes for the occasion and for the future of the school." [67] He later visited the school as a guest speaker, and also proved to be an important crusader on its behalf during a later, more tumultuous, period in the school's history.

At Commonwealth College, George S. Counts, another progressive educator, served on the school's advisory board. His support for workers' education is evident in the following passage, written in 1927:

> The laboring classes are becoming interested in the social and economic order in which they live and work; they are convinced that they are the objects of exploitation by the favored classes; they desire the power which comes from clear insight into the forces which surround them; and they do not trust the instruction which society provides for them through schools controlled by boards of education composed, for the most part, of persons representing the employers' point of view. In no other way can the establishment and support of schools of their own on the part of organized labor be understood. [68]

Both Counts and Dewey sent modest financial contributions to Commonwealth.

Therefore, liberal support and educational theories, in these cases, seemed to be compatible with working-class visions of a radically new social order. Liberals, on the one hand, espoused social reform and argued that educational reform, possibly in the form of workers' education, could mitigate social problems. Working-class radicals, on the other hand, articulated the need for fundamental social change and recognized that workers' education, as part of the labor movement, could contribute to the change process.

But disharmony affects all communities, as it did the labor colleges. Some of it can be attributed to external forces. In other cases, internal disputes over personal and political matters created serious problems.

Part III
Conflict and Struggle

5

Harassment

> I love workers' education, but I am not going to stand by and see the funds of the American Federation of Labor used to equip young men to come home and fight us if I can help it.
>
> —William Green, *Proceedings of the Forty-Eighth Annual Convention of the AFL* (1928)

THE LABOR colleges' radical social and educational goals and programs provoked many attacks and generated a great deal of turmoil. As an integral part of the labor movement, the labor colleges reflected the movement's political diversity and became embroiled in its turbulence. During the 1920s and the 1930s, various factions on the political left competed among themselves and with the AFL for control of the organized labor movement. Federation leaders reacted to these threats by attacking radicals and by consolidating their own power and ideological base within the labor movement. These conflicts sometimes involved efforts to dominate the labor colleges. In addition, the radical objectives and activities of the labor colleges incurred the wrath of employers, reactionary groups such as Christian fundamentalists and the Ku Klux Klan, and an occasional politician, mobilizing the resources of the state. What impact did these events have on the labor colleges?

Assaults on Work People's College

Finnish radicals in general, and Work People's College in particular, encountered political problems which, in the long run, isolated them from the larger Finnish community and eroded their ideological base on the American left. Finnish Socialists first earned the enmity of elements within the Finnish community from 1906 to 1907, when they usurped control of the school from the Finnish Evangelical Lutheran National church. That church, too conservative and inflexible to tolerate the existence of Socialists, assailed the radicals at every opportunity. Socialist agitators, violently anticlerical and atheistic, likewise refused to reconcile their differences with the churchmen.

The 1907 Mesabi Range strike further polarized the radicals and the larger community. During the walkout, some Finnish merchants denied credit to striking Finnish miners. Following the strike, when anti-Finn attitudes were running high in the area, Finnish businessmen remained insensitive to the miners' plight. They openly condemned the Socialists for the walkout, and in an effort to mitigate attacks on the Finnish community in general, in February 1908 they formally dissociated themselves from the radical Finns and their ill-fated strike by organizing the "True Finns" movement. As the "true" spokesmen for Finnish-Americans, conservative Finns beseeched the steel trust and the newspapers not to judge all Finns by the actions of the radicals. Equating socialism with atheism, they reaffirmed the Finns' Christianity and assured employers and political officials alike that religion was the best guarantee of loyalty.

Despite blacklisting by the steel companies and repudiation by their conservative countrymen, Finnish radicals remained unflinching in their resolve. At their 1909 national convention, leaders of the Finnish Socialist Federation refuted the charges of anarchism and atheism, reasserted their rights of free speech and organization, and encouraged their members to adopt U.S. citizenship. Proponents of the True Finns movement, they argued, had underestimated the significance of economic injustice and the need for unionization. It was not the fault of their radical leaders, as the True Finns charged, that the Finnish miners were blacklisted; instead, the miners' problems were caused by the political economy in general and the steel trust in particular. Furthermore, because so many Finns were not naturalized and had no access to the ballot, unionism served as the only means for Finnish immigrant workers to wield any political clout. Eventually, the lack of sympathetic response by bourgeois Finns persuaded Finnish miners that the True Finns were as the real betrayers of the Finnish workers' cause.

Conservative Finns remained similarly unsupportive during the

1913 copper miners' strike on the Michigan Upper Peninsula. Finnish business leaders formed the Finnish Anti-Socialist League, shortly after the ill-fated strike ended, to eradicate radicalism in the copper country. The league launched a propaganda drive against socialism and even offered its assistance to the mining company in its campaign to blacklist workers. These efforts proved to be short-lived, however. Effective radicalism in the region had already been obliterated by the mining interests.

Radical Finnish opposition to America's entrance into the First World War intensified the antiradical feelings of the bourgeois Finnish community. Shortly after America's declaration of war in 1917, the state of Minnesota established a Commission of Public Safety, which attempted to resolve troublesome labor unrest in the northern part of the state, investigate general opposition to the war, and enforce the registration drive under the authority of the unpopular draft law. Seeing the IWW and Work People's College as primary targets, the commission sought, and received, the enthusiastic backing of several prominent Finnish businessmen and lawyers in its efforts to expunge radicalism. Replicating the pattern it had followed in 1907 and in 1913, the Finnish conservative community founded the Finnish American Loyalty League in Duluth and obtained professions of loyalty and support for the war from many cautious Finns. The commission also encouraged the Justice Department to conduct nationwide raids on IWW headquarters. Not surprisingly, Leo Laukki, a teacher and administrator at Work People's College, became an early victim. And, as Peter Kivisto points out, troops from Minnesota's National Guard, which had recently returned from the Mexican campaign against Pancho Villa, attacked numerous Finnish socialist halls and demolished the IWW offices in Duluth. He further hints that a mysterious fire that destroyed the newly constructed building, as well as damaged the main building, on the school's campus may be attributable to the patriotic fervor of the soldiers.[1]

Anti-red hysteria found further expression in the form of the Lusk committee, created by the New York State legislature in May 1919, during the aftermath of the Russian Revolution, to investigate Bolshevism in the state of New York. Of course, the Lusk committee, chaired by Senator Clayton R. Lusk, never set out to scrutinize either the Finns or Work People's College in Duluth, Minnesota; but it did. During the ensuing weeks and months, the committee's wide-ranging investigation would marshal all of the state's resources, including the governor and the state supreme court, and its findings and accusations would produce sweeping headlines and sensational articles splashed across the front page of the *New York Times*, which sympathized with the committee's efforts.

The committee opened its hearings in New York City during the first week of June, with Lusk's declaration that "a considerable number of men and women are actively engaged in advocating radical doctrines in New York State," and this plot was carried out "systematically by shrewd, capable men and women who seem to be co-operating in their efforts and who have been so successful that their followers and sympathizers in New York City numbered by the hundreds of thousands."[2] He pointed, in particular, to foreign-language organizations and their presses as the chief culprits. The Deportation Bureau of the Department of Immigration became interested in the scope of the Lusk committee's investigation, and in its crusade to root out seditious aliens, assigned an agent to the committee. Lusk organized a "secret service force to gather information for the committee," and sent it, in mid-June, to raid the Russian Bolshevist Mission (that is, the Soviet Embassy), the Rand School for Social Science, and the IWW's local headquarters. As a result, the Lusk committee acquired truckloads of documents, letters, and other supposedly traitorous materials in, as the *New York Times* proudly reported, "the biggest raid of the kind in the history of the city."[3] The committee intended to use these incriminating records to indict the radicals and to destroy their organizational infrastructure.

The Lusk committee took special interest in Russian radicals and the IWW, and this naturally led it to examine the radical Finns and their school, Work People's College. Throughout the hearings, the committee called upon countless witnesses to provide "impartial" testimony. Hugh Frayne, a general organizer for the AFL, gave evidence against the IWW, maintaining that its alleged goal was to overthrow the federal government. Ultimately, on December 28, 1919, the article "Says 300,000 Finns in U.S. Are 'Red'" appeared in the *New York Times*, reporting that the committee had asked Miss Meta Rumel, the official interpreter for the Lusk committee, to testify. She translated some radical Finnish newspapers and periodicals for the committee, and then boldly proclaimed that 300,000 Finns in this country were either Socialists, members of the IWW, or involved in some similar disloyal activity. Rumel added, "It is alleged that William D. Haywood, who says he was the organizer of the Red Finns in this country, picked out that nation [the Finns] as likely to be the most susceptible to his ideas." As Carl Ross, a Finnish-American historian, soberly observes, this testimony presented "feeble evidence for the inference that every man, woman, and child of Finnish descent in America was a 'Red.'" Perhaps the only credible statement in Rumel's highly questionable testimony was that the "Finnish Working People's College . . . [was] one of the mainstays of Finnish radicalism in this country." She likened it to a "Finnish Rand School," which the Lusk committee had raided and was going to great lengths to eradicate.[4]

The Lusk committee's comprehensive investigation and subsequent four-volume report, published in 1920, included a section, "Academic and Scholastic Socialist Activities," that illustrated how "radical" instructors had infiltrated the education system and used their positions to spread red propaganda. It pointed to two faculty members in particular, Arthur Calhoun, then at Ohio State University, and William Zeuch, teaching at Cornell and the Rand School, and printed the entire text of a 1919 letter written by Calhoun to Zeuch, providing indisputable proof of their plot to teach Bolshevist principles. The report continued by implicating scores of other professors, including Scott Nearing and Charles Beard, and condemned the ACLU, Intercollegiate Socialist Society, and Bureau of Industrial Research. The Union Theological Seminary represented one of "two dangerous centers of Revolutionary Socialist teaching of a university type in ecclesiastical institutions." The committee's accusations knew no moral, ethical, legal, or geographical bounds.

The report further offered remedies to the growing menace of radicalism in another section titled "Constructive Movements and Measures in America." First, and most urgent, the committee recommended "stringent" federal legislation restricting immigration, especially from southern and eastern Europe. Unlike their northern and western predecessors, these immigrant groups appeared to be the least familiar with democratic institutions and the most susceptible to radical dogma. Second, for the immigrants already here, the committee encouraged extensive education sponsored by the private and public sectors; bourgeois hegemony had to be served. Specifically, the report hailed education efforts such as the Goodyear Industrial University, opened in 1920, in Akron. The most ambitious endeavors consisted of a variety of Americanization programs sponsored by the states and by local school boards, social settlements, and churches:

The problems affecting public peace and public safety which have been created by the propaganda of social unrest are in large measure the product of subversive doctrines. One of the most effective measures for nullifying the effect of such teaching is, therefore, education designed to train the citizens of this State to assume the responsibilities and duties of citizenship. . . . Such education must be endorsed by a sincere, sympathetic and courageous citizenry. America will not be the land of the too free so long as it is the home of the sufficiently brave. [5]

After this ominous warning, the report continued by prescribing teacher requirements, curricula, "regulated attendance" procedures, and appropriations. Indeed, the Lusk committee, through blatant use of state power, had served early notice to radicals and their education efforts.

Political developments during the war also altered the character and form of Finnish radicalism and, eventually, isolated Work People's College within the radical community. Membership in the Finnish Socialist Federation had peaked at 13,000 just prior to the war but had dropped to 8,859 in 1915 after the split over industrial unionism; by 1919, membership had recovered slightly and rose to 10,884. The Finnish Socialist Federation weathered the war years by maintaining a low profile, sponsoring cultural activities, and shifting from labor union agitation to setting up cooperatives. Finns had been active in cooperative endeavors since 1903 and organized the Eastern Cooperative League in 1914, the national Finnish American Cooperative League in 1916, and the Cooperative Central Exchange in Superior, Wisconsin, in 1917. In 1920, the combined worth of the cooperatives and the network of Finn halls amounted to an estimated $720,000. With these, three daily newspapers, and a journal of political satire, Finnish Socialists managed to retain and influence a substantial following. [6]

In spite of its political fragmentation in 1919, the Socialist party still attracted—at least temporarily—the loyalty of the Finnish Socialist Federation. But the heady atmosphere bred by the Russian Revolution and the bold polemics of communist doctrine began to lure some Finns away from the Federation. Consequently, during the 1919 convention of the Finnish Socialist Federation, a split occurred between the eastern delegates (primarily from Massachusetts), who remained loyal to the Socialist party, and the midwestern, western, and a minority of the eastern delegates, who identified with the Third International. In 1922, this latter group officially affiliated with the Workers' (Communist) party and contributed $25,000 for the establishment of the Communist daily newspaper, the *Daily Worker*. The Finns also represented the largest component, some 7,000 members, or 40 percent of the total party membership.

In 1924, the Communist International ordered the bolshevization of the U.S. Workers' party in order to place American communists under its direct authority, and mandated that the immigrant worker–members become American citizens. This directive implied that the foreign-language federations had to be dissolved. This was much easier said than done, especially in the case of the Finnish Socialist Federation. The Finns clung to their ethnic identity and, at first, simply refused to obey the Comintern's orders. They rightly feared that the reorganization would expel foreign-born party members, destroy Finnish cohesion, and eliminate the social functions of the Finnish branches of the party. Nevertheless, the Finns relented and agreed in 1925 to support the spirit of the plan. Meanwhile, they cleverly circumvented the formal bolshevization process by scuttling the Finnish Socialist Federation and creating the Finnish Workers' Federation, which would function to protect their halls and property and, more importantly, keep their control in Finnish hands. They also maintained their allegiance to the Communist party through membership in local branches instead of direct membership in the party. Meanwhile, the Finnish Workers' Federation operated as the central organization of the locals. In essence, the Finns placated the party by accepting bolshevization in its form without necessarily subscribing to its substance. [7]

Yet, for all of the Finns' cunning, the Finnish Workers' Federation only retained nominal independence from the party. It was largely controlled and managed by party members who took their orders from the Finnish Party Bureau, a department of the Communist party. Hence, the party could, and did, censure any derogatory remarks made by Finnish members about it. Resolutions passed by local societies that contained any criticisms of the party were simply not published by the party-controlled newspapers. Moreover, the expulsion of dissenters became commonplace.

Although greatly weakened by periodic purges, the Finnish Workers' Federation remained active for a few years. On the other hand, the Comintern's reorganization plan for the Finns largely failed. While the Workers' party claimed some 25,000 members in 1923, the banishment of immigrant workers slashed the total membership to 16,326 by 1926. This total continued to decline rapidly, until 1928 when, according to the Comintern, the party could count only 7,277 members. By 1929, the membership had shrunk further to 3,000.[8]

As an integral part of the Finnish radical movement, Work People's College became the target of the conservative Finnish community as well as being swept up in the nationwide suppression of the IWW. The school experienced further problems when the Finnish radical community splintered into competing factions. By the early 1920s, Finnish radicals directed their allegiances to any one of three different organizations: the Socialists, the IWW, and the Communists. This political fragmentation undoubtedly contributed to the erosion of the political and financial base of Work People's College. While the school remained ever loyal to the IWW, the union was fading as a viable force among Finnish radicals. Many Finns associated with the school rejected communist doctrine, which affirmed the inevitability of violent revolution.[9] Through their complete intolerance of socialist and communist ideologies and unswerving allegiance to IWW tenets, the supporters of Work People's College effectively isolated the school from the mainstream of Finnish radical activities.

Controversy Surrounding Brookwood
Labor College

In contrast, Brookwood Labor College earned wide support and respect in the labor movement as well as in the workers' education movement itself after its founding in 1921. On February 10, 1928, at a dinner given in honor of Brookwood by its New York City alumni, the school received over $12,000 in contributions and another $37,000 in pledges to the building and endowment fund from the local of the United Textile Workers as well as those of the mine workers, carpenters and joiners, electrical workers, plumbers and steamfitters, machinists, and other unions. This event represented an important step in Brookwood's efforts to raise $2 million to expand the school's facilities, provide for research work, and increase its summer institutes and extension work. Jane Addams, Stuart Chase, and John R. Commons, prominent liberals, endorsed Brookwood's fund drive, which had been initiated in 1926. Brookwood normally accepted forty to fifty students a year, but because of limited accommodations turned away almost as many more. With the addition of two new dormitories, a library, an academic building, and another dining room and more kitchen space, Brookwood's supporters hoped to enroll nearly a hundred students a year. Later that spring, a conference of teachers and representatives of workers' education, held annually at Brookwood, called upon the school to train more teachers and to furnish more materials, such as course syllabi and texts, for the workers' education movement.[10] Thus, by 1928 Brookwood had become one of the most outstanding institutions among some forty workers' education enterprises affiliated with the Workers' Education Bureau, with praise for its achievements and calls for training even more students and expanding its services for the labor movement.

At the same time, by the end of the decade Brookwood had also become an irritant to AFL leaders through its classroom training in labor activism, its institutes and conference programs, and its dominant influence in the Labor Publication Society, which had come to regard the AFL as coopted by bourgeois society. In 1921, the LPS had inaugurated *Labor Age*, the official organ of "labor progressives" throughout the twenties. The journal's editor was Louis Budenz, an attorney with extensive experience in the labor movement dating from 1912.

Like Brookwood Labor College, the LPS was the creation of an impressive group of Socialists and various other radicals, who also served on its board of directors (see Chapter 2). The group included Harry Laidler, Elizabeth Gurley Flynn, Stuart Chase, A. J. Muste, and leaders of fifteen state AFL branches and twelve national unions. James Maurer was the society's president; Joseph Schlossberg, president of the ACWA, and Thomas Kennedy, secretary–treasurer of the UMW, served as vice-presidents. In addition to founding Brookwood, the LPS, and *Labor Age*, this group had been instrumental in creating the WEB and, in 1929, the Conference for Progressive Labor Action. [11]

Since 1926, *Labor Age* had been publishing increasingly biting criticisms, often penned by Muste, about the AFL's policies. *Labor Age* favored the organization of the mass production industries and urged special attention to the plight of black and female workers, often ignored by the craft unions. These attacks, of course, did not escape the attention of Federation officials. Indeed, while Brookwood gained popularity during the 1920s, AFL leaders grew ever more defensive and conservative. Smarting from frontal attacks by employers and their antiunion American Plan, as well as from the challenges of the communist policy of dual unionism and of the Trade Union Unity League, the Federation hierarchy defended the AFL by advertising it as both a steadfast friend of capitalism and as a staunch enemy of Bolshevism. AFL officials expressed their conservative policy through their support of union–management cooperation, scientific management, a wage policy linked to productivity, labor banking, union-sponsored insurance companies, and its ongoing close association with the National Civic Federation. The NCF noted in 1921 that "Socialism in some form" was "everywhere," that "as a cult it [had] never been stronger." [12]

The AFL's growing disenchantment with workers' education, particularly with that at Brookwood, further characterized this reactionary mood. And Muste's position of keeping Brookwood nonfactional, which resulted in the admission of communist students and faculty, only served to exacerbate the situation. In a faculty memorandum dated August 4, 1927, Muste clearly reiterated the school's longstanding policy: "Brookwood desires only such students as are fundamentally loyal to the labor movement and does not want incompetents, cranks or destructionists in its student body. Every effort is made to keep out the latter." Muste also used the memo to respond to criticisms of Brookwood's acceptance of communist students as unjustified because, as he ironically pointed out, the screening process for student admission usually involved union endorsement: "In every single one of these instances, endorsements were given these applicants by the highest officials in the unions involved and the school was even positively urged by these officials to accept these applicants." [13] While Muste's nonfactional stance appeared statesmanlike and non-sectarianism served as a means to avoid state scrutiny, it ultimately contributed to Brookwood's split with the AFL and, eventually, the WEB.

Actually, Federation leadership had long cast a jaundiced eye in the direction of the college in Katonah. As early as fall 1924, Muste had received disturbing word that the AFL's Executive Council perceived the school in a somewhat suspicious light. In May 1926, at the request of William Green, Ralph M. Easley, chairman of the executive council of the NCF, forwarded confidential information to Green concerning the communist background of Arthur Calhoun, a Brookwood social science instructor. [14] In subsequent months, Federation officials grew even more irritated with Brookwood when several students and teachers joined John Brophy's save-the-union movement to wrest the UMW's leadership from John L. Lewis. Brophy had served on the school's Labor Cooperating committee from its inception, and Brophy's UMW District No. 2 union had provided scholarships for miners to attend the school. His campaign for the presidency of the

UMW represented a direct assault on Lewis and his status quo policies. In Brophy's own words, "In August 1926, I announced my candidacy, pledging myself to organization of the unorganized fields, advocacy of nationalization of the mines, and support for a labor party." [15] Lewis responded to Brophy's challenge by ignoring the issues and launching a red baiting crusade. Brophy strongly denied that he solicited communist support for his campaign. However, as Melvyn Dubofsky and Warren Van Tine insist, "There is no doubt that he allied with Communists against Lewis. And well he should have, for both the Communists and Brophy criticized Lewis for similar reasons and sought similar objectives." [16] Lewis won, with a victory that Brophy and his supporters claimed was stolen.

In spring 1927, Green delegated Spencer Miller, secretary of the WEB, to inquire into Brookwood's activities, such as its celebrations for May Day, the international labor holiday that was especially significant to Socialists and Communists. Miller, somewhat rankled by progressive criticisms directed at the bureau, reported to Green that Brookwood maintained definite radical tendencies and that Calhoun represented "a most destructive influence." But, as James O. Morris reveals, "Miller's greatest apprehension was over the growing importance Brookwood was assuming in the field of workers' education." [17] Furthermore, Brookwood was completely autonomous, that is, outside the sphere of Federation influence in devising its educational programs and activities. At the May 1927 meeting of the AFL Executive Council, Green received a letter from the president of the Brotherhood of Railway Carmen criticizing Brookwood's radical leanings.

Matters came to a head in April 1928, when five Brookwood students objected, at a student body meeting, to plans being made for a May Day celebration at Brookwood. When their resolution in opposition was defeated, however, one of the students, R. M. Ware, not coincidentally a member of the Railway Carmen, promptly contacted Green about the incident. Green complimented Ware on his report and requested more information about the matter. Ware dutifully complied and, with the aid of another student, Hector Daoust, also of the Railway Carmen, sent a detailed account to Green. Green now believed that he had irrefutable "proof" of the radical nature of Brookwood's teachings and appointed Matthew Woll, vice-president of the AFL and chairman of the WEB's executive committee, to conduct a full-blown investigation of the school. Woll soon completed his secret inquiries and shared the findings with the Federation's Executive Council. [18]

On August 1, 1928, the Executive Council, without warning, advised its affiliated unions to withdraw their support from Brookwood. Federation officials complained that Brookwood sponsored "pro-Soviet demonstrations"; taught "doctrines contrary to the American Federation of Labor policies"; and encouraged "anti-religious doctrine." [19] Muste and Brookwood's teachers and board of directors wrote to Green requesting a hearing to examine the evidence and refute the charges. The Federation's arbitrary action also sparked sharp rebukes from labor newspapers, liberal journals, many prominent educators, and unions such as the Massachusetts State Federation, the Rhode Island Federation, the Denver Central Labor Union, the IAM, the Hosiery Workers Union, and the AFT, as well as others. Because of the uproar triggered by the apparently unwarranted action of the Executive Council, Green appeared to delay "final action" on Brookwood "until members of the Council . . . had ample opportunity to acquaint themselves with the protests filed." [20]

William Zeuch's editorial in the *Commonwealth College Fortnightly* exemplified the protests labor educators lodged against the AFL:

> The action of the executive council puts the American Federation of Labor rather than Brookwood on trial. We will soon know whether American labor leadership as typified by the membership of the executive council is intelligent enough to comprehend the real meaning and import of education; whether it is broadminded enough to perceive the catholicity necessarily inherent in the curriculum of any program of workers' education; and whether it is tolerant and liberal enough to be entrusted with a dominant and controlling position in the development of labor education projects. [21]

Commonwealth's purposes as well as the role of "self-supporting workers' education under absolute self government" in the labor movement were also restated. Zeuch lamented, almost prophetically, "We have grave doubts whether the officialdom of the American Federation of Labor will resolve the Brookwood affair wisely."

Green's duplicity remains hidden in the AFL proceedings, but becomes visible in a three-cornered correspondence between him, Muste, and E. C. Carter, a Brookwood sympathizer. In an exchange of letters with Green, Muste again requested a copy of the formal charges lodged against Brookwood as well as a hearing for the school before the AFL's Executive Council. On September 6, Green sent a response to Muste's August 30 communication. Green appeared to be less than candid with Muste, denying that he was the source of adverse publicity towards Brookwood: "The International Labor News Service is wholly responsible for the publicity given to this matter through the general story which it sent to numerous labor papers." Green further hedged his accusations: "The same news service is responsible for any criticism which it may have directed toward alleged red activities which have taken place at Brookwood College from time to time." However, he concluded by reiterating that the AFL was "within its right in withholding approval of the educational policy pursued at Brookwood if in the judgement of the officers and members of the American Federation of Labor such policy is not in accord with the policies of the American Federation of Labor." Muste responded, on September 11, by agreeing with this latter assertion. Still, Muste appealed to Green to suspend "decisive action" until a hearing was arranged before the Executive Council. Moreover, Muste petitioned Green, a third time, for a copy of the formal charges. By this time, it appeared that Muste suspected Green's stalling tactics and the ultimate outcome for Brookwood. On September 15, Muste wrote to the members of Brookwood's board of directors, warning them that Green's most recent letter blatantly omitted any reference "to his postponing decisive action until the protests and appeals for a hearing had been placed before the Executive Council." Muste concluded, from Green's correspondence, "that all that remains to be done is [for Green] to complete Mr. Woll's report and then give full publicity to it." Muste's concern was not unfounded, because he had been alerted by Carter. Green had sent a letter to Carter the day after Green had written to Muste, thanking him for his letter "regarding Brookwood College" and informing him that "the partial report shows that the investigation has been most thorough and comprehensive. . . . As soon as this report shall have been completed it will be given full publicity." [22]

Meanwhile, on September 20, the NCF held a luncheon at the Bankers' Club in New York City. The Subversive Movements Department of the NCF appointed a committee at the gathering "to investigate the activities of Communists in this country." Woll, vice-president of the AFL and acting president of the NCF, emphasized in his speech that the labor movement in America was "in grave danger as a result of the 'boring from within' tactics of the Communist party, directed from Moscow." Ralph B. Goddard, of R. G. Dun and Company, added that

the investigation should "include an inquiry into subversive movements in the schools and colleges of this country."[23]

Not long thereafter, Woll requested that individual members of
Brookwood's board of directors appear before him to "answer certain
questions." On behalf of the "Labor Directors of Brookwood," Fannia
Cohn drafted a response to Woll on October 16 in which she refused
to comply with his directive. Her letter stressed the fact that the board
of directors, many of whom were Federation members, still had not
received in writing the charges against the school: "We are not in a
position, either individually or collectively, to present 'Brookwood's
side of the case' unless we know what are the charges against Brookwood, the evidence upon which they are based, and the source of
such evidence." Cohn also noted that Woll's lack of regard for due
process smacked of "Star Chamber proceedings." She soberly pointed
out to Woll, "If your letter were part of the beginning of an investigation, it might be proper for individuals to furnish information. But
in this case the investigation was presumably held; you came to an
adverse conclusion; the Executive Council took action based on your
report, and this action was given widespread publicity both in the
general and in the labor press."[24] Cohn ended the letter asking, again,
for a hearing before the Executive Council.

Within days Green sent a letter to all national and international
unions affiliated with the AFL and urged them to withdraw their
financial support and scholarships from Brookwood. He charged, in
the *New York Times* excerpts of his letter, "that an avowed Communist
may be employed as a professor at Brookwood College and the cause
of Communism extolled through example, teachings and writings."
The students lived, Green continued, "in an atmosphere antagonistic
to the American Federation of Labor and are taught theories which
are in contradiction to the philosophy of the American Federation of
Labor." He further emphasized that "the college authorities did not
ask to present their side of the case."[25]

The controversy continued to rage, with the *New York Times* as a
public forum for the debate. Muste quickly responded to Green by reminding him of Brookwood's persistent requests for a hearing: "This
is an utterly incredible statement and we expect a prompt denial of
it from President Green. By telegram on Aug. 8 and by letter dated
Aug. 9 he received a request from the Brookwood Board of Directors
that they be given a hearing before the Executive Council before the
threatened action could be put into effect." Muste added indignantly

that Green had replied to these and other communications related to the Brookwood affair and had agreed to "refrain from taking any decisive action in this case until members of the Executive Council [had] had ample opportunities to acquaint themselves with the protests filed and the requests made for a hearing by the Board of Directors of Brookwood College." [26]

On November 5, 1928, the *Times* printed excerpts from an "open letter" released by Brookwood's board of directors. Basically, the letter reiterated the school's purposes and called for a hearing at the forthcoming AFL convention to be held in New Orleans during the last week in November "in order that we [the board of directors] may have the elementary privilege so far denied to us of studying these charges, replying to them and submitting our own evidence as to aims, activities and achievements of Brookwood." The statement further pointed out that Brookwood's board of directors consisted of "members and, in many cases, officers of long standing in A F of L unions" and, because of this fact, deserved a fair trial. [27]

The noted educational philosopher John Dewey also came to Brookwood's defense. The AFT, which included Brookwood's teachers as Local 189, joined the fray on November 9, when Local 5 sponsored a rally to support Brookwood in New York City. Among the speakers, Dewey, professor at Columbia University and a member of the teachers' union, lauded the educational efforts of Brookwood: "There is a need for a certain type of workers' school which shall lead the way, shall be the pioneer and show the other schools what they might do. I am very glad to pay my regards to the work Brookwood has done precisely in blazing the way as a pioneer so as to show exactly what expansion our other schools are capable of." [28] Speaking before an audience of five hundred people, Dewey urged that the public schools adopt some of the philosophy and programs of Brookwood. He then turned his attention to the AFL, which assailed Brookwood, Dewey contended, because it "was not sufficiently subservient to the administrative officers of the Federation." [29] Yet, as Dewey saw it, labor education would be ineffective if totally controlled by unions:

You can have training without mental freedom, but you do not have education. Education is awakening and movement of the mind. To take hold actively of any matters with which it comes in contact, and to be able to deal with them in a straight-forward manner is the condition under which the mind develops.

It is obvious that that is the spirit in which Brookwood has been conducted. It seems to me that it shows loyalty to the labor movement, to the cause of the workers, when a school really believes that the interests of organized labor are going to be advanced and not set back by this full and honest discussion. [30]

Dewey readily perceived the crux of the Federation's grievance against Brookwood; that is, AFL officials wielded little, if any, control over Brookwood's affairs.

This point became evident at the Federation's 1928 convention in New Orleans, when the Federation simply rubber-stamped Green's condemnation of the school. The Brookwood issue did not surface until the convention's seventh day, and came to the floor for discussion in an esoteric manner. One gets the sense that AFL officials carefully orchestrated the proceedings. Harry W. Fox, of the Wyoming State Federation of Labor, rose to recommend a resolution that the Executive Council consider the establishment of a national labor college under the direct auspices of the Federation. Delegate P. J. Shea, of the Street and Electric Railway Employees Union, voiced his objection to Fox's resolution. As Muste recalls, Shea held Brookwood in low regard. According to his account, an agreement by Shea's "union with the Mitten interests in Philadelphia was widely regarded as having played outrageously into the hands of the street car companies. It had been severely and effectively criticized by Brookwood graduates at a Pennsylvania Federation of Labor convention." Muste had also criticized the Mitten agreement in *Labor Age* the previous May. [31]

It was not surprising, therefore, when Shea addressed the delegates: "I arise at this time to oppose this resolution; . . . if our national college is going to take the same course as Brookwood, I am opposed to it; . . . let the delegates know, not venture into some other institution of the same nature without knowing what happened to Brookwood." As if on cue, Matthew Woll responded to Shea's request. Woll admitted that he had been delegated by Green and the Executive Council to "investigate" Brookwood's "organization, methods of operation, etc." The results of Woll's inquiry had been released to the public during the previous August, and he had been severely criticized for his report by Brookwood's supporters. Thus, he asserted indignantly, he had "the right on this occasion to advise this convention and to advise those who wish information upon it just what the situation is."

Woll proceeded to list the grievances against Brookwood, basing them upon evidence obtained from some former students. First, Brookwood functioned as a communist institution, he claimed, because its director, A. J. Muste, maintained communist views. Woll found Muste's criticisms of capitalism as an inefficient and inhumane "system of industrial and social organization" and Muste's support for "a cooperative commonwealth under the control of the producers" as a clear-cut "definition of Communism." Second, in what appeared to be the main thrust of his attack, Woll accused Brookwood and its teachers and students of unrelenting assaults on the AFL's leadership and policies. At Brookwood, Woll proclaimed, "the American Federation of Labor is constantly ridiculed and not a word of favor [is] spoken in its behalf and . . . the Third Internationale is lauded as the great institution that will save labor and the workers the world over." Third, Woll expressed grave doubts about the content of the courses taught at Brookwood. For Woll, the subject matter smacked of communist dogma, encouraged criticism of the Federation, and promoted an "anti-religious point of view." Moreover, courses such as psychology taught "sex impulses, sex behavior, and kindred spirits." Woll revealed an anti-intellectual streak when he condemned many of the courses as too abstract and theoretical and wholly inapplicable to the labor movement. He concluded, "I think I have indicated enough to you to make clear what sort of an institution Brookwood is, and enough to warn you to be careful that hereafter organized labor will not give support, silent or otherwise, to such an institution."

John H. Walker, a delegate and chairman of the AFL's Education Committee, conveniently followed to support Woll's accusations. Walker, like Woll, was as "fearful of a theorist as anything that might be created." Brookwood was too abstract in its approach to workers' education. Instead, Walker recommended the formation of a "safe" labor college under direct AFL supervision. Walker ended his comments by urging the convention to adopt Woll's recommendation.

President Green spoke next and stressed that the Executive Council did not want to give the impression that Brookwood had been placed on trial: "We make no charge against Brookwood. We have never placed Brookwood on trial. We made an inquiry, however, regarding the academic course given students in Brookwood, its general surroundings and environment, and we were shocked and amazed at the revelations that were made." Still, while Green refused to admit that Brookwood was on trial, he did not hesitate to judge the school. He accused Brookwood instructor Arthur Calhoun of being a Communist, and appeared especially incensed over criticisms of Federation policies by Brookwooders. The investigation found, according to Green, "that the students were being taught doctrines antagonistic to the American Federation of Labor and were living in an atmosphere antagonistic to our movement." Green substantiated his accusations by reading a letter from a former Brookwood student.

Thus, the apparent threat of Brookwood producing students who maintained a critical view of AFL policies, practices, and leadership represented the essence of Green's—as well as Woll's—stinging attacks on the college. Indeed, an enlarged and increasingly popular Brookwood would have created further headaches for Federation officials. Not only would it have provided a broad forum for analyzing and criticizing AFL policies, it would produce more labor leaders and activists who opposed Federation leadership. As Green cogently summarized his case, "I love workers' education, but I am not going to stand by and see the funds of the American Federation of Labor used to equip young men and women to come home and *fight us* if I can help it."

When Green concluded, William D. Mahon, president of the Street and Electric Railway Employees' Union and a member of the NCF, moved that the "Convention endorse the position taken by the Executive Council in connection with Brookwood College." His motion was perfunctorily seconded, but several delegates rushed to the school's defense. Charles L. Reed, a delegate from the Salem, Massachusetts, Central Labor Union, protested that the charges brought against Brookwood were exaggerated: "I went through that institution and I know something about it. One hundred and twenty-five or more students have graduated from Brookwood, and it doesn't seem fair to me to indicate, because four or five of these graduates have sent out these letters, that the school should be judged accordingly." Reed further objected to the indirect manner in which the Brookwood issue had been raised, and astutely recognized the proceedings for what they really were: "They say Brookwood has not been placed on trial. Maybe it has not. Maybe Brookwood has been placed on trial, but the results of the action taken will be just the same as if Brookwood was placed on trial. . . . It is injected into a subject matter having no reference to Brookwood. What is the result? I know and you know what the result will be." After Reed completed his remarks, the motion was referred to the Executive Council for consideration.

The debate continued the following day, November 28, 1928. Delegate Florence Hanson, AFT secretary–treasurer, made an apparent attempt to secure an open hearing for the school by requesting a full investigation of Brookwood as an AFT local. Green ruled her motion out of order. Later, Mahon moved that the Executive Council's report on Brookwood, as presented by Woll the previous day, be officially adopted by the convention. Delegate Victor Olander, secretary of the Illinois Federation of Labor, seconded the motion, and a debate ensued. Charles Reed and Abraham Katofsky, of the ILGWU, entreated the Executive Council to hold "a full, fair and impartial investigation and report its findings and decision to the affiliated organizations." Such an inquiry, they reasoned, would hear both sides and examine the relevant evidence. President Green and Jacob Goldstone, of the Bakery and Confectionary Workers, opposed the proposal. Goldstone contended: "The Communists both in America and Europe usually asked for investigations, and the more investigations they get the better they are satisfied, because they know that any scheme that occupies the time and attention of the trade unionists allows them a better chance to sabotage the labor movement."[32] The delegates overwhelmingly adopted Mahon's motion.

Many of the statements made about Brookwood Labor College were quite true. It did not necessarily follow, however, that the school was irreligious, subversive, or anti-American. Calhoun did teach social science from an evolutionary perspective, but his action alone was not proof that Brookwood as a whole functioned as an antireligious community. In fact, the school provided free transportation for anyone who wanted to attend Sunday services in Katonah. As to the communist charges, Brookwooders indeed celebrated May Day as a labor holiday. Yet this was not so unusual, considering that workers in most industrial countries, communist as well as noncommunist, likewise honored May Day as the international day of the worker. The lone exception was the main body of American trade unionists. Moreover, it would have been ludicrous to portray Brookwood's observance of May Day as anything but benign. For example, the notice posted for faculty and students for the 1925 May Day festivities announced that activities would begin promptly at 8:15 A.M. with speakers on Karl Marx, followed with a picnic supper and capped with a baseball game. Certainly, Brookwooders commemorated the deaths of Lenin in 1925 and Debs in 1926. Still, these memorial services did not affirm a communist orientation for the school; in 1924, Brookwooders also paused to note the passing of AFL president Gompers. It was also true that many communist students attended the school. But they were merely seen, by Socialists and progressives alike, as nothing more than "socialists in a hurry." Furthermore, in the opinion of many faculty and students at Brookwood, the dogmatic nature of the Communist party had begun to wear thin after a while, and the later Stalinist purges in the U.S.S.R. horrified many Brookwooders. By the time of the 1928 convention, it was a moot issue anyway, since the school had already decided to stop admitting communist students. Katherine Pollak, who arrived on the campus in the fall of 1929, observed that the faculty "had found, increasingly, that the communists who came as students had apparently gotten party approval for their coming and that they came to teach, not to learn, and Brookwood's faculties were being wasted on them." Similarly, Brookwood's teachers were not completely "red." Muste and Saposs lectured occasionally at the (communist) Workers' School in New York City, but neither of them was a Communist. Calhoun, however, not only taught at the Workers' School, but also admitted to voting for the Communist ticket in the 1924 and 1928 elections. Hence, Brookwood was not entirely free from communist influence; but it was likewise not controlled, let alone dominated, by Communists. Ironically, during the previous August, the Communists, through the *Daily Worker* and the Young Workers' League, denied any connection with Brookwood and condemned its teachings as "class-collaborationist."[33] Thus, Brookwood's moderate-left political position in the labor movement crystallized. While the conservative faction of the labor movement (the AFL leadership) censured the school for being radical, the radical segment (the Communists) lashed out at Brookwood for being too bourgeois.

Although Brookwood's "guilt" or "innocence" remained clouded on most issues, Brookwooders could not deny their activist role in the labor movement. After all, it was their avowed aim to reform the labor movement and, ultimately, society. It was therefore natural for Brookwooders to support such activities as the save-the-union movement. These reform efforts also manifested themselves through open attacks on the staid strategies of Federation leaders. AFL officials reacted in kind. They clearly wanted to arrest the growth and progress of Brookwood as a source of opposition to their policies, and they succeeded. As James Morris has noted, "This charge raised perhaps the most significant issue of the controversy—academic freedom versus union control of policy making."[34] Of course, academic freedom lost, and the outcome proved to have profound and far-reaching implications for the future of workers' education.

While the carmen's, machinists', painters', and miners' unions and the state and city central bodies promptly withdrew their support from Brookwood, some two hundred individuals—namely, union officers and members, educators, editors, social workers, and ministers —along with the AFT, the UTW, and the hosiery workers', railway clerks', and lithographers' unions, protested the Federation's actions and rallied to the school's cause. Three Commoners witnessed the condemnation of Brookwood at New Orleans, and two articles appeared in the *Fortnightly* criticizing the actions of the AFL hierarchy. One characterized the proceedings as "jabberwockian confusion," but the main attack, and the most biting, was reserved for Woll.

> The disinheritance of Brookwood was largely the doing of Brother Matthew (Wolf! Wolf!) Woll who, having deputized himself an investigation committee of one, donned false whiskers and colored specks, hawkshawed and sherlock-holmed here, there, and everywhere, *but* the Brookwood campus, until he had satisfied himself that his hunch about Brookwood's being Communistic, antireligious, and a disseminator of propaganda antagonistic to the A F of L was correct.

Another article cleverly reproached Green by citing two pages of direct quotations from his speeches and writings that had appeared in the *American Federationist* from May 1925 to June 1928. Green's quoted words extolled the virtues of and the need for academic freedom.[35] Coincidentally, this same issue of the *Fortnightly* had the following headline emblazoned across the front page: "Arkansas Federation of Labor Endorses Commonwealth College." In the uneasy atmosphere for workers' education following the New Orleans convention, Commoners sought refuge by allying themselves and their school with the Arkansas Federation of Labor.

Brookwood received widespread union backing as well. The AFT reaffirmed its affiliation and support of the Brookwood branch, Local 189. In addition, "Local 706 of the Full Fashioned Hosiery Workers in Philadelphia," the *Brookwood Review* proclaimed, "voted to continue friendly relations with Brookwood and to send $500." The Federation's attack on Brookwood likewise generated many small individual contributions. The school also received and published letters criticizing the AFL and supporting Brookwood.[36]

Among the liberal supporters of Brookwood, perhaps John Dewey offered the most incisive and perceptive analysis of the Federation's action. In an article that appeared in the *New Republic* shortly after the convention, Dewey chronologically recounted the events leading to Brookwood's censure. He recalled the August resolution of the Executive Council, which called upon affiliated unions "to cease support of the Brookwood school" because of its subversive teachings and "disloyalty" to the AFL.[37] This "action," Dewey stated, "was taken without any investigation of the school; without submitting charges to the faculty and students; and without giving opportunity for reply." At the New Orleans convention, Federation officials further denied that Brookwood fell under their jurisdiction and therefore refused to grant the college a fair and open hearing. In so doing, the AFL leadership rejected the supporting testimony of 125 former Brookwood students. Yet the letters of five former students hostile to the school's criticism of the AFL and discussion of socialism and communism became admissible evidence for the Federation's judgment against Brookwood. "Anybody who knows anything about schools and students," Dewey pointed out in an exasperated tone, "is aware that five out of a total hundred and twenty-five students, present and past, is a small number to become disgruntled." Nevertheless, it was these "star-chamber" tactics, as Dewey termed them, that produced the indictment against Brookwood.

Dewey expressed his unqualified support for Brookwood. Citing the school's official statement, he endorsed its desire for "a social order free from exploitation and based upon control by the workers." Dewey favored these "liberal ideas and ideals" and Brookwood's educational practices, which encouraged "free discussion" and freedom of thought. Echoing Commonwealth's argument, he recognized that the Federation's hierarchy feared this type of education. According to Dewey, "The action of the American Federation of Labor's administrative machine, in itself and in its mode of execution, is a warning that it does not want this sort of education, it regards it as a danger and a menace."

Dewey, again like Brookwood's supporters at Commonwealth, focused his sharpest attack against Woll. Dewey emphasized that the NCF functioned to sabotage "the aims of aggressive unionism" and noted how Woll "subtly employed his dual official position to cramp or paralyze action on the part of the Federation of Labor that is not in line with the Civic Federation." Because of its association with the NCF, Dewey argued, the AFL "is no longer cursed as revolutionary and subversive but is blessed as a constructive, safe and patriotic organization." But such a comfortable accommodation to the status quo was most unfortunate, because "organized labor should be a great force in social reconstruction." If organized labor possessed a politicized and critical leadership, Dewey contended, it could be instrumental "in bringing about a better social order." Brookwood, if left to its own devices, would have produced this cadre. Dewey saw this as the fundamental reason why the AFL ostracized Brookwood: "The facts cited are relevant to the inert character of the present labor movement and to the charges brought against a Labor College guilty of believing that an educational movement should train leaders who think independently and should thereby help in ushering in a social order free from exploitation."

Dewey concluded by making two basic points. First, the AFL's censure of Brookwood served as a warning to other institutions involved in workers' education:

It cannot be too generally understood that the condemnation of Brookwood is no isolated event. It is part of the policy to eliminate from the labor movement the schools and influences that endeavor to develop independent leaders of organized labor who are interested in a less passive and a more social policy than that now carried on by the American Federation of Labor in its close alliance with the National Civic Federation.

Dewey's second point involved the implications of the AFL's policies and its kinship with the NCF. As Dewey explained it, any "opposition to the [AFL] political machine . . . is to be interpreted as enmity to organized labor itself; that any opposition is ascribed to Bolshevist sympathies is in line with the resort to cheap epithets currently employed to discredit any liberal movement."[38] Therefore, for Dewey the Brookwood incident symbolized an important episode in the AFL's efforts, with the backing of the NCF, to purge militancy from the labor movement in general and from the workers' education movement in particular.[39]

Muste too recognized that the AFL's hostility toward Brookwood could spread to other targets. He expressed his fears in an article in *Labor Age* in which he described the role of education in a social movement: "A school or educational system is always in the last analysis a child or instrument of some social group. Workers' education, Brookwood, all similar enterprises, are the children of and the instruments of a militant labor progressivism, or if the expression be preferred, a noncommunist left." Muste reiterated the definition of "militant labor progressivism" as an

> aggressive effort to organize the masses of unskilled and semi-
> skilled workers in the basic industries into industrial unions,
> with special attention to such groups as women workers, young
> workers, negro workers, immigrant groups; determined resistance
> to injunctions and yellow-dog contracts, with recognition of the
> fact that mass resistance to judge-made law on the picket line is of
> fundamental importance.

Militant labor progressivism also entailed a

> presentation of the labor movement as not only a business propo-
> sition but a great idealistic force, having for its ultimate goal the
> good life for all men, in a world controlled by the workers; . . . and
> finally, [it means] a workers' education movement that has for its
> primary aim not extending to workers the same cultural advan-
> tages now enjoyed by other classes, but equipping them for the
> struggle against the company union, the open shop, the injunc-
> tion, the labor spy, the struggle to improve their conditions and to
> gain control of industry.

Like Dewey, Muste believed that AFL officials intended to subvert efforts to achieve such objectives. Recalling the Federation's "lynching of Brookwood," Muste further warned that the Workers' Education Bureau would perhaps be its next victim. [40]

Indeed, Federation leaders wasted little time in their attempts to emasculate the WEB. At the bureau's annual convention in the spring of 1929, Green, in his opening remarks to the delegates, rebuked the "so-called progressive movement" in labor—which, of course, included Muste and the supporters of Brookwood. Maurer, the WEB's president and one of Brookwood's founders, defended Brookwood and attacked Federation policies and officials:

> It is our duty, convening as a body interested in the spread of
> educational activity in the American Labor Movement, to protest
> most vigorously against the action of the American Federation
> of Labor towards Brookwood. We must do so, not primarily for

Brookwood's sake, but for the sake of the cause which we here represent. If the Workers' Education Movement, in convention assembled, will condone the suppression of one of its most successful and influential enterprises, and not make effective protest to the labor movement, it may just as well as fold up its tents and go home.

Maurer cautioned the assembly not to adopt two measures that had been approved at the New Orleans convention that proposed profound alterations in the structure of the WEB. The first proposal, an amendment to the bureau's constitution, restricted representation on the Executive Board of the WEB to members of the AFL. Maurer feared that if the amendment was accepted, the perspective of the bureau's Executive Board would be narrowed, and rank-and-file participation would be eliminated. The second measure, again in the form of a constitutional amendment, urged the establishment of a cooperative relationship between the bureau and university-sponsored workers' education activities. Maurer, to be sure, reminded the delegates that universities

are built to develop the individual to personal advancement, to "getting ahead in the world." Workers' education, however, is a social process, organized to develop the individual for the sake of his group. The universities . . . reflect the dominant views of big business, of the militarists and imperialists. Workers' education functions to rip free the dogmas and illusions which clutter up the social sciences and present to the workers an understanding of social life that will make possible an analytical survey of existing institutions. [41]

In spite of Maurer's plea, the convention approved the amendments. Maurer, in protest, refused "to preside over a convention which had repudiated every recommendation he made in his opening address." Muste, accompanied by several Brookwood delegates, followed Maurer out of the hall. Not surprisingly, Woll assumed the chairmanship of the convention.

By the close of the 1920s, the AFL had taken the necessary steps to throttle the type of workers' education that had been critical of Federation leaders and their policies. To further curtail the independence of future labor education, it had endorsed the extension departments of universities, rather than the labor colleges, as the future source of workers' education. David Saposs perceived at the time the significance of the AFL's usurpation of the WEB.

> Since most of the interest and enthusiasm in workers' education has always come from the bottom rather than the top; since it is the more alert and critical-minded that have been interested in workers' education, both among teachers and students; and since it is known that the leaders look with suspicion even upon their own brand of workers' education because it may be difficult to confine it within the narrow limits they have set, the action of the recent convention of the Workers' Education Bureau is a serious challenge to vital and effective workers' education in this country.

The WEB never held another regular convention after its cooptation by the AFL. In addition, the Federation censored textbooks. As Muste lamented, "The idea that labor might need a 'culture' of its own and could not depend on the cultural material provided in the universities was condemned." In retrospect, James Morris concludes that "workers' education was thereafter recognized and treated, more than ever before, as a staff operation under the strict control of union officers."[42]

The impact of the Brookwood–AFL conflict proved to be equally damaging to Brookwood. Although the school would continue to operate in an effective manner for another eight years, the ordeal left strained relations among the faculty, undermining any cohesion that may have existed. Throughout the entire AFL episode, the teaching staff had vigorously debated over what strategy to employ in Brookwood's defense. Muste had attempted to keep faculty in line in order to project a united front, but his memos to faculty members occasionally took on harsh tones, revealing some stress. The fundamental question arose over the use of communist criticisms of the school: that is, should Brookwooders point to communist attacks on Brookwood as proof positive that the school was really not "red"? For instance, Cara Cook, a Brookwood instructor, supported the use of communist propaganda to defend Brookwood. David Saposs, however, wanted to cast Brookwood in a more academic light by emphasizing that the school accepted "students of all points of view" and was not "interested in converting them to the policies and tactics of any faction or group in the labor movement." Finally, while both Muste and Calhoun opposed the use of communist comments about Brookwood, Calhoun saw Brookwood as "furthering a Bolshevist attitude"—which did not deviate too far from a communist position.[43] Indeed, as Calhoun would soon discover, this dissension would have a lasting and profound effect.

Troubles at Commonwealth during the 1920s and 1930s

Commonwealth College, unlike Work People's College and Brookwood, survived the first of many attacks soon after it was moved to Arkansas in 1925. In August 1926, at the state convention of the Arkansas American Legion, an antiunion Legionnaire, Joseph Morrison, charged Commonwealth with receiving "red gold" in the form of $100,000 from the IWW and $50,000 from the Soviet Union. "Once having gone as far as that," the *Fortnightly* observed, "the phrases 'Bolshevism,' 'sovietism,' 'communism,' and the inevitable 'free love' were also introduced and freely flourished." Morrison based his accusations on an alleged Department of Justice report which he did not present for public scrutiny. The convention voted to table a resolution demanding that the state legislature enact a bill to bar Commonwealth from operating in Arkansas. Some members of the executive committee remained undaunted in their investigation of the school and decided to solicit information about its founders, teachers, courses, religious affiliations, and sources of income from Commonwealth's director, William Zeuch. They phoned Zeuch to inquire into the college's "connections to 'red' Russia." Zeuch treated the call as a prank, but the operator interrupted to assure him that "this matter is really serious. This is no joke, the people calling are in earnest." Zeuch refused to comply with their demands and refuted the charges. The committee members further delegated an overzealous Legionnaire to form an investigating team to visit the campus. Newspapers published the charges extensively, and rumors about plans to attack and burn the "radical" school abounded. Many neighbors and friends sent word to the college that they had made preparations to defend the "premises" by whatever means. The Arkansas State Federation of Labor, most of the state's newspapers, local townspeople, and the ACLU likewise rushed to Commonwealth's defense—albeit not in the same sense as the school's neighbors. Some of the members of the Arkansas American Legion even sent letters of support to the school. Ultimately, in a response to an inquiry by Commoners themselves, J. Edgar Hoover, the director of the FBI, flatly denied the existence of any Department of Justice report condemning Commonwealth. Not only did this statement silence the Legionnaires, but the legion also publicly reprimanded Morrison and others involved in the witch hunt. [44]

Regardless of the favorable outcome, this early attack permanently scarred Commonwealth College. The episode had branded the school as "red" and, as a result, alienated many of the older, more conservative residents of Polk County. As one manifestation of this red baiting, the Daughters of the American Revolution (DAR) in 1928 blacklisted Commonwealth, Brookwood, and numerous other organizations, including the League of Nations. The DAR based its censure of Commonwealth on its "pacifist or communistic leanings." In addition, many of Commonwealth's benefactors experienced harassment. Because of the American Legion's fallacious charges in 1926, Commoners had instituted a policy of regularly disclosing the names of donors and the amount of each donation given to the school. As the *Fortnightly* recalled, "It was thought best in the future to publish . . . the receipt of all funds so as to avoid such absurd rumors." Yet this scrupulous practice became a weapon in the hands of the school's enemies. In 1930, the *Fortnightly* reported: "A college professor who is a member of our Maintenance Fund writes that he was called in by his president a couple weeks ago and informed that a protest had been made because he was contributing to Commonwealth. The professor remarked that he presumed that that would be sufficient cause in his college for the recommendation of his dismissal." [45] Nevertheless, the school continued to retain an extensive list of contributors, which included such distinguished liberals as Justice Louis Brandeis, Roscoe Pound, and John Dewey.

Commonwealth encountered another, more serious, threat on February 13, 1935. Because the school's activities in support of the Southern Tenant Farmers' Union in eastern Arkansas had angered numerous influential planters, the Arkansas House of Representatives adopted a resolution calling for a legislative investigation of alleged communist activities at Commonwealth.

Whereas, persistent rumors recur concerning Commonwealth College . . . to the effect that said College fosters communism and permits the teaching of un-American doctrines, and whereas, from newspaper accounts its instructors always attend meetings where it is possible to incite hatred; . . . therefore be it resolved . . . that

a committee of five members of this general assembly . . . be . . .
authorized to conduct an investigation of the said college to the
end that any condition existing there which fosters un-American
ideas may be corrected. [46]

The investigating committee began its hearings in Mena, and sub-
poenaed Lucien Koch, along with other Commoners, to testify. Koch
cooperated fully and gave six hours of testimony on February 16, only
days after the Marked Tree episode (see Chapter 4). A sample of the
questions the committee asked Lucien follows:

Q: Do you believe in God?
A: No.
Q: You do not believe in God?
A: I am giving my personal opinion and I am not representing the
position of the school.
Q: . . . May I ask do you believe in the Constitution of the United
States?
A: I am convinced that I believe in it more thoroughly than the
planters of Eastern Arkansas.
Q: Do you believe in the Bible?
A: I am interested in the Bible as a social document.
Q: Do you believe in the Bible?
A: I am not sufficiently acquainted with the Bible to state whether
or not I believe in the Bible. I believe, however, I would have
many disagreements with passages in the Bible.
Q: Do you believe in Communism?
A: I have an intellectual curiosity towards Communism, as I have
an intellectual curiosity towards all other opinions including
Capitalism, Fascism, et cetera.
Q: Do you have a Socialist faction in your College?
A: We do.
Q: Do you have a Communistic faction in your College?
A: We do.
Q: Do you have a Fascist faction in your College?
A: We do not. At the present time the Fascist faction seems to be
in Eastern Arkansas. [47]

The committee refused to allow the Commoners to have legal coun-
sel present or to bring their own stenographer. Commoners were also
denied the right to hear or to question witnesses hostile to the school.

The committee visited the campus, observed a class in session, and toured the Museum of Social Change. Later, Mena residents testified that they were mainly concerned with the school's "violations" of their fundamentalist beliefs. Several witnesses expressed horror that mixed swimming was tolerated at the school. The committee completed its inquiry in Little Rock, where it heard the testimony of leading citizens of the planter group. Unabashedly hostile towards Commonwealth, they were equally angry with the state because it bothered to give this "atheistic, free-love" school even a semblance of due process. [48]

While the committee pursued its investigation, Commonwealth not only received violent threats but also experienced state interference. The Ku Klux Klan in Little Rock released a press statement to United Press renewing its declaration that the "activities of the labor school which has been the storm center of several workers' uprisings at least have attracted the attention of the Klan." Further, state representative S. A. Gooch introduced a bill, directly aimed at Commonwealth, to outlaw and punish sedition in the state. The proposed bill attracted national attention. Many prominent supporters of the school, including Jane Addams, Mrs. Edward Bellamy, Alexander Meiklejohn, and H. L. Mencken, sent telegrams and letters to the Arkansas legislature condemning this action. Tucker Smith, then director of Brookwood, also backed the college. The ACLU likewise expressed its objections to the measure and offered legal assistance to Commonwealth. On March 6, 1935, the legislature killed the Gooch bill as well as another "nuisance bill" directed at the college.[49] Certainly, the protests lodged by Commonwealth's liberal supporters appear to have been instrumental in dissuading the Arkansas legislature from passing these punitive measures.

On March 11, the investigating committee submitted its findings to the Arkansas General Assembly. The committee found that Commonwealth's teachers and students, "although committed to the Communist theory," did not advocate the violent overthrow of the United States government. However, the committee did recommend that a "close check" be made on the school's "principles" and teachings. [50]

The conflict appeared to stimulate union and liberal endorsements of Commonwealth. Tucker Smith visited the campus in 1936 and professed that Brookwood was "similar to Commonwealth in many respects." Commonwealth also received donations from the ILGWU, ACWA, and the Hosiery Workers. J. B. S. Hardman, Mark Starr, Oscar Ameringer, George S. Counts, Clinton S. Golden, Alexander Meiklejohn, and Scott Nearing agreed to serve on the college's advisory board. Albert Einstein supplied a scholarship in 1935 and sent a donation in 1936. [51]

Commonwealth, after only a brief respite, suffered another attack. In December 1936, an inflammatory article, "Rah, Rah, Russia," based largely on the investigating committee's evidence as well as KKK propaganda and hearsay, appeared in *Liberty* magazine and revived the tired old charges of atheism, free love, and, of course, communism at the school. The sensational exposé triggered violent threats against the college. In defense of the school, Charlotte Moskowitz, the new temporary director, sent a letter to Wisconsin's senator Robert La Follette, chairman of the Senate's Civil Liberties Committee, requesting an investigation of the magazine and conditions in Polk County. The Reverend L. D. Summers, pastor of the First Baptist Church in Mena, organized a citizens' committee, obtained the signatures of 914 Polk County residents, wrote a pamphlet titled "Communism and Commonwealth College Unmasked," and announced that he would attempt to have the school closed "in a legal way." Relying again on information gathered by the investigating committee and KKK literature, Summers claimed that the college was "a den of iniquity" and, perhaps worse yet, was a proponent of "negro equality." In closing his pamphlet, Summers submitted the following as proof of the school's guilt: "To further convince you, my friend, that Commonwealth College . . . is a Communist institution, they send their students and teachers to every section of the country where there is confusion or disturbance between the employer and the employee, where there are strikes, farm troubles or race troubles." He was correct. For as the *American Teacher*, the AFT's official organ, surmised, the reasons for the renewed attacks on "Commonwealth College [Local 194] can be discovered in the encouragement and assistance which Commonwealth College has given to the organization of the embattled Tenant Farmers Union and in the numbers of militant trade unionists among its graduates." [52]

Invariably, the Arkansas legislature became embroiled in the controversy that attracted national coverage by the *New York Times*. State representative Herman Horton prepared "a bill to prohibit any one refusing to pledge allegiance to the American flag from teaching in an Arkansas school and to declare the teaching of communism or free love a felony." Horton readily admitted that the measure "was prompted by published criticism of Commonwealth College, a cooperative labor school at Mena, and by personal inquiries into the conduct of the institution." As in 1935, this antisedition bill, first introduced to the legislature in January 1937, sparked widespread protest from many of Commonwealth's liberal supporters. Forty-one Rhodes Scholars at Oxford University cabled the governor to condemn the bill. Arkansas legislators likewise received numerous letters and telegrams of admonishment. Indeed, many state legislators themselves objected to the bill and defeated it. Again, as in 1935, Commoners realized that liberal support and protest represented a significant factor in sustaining the college.[53] Commonwealth continued to survive, but after eleven years of almost constant harassment, the school's liberal supporters began to lose interest, and donations dwindled.

The social and educational purposes and programs of the labor colleges challenged employers, politicians, the clergy, and even a few union officials. As in the cases of Work People's College and Commonwealth, some of these groups joined forces and employed the limitless power of the state in attempts to eradicate these modest educational institutions. This red baiting even encompassed mixed swimming; a simple, innocent activity in any other setting assumed an exaggerated, licentious quality when practiced at a left school like Commonwealth. The schools endured, however. Liberal supporters at Brookwood and Commonwealth played key roles in ensuring the schools' survival, while Finnish radicals protected Work People's College. Still, these attacks took their toll, sapping valuable energy and resources and forcing the schools to assume a defensive posture.

The Brookwood–AFL clash illuminated a fundamental point in the history of workers' education. First, Brookwood's desire for a new social order and an aggressive cadre sharply contrasted with the status quo—the business unionism of the Federation leadership. This incident illustrated that militant examples of workers' education would not be tolerated by the AFL hierarchy. Second, Federation officials appeared intent on obliterating workers' schools that offered any criticism of their leadership. Third, Green and the Executive Council revealed their preference for a controlled version of workers' education, under the direct auspices of either a union or a university. Independent workers' education would simply not be tolerated by Federation officialdom. Fourth, the dispute illustrated the emasculating effect the NCF had on the organized labor movement in general and on workers' education in particular.

In sum, the Brookwood–AFL episode indicated the defensive posture that the Federation had assumed by the 1920s. AFL officials knew that, within the context of hostile antiunionism, they had to protect the union at all costs. This meant, in some cases, purging those elements that antagonized bourgeois interests. As David Montgomery observes, "AFL leaders liked to depict themselves as fighting a two-front war against mindless revolutionaries who threatened to tear down the 'house of labor' by flouting its 'tried and true ways' on the one side and 'reactionary industrialists' on the other."[54]

Unlike the AFL, the labor colleges, during this same period, remained aggressive in their goals and in their training programs. In fact, beginning in the late 1920s and continuing through the 1930s, some teachers and students began to question even these, criticizing them as not radical enough. These internal disputes would likewise exact their toll on the schools.

6

Fratricide

> We feel very sorry that the followers of the Communist Party on campus have not been content with their opportunity freely to propagandize their economic and political beliefs, which this school, with its prevailing "left" philosophy, was so willing to grant them.
> —Lucien Koch, *Nation* (1933)

IN ADDITION to assaults from outside forces, the labor colleges suffered through many in-house political and financial struggles. Work People's College, as already noted in Chapter 2, shifted from the socialist ranks to the IWW camp. At Brookwood Labor College, A. J. Muste and several of the school's progressive unionists had decided to regroup after the split with the AFL; however, this decision also brought with it new sources of conflict. Finally, Commonwealth College was torn by student criticisms, ending in a strike and resignations from the school, concerning alleged racism, ideological softness, and the exclusion of students from campus governance.

These battles assumed a distinct sectarian nature. This proved tragic, since a semblance of a united front had generally existed on the left throughout the 1920s. Gloria Garrett Samson's analysis is revealing on this point: "While socialists and communists certainly did compete for the allegiance of the working class, disagreed about tactics to achieve the new social order, and engaged in scathing denunciations of each other, as individuals they often seemed like attorneys who attack one another in the courtroom but retain a personal and friendly relationship."[1] However, by the late twenties, costly and tortuous internecine wars drained the labor colleges' intellectual vitality and narrowed their political base of support. These internal ruptures, combined with external oppression (as we have seen), contributed to the schools' demise.

Brookwood and the Founding of the CPLA

A significant cause for the political imbroglios at Brookwood, and one that eventually became a great source of turmoil for Brookwooders, was the formation of the Conference for Progressive Labor Action (CPLA) in 1929. In the weeks and months after the AFL attack, Brookwooders scrambled to reorganize. Muste recalls that the censuring of Brookwood "made it virtually impossible for the progressives, in workers' education and other fields, to maintain a base within the AFL." As a result, progressives had to formulate "a base which would be prepared to incur the hostility of the Federation leadership but, at the same time, be independent of the Communist party. Brookwood, on its part, had to build such a base or die for lack of constituency from which students could come and into which they could return to carry on the labor struggle."[2] After a series of informal debates and conferences, Muste and several of the Brookwood staff scheduled a two-day formal meeting of labor progressives to be held at New York's Presbyterian Labor Temple in May of 1929. Some 151 delegates from eighteen states attended the meeting. They included Socialists and trade unionists associated with twelve educational institutions and thirty-three unions—the majority of them AFL affiliates.

Under Muste's leadership, those delegates founded the CPLA, the avowed aim of which was to expand the labor movement by broadening its representation. They voted to adopt *Labor Age* as the new organization's official organ. Reaffirming the goals of progressives within the labor movement, the CPLA platform contained, among others, the following planks: (1) organization of as yet unorganized workers into industrial unions; (2) elimination of racial and religious barriers to union membership—still a sore point for the labor movement; (3) institution of unemployment benefits and other forms of social insurance for union members; (4) formation of a U.S. labor party along the lines of the British Labour party; (5) recognition of the Soviet Union; and (6) propagation of an anti-imperialistic and antimilitaristic labor movement in the United States. Membership in the CPLA would be open to all labor and farm organizations of a trade-unionist, educational, cooperative, or political character. Individuals were also invited to join. The delegates created a national executive committee and elected Muste chairman, Maurer vice-president, A. J. Kennedy treasurer, and Louis Budenz executive secretary. Also on the executive committee were representatives of the machinists, jewelry workers, hat and cap makers, and the sleeping car porters, and from the ACWA, AFT, UTW, and other unions. The CPLA also attracted the Socialist party's unofficial endorsement, signaled by Norman Thomas's presence on the executive committee. Brookwooders were well represented in the group. They included Clinton Golden, Brookwood's field representative; Leonard Craig, education director of the Pennsylvania Federation of Labor; Charles V. Maute, president of a New York City local of the Railway Clerks Union; and Walter Wilson, a leftist Brookwood student. The CPLA opened its national headquarters in New York City on June 10, 1929. Some seventeen branch organizations were set up during the next two or three years, located in such strategic industrial cities as Philadelphia, Pittsburgh, Cleveland, Detroit, Chicago, and Youngstown, Ohio.[3]

At its inception, the CPLA served as a rallying point for the noncommunist left by articulating the goal of broad-based reforms for the labor movement in particular and for society in general. The CPLA was never conceived as a narrow, sectarian organization in and of itself, and the seemingly diverse membership attested to that fact. As such, the CPLA acted to recapitulate, in many ways, Brookwood's social and educational goals.

Not all Brookwooders rushed to join the CPLA, however. Calhoun, who earlier had been denounced as a Communist by AFL officials, opposed Brookwood's alliance with the noncommunist left. Instead, Calhoun urged that Brookwood adopt an ideological position more in tune with that of the Communist party. Calhoun responded to a draft of the lengthy, unpublished CPLA statement, "Memorandum on Brookwood History and Policy," which Muste had circulated among the Brookwood faculty, by suggesting that the school align itself with the Soviet cause. Calhoun offered the following terse proclamation as an alternative statement of Brookwood's social and educational goals: "Standing as Brookwood does for the acquisition of all power by the workers, it hails the Russian Revolution as the one notable achievement of modern times, and it insists that all who have the cause of Labor at heart must support unqualifiedly the struggle of the Russian workers carried on under great odds in the face of a capitalistic world." He continued, in equally dogmatic terms, to call for Brookwood's involvement "in an international Labor front" and commitment to "a comprehensive organization of the workers," that is, "a political party committed to the battle against capitalism the world over." There seemed little doubt that Calhoun referred to the Communist party. Muste realized this, of course, and bluntly rebutted Calhoun's diatribe, concluding with a sarcastic question: "And in order to serve [the workers], is it not necessary to distinguish ourselves from the CP as from the NCF?"[4] Here Muste reiterated Brookwood's noncommunist left position.

Calhoun's disaffection ran much deeper than this political spat indicated. As early as 1926, Calhoun appeared to be dissatisfied with his prospects at Brookwood and began a correspondence campaign in an attempt to secure a traditional faculty position. The replies that he received from faculty at the universities of Chicago, Nebraska, North Carolina, Michigan, and Kansas generally sympathized with Calhoun's expressed anxiety over his lack of a formal academic job. Nevertheless, a few also warned Calhoun that unless he tempered his "wildness," that is, his "radical political" tendencies, he would never find employment in higher education. Calhoun continued his quixotic quest through 1927, but without success. One respondent, from an Ivy League college, referred to Calhoun's "apparent 'blacklisting' " by the field. Brookwooders were quite aware of Calhoun's disenchantment with Brookwood because students collected signatures, during the 1925–26 school year, for a petition discouraging Calhoun's resignation.[5] Thus, with Calhoun's attempts to leave Brookwood doomed to failure, it appears that he couched his personal disappointment in political terms; Calhoun, a Communist, saw himself trapped at Brookwood, which was moving quickly to disavow any connection with the Communist party.

Calhoun's constant criticisms and biting remarks about Brookwood's perceived growing conservatism alienated his colleagues, and in June 1929, the Brookwood faculty unanimously voted to ask the board of directors to terminate his appointment. Calhoun reacted by denying that he maintained membership in the Communist party and accusing Brookwooders of "veering to the right" ideologically. The board accepted the faculty's recommendation and voted to relieve Calhoun of his teaching responsibilities. The board also issued a statement disclaiming any abuse of academic freedom, and reiterated that Calhoun's competence as a scholar and teacher was unassailable. The issue of tenure remained similarly a moot point. In fact, the board cited Calhoun's own written statement refusing tenure in 1927, when he had informed the board that he preferred to teach in a conventional educational institution because, as he reasoned, his "years at Brookwood [had] been a dreary void." With all of this aside, the board then delineated the sole reason for Calhoun's dismissal; his stubborn, dogmatic stance was severely hindering Brookwood's efforts to right itself in the wake of the AFL clash:

> The attacks made upon Brookwood during the past year by extreme right and extreme left elements in the labor movement, have compelled Brookwood to restate and clarify its policy.
>
> In this situation Dr. Calhoun contends that Brookwood should adopt a policy of Communism, and that those who take a contrary position are betrayers of labor.
>
> In view of his temperamental inability to cooperate with the members of the Faculty in the achievement of the aims for which Brookwood was established; and in view of his declaration that he regards it as his duty to frustrate the achievement of these aims, the Board of Directors deems it necessary to adopt the recommendation of Dr. Calhoun's colleagues. [6]

Muste publicly summarized the reason for Calhoun's release in a letter printed in the *New York Times*: "The issue, in so far as it is one of policy, hinges on the fact that Dr. Calhoun desires to see the school committed to a Communist policy. Dr. Calhoun would have the school place as the basis and forefront of its teaching the proposition that fundamental social change can be accomplished only by a violent revolution." Calhoun responded, in another letter to the *Times*, that Brookwood's progressives were simply intolerant of "minority viewpoints about labor policy. If [Muste] would come out squarely with such a declaration, it would be unnecessary for him to frequent further the columns of the daily press and to burden the mails with frantic publicity." [7]

Brookwood incurred sharp rebuke from a variety of quarters for Calhoun's expulsion. Zeuch "deplored" Brookwood's action because it suggested that the school had sacrificed academic freedom and had moved ideologically to the right: "It reveals the fact either that the school is not big and broad enough intellectually and spiritually to tolerate widely divergent labor points given or else that the school is adopting a new policy which junks free workers' education. In either case Brookwood ceases to be what we thought she was and becomes just another 'seminary' of a faction." (Zeuch, as a student and acquaintance of Calhoun's, of course, was anything but objective.) V. F. Calverton, a philosopher–educator, similarly reproached Brookwood in a lengthy letter that appeared in the *New Republic*.

> Something has happened at Brookwood this year. A change of policy! A new affiliation! The affiliation, as Dr. Calhoun himself points out, is with the Council [sic] for Progressive Labor Action. That Brookwood has a right to affiliate wherever it wills no one can deny, but when such affiliation results in such a revolution in policy as to make it go back on its entire ideal of Independent workers' education, it opens itself to the condemnation of every liberal and radical in the United States. [8]

John C. Kennedy, the socialist educational director of Seattle Labor College, with a long record of labor activism, agreed to fill Calhoun's position at Brookwood.

Muste's own politics further strained Brookwood's liberal support. On December 30, 1930, Muste resigned from the executive committee of the League for Independent Political Action (LIPA) in protest over John Dewey's recommendation that a third political party be formulated, "a liberal third party movement built around a few men of prominence." Dewey had invited Senator Charles W. Norris of Nebraska to join the LIPA in its efforts to form a liberal party, but Muste balked at this suggestion and argued that only a labor party could function as an effective third party. More importantly, Muste wryly commented, instead "of seeking messiahs [that is, Norris] who are to bring down a third party out of the political heavens, . . . [a] soundly built labor party in the process of its growth will develop its own leaders." In spite of their differences, Muste still maintained "the utmost respect for Dr. Dewey." [9] Nonetheless, Muste was clearly evolving away from liberal alignments.

Dewey and other liberals continued to endorse Brookwood, and their support proved critical during a financial crisis in 1932. Enrollment had begun to decline because many unions were unable, due to the deepening depression, to subsidize the education of their members. Dewey, Stuart Chase, Sinclair Lewis, and other members of a sponsoring committee of about eighty educators, labor officials, editors, authors, and publishers requested donations for Brookwood in an article in the *Nation*. The appeal emphasized Brookwood's accomplishments.

> In every section of the country its graduates are giving creditable, in some cases noteworthy, service to labor, progressive, and radical movements—in unions, labor colleges, cooperatives, labor political organizations, unemployed leagues. It has given inspiration and help, has been a rallying center, for other workers' education enterprises, such as summer schools and local labor colleges and classes. The members of its staff have written books and pamphlets which are used throughout the workers' education movement. The need for more such material is keenly felt. Through extension classes and lecture services the school reaches each year thousands of workers who cannot take a residential course.

Dewey, George Counts, John R. Commons, William Kilpatrick, and other noted liberals continued their quest to secure funds for Brookwood. [10]

Meanwhile, between 1929 and 1933, the CPLA maintained an activist mode. It sponsored reform movements among mine workers, initiated organizing efforts among textile workers and steelworkers, attacked labor racketeering, and campaigned for a program of government-sponsored unemployment insurance. The CPLA, however, lost whatever credibility it had with trade unionists when it revised its statement, redefining itself as an avowed left-wing political group. This issue, coupled with the serious financial problems plaguing the school, portended a rupture between Brookwood and the CPLA, with devastating and lasting effects on the school, as we shall see.

The eventual rift between Brookwood and the CPLA had long been brewing. Fannia Cohn was conspicuously absent from the CPLA rolls. She had worked with Muste in the creation of Brookwood Labor College, the Workers' Education Bureau, and the Labor Publication Society, but parted with him over the CPLA. Cohn believed a new so-called militant group was not what the labor movement needed at that time; it was already too fragmented. She further demonstrated her displeasure with the CPLA by resigning from the publication board of *Labor Age*, which had been designated as the CPLA's official organ. [11] That parting signaled the early estrangement of a long-time Brookwood sympathizer and important potential supporter of the CPLA.

Moreover, CPLA activities over the years seemed either to end in defeat or to alienate key supporters of Brookwood, particularly the few remaining trade unionists who supported the school in the wake of the AFL clash. While CPLA organizers busied themselves in the coal fields of Illinois and West Virginia, their efforts consistently proved futile. Further, many Brookwood faculty members saw CPLA attempts to stamp out racketeering in unions as an unwarranted intrusion into the AFL's internal affairs, thus further antagonizing what little trade-union support existed for Brookwood. Another of the CPLA's disturbing characteristics stemmed from its organizing campaigns, which often ended in violence. In this latter regard, Jo Ann Ooiman Robinson observes that "Muste had begun to weaken his ties to the Fellowship of Reconciliation and had adopted a stance of qualified defense of labor violence."[12] With some Brookwood faculty and students sympathetic to the CPLA cause becoming more and more involved in violent conflicts, and with Muste's apparent shift away from strict pacifism, other Brookwood faculty members expressed concern.

This concern turned to alarm when, in the August 1931 issue of *Labor Age*, the CPLA attacked the Socialist party because it "lacked vigor and aggressiveness." The situation between Brookwood and the CPLA continued to deteriorate and by March 1932 became a comic opera. The presence in the organization of Ben Mandel, a dissident Communist admitted to the CPLA in the summer of 1931, bewildered many Brookwooders. Mandel, who served in the CPLA's national office, tended to operate in an arbitrary manner and enraged them when he wrote, as these Brookwooders stated it, "a venomous and inaccurate review" of the Brookwood labor pamphlets in March 1932 for publication in *Labor Age*. Of course, this proved to be an embarrassing blunder for Muste, since the Brookwood labor pamphlets were written and edited, with Muste's approval, by Katherine Pollak, David Saposs, Helen Norton, and Tom Tippett—all Brookwooders active in the CPLA. Muste claimed, "This review proposes in *Labor Age* to make a public attack on the chairman of the CPLA and two of its NEC [National Executive Committee] members. . . . The issue . . . will have to be met at the earliest possible moment." Although Muste promised to dismiss him immediately, Mandel continued in his CPLA staff position for five more months, after which he attacked both Brookwood and the CPLA. His denunciation of Brookwood was the most telling, for he labeled Brookwood as "an expensive luxury for the labor movement"—a painful charge to be leveled at the nadir of the Great

Depression. Worse yet: "The tapping of financial resources by Brook-wood was one of the factors which tended to hamper and cripple the activity of the CPLA."[13]

The CPLA further shocked Brookwooders when its national executive board formally revised its position on the Socialist party, among other issues, at the organization's first national convention, held in New York City from September 3 to September 5, 1932. Maintaining a decidedly more militant tone, the NEC, with Muste as chairman, released a statement delineating the CPLA's "revolutionary task": "to abolish, not reform, the capitalist system," and in its place, "establish in the U.S. a planned economic system operated in the interest of the workers and not of the few, and a workers' republic affiliated with workers' republics throughout the world." The CPLA recognized the "Russian Revolution as the great turning point in modern history" and supported the Soviet Union "against its capitalist and imperialist enemies." Yet, for Muste and the other members of the NEC, the fundamental defect of the existing "revolutionary movement" lay in its alien character—that is, "The American section of the world-wide movement of labor must be built by the solidarity, courage and brains of American workers." Further, the CPLA declaration arrogantly dismissed the existing American labor organizations as inept. It saw the Socialist party as gradual and naive, the Communist party as hasty and haphazard, and the AFL as bureaucratic and subservient. Since Brookwood depended upon retaining what little support it still had among members of AFL affiliates as well as the continued loyalty of its socialist backers, the CPLA's excoriation of the AFL and the Socialist party estranged a large portion of Brookwood's constituency, thus seriously jeopardizing the school's very existence.

That proclamation continued by tracing the metamorphosis of the CPLA from a "vaguely progressive" association, with a membership encompassing all factions of the noncommunist labor movement, to a "definitely militant" organization, with no room for "lukewarm or hostile" elements, particularly from the Socialist party. In addition to purging undisciplined members, the CPLA predicted that it would undertake more aggressive organizing actions. Although that declaration did not promote violence as such, it noticeably deleted negotiation as a tactic. Furthermore, the CPLA, which had originally "advocated independent political action," now sought a "mass labor party," but not like its "collaborationist and corrupt" European counterparts. Finally, the CPLA endorsed workers' education that strove "to teach [workers] the facts about the present system, to give them a vision of a better world, and to train them for more effective service in all branches of the labor movement." The CPLA appeared to recapitulate Brookwood's social and educational goals. Yet, in an obvious swipe at Brookwood's traditional position, the statement later called for an emphasis "less on general education and more on concrete action." This would prove to be an important distinction for the pro-CPLA Muste and for loyal Brookwooders.

The CPLA pronouncement closed by evoking a messianic image. It pointed to the "three major struggles in American history," the Revolutionary War, the Civil War, and, finally, the social-class war, now exacerbated by the Depression. The CPLA was ready to assume its role as the self-appointed redeemer of the working class. As Muste boasted in *Labor Age*, "The Conference for Progressive Labor Action has ceased to be a committee and has become an organization."[14]

Personality clashes certainly intensified the political differences between the CPLA and Brookwood. As Muste pointed out, in retrospect, Brookwood's "pretty closely knit community" was already disintegrating. First, the earlier AFL censure had an unsettling effect, and according to Muste, it eventually led to Calhoun's dismissal. Second, the deepening Depression reduced Brookwood's revenues, forcing it to make drastic cuts in its budget. Often these decisions assumed the guise of an ideological contest. In Muste's words, "Issues of policy were exasperated because problems of who should be dropped, and so on, arose. The whole political atmosphere was highly charged." Hence, the pressures and uncertainties of the depression magnified the political differences. Third, Muste pointed to his age, forty-eight, as being yet another factor: "I was inwardly somewhat less assured than in earlier and later crises."[15] Muste perhaps overcompensated for his self-doubt, brought on by his midlife crisis, by conducting an overly zealous, and at times downright malicious, campaign for the CPLA among Brookwooders.

Other signs of stress began to surface as well. Since 1929, Muste had divided his time between serving as CPLA chairman and as Brookwood's director. In June 1932, the American Fund for Public Service, which in 1926 had committed a ten-year subsidy to the school, chastised Muste and threatened to terminate its financial backing because of Brookwood's affiliation with the CPLA. The AFPS specifically charged that Brookwood had become a mere appendage of the CPLA, evolved to an increasingly anticommunist position, and lost its broad trade-union support. The Fund based its allegations on articles that had appeared in *Labor Age* as well as on Muste's numerous speeches and writings on behalf of the CPLA. Further, the AFPS accused Brookwood of consistently praising the CPLA in its publications. For evidence, the Fund ironically pointed an accusing finger at the Brookwood labor pamphlet *Our Labor Movement Today*, written by Katherine Pollak, a Brookwood tutor and active CPLA member, and edited by Muste, Tippett, Saposs, and Norton. The AFPS also expressed consternation over the fact that too many Brookwood teachers and students were becoming increasingly involved in solely CPLA activities. The Fund's statement concluded by warning Brookwood that the AFPS had committed itself to a long-term financial contract that would gradually decrease every two years. The original agreement had stipulated such an arrangement in the hope that Brookwood would attract trade-union contributions to offset the reduced subsidy. "Instead of that," the AFPS complained, "Brookwood's sectarianism has produced the contrary effect, thus leaving it with middle-class support, and with no prospect of carrying out its professed purpose of building up workers' education, supported by trade unions, for all branches of the [labor] movement." Muste retorted by imperiously denying the accusations. The Fund promised to fulfill its financial obligation, but steadily fell into arrears. [16]

Brookwood's board of directors, unlike Muste, took a more sober approach. In an obvious attempt to assuage the AFPS, the board released a declaration in June 1932 that reaffirmed Brookwood's traditional position and reiterated its autonomy from the CPLA. Brookwood was suffering through a dire financial crisis and could not afford to antagonize the Fund. To further address this problem, the executive committee appointed a special finance committee and urged Muste to concentrate on raising funds for the school. However, the executive committee, as well as the rest of the faculty, realized too that the CPLA represented a drain on precious Brookwood income. This made for an awkward relationship between Muste, chair of the CPLA, and the Brookwood community, particularly in light of Mandel's unfounded accusation that Brookwood was a financial burden on the CPLA. In reality, Muste had long used Brookwood's facilities, clerical help, and materials, including the Brookwood letterhead, to promote and sustain the CPLA. [17]

Thus, Brookwood's close identification with the CPLA because of Muste's dual roles was proving self-destructive. Brookwood's trade-union support dwindled as the CPLA continued to excoriate the AFL. Socialists, offended by CPLA attacks, had not only withdrawn from it, but began to cast a wary eye in Brookwood's direction; Norman Thomas resigned from the CPLA's National Executive Committee. Brookwood's affiliation with the CPLA was also jeopardizing its principal source of revenue, namely the AFPS. This dilemma produced internal tensions, to be sure. Many of Brookwood's faculty began to grumble that Muste did not give enough attention to the school's tenuous fiscal state, made all the more perilous by the Depression. At the same time, Louis Budenz, executive secretary of the CPLA, chided Muste for not devoting sufficient time to the CPLA. Things soon came to a head.

In the wake of the CPLA's revised statement of aims, strategy, and tactics, several Brookwood faculty confronted Muste about his divided allegiances at a faculty and executive staff meeting that took place in late October 1932. Two solutions were proffered. Josephine Colby, John C. Kennedy, Helen Norton, David Saposs, and Mark Starr suggested that Muste should resign as Brookwood's director. On the other side, Cal Bellaver, Cara Cook, and Tom Tippett recommended that "A. J." resign his CPLA post. Responding in a November memo to the faculty, Muste saw his first and foremost job as sustaining Brookwood "through the immediate crisis" in order "to save Brookwood for the labor movement." He further proposed a compromise; he would take a temporary leave of absence from the chairmanship of the CPLA.[18] The faculty, for the time being, appeared placated.

Nonetheless, factionalism had exacted its toll. Brookwood teachers Colby, Norton, Pollak, Saposs, and Starr became increasingly sensitive to the CPLA's growing political aspirations and what they implied for Brookwood. Two members of the CPLA's national office had gone so far as to broach the subject of Brookwood's formal integration into the CPLA. This certainly did not alleviate the faculty's suspicions. The CPLA, on the one hand, was immersed in organizing and strike campaigns and in political party activities. Many of the faculty and students at Brookwood, on the other hand, saw the college's main purpose as one of educating, or training, activists to carry on labor's struggles. Muste's November memorandum appeared to put this debate to rest by underscoring his endorsement of Brookwood's neutral role in the training of labor leaders; in Muste's words, Brookwood was "not a 'party' school, whether SP, or CPLA, or anything else." According to the minutes taken at the December 6, 1932, faculty meeting,

Muste formally declared that he was taking a leave of absence from the chairmanship of the CPLA and would not be responsible for the executive, administrative, or fund-raising activities of the CPLA. [19]

Still, Muste's assurances failed to mollify all of Brookwood's faculty, and some began to abandon the CPLA. On January 4, 1933, Kennedy submitted his resignation to Budenz, stating that he could no longer support an organization involved in "futile factional controversies." The trend continued, on January 17, with Pollak and Saposs expressing their concerns about the CPLA's new direction. [20]

In spite of Muste's announced leave of absence from the CPLA, his dual roles still irritated many Brookwooders, particularly since he never relinquished the CPLA chairmanship. At a faculty meeting in January, Abraham Lefkowitz, now chairman of Brookwood's board of directors, called Muste's attention to the fact that by remaining as the CPLA's chair he had violated the spirit of the November agreement to keep Brookwood and the CPLA separate. Muste reminded Lefkowitz that he had agreed merely to surrender his executive, administrative, and financial duties "so as to be free to give his full time to Brookwood." Muste had never promised to remove his name as chairman from the CPLA letterhead. According to the minutes taken at the meeting, "The faculty unanimously sustained Abe's interpretation of the agreement and document. . . . It was decided to refer the matter to the Board for final determination, especially after A. J. admitted the inevitable confusion resulting from his dual capacity." [21]

The plot thickened and the pace quickened in the tragic little drama, producing both contradictory statements and more ill feelings. On February 2, Muste announced that he, Cook, and Tippett saw an irreconcilable difference of opinion over policy between them and the rest of the faculty, and that they would draw up a statement to present to a special meeting on February 11 in order to settle the matter. Meanwhile, student morale had plummeted. Brookwood students held a meeting and submitted a letter formally requesting a clarification "on the differences of opinion among the faculty." [22] To further confuse matters, Lucien Koch, who was visiting Brookwood that winter, remarked that at Commonwealth and among labor educators "Brookwood was generally assumed to be a CPLA school." [23] Finally, on February 7, Muste released a statement stressing that there was "no official connection between Brookwood and the CPLA." [24]

But Muste caused the final breach when he contravened this statement at a faculty and student meeting held on February 11. The gathering quickly deteriorated into a brutal, name-calling melée. The issue debated was: "Shall Brookwood become a CPLA school?" Muste, speaking for Bellaver, Cook, Tippett, and other CPLA sympathizers, emphasized "labor action" and "wanted to relate Brookwood and the educational process going on there directly to the day-to-day battles in mining, textiles and steel, and automobiles—the great unorganized industries of that era." As Muste saw it, this would be manifested in a fundamental departure from Brookwood's traditional educational program. Brookwood would rely primarily on extension courses and, more importantly, Muste further recalls that he argued "that it might be advisable, if trying to maintain a resident institution in Westchester County under depression conditions absorbed all the energies we had and all the money we could raise, to sell the Brookwood property and to move the school to less expensive quarters in an industrial center" —preferably Newark, New Jersey. [25]

As expected, Colby, Kennedy, Norton, Saposs, Starr, and other Brookwooders loyal to the traditional notion of the school balked at Muste's plan to move Brookwood to Newark and to affiliate with the CPLA. Muste leveled two charges at these obstinate Brookwooders, "whose primary interest was an institution devoted to education in some sort of relationship to the labor movement." [26] First, he said their obsession with Brookwood's finances reflected nothing more than a self-serving concern for their own "safe nests" on the "fair hill." Second, Muste claimed that their blind stubbornness over Brookwood's direction would cause the college to "become rightwing, isolated and ineffectual." Muste likewise resorted to personal invective, sprinkling such epithets as "numbskulls," "traitors," "turncoats," "academicians," and "reactionaries" throughout his attack. [27] In retrospect, Muste admits that he went too far, especially in the case of Colby, Brookwood's most devoted teacher. According to Muste's recollections, "I used Bernard Shaw's familiar sentence: 'Those who can, do; those who can't, teach.'" Colby cried out, "I protest." Muste immediately regretted that statement. As he said later, he quickly realized that "it was one of those moments in a controversy when you sense that it cannot be 'patched up' any more. Josephine Colby, I know, was deeply wounded by my remark." [28]

In March, Muste met with Brookwood's board of directors and repeated his proposal. The labor directors, five of the seven faculty, half of the graduates present, and nine of the twenty-eight students voted to keep the school nonfactional. Muste, Tippett, five administrative officers, and nineteen students left Brookwood in protest, completely severing their connections with the school. Their rallying cry was "Brookwood turned right, and we left." Muste further argued that Brookwood's directors voted against affiliation with the CPLA in order to "play safe" and ensure the continuation of the school's financial support. He wrote at the time, "Economic conditions are at the root of the whole thing. If the institution had not been pressed for funds, and if conditions were as good as they were two years ago, I dare say this sudden outburst of conservatism would never have been manifest. The purpose of the directors seems to play safe and conserve what they have."[29] Thus, in the immediate aftermath, Muste grossly oversimplified the complex political, economic, and personal reasons for the Brookwood–CPLA split.

Brookwood's board of directors acted quickly to repair the damage and restore continuity. In an official statement published in the May 1933 issue of the *Brookwood Review*, the board of directors, which included Lefkowitz, Cohn, and Brophy, reiterated Brookwood's position:

> As an educational agency, Brookwood refuses to be diverted from its established educational programs and become subordinated to any particular theoretical or political faction. . . . Brookwood must be preserved . . . because it is the educational hope of that part of the labor movement which is committed to the establishment by the workers of a new social order through militant, cooperative efforts both on the industrial and political fields.[30]

The board asked Kennedy to serve as Brookwood's acting director until it appointed Tucker P. Smith, a Socialist, pacifist, and executive secretary of the Fellowship of Reconciliation, as the new director in June 1933. Smith had been born and raised in Missouri, attended the University of Missouri and Columbia University, as a graduate student, specializing in economics, sociology, and international relations, and taught at New York University, Springfield College, Haverford College, and Northwestern University. As Brookwood's director, he proposed an expansion of the summer program, ten-day institutes, and chautauquas in order to better reach workers and the unemployed. The school accordingly deemphasized its political activities and revitalized its economic and industrial pursuits.[31] Nevertheless,

Brookwood was, in the end, the victim of factionalism, exacerbated by the drastic economic conditions of the era.

Regardless of the political and personal reasons and financial pressures for the dispute, Muste recalls, in fatalistic tones, that a falling-out was inevitable—if not in 1933, then later. As he recollects, fundamental ideological realignments were already under way at Brookwood. Many of the faculty and students who opposed Muste eventually found jobs in the government or joined the CIO. In Muste's words, "To have become identified with the New Deal, with the CIO top leadership and, presently, with support of the [Second World] war— this would have been for me the abandonment of my deepest convictions and the collapse of inner integrity. In this context, my instinct that those who disagreed with me wished to carry Brookwood in a conservative direction seems to me to have been validated. . . . Of necessity, my 'detour' had been to the Left." [32]

The rupture hurt both Brookwood and the CPLA, which dissolved shortly after the Brookwood schism. Within eight months, Muste and his followers established the American Workers party, eventually merging with the Communist League of America, a Trotskyite organization, in 1935. [33] More importantly, because of this splintering of the noncommunist left, Brookwood never regained its former stature and vitality.

Internal Problems at Commonwealth College

The year 1932 proved to be a dark time for Commonwealth as well as for Brookwood. A major internal struggle at Commonwealth exploded on December 2, 1932, when several students struck for two days. According to the protesting students, the main issues centered on student representation and their right to control student discipline, the admission of black students, and the dismissal of certain teachers. Personality conflicts were important to that dispute. School administrators conceded on the issue of student discipline but refused to budge on the other demands and, further, suspended the two "communist" student leaders, Jack Copenhaver and Henry Forblade. Thirty-four students struck in protest. Seventeen other students chose not to participate in the protest and earned the label of "scabs." One "scab" maintained that some of the protesters' requests, such as that students be allowed to participate even more in outside labor activities and that the ten o'clock curfew be rescinded, were justified, but characterized the two student leaders as generally disruptive and wholly unreasonable in their demands.

Lucien Koch, the school's director, held a contrasting view. For him, the strike was more than a personality dispute; it symbolized an ideological conflict. As he wrote for the *Nation*:

> The basic issue of the strike . . . was not student representation but an attempt to force the school to abandon its non-factional position and adopt the position of the Communist party. That not all the strikers were Communists or even completely aware of the aims of the two students against whose suspension they protested is merely a testimonial to the clever strategy of the Communist group in bringing extraneous issues to the fore.

Koch abhorred the demand for the elimination of "certain teachers whose political views did not square with the brand of Marxism held by the protesting students." He attempted to justify the exclusion of students from the college's leadership by reiterating that students had always maintained representation on the Commonwealth College Association, but that "lately, on account of economic conditions, the ration of student members [had] become smaller, and plans [had] been under consideration for reducing the period for eligibility." Koch, nonetheless, appeared conciliatory:

> We feel very sorry that the followers of the Communist Party on campus have not been content with their opportunity freely to propagandize their economic and political beliefs, which this school, with its prevailing "left" philosophy, was so willing to grant them. We merely objected to being mistaken for the capitalist system and made a target for Communist wrath.

This was not enough to mollify one of the strikers, who sharply rebuked Koch, asserting that he could not be duped, and that student representation and teacher dismissals were indeed legitimate issues.

Jane Addams volunteered to mediate the dispute, but it was in vain. Commonwealth's administrators had warrants issued for the arrest of the strike leaders, and the local sheriff removed them from the campus. As a result, thirty-four students abandoned the school in protest. In spite of the "Communist-led insurrection," the school's administrators continued to welcome the enrollment of avowedly communist students. [34]

Although different in character, the conflicts and struggles of the labor colleges had common elements. The inherent contradiction between ideological orientation and academic freedom is nowhere better demonstrated than in the strenuous conflicts and clashes of ideals at the labor colleges. Problems arose over the schools' political and social goals and practices and, to some extent, over the sources of their control. The labor colleges not only battled conservative threats from the right (as we saw in the previous chapter), but also had to cope with communist disruptions from the left. While Work People's College and Brookwood aligned themselves with the noncommunist left, Commonwealth, in spite of the 1932 insurrection, tolerated this and other radical groups on campus.

In spite of the turmoil, the labor colleges maintained, for better or worse, their basic goals and educational programs. Work People's College, of course, remained steadfastly loyal to the IWW. Brookwood's ideological base narrowed somewhat with the formation of the CPLA and the subsequent expulsion of Arthur Calhoun, but it appeared to again broaden its political perspective with Muste's departure. Meanwhile, Commonwealth drifted steadily leftward. Yet it did not become communist. Although it tolerated the presence of communist students, Commonwealth preferred to remain factionally independent, as its response to the 1932 student strike clearly illustrated. But it was just such independence that spelled doom for the schools.

7

The End of the Labor Colleges

There are few of us now, soon
There will be none. We were comrades
Together, we believed we
Would see with our own eyes the new
World where man was no longer
Wolf to man, but men and women
Together. We will not see it
It is farther off than we thought.
            —Kenneth Rexroth,
                "For Eli Jacobson" (1956)

THESE THREE labor colleges never expected to survive; rather, they were to become unnecessary with the hoped-for social revolution. Nor were they expected to work miracles overnight: they were, after all, not founded by starry-eyed dreamers or dogmatic ideologues with false illusions. Arthur Gleason, present at the founding of Brookwood in 1921, sensed the long and difficult road that lay ahead for workers' education, which he viewed as a "humanly imperfect effort to meet the situation." He continued: "Workers' education does not say 'Come and be comfortable.' It cannot be dressed in the garments of success. It demands the impossible. It calls for hard and clear thinking, for lonely work, for slow results and unregarded growth. The faithful servant of this calling may read 'his victory in his children's eyes,' but he will not live to see the day of its advent. He is building for a long future."[1]

Many critics saw the schools as elitist, expensive, and out of touch with the everyday trials and events of the factory, farm, or other work-

222

place. The concept of a residential labor college built on the lines of other institutions of higher learning was far from an answer to the problems of the vast majority of workers. Many opponents favored community-based workers' education instead, and questioned the efficacy of residential programs. First, some charged, labor college achievements remained limited. They could accommodate only a few students and consequently had to be extremely selective. Second, residential programs often became disadvantageous to the worker–students, who had to temporarily withdraw from their communities, their families, their jobs. They lost valuable experience and contacts, and on their return they had to readapt to their former lives. Third, residential colleges appeared expensive compared with part-time, in-service education. Because of their relatively high operating costs, the residential labor schools relied heavily on donations from liberal sympathizers and contributions from unions and foundations, such as the AFPS. This caused labor advocates to fear that the colleges' educational programs and ideology might lose their independence, might be forced to defer to special groups. [2]

Many of these criticisms of the labor college concept evidenced valid concerns. Indeed, only a few worker–students could make the necessary sacrifices to attend a labor college, and the expense and selectivity entailed in their training meant that the working masses could be affected by the schools only indirectly, if at all. However, there were also clear justifications for modeling the labor colleges on "mainstream" institutions of higher education. Immersed in a stimulating environment, becoming socially acquainted and working side-by-side with others like themselves, studying under trained academics and experienced labor activists who could bring an intellectual and ideological ballast to their socialistic convictions, the labor college students could benefit from an intense, comprehensive learning experience far beyond the possibilities of part-time or community-based education. The number of graduates from the colleges who significantly shaped and enriched the labor cause attests to the validity of the concept. For this reason, in spite of the schools' alleged shortcomings, it can be convincingly argued that the labor colleges carried out their mission. They succeeded in training a cadre of labor educators, writers, editors, organizers, union officers, and other activists who participated in countless labor struggles and played important roles in the development of the CIO.

The End of Brookwood Labor College

On January 18, 1936, a celebration was held in New York City to honor Brookwood's fifteenth anniversary. More than five hundred people gathered for the commemoration, including graduates, supporters, trade unionists, workers' education teachers, and members of the board of directors. In reviewing Brookwood's record, director Tucker Smith pointed out that Brookwood's experience had answered several questions vital to the labor movement:

> We have shown that workers will take time off to go to school. The Brookwood graduates' achievements prove that workers' education does pay. We find them in every field of labor activity; leading picket lines, writing labor's news, teaching classes, and organizing cooperatives. We have shown that a non-factional school can be successful. Perhaps most important of all is the fact that throughout its entire history, Brookwood has been able to keep up its fight for a progressive labor movement.[3]

Brookwood's *Fifteenth Anniversary Review* contained many congratulatory notes from various unions and other supporters. Commonwealth College sent its greetings along with those of such unions as the ILGWU, the ACWA, and the AFT. Similarly, the July 1936 *Brookwood Review* painted an image of stability and growth during this period. The Hosiery Workers' Union had voted to supply a scholarship.[4] The *Review* also recorded that Smith "reported an increase in the Brookwood extension activities, telling of the agreement to cooperate with the United Auto Workers, and the possibilities for classes in New England and the Midwest. These included negotiations now going on for the setting up of a branch of Brookwood in Detroit, with Roy Reuther in charge."[5]

In spite of this ostensible optimism, Brookwood's administrators wrestled with a grim fiscal situation in 1936, as alluded to in Chapter 6. According to the Executive Committee's minutes, contributions to Brookwood had fallen to a "dribble," and necessary loans had been delayed because of "red tape." These financial exigencies had consistently plagued Brookwood. Of course, there had always been scholarships from various unions, among them the ILGWU, the ACWA, the Machinists, and the Illinois and Pennsylvania Mine Workers, but these depended on the political outlook and financial health of the sponsoring union. And the AFL–Brookwood clash and the sectarian battles at the school further jeopardized this tenuous support. Muste had also exploited his contacts among his socially minded and well-to-do acquaintances to generate some income for the school.

Muste implemented a systematic, and somewhat manipulative, fundraising campaign among his liberal supporters. He maintained an extensive list of past donors as well as the amounts and dates of their contributions. Muste also composed a series of form letters on the Brookwood letterhead, and designated which kind of letter should be sent to which former or potential benefactor; the choice depended largely on whether the request was being directed to an organization or an individual. Some letters were written in calm, sober tones, such as one, dated March 23, 1931, to Miss Ida Oppenheimer of New York's Lower East Side Community Council: "You can readily imagine that it is a mighty tough year for us . . . we have to scramble to get every bit of possible aid from liberals who have vision enough to realize the importance of developing an intelligent leadership for the labor movement." However, other letters displayed a hysterical, melodramatic approach, as illustrated in a letter, dated February 21, 1933, to Mrs. Ethel R. Allen: "Please let us hear from you. Anything you may be able to do now may mean the difference between going on or shutting down."

Muste's successor maintained the letter campaign, but donations continued to dwindle. Some contributors supported Brookwood solely because of Muste, and their backing ceased when he suddenly departed in 1933. The Depression curtailed many such philanthropic activities, to be sure. Apathy likewise exacted its toll. As sympathy for socialist causes became passé among the more educated and affluent, contributions from bourgeois idealists fell off sharply. But this appeared to be more than just indifference; as Lawrence Rogin, a Brookwood instructor, points out about the CIO campaigns, when "the wave of organizing started . . . when they saw agitation, the real thing . . . when it was no longer romantic but real, [the liberal contributions] disappeared."

Nonetheless, Smith employed the same approach as Muste. Writing to the League for Industrial Democracy in December 1935, he stressed the activities of Brookwood in positive terms: "Roy Reuther is conducting a very successful circuit of classes in the Massachusetts–Rhode Island area." Still, in other personal appeals for individual donations, Smith presented a gloomy side, as in the case of a letter to

Fanny Cochrane: "At the present time we have seven dollars in the bank, and must buy groceries and coal at once—not to mention the fact that our staff faces Christmas with no salary since spring."[6]

The AFPS became the largest and most stable benefactor; in fact, Brookwood was considered one of its "chief enterprises." Subsidies from the Fund were critical to Brookwood's existence during the 1920s and represented a substantial portion of the school's budget. Brookwood's budget for 1923–24 totaled $38,000. Between 1924 and 1926, this increased to $45,000 per year. For the six-month period from June 1925 to January 1926, the AFPS contributed almost $14,000 to Brookwood. Yet relations between the school and the Fund were uneasy, at best, during the early 1920s. Muste, who constantly petitioned the AFPS for money, callously referred to its management as a "hard-boiled lot to deal with!" Not only were funds difficult to acquire, but Brookwood also faced many problems in repaying its loans to the Fund and barely serviced the interest. Muste regularly pleaded for extensions and attempted to refinance previous loans; the AFPS usually just canceled the college's notes.

But the AFPS did not want to continue such piecemeal, massive funding, hoping to encourage Brookwood's greater independence. In February 1926, the Fund arranged a long schedule of generous payments to the college, beginning with $25,000 each year during 1926–27 and 1927–28 and decreasing by $5,000 every two years thereafter. The payments were to end in 1936. The total grant amounted to $150,000 over a ten-year period. As Helen Norton recalls, "The theory [was] that in ten years the school should have become established firmly in the labor movement and, if it hadn't done it by that time, it probably wouldn't." Thus, the AFPS, during this period, subsidized scholarships for the dependents of worker–students, for blacks, for publications, and for summer institutes. Fund money also underwrote the work of the college's field agent, Clinton Golden, and research projects, providing Brookwood instructor David Saposs with a research assistant for his work on a manuscript titled "Methods of Trade Union Organizational Work." During the AFL–Brookwood conflict in 1928, the AFPS granted an additional $2,000 for the school's campaign against the Federation. This donation financed the travel and lodging expenses for three Brookwooders who represented the school at the annual AFL meeting in New Orleans.

The Depression eroded Brookwood's tenuous solvency. Union scholarships dried up, and liberal backers were hard-pressed to make up the difference. Besides, fewer and fewer students were able to pay their own fees. Ironically, Norton recalls, "Brookwood, rather than having income from the students, found itself paying for [their] dental bills." Muste exacerbated the situation when, beginning in October 1929, he began to submit applications to the AFPS on behalf of the CPLA, founded that same year. But the Fund had already announced, the previous April, that it had committed all of its remaining assets and could not accept any more applications for loans or grants. The AFPS later chastised Muste and threatened to discontinue its financial support because of Brookwood's close affiliation with the CPLA. To make matters worse, the Fund began to send its monthly installments to the school on an irregular basis because of other loan defaults. By 1932, after the AFPS's appropriation to Brookwood had continued to fall in arrears, the college appeared to be in dire financial straits. In October 1932, Muste begged the Fund for $500 so Brookwooders could eat. Spinach had already become a staple of the Brookwood diet. Muste slashed the school's budget to cope with its tenuous finances. Between 1928 and 1930, the annual budget averaged $62,000, but by the 1932–33 school year Brookwood's budget amounted to barely $27,000. These budget reductions often came at the expense of the faculty members, whose salaries were cut by as much as 52 percent between 1932 and 1934. Sometimes faculty went without pay or simply worked for room and board; unpaid salaries amounted to over $7,000 for the 1934–35 school year alone.[7]

Apparently revenue was so scarce that a faculty skit, presented in September 1932, poked fun at Muste's seemingly quixotic quest for money to maintain the college. The play opens with a faculty meeting, set in Muste's study, that is preoccupied with the nagging shortage of money. The shortfall has produced profound consequences that begin to assume ludicrous proportions as the faculty lists the problems, including insufficient texts, overdrawn checking accounts, poor credit with the iceman, defective tires on the school truck, lack of coal for the furnace, shutoff notices from the telephone company, stranded teachers who have run out of gas, and so on. The "crisis" over deficient funds even takes priority over other issues, such as the recruitment and acceptance of students. The play ends with the following analysis, by Muste, for admitting a student:

AJ: Yes, and here's Natrig Pederson from Norway who's a teacher. He can teach . . . the students can look after the place, and that will leave the rest of us all free for our real job of:
All: RAISING MONEY![8]

Tucker Smith, director after 1933, continued to prod the AFPS for money. Brookwood's budget for the 1933–34 school year totaled $25,000; the Fund supplied $10,000 of it, but the remainder had to come from other sources. While it was the director's task to find additional monies, Smith's leadership abilities, particularly in fundraising, appeared to be weak. Moreover, he feared compromising the school's principles in the search for financial security. Although the college faced serious fiscal problems, Smith refused, in early 1937, to endorse a proposal to form a joint effort to raise funds for Brookwood and two southern labor schools, Commonwealth College and Highlander Folk School in Tennessee. He contended that the proposed fundraising campaign, which was to be waged in the South, favored the two southern labor schools. He further reasoned that Brookwood required immediate financial relief and could not afford to wait. Brookwood's educational offering had deteriorated, as Rogin recalls, to "a six-month program plus two months in the chautauqua."[9]

Brookwood's Executive Council prepared a contingency plan for the 1937–38 school year. The proposal outlined a three-part program that, in an attempt to reduce operating costs, drastically curtailed the school's educational endeavors. First, the Katonah campus would host only summer institutes, short courses, and a publishing center for workers' education materials. Second, extension courses would be expanded. Third, labor drama, the school's most popular and profitable component, would be retained. The proposal had a desperate, if not sad, tone. As the closing comment emphasized, the goal was to maintain "Brookwood," no matter what form it might assume: " 'Closing Brookwood' would be a severe moral blow to progressive forces in America. We must adopt some scheme for keeping the idea, tradition and name alive, even though financing it may be difficult for several years."[10] Indeed, this optimism, as futile as it seemed, did not appear to be totally unfounded. Many of Brookwood's graduates were beginning to assert themselves, in highly visible ways, in the unfolding CIO movement. In his fundraising letters for February 1937, Smith extolled the efforts of Brookwood students at the General Motors strike in Flint, Michigan:

Two Brookwooders inside the plant organized a "resident labor college" twenty-four hours after the first great sit-down strike started. The educational director, the publicity director of the union, organizers in Detroit, Flint, Anderson, Tarrytown and elsewhere, and the publicity director of the CIO—all are Brookwood grads. All auto workers in the present student body are out organizing. *Brookwood training, once more, is proving its value—in effectiveness, in loyalty, in enthusiasm for the labor movement.*[11]

However, many of Brookwood's faculty felt differently about the school's future. For them, Brookwood's proud legacy meant more than an emasculated existence. They took the initiative and appealed to the Brookwood board of directors for help. Yet the board was scattered, and the situation looked hopeless. Fannia Cohn, a staunch supporter of the college and the most active member of the board, finally consented to the faculty's request to close the school. Facing insurmountable financial obstacles and a declining enrollment—only nineteen students would graduate in the spring of 1937—the board voted to suspend operations. Still, Cohn had one personal request: she persuaded the teachers to remain at the college until after graduation. As she promised them, "We will try to end Brookwood with honor as it deserves."[12]

The *New York Times* announced Brookwood's official closing on November 21, 1937. In a statement released to the newspaper, Julius Hochman, president of the board of directors, noted several reasons for the school's demise, primarily related to changes in the labor movement, which for so long had supported the school, both materially and otherwise. First, large-scale organizational drives to establish new unions, encouraged by New Deal programs, had drained union funds normally designated for educational purposes. Thus, when Brookwood's board appealed to the CIO to adopt the college as the "workers' education bureau" of the "new federation of labor," John L. Lewis refused because of a lack of money for the project. Second, union officials needed their "best people" to participate in and direct organizing efforts, and refused to spare them for an extended period of training. Brookwood's enrollment plummeted as a result. Third, harking back to the longstanding rift between many unions and the labor colleges, alleged to be "too radical," union leaders preferred to rely on their own educational departments rather than send students to Brookwood. The ILGWU's educational program, for example, was more popular than intellectual—it included public lectures, motion pictures, musicals, dramas, radio programs, and hikes and excursions. The ILGWU, a long and faithful friend of Brookwood, briefly flirted with assuming full responsibility for the school, but canceled the proposed arrangement at the last minute for fear of offending AFL officials who favored the school's extinction.[13] Brookwood's problematic connection with the labor movement ultimately brought about the school's demise.

One concrete legacy of Brookwood remains, however. After the school closed, Local 189 opened its membership to anyone involved in workers' education. Its objectives were "to bring workers' education personnel together for their mutual benefit, and to strengthen workers' education through collective bargaining and through protecting and advancing the technical and economic standards of its personnel."[14] Governed by an elected board, Local 189 continued to distribute workers' education materials, develop workers' education histories and bibliographies, and survey directors and teachers in the field. During the 1960s and 1970s, Local 189 members criticized the Vietnam War and the Nixon administration and served in the civil rights movements. Their battles against antidemocratic tendencies in the AFT earned them the enmity of the Federation's president, Albert Shanker, forcing Local 189 to withdraw from the union in 1977. The local presently maintains chapters throughout the country.

The Demise of Commonwealth College

Like Brookwood, Commonwealth College struggled with a number of fiscal crises during the Great Depression. Although it opened on a shoestring, the college managed to avoid serious financial problems for many years because the AFPS largely subsidized the school's daily operations, as it did with Brookwood. The Fund donated an initial $2,000 to establish the college and continued its support throughout the 1920s, amounting to a total of $28,000, $24,000 of which went to the building program, completed in 1928. The AFPS provided smaller grants in the 1930s to overcome the drought years. For its subsidies to the labor colleges, as well as its financial support of other activities in the labor movement, the AFPS earned the reputation of being a "red" organization. Moreover, Commonwealth was partly self-supporting, using student and faculty labor to offset the costs of food, housing, and other necessities. The depression years, however, severely strained the school's economic resources. Ironically, the school expanded to 320 acres in the hope of ensuring its independence through self-support, but this proved a liability, only guaranteeing its dependency on liberal donations. Between 1931 and 1935, the *Fortnightly* frequently announced that unless Commonwealth received desperately needed funds it would cease operations. The college managed to survive, but fiscal problems continued to plague it. [15]

As if that were not enough, local union officials grew anxious over the existence of a communist faction at Commonwealth, and also complained that the school tended to favor students from other sections of the country and failed to address regional problems. Consequently, Commonwealth and the Southern Tenant Farmers' Union maintained a stormy relationship, both reflecting and exacerbating existing factionalism at the school. The lack of consistent historical accounts clouds their relationship.

The deep-rooted problems of southern sharecroppers symbolized a natural cause for the Commonwealth militants to espouse. By 1935, 60 percent of Arkansas's farms were tenant operated, and almost 70 percent of the sharecroppers were black. Croppers surrendered from 30 to 50 percent of their crop production to the landowner. Planters meanwhile disposed of the sharecroppers as they pleased, continuously squeezing them for debts or callously discarding them after the harvest. Indebted croppers paid the owners 7 to 8 percent interest on their debt, a tidy sum during the Depression. While the croppers earned a mere $250 to 300 a year in wages, the planters reaped gross incomes ranging from $51,000 to $95,000. Commonwealth instructor Covington Hall described the sharecropper's plight:

Sloughfoot Sam and his gal, Lou,
Rode up thar on a kangaroo.
You've seen yore share of Hell on Earth
Said old St. Pete,
So come right in and rest a spell,
Cause you paid more rent and interest too
Than God in Heaven can count for you. [16]

The Agricultural Adjustment Act (AAA) intensified the sharecroppers' dilemma. The AAA's acreage reduction program pushed croppers off the land while rewarding landowners with parity payments, compelling planters to shift from sharecroppers to day laborers. Between 1930 and 1935, the number of tenant-operated farms in Arkansas declined for the first time since the Civil War, a particularly difficult situation for black croppers, who had absorbed the brunt of displacement. During 1932 and 1933, Commoners participated in the organization of the National Farmers' Holiday Association and the Farmers'

National Relief Conference. They soon discovered, however, that alleviating the sharecroppers' plight demanded a much larger organization, with the school relegated to a supporting role.[17] That discovery led Lucien Koch, then Commonwealth's director, to make overtures to the STFU.

The STFU had grown out of the sharecroppers' adverse conditions and received inspiration and support from Socialists such as Norman Thomas, who frequently visited Arkansas to speak on behalf of the union. By 1935, the Depression had produced an increasingly militant left wing in the Socialist party, and in that year the party, under the leadership of Thomas, denounced racial discrimination and called for the active organization of unions and the unemployed. Growing numbers of Socialists adopted the struggle for black rights as part of the struggle for union rights and social change.

In the South, as Michael Honey points out, left-wing socialists—strongly reflecting the Debsian brand of socialism—along with religious radicals like Howard Kester and Claude C. Williams, "condemned capitalism and racism as militantly as any Communist." Arkansas, Louisiana, Oklahoma, and Texas had long hosted a strong socialist movement, drawn from the more radical elements of the Populist party, the UMW, and the refugees from the 1894 Pullman strike led by the Debs. In Louisiana, the Brotherhood of Timber Workers, an interracial organization, had been formed in 1910, and joined the IWW. At one point prior to the First World War, Oklahoma had had the strongest state party in the nation, with some twelve thousand Socialist party members in 900 locals, electing many local and county officials. In eastern Oklahoma, the Working Class Union, an antiwar organization led by Socialists, sparked the Green Corn Rebellion in August 1917. Hundreds of sharecroppers started to march, first on Oklahoma City, the state capital, and eventually on to Washington, D.C. The governor of Oklahoma activated the state militia and jailed the movement's leaders. Later, Oscar Ameringer organized renters' unions in Oklahoma and Texas that clamored for dwelling standards to be implemented by planters for their tenant farmers. In July 1934, eleven white and seven black men met in an abandoned one-room schoolhouse just south of the little town of Tyronza, in the Arkansas Delta, and organized the Southern Tenant Farmers' Union. Many of them had just been notified that they had to move off the plantation on which they worked.[18]

H. L. Mitchell, an active Socialist and a founder and leader of the new union, saw sharecropping as "a new form of slavery." Experience had shaped his outlook. Mitchell, born in a sharecropper family in Tennessee in 1906, had worked as a newspaper boy at an early age, graduated from high school, and later labored as an itinerant worker and sharecropper. He adopted socialism in 1920 after hearing speeches given in support of Debs's presidential candidacy, and became immersed in local socialist politics while working as a dry cleaner in Tyronza. After the 1932 elections, Mitchell played an instrumental role in organizing the Tyronza Unemployed League and attended, as a delegate, the Continental Congress of Farmers and Workers, a Socialist-inspired national conference held in Washington, D.C. Local plantation owners, fearing "red agitation," boycotted his dry-cleaning business, forcing him to close. In 1934, Mitchell won election as the state secretary of the Arkansas Socialist party. he also became an Arkansas delegate to the 1934 national convention of the Socialist party, held in Detroit, where he first encountered the Reuther brothers (see Chapter 8).

The STFU claimed one thousand members by the end of 1934 and generated strong opposition. Deputies, riding bosses, and planters padlocked churches and removed the floors or burned the schoolhouses where the union met. They evicted prounion sharecroppers from the farms and hauled active organizers off speaking platforms and out of cars to beat them. Arrests and defections of many organizers further decimated the union's ranks. Facing a desperate situation, Mitchell, by now the union's executive secretary, finally accepted Commonwealth's offer of aid in January 1935. However, according to William Cobb and Donald Grubbs, Mitchell only reluctantly turned to the college for assistance. They argue that the school's statewide reputation among labor leaders had become tainted. As we have seen in Chapter 5, widely publicized attacks had inappropriately branded the school as a hotbed of atheism, communism, and free love. Cobb and Grubbs insist that the fledgling STFU remained cautious, hoping to avoid more problems through its association with the "radical" little college. Yet Mitchell's personal account never makes such an allegation. [19]

Commoners responded enthusiastically to the STFU's appeal. Both the communist and socialist factions at the school agreed to a united front in assisting the union's organizing campaign. This reflected a broader experience. As the Socialist party grew more militant during the 1930s, common action with the Communist party became feasible.

Likewise, many Communists desired a united front with Socialists, and they began to coordinate activities and form joint organizations, such as the Workers' Alliance in 1936. Further, as Honey asserts, the left in the South included a broad range of people with anticapitalist and antiracist sentiments who did not necessarily claim any allegiance to either party. "Indeed, anti-capitalist and anti-employer feelings were so strong among many workers during this period that identifying the left by party affiliations can be misleading." [20] It was this assortment of radicals—Socialists, Communists, religious radicals, and unlettered white and black workers—that comprised the united front and provided the base of support for the STFU's organization. Nevertheless, sharp disagreements still remained between the two parties and, as events would soon demonstrate, dogmatism would prove to be the downfall for both the college and the union.

Commoners, led by Lucien Koch, embarked on a campaign of aggressive field work and immediately encountered planter retaliation in eastern Arkansas. "Nightriders"—a euphemism for Ku Klux Klan members—disrupted STFU meetings, often held in black churches, and clubbed union members. Commoners were likewise beaten and jailed. Reported shootings also caused many STFU leaders to flee across the Mississippi River to Memphis, a natural haven for them. Memphis claimed a sizable socialist base with respectable support for Norman Thomas in the 1932 election, leading one Socialist to boast that the city would soon become socialism's capital in the South. According to Mitchell, "This became the place of refuge for the sharecropper leaders and their families. The union was forced underground. All meetings were suspended." [21]

Commonwealth's contribution to the union's initial organizing campaign remains a point of contention. For Cobb and Grubbs, Commoners, though well intentioned, caused too much trouble for the union and, in fact, hampered union efforts to organize sharecroppers. They assert that the presence of "outsiders" and "reds" infuriated landowners, resulting in such conflicts as the Marked Tree incident (described in Chapter 4). In several instances, therefore, the union had to rush to the aid of Commoners, often snatching them from the clutches of the planters or bailing them out of jail. Yet, Raymond and Charlotte Koch recall Commonwealth's work with the STFU as one of the college's major accomplishments. Moreover, Mitchell's autobiography, which admits that the union did in fact assist Commoners, reveals no such animosity by the union towards the college, at least at this point.[22] After several more such organizing incidents, Commoners withdrew to their school, ending their first formal association with the union.

Liberals and sympathetic organizations hastened to assist the struggling STFU. A variety of northern and southern church groups, the AFPS, the NAACP, and the ACLU provided both moral and financial support. Norman Thomas, appalled at the illiteracy and poverty of the sharecroppers, became the "godfather" of the STFU, raising 75 percent of the union's 1935 budget alone. The AFPS contributed $2,000 and subsidized fourteen field organizers. This backing proved to be invaluable. By August 1935, the STFU had recovered, and in response to a sharp wage cut for cotton pickers, Mitchell called a strike. The membership approved by a margin of 11,186 to 450. The strike ended in October with the planters raising the wage rate and Mitchell declaring a victory: "Confidence in the union returned. New areas were opened up to organization in Arkansas, Missouri, Mississippi, Tennessee, and Texas. Soon I was claiming 25,000 members of the Southern Tenant Farmers' Union."[23] Mitchell admits, however, that this represented an exaggerated figure. The strike strengthened the support and interest of the union's wide range of sympathizers; liberals such as Reinhold Niebuhr, various branches of the Socialist party, and various union locals, responding to an appeal from AFL president Green himself, sent contributions for strike relief.

Meanwhile, Lucien Koch had departed Commonwealth College, and Richard B. Whitten, executive secretary of the New Orleans local of the Socialist party, replaced him as director. Characterized by Cobb as a weak director, Whitten adopted the farm labor problem as the focal point of the school's educational organizing mission. Beginning in October 1925, the college initiated a drive to furnish the sharecroppers' union with scholarships. In return, the STFU passed a warm resolution of appreciation during its state convention in January 1936. Shortly thereafter John R. Butler, president of the union, joined the Commonwealth faculty in order to create a new course in southern farm labor problems. The union also sent seven of its members to the school, and by the spring quarter of 1936 fifteen more southerners, including eight tenant farmers, were enrolled at the labor college.[24]

Butler became active in all aspects of Commonwealth life. Prior to Commonwealth, he had worked as a tenant farmer, an oil field hand, and a country schoolteacher. He also earned a reputation as a fine speaker, which aided his organizing work for the STFU. Butler remained ever loyal to the union. He had written its constitution and refused to draw a salary for his union work during his first two years of service. Butler's course at Commonwealth attracted many students, quickly becoming the most popular, and in April 1936, he organized the STFU's Mena local. On May Day, he spoke at the school's annual celebration, and, in June, Butler and Whitten, as the college's delegates, attended both the Socialist party convention in Cleveland and the Minnesota Farmers and Laborers Association Convention in Chicago. In August 1936, Butler, still a Commoner, accepted the nomination as Socialist candidate for governor, along with Claude Williams for U.S. Senator, at the Socialist state convention held in Little Rock. As the *Fortnightly* boasted, the convention also passed a resolution commending "the efforts of Commonwealth College to orient itself toward the southern labor movement and to train workers and farmers for more effective work in the labor movement."[25]

Others were not so impressed. Mitchell, as well as other STFU officials, guarded a deep concern over such a close affiliation with Commonwealth. As loyal Socialists, they feared that union members, including Butler, would fall under the Communists' spell at the labor college. Reports from Mitchell's brother, Edwin, who was enrolled at the school, confirmed Mitchell's suspicions. Indeed, many Commoners maligned the STFU by criticizing Mitchell, a Socialist, and other union officers for not cooperating more with the Communist party. This factionalism culminated, in July 1936, in a comic-opera attempt by an overzealous and grossly misinformed sharecropper student to shoot Mitchell when he visited the school. Fortunately for Mitchell, the assailant proved to be a poor marksman, missing with all his pistol shots; Mitchell wisely fled the scene when the attacker went for his shotgun. This incident convinced Mitchell, along with other union leaders, that a plot was afoot by the Communists at Commonwealth to expropriate the union. Mitchell recalls with alarm: "This was the beginning of my anticommunist paranoia. Prior to that time, I had welcomed communists and socialists alike, considering them to have the same ideas. However, assassination of political rivals had never been a part of the Socialist party program in America or elsewhere in the world." Whitten, as Mitchell recollects, "was fearful that both the college and the union would be hurt if it became known that a union member had tried to kill the secretary of the STFU at Commonwealth."[26] The STFU reluctantly acceded to Whitten's plea not to publicize the unfortunate affair.

Relations between the union and the school, however, experienced a major setback as a result of the incident. Mitchell and the STFU hierarchy made preparations to sever their ties with Commonwealth. And another round of political attacks by the Arkansas legislature on the school only made matters worse. Commonwealth, according to Cobb and Grubbs, was well on its way to becoming an outcast from the southern labor movement. Of course, overlooked was the fact that one of the reasons the state legislature harrassed the school was because of its assistance to the STFU. STFU officials, as well as officers from other unions, complained bitterly about the existence of a communist faction at the labor college, and further criticized the school for favoring students from other sections of the country. Because of this tendency, they reasoned, Commonwealth failed to come to grips with fundamental regional problems and commit itself totally to the southern labor movement. Amidst this turmoil, Whitten resigned as the school's director, and Commonwealth teetered on the brink of oblivion. [27]

Commonwealth's critics further castigated the school as politically and culturally chauvinistic towards the South. Yet this characterization of the school represented an exaggeration. Indeed, Commonwealth did concern itself with the problems of southern workers and farmers, but within the context of the larger labor movement. Commoners were all too aware of the liabilities of being provincial. Instead, the problems of southern workers, as they saw it, stemmed from broader social relationships, and worker solidarity served as the ultimate solution for southern workers. This was why the labor college strove for the expansion of the labor movement and the dream of a new social order.

By December 1936, Mitchell and other concerned southern union leaders had made a decision about the future of Commonwealth; they would reorganize the school and formally integrate it into the southern labor movement. They approached the Arkansas, Oklahoma, and Texas state labor federations and the UMW to request that these unions assume control of the college. That proposal elicited only a lukewarm response. Commonwealth's communist reputation, although wildly exaggerated, proved the stumbling block.

The correspondence of Howard Kestor, an STFU official, clearly prescribed Commonwealth's new direction. Kester's father had been a small businessman and active church member in Beckley, West Virginia. Kester graduated with honors from Lynchburg College in 1925 and entered Princeton Theological Seminary, but was asked not to return for a second year because of a sermon he had delivered to the student body denouncing the National Association of Manufacturers. Kester enrolled at Vanderbilt University's divinity school in 1926. He became secretary of the YMCA, led a protest against imperialism in China, and promptly lost his job. For several months, he worked as southern secretary for the Fellowship for Reconciliation. Kester began his work for the STFU on a full-time basis in November 1934. By that time, he was, in Mitchell's words, "a legend in the South." An obvious embarrassment to his bourgeois and pious father, Kester had run for Congress as a Socialist, investigated lynchings, and participated in a coal miners' strike.[28] According to Kester, Commonwealth's "revolutionary" posture proved to be the sore point for STFU officialdom, but he wanted to avoid Commonwealth's becoming "just 'another labor school' in the hands of reactionary trade unionists which would not serve the cause in the forthcoming industrialization of the South." Rather, Kester and other STFU officials desired the labor college to "be progressive and substantially militant," surely reflecting the noncommunist left.[29] To facilitate this transition, Roger Baldwin, of the ACLU and the school's advisory council, suggested that Claude Williams, a defrocked Presbyterian minister and radical labor leader in Arkansas, should be considered for the job as director of Commonwealth. Mitchell at first opposed William's appointment because of his alleged communist leanings, but later relented.

Williams, much like A. J. Muste, had experienced a profound spiritual and intellectual transformation from fundamentalist religious beliefs to social activism. Born and raised in Tennessee, Williams prepared for the ministry in the traditional manner, attending Bethel College and the cumberland Presbyterian Church's seminary school. He began his ministry, upon graduation in 1924, in a small Tennessee town and soon achieved a reputation as a spellbinding preacher. By the late 1920s, Williams, feeling restless, took a leave of absence to attend the Vanderbilt University divinity school, where his conversion to the social gospel began to unfold. Returning to his tiny conservative flock, Williams quickly alienated them by preaching about racial and social equality, trade unionism, and social activism. In early 1930, Williams moved to a new church in Paris, Arkansas. Here he found a poor and demoralized congregation with a church in need of extensive repairs. The congregation needed to be rebuilt spiritually and politically. Departing from the fundamentalist path, Williams and his wife, Joyce, organized social activities and recreational events, opened a library in the church, and assisted coal miners in their unionizing campaign. With his religious beliefs now translated into social activism, Williams's church became a focal point for the entire community—a place for meetings, a refuge from repression, a retreat for study and self-improvement. These activities, of course, antagonized the local Presbyterian elders, mine operators, and businessmen. Williams, for all of his good intentions, was removed from his pastorate by the Presbyterian General Assembly in 1934.

Williams now totally committed himself to social activism. He and his wife moved to Fort Smith, an industrial city in western Arkansas, where they joined in the organization of the unemployed into the Workers' Alliance. Authorities arrested Claude for organizing and participating in a hunger march, and sent him to jail for a month. After his release, he moved to Little Rock and was commissioned by the STFU's leaders, the Workers' Alliance, and Socialists and Communists alike to organize a training school for black and white leaders of the labor movement in Arkansas. The school, opened in 1936 with the pretentious title of the "New Era School of Social Action and Prophetic Religion," blended social and religious views with field work. Courses included labor history, drama, union democracy, political science, "prophetic religion," race and class relations, imperialism, and trade-union organization.

Williams's success with this educational venture and his newly acquired prominence—due to a highly publicized flogging by planters for his organizing efforts among sharecroppers—led him to be recommended for the directorship of Commonwealth College.[30] Williams appeared before the STFU's national executive council on June 18, 1937, with a proposal to realign Commonwealth College on a strictly union basis. The council endorsed his plan and appointed him to the council. The linkage between the STFU and the labor college appeared to be institutionalized, and the reorganization officially took place on August 15, 1937.

According to Williams's proposal, which strongly echoed Kester's recommendations, Commonwealth would devote itself to a direct alliance with regional trade and agricultural unions. The plan, as outlined in the November 15 issue of the *Fortnightly*, called for the addition of nine nonresident members to the school's executive board, specifically representatives from the United Cannery, Agricultural, Packing, and Allied Workers of America, the International Typographical Union, the Bricklayers' Union, the United Electrical and Radio Workers, the Citrus Workers' Organizing Committee, the AFT, and the STFU. Further, Commonwealth now recruited 75 percent of its student body from the South, ensuring that it trained local worker–students as organizers. Commonwealth's efforts earned it national recognition, with *Time* magazine hailing the move: "Southern labor organizations will be asked to help in Commonwealth's activities, which will include establishing close educational relations with city and rural unions of garment workers, miners, oil, textile, lumber, maritime, iron, steel, and automobile workers." In conjunction with the STFU, Commonwealth agreed to provide extension courses for sharecroppers, both white and black. In addition, Williams promised "publicly that political organizations would no longer be permitted to function on campus."[31] The nagging problem of a communist faction at Commonwealth appeared to be finally resolved.

Relations between the school and the union remained far from harmonious. STFU socialist officials appeared skeptical about Williams and Commonwealth, especially since Williams had reportedly appeared at a union meeting in September 1937 brandishing his Communist party card. Still, during that fall quarter, Commonwealth seemed to have become a genuine resident labor school strictly devoted to southern labor. The college conducted an extension course in October, and the STFU sent several people to the school in November for a special six-week course on sharecropper problems. In January 1938, the college sponsored a special four-week session for farm organization members. This cooperation between the school and the union was shortlived, however. Throughout the next several months, STFU officials complained that Williams had failed to closely coordinate his activities with the union. For example, during National Sharecroppers' Week, March 6 to 13, 1938, Williams made speeches that conflicted in intent with those scheduled by STFU leaders. Finally, in August 1938, J. R. Butler, president of the Tenant Farmers' Union, claimed that he had accidently discovered a document, in Williams's possession, outlining a plot by Commonwealth's communist faction to subvert the union.[32]

The story broke in numerous newspapers on August 22, 1938, generating a heated exchange of letters between the union and the school. Butler, feeling betrayed, wrote to Williams that same day demanding his resignation from the STFU executive council.

> Ever since the reorganization of Commonwealth College when
> you became its Director I have defended you against all charges of

Communism and against all charges of attempting to disrupt the Southern Tenant Farmers' Union. I did these things on the basis of your word of honor (such as it was) to me. . . . The enclosed report shows conclusively that you have connived and that you are still attempting to connive with the Communist party to "capture" the Southern Tenant Farmers' Union for the Communist Party.

Butler also submitted his resignation to Commonwealth. Williams responded to Butler on August 25 by admitting that a document, formulated by a communist student at the school, did exist and that it did indeed delineate a plan to infiltrate the STFU. But Williams added that he had officially disapproved of the idea and, moreover, it had represented nothing more than an abstract exercise: "It was merely a tentative proposal of an individual in class work of the school's program as a possible basis for and a suggestion of a possible source of support and was submitted along with several other individual appraisals for and suggestions of possible sources of support." Williams concluded by stressing that neither he nor Commonwealth's faculty desired to "move into" or "capture" the STFU. Williams's assurances appeared to mollify Butler, who promptly withdrew his request for Williams's resignation from the executive council of the union. [33]

Kester, however, remained unconvinced and intervened, pressing charges himself against Williams. Butler subsequently renewed his request for Williams's resignation from the union's executive council, but Williams refused. The exchange of letters and stream of press releases echoed what had transpired between Brookwood Labor College and the AFL a decade earlier, with a similar outcome. Williams appeared before the STFU executive council on September 16 and 17, 1938, and flatly denied all the charges lodged against him and the school. He submitted notarized documents substantiating his assertions and presented Ralph Fields, the Commoner who had authored the incriminating statement. Fields readily admitted to writing the document as a class essay. But Butler testified against Williams, calling him a Communist and accusing him of directing the communist conspiracy against the STFU. The council voted unanimously to expel Williams from the union. Williams attempted an appeal and wrote to Roger Baldwin, a key member of the school's advisory board, rebutting the union's charges. It was all in vain. [34]

Not all of the blame can be heaped upon Commonwealth. Grubbs points out that, in addition to Williams, the union purged three other members of the union's executive council. Williams claimed that he and the other expelled members had voiced opposition to the union's growing bureaucratic tendencies. As Grubbs explicates it, STFU officials had approached the CIO for recognition and help in its organizing campaigns. CIO officials "ordered the public disavowal of Commonwealth as the price of discussing CIO affiliation, [and] the STFU leaders obeyed."[35] Raymond and Charlotte Koch corroborate this view; that is, the socialist STFU, not "communist" Commonwealth, broke with the united front, the rationale being that the STFU needed to do this to ensure affiliation with the CIO. In spite of the tragic outcome, the Kochs fondly remember their assistance to the sharecroppers, not all of which was academic or political:

> How would it be possible to measure what it meant to several cotton croppers to experience brief surcease from unrewarding backbreaking labor and substandard eating; to sit in a dentist's chair and have the innards of their mouths probed and reconstructed without being first asked whether they could pay; to be professionally fitted for glasses instead of picking a pair in the dime store; to associate so intimately with people from all over the world; to have their agonies, struggles, and accomplishments understood and appreciated by scholars whose fingers have never touched raw cotton bolls.[36]

Regardless of the perspective, relations between the STFU and Commonwealth, from the beginning, proved to be unsteady at best and destructive at worst. Factionalism assuredly contributed to the final rupture, but neither the union nor the school benefited. The communist United Cannery, Agricultural, Packing, and Allied Workers of America (UCAPAWA) absorbed the STFU in September 1937, but by March 1939 the STFU had seceded. Commoners gleefully claimed that the STFU broke from the CIO for the same reason that the union had parted ways with Commonwealth; as Williams pointed out in the *Commoner*: "The 'secession' from the CIO was to be expected. It has been apparent for some time that the Memphis [STFU] leaders were planning to do just this. Their red-baiting of the cannery workers and the CIO is in line with their red-baiting of Commonwealth College and progressive leaders of the sharecroppers."[37] However, Grubbs and Honey soberly point out that the differences between the STFU and UCAPAWA appeared more complex, encompassing dues rates, jurisdictional questions, autonomy, and internal bickering within the STFU itself. Sadly, the union withered away, maintaining only its name for several years. Meanwhile, Commonwealth lost what little legitimacy it had in the southern labor movement. Other unions followed the STFU example and withdrew their support from the college. The result proved to be tragic; the school's very reason for existence depended on a close alliance with organized labor. The remainder of the college's history, from 1938 to 1940, was little more than a death struggle.

Besides factionalism, other factors contributed to Commonwealth's demise. The school, in its latter years, lacked strong leadership, the result, to a great extent, of its nagging financial problems. The formal curriculum had disintegrated. Raymond and Charlotte Koch recall that "some dramatic expeditions, a few lecture junkets, and a single, successful, off-campus interracial conference were the high points of educational achievement during this period."[38] Instead of providing the intellectual leadership so desperately needed, Williams spent most of his time scouring the country in vain attempts to secure financial support for the school. The fiscal problems dominated his correspondence: "The college has been living principally on fried egg-plant for the last three weeks excepting a neighbor's cow which fortunately got choked to death day before yesterday, the carcass of which we purchased on credit for ten dollars providing meat over the weekend."[39]

Although the *Commoner* attempted to paint an optimistic picture between 1938 and 1940, the school was slipping into an abyss. In August 1939, Williams resigned as director, claiming health reasons. Yet, as Grubbs emphasizes, "Communist party members at Commonwealth became so blatant about their affiliations in 1939 and 1940 that Claude Williams, fearing legal reprisals and resenting Communist as well as Socialist 'sectarianism,' resigned as director."[40] Commonwealth appeared to be saved once more from oblivion when the *Commoner* announced in July 1940 that the New Theatre League would assume control of the school's facilities in order to create "a southern labor theatre." Based in New York City, the league served as a clearinghouse for 400 "new theatres" spread throughout the nation.[41] This last-gasp effort to sustain Commonwealth proved to be futile, however. Another, yet more ominous, political threat loomed on the horizon.

Before the merger could be consumated, Commonwealth confronted another reactionary onslaught, but unlike previously, the school lacked both labor and liberal support. The Arkansas American

Legion demanded that Commonwealth be closed immediately. Reverend L. D. Summers likewise intensified his agitation. Finally, on September 12, 1940, the state filed an anarchy charge against the college; Commonwealth allegedly had disseminated propaganda which encouraged the overthrow of the U.S. government. Five days later the first of a series of raids was conducted on the school to gather further incriminating evidence. On September 23, 1940, two more charges were brought against the college. Commonwealth, it was claimed, had failed to comply with a state law requiring all educational institutions to fly an American flag. Furthermore, the school had displayed an unlawful emblem; this consisted of a hammer and sickle, made from iron scraps, innocuously embedded in a concrete slab at the base of the water tower. The court denied the college's request for a change of venue, ruled Commonwealth guilty of three misdemeanors, and levied a $2,500 fine. An appeal to the Arkansas supreme court failed. The school's property was auctioned at a public sale on December 4 to pay the fine. Summers purchased the school's library collection, containing 5,442 volumes, for $360; it has never been seen since that day. [42]

Work People's College Closes Its Doors

Unlike Brookwood and Commonwealth, Work People's College withstood the financial hardships of the Depression but, like its two counterparts, finally fell victim to sectarianism, a lack of sustained leadership, and the growing acculturation of its Finnish constituency.

Work People's College had reached its apex prior to the First World War, before Brookwood and Commonwealth even existed. Student enrollment steadily increased from 130 in 1911–12 to 147 in 1913–14. Guss Aakula recalled, "These years were indeed the most flourishing ones in the history of the Institute, and at the peak, the faculty consisted of eight members." After its transition from socialism to industrial unionism, attendance dipped to 38 but climbed to 65 students during the 1916–17 school year. Although Work People's College managed to attract some non-Finns, it never recaptured its prewar following. Between 1920 and 1925, the average annual enrollment numbered some 70 students. This figure decreased to 48 between 1926 and 1930. By 1936, that total had dwindled to a mere 36 students. [43]

Work People's College declined because it isolated itself from contemporary radicalism, the New Deal, and its ethnic base. Its unswerving loyalty to the IWW had alienated it from the Finnish radical community. The college had disavowed any connections with the Socialist party and Finnish Socialists by 1917. The school also played no direct part in the vital Finnish cooperative movement of the 1920s and 1930s. Communism too was anathema to the Finnish Wobblies during the 1920s; indeed, this reflected the stand of most Wobblies, as Melvyn Dubofsky has summarized:

> Still dedicated to syndicalism and to nonviolent direct action, they found repugnant a movement based upon control of the state and the violent seizure of power. Committed to the concept of industrial democracy, they found alien the Bolshevik principles of the dictatorship of the proletariat and democratic centralism. Opposed to all forms of coercion and bureaucracy, they looked upon the Soviet system with deep suspicion.

The IWW and Work People's College likewise rejected the New Deal legislation of the 1930s and refused to support the CIO movement of the 1930s. Wobblies criticized both Section 7a of the National Industrial Recovery Act (NIRA) and the 1935 Wagner (National Labor Relations) Act for placing government precisely where it did not belong, in labor-management relations. Ironically, Dubofsky writes, "the IWW's critique of the Wagner Act was in fact remarkably like that issued by the National Association of Manufacturers!" As a result, the IWW was left behind in the successful campaign for industrial unionism. [44]

Other problems plagued the college. By 1930, almost 90 percent of all Finnish immigrants ten years of age or older could speak English. Second generation, English-speaking Finns avoided Work People's College, not only because, like virtually all children of immigrants, they wanted to escape Old World influences and to be "real" Americans, but also because, as Douglas Ollila argues, they "were often deeply ashamed of their immigrant parents' radicalism." They chose, instead, to attend the public schools, since "attendance at the Work People's College was not calculated to give Finnish-American youth status in their own peer groups." [45] The hegemony that their parents and grandparents had tried so desperately to counteract proved to be too powerful and pervasive. In addition, Carl Ross suggests that the school, like Brookwood and Commonwealth, suffered because of lack of stable leadership. The arrest of Leo Laukki and his subsequent flight to the Soviet Union, eliminated the last real Marxist theoretician at Work People's College. And except for Fred Thompson, the record is unclear concerning sustained leadership at the college. Finally, and perhaps most importantly, unlike Brookwood and Commonwealth, Work People's College never cultivated a broader base of ideological support that extended beyond the Finnish-American community of the Midwest. The destiny of Work People's College rested, for better or worse, on the attitudes and situation of the Finnish radical community. And since the school depended on Finnish radicals, yet had declared its independence from Finnish Socialists and Communists, it had really narrowed its base.

Work People's College evaded death stubbornly, however. Although regular classes were suspended in September 1941, summer classes continued for a while. Because of a housing shortage during the Second World War, the federal government leased the remaining building in 1941 and converted it to an apartment dwelling for war industry workers. The government terminated its lease in 1950, and the school's board of directors elected to sell the building for $14,000 in 1953. The board continued to purchase outstanding shares from stockholders and in 1963 dispersed the remaining college funds.[46] Work People's College, which had avoided the fiscal woes that plagued Brookwood and Commonwealth, had fallen prey to sectarianism.

Financial instability as well as political repression and sectarianism contributed to the demise of the labor colleges. On the one hand, the institutional autonomy of Brookwood and Commonwealth caused these schools to rely on union scholarships and sponsorship, AFPS subsidies, self-sufficiency efforts, and liberal donations. The Great Depression dissolved these sources of support, exacerbating an already tenuous fiscal situation. On the other hand, Work People's College maintained a unique and effective cooperative arrangement. Still, funding concerns never remained totally divorced from political harassment and factionalism. Bourgeois opposition, sometimes relying on state mechanisms, forced the schools into a defensive posture, diverting precious energy and resources to combat these attacks. As we saw in Chapter 5, the colleges' political and financial bases of support narrowed as a result. Sectarianism, reflecting general left fragmentation, as described in Chapter 6 and this chapter, distracted labor college supporters, teachers, and students from their larger social and educational goals and further constricted political and fiscal backing.

Part IV
An Educational Legacy

8

Achievements of the Labor Colleges

We are both engaged, body and soul, in our local's activities.
—Fritz Hohn, former Commonwealth
student, *Fortnightly* (1927)

HOW SUCCESSFUL were the labor colleges? Did they achieve what they had been set up to do? The schools' founders had formulated two basic objectives that reflected, they believed, the social and educational needs of the working class. First, the schools were expected to become indispensable to the training of labor leaders and activists, who were needed if workers were to be organized and brought into the union movement. Second, they hoped that with strong and inspired leadership, the working class could acquire the vision and the solidarity that would culminate in a new social order—an economy controlled by workers and free from exploitation.

Labor Leaders and Activists

A good way to evaluate the colleges' success in educating a cadre is to review the observations of those students who kept a record of their educational experiences and their activities after leaving school. Although we are able to trace the achievements of only a few, school notebooks and other accounts—such as teachers' course outlines— give us a glimpse of the intellectual and political development of the labor college students. Acknowledging our limited resources, we can attempt to answer two questions: What did the students learn at the labor colleges? and, How did they use what they had learned?[1]

249

One Brookwood student, Joseph Ozanic, who took copious notes, gives us a rare personal glimpse into the student's perspective.[2] Born of Polish immigrant parents in 1895, Ozanic followed his father and brothers into the Illinois coal pits at the age of eight and did not become a Brookwood student until his mid-thirties. Spanning the period between December 1930 and April 1931, his notes reveal an intense educational experience, with considerable reading and many writing assignments. Ozanic's notebook contains a daily schedule that gives evidence of a long and hard school day: Classes began at 8:45 A.M. and, except for breaks for lunch and dinner, ran until 9:00 P.M. When compared with his instructors' course outlines, Ozanic's notes, replete with definitions, statistics, flow charts, and occasional doodles, indicate that he gained a clear grasp of the basic concepts underlying each course of study.

Ozanic's notes reveal much about the theoretical courses in the Brookwood curriculum. The notes for Ozanic's economics course, taught by J. C. Kennedy, reflect a distinct Marxist orientation in Kennedy's criticisms of capitalism and his emphasis on cooperation instead of competition as a basis for a healthy economy. Ozanic's records for a course entitled "The Trade Union Movement" stress an "international" approach to unionism. Clearly, the instructor's focus was meant to instill in Brookwood students—and, by extension, American workers—a sense of solidarity with workers in other countries. Ozanic's comments on David Saposs's course in American labor history tended to be critical of the AFL—a longstanding Brookwood attitude. According to Saposs, the Federation wielded seemingly "complete power" over its locals through a false claim to wide authority. When Saposs's students closely examined the AFL constitution, they learned that the Federation was actually quite restricted in its power. This was a revelation for Ozanic; he wrote in his notebook that the AFL had "no right to dictate any local policy." Furthermore, Ozanic learned that many of the assumptions of Federation leaders were unfounded. They opposed industrial unionism because they believed "that the machinery of present Trade Unionism is sufficient if handled properly." The AFL hierarchy, Ozanic's notes continued, "claim it is impossible to organize [industrial-union] membership if labor organizations fluctuate according to industrial conditions." Ozanic disputed these assumptions. In "Basic Industry," a quasi-economics course also taught by Kennedy, Ozanic learned the principles of industrial organization from the top down. His notes provided a detailed breakdown of the

components of an industrial complex, including the relationships between location, raw materials, and distribution. The rudiments of scientific management were also reviewed. Ozanic's information about
the workplace encompassed ethnic and racial data as well.

Ozanic enrolled in several practical courses, public speaking and
English among them, but his entries on "Field Work," principally directed by Louis Budenz, appeared to dominate the notebook. The
course centered on the basics of carrying out a successful strike campaign. Ozanic listed committees—for example, steering, publicity, relief, and demonstration—as essential. Subsumed under his notes on
field work was a brief comment on "What a Labor Leader Should Be in
Public Life and in Private Life." The comment included the following
admonitions: labor leaders were to remain above reproach and ever
watchful for potential entrapments, planned by capital and the press,
intended to defame their character. Labor leaders, particularly during
a strike, were to present a model of behavior by avoiding alcoholic
beverages and "sex snares." Labor wars, to be sure, were fraught with
many dangers. On a more sobering note, a successful organizer was
always to be methodical. As Ozanic wrote, "A knowledge of human
nature [is] more essential than technical knowledge." He further commented: "When going out to organize, always learn psychology of
constituency. Don't have [a] set cock and bull idea to put over on anyone. . . . Be a worker; be with them; be one of them. Learn to know
them. Eat when they do. Sleep when they do." One of Ozanic's last
notations, on April 1, 1931, spelled out, in no uncertain terms, the
mission of the labor college student; that is, to go "from education to
Action. Build a rank-and-file organization of dues paying [members]
. . . build a real movement to offset capitalism."

Ozanic's notes, containing such inspired directives, witness to the
seriousness of his ambitions, which he largely fulfilled. In 1932, upon
leaving Brookwood, he became a charter member and active supporter
of the Progressive Mine Workers of America (PMWA), founded by
rank-and-file Illinois miners opposed to the UMW. Ozanic helped to
direct the PMWA's organizing drives in Illinois from 1932 to 1935 and
won recognition from his fellow unionists as a leader. He became a
member of the PMWA's District No. 1 executive board in 1935, and in
1936 won the presidency of District No. 1. [3]

Other labor college students put their knowledge to use as well.
C. Mauritz Erkkila, a former student at Work People's College, insists
that his labor college background gave him "insight into the society

in which we live." "The economic system," he adds after a lapse of more than fifty years, "has not changed much." He points out further, "Work People's College, with its few teachers and small student body, has made [an] outstanding contribution toward creating a more just and equitable society." After his graduation from Work People's College in 1935, Erkkila went on to serve as the executive director of a federation of twenty-six consumer cooperatives in Minnesota, and today remains active in the cooperative and nuclear freeze movements. He credits these continuing economic and political interests to his early training at Work People's College.

For Erkkila, it "was no accident that many students of Work People's College became activists and leaders in union, cooperative, and local civic affairs." The school supplied thousands of graduates who became organizers, newspaper reporters, speakers, propagandists, and managers for local consumer cooperatives in Minnesota, Wisconsin, and Upper Michigan. John Wiita, for instance, became the editor of important radical Finnish publications, such as *Socialisti* and *Tyomies* ("Worker"), and generally offered outstanding leadership in the Finnish-American labor movement. Other activists who were trained at the school and offered direction to the IWW movement were August Wesley, Guss Aakula, Ivar Vapaa, George Humon, Fred Jaakola, Matti Kainu, and Jack Ujanen. Many social halls among the Finns are still going strong today, largely thanks to the efforts of former Work People's College students.

Not all students, of course, fulfilled the school's stated objectives. Fred Thompson expresses disappointment with the results of the school because "it did not give the IWW a flock of well-trained, effective organizers." Yet even Thompson admits that the school supplied numerous managers for the cooperative movement, as well as others to organize workers for the IWW in the Iron Range and in Cleveland. Still others worked for the CIO. As Thompson recalls, "the students provided the leaven for the labor movement through their work in the CIO organizing campaigns." Finally, a few students pursued conventional careers in academia. After completing his studies, Walfrid Jokinen went on to attend the University of Minnesota and to teach sociology at Louisiana State University. In spite of his apparent academic ambitions, he remained loyal to his past. Jokinen wrote extensively about Finnish immigrants and their various social and economic activities.[4] Thus, Work People's College not only grew from the socialist inspiration and leadership that came from Finland, but it also supplemented it, with a few exceptions, by developing new leadership in the United States.

Commonwealth students also went into other meaningful careers. The November 15, 1932, issue of the *Fortnightly* reported that several former students had organized a workers' theater, worked at Hull House in Chicago, and participated in unemployed councils and demonstrations, hunger marches, and farmers' movements. The article concluded, "Besides the above, Commonwealth learns that its former students are working for the cause of the common people in the spheres of activity where they can be of most use to the labor movement."[5] This involvement encompassed workers' education, with Bill Buttrick joining the staff of Highlander Folk School in Tennessee; and the labor press, with Jackie Kwallek editing the *Wheel* for the Teamsters Union in Lexington, Kentucky. These activities extended to other countries as well. Bobbie Reed fought in the infamous Spanish Civil War, and in June 1938 it was reported that John Field, a former Commoner, had died in Spain as a member of the Abraham Lincoln Brigade.

Yet, as with Work People's College, a few graduates, in spite of the school's claims, chose not to return to the labor movement. Irving Weissman, for example, originally from Brooklyn, attended Commonwealth for four years and later enrolled for graduate work in sociology and labor history at the University of Wisconsin. However, the majority of Commonwealth students appeared to fulfill their projected roles, selflessly serving workers. Fritz and Gertrude Hohn strongly reflected the activism that they had learned as students at Commonwealth, writing to the *Fortnightly* about their organizing experiences in Paterson:

> We are both engaged, body and soul, in our local's activities. Gertrude is secretary of the lady members' branch, and is trying to make this rather novel enterprise a success. I have been elected to the position of vice-president of our union. Both of us belong to various committees, and we are busy with some sort of a meeting almost every night. Just now we are organizing basketball and bowling teams. We find it difficult to keep the membership interested in the movement, and we introduce as many social activities as possible because we must prove that the union means more to its members than just a machine for securing higher wages and better working conditions.[6]

Of all of the labor colleges, Brookwood earned the most outstanding reputation for producing numerous labor leaders and activists with significant roles in the labor movement. In the course of more than fifteen years, Brookwood trained six to eight hundred persons who later occupied responsible positions in labor and social movements as organizers, business agents, union officials, labor educators, and labor journalists. As one graduate wrote in the Brookwood anniversary review in 1936:

When Akron [Ohio] rubber workers go on strike, Brookwood grads are there to do their part. We have organized auto workers in Detroit; shirtworkers in New York and Pennsylvania; hosiery workers in the South; machinists in Los Angeles; coal miners in Illinois; garment workers throughout the United States. Every available Brookwooder was called on during the organizing campaigns following the NRA. . . . The nationwide textile strike also kept us busy.

When workers' education, almost dormant, took a spurt in the last few years, graduates of Brookwood helped supply the need for teachers. Heading local labor colleges, teaching for international unions or on the federal relief program we have done our share to bring the message of trade unionism to the millions of new recruits to the labor movement.

In the columns of the labor press you will find the names of many Brookwooders. They are Federated Press pages, or, perhaps, handling publicity for a strike in which they are active.

In a survey conducted that same year, a hundred graduates responded. The results were as follows:

Eighty-four of us have recently participated in strikes or organization campaigns; 54 have held full-time positions in unions; 49 have been arrested for labor activity; 65 have written for or edited labor papers; 76 have taught workers' classes and organized workers' education centers; 74 have been active in labor political organizations; 41 have helped in the organization of the unemployed; 17 have taken part in the consumers' cooperative movement; and the same number have worked in farm organizations. [7]

Individual accounts of Brookwood graduates further attest to their devotion to the labor movement. According to the *Brookwood Review*,

Bob Roberts, a 1932 graduate, had been arrested and sentenced to six months at hard labor for organizing activities for the National Miners' Union in Gallup, New Mexico. The same issue also carried a story of how three Brookwooders had been accused of conspiring to incite to riot, as well as rioting, trespassing, and vagrancy because of their organizational work among hosiery workers in High Point, North Carolina. Found innocent, they established the Carolina School for Workers after their release from jail. It was patterned, of course, after Brookwood. Although not a residential college, that school replicated Brookwood's curriculum and used its classroom materials.

Many Brookwooders also distinguished themselves as workers' education teachers. Four Brookwood graduates held classes in the Kanawha Valley of West Virginia for coal miners during the summer of 1932. Brookwood sent two faculty members to assist in the educational effort. "Your Job and Your Pay," a Brookwood publication, was used as a text. Later, Elizabeth D. Hawes, a 1933 graduate, became the extension director of the Highlander School. Brookwood graduates also helped to found or gained influential positions in six eastern labor colleges, located in Philadelphia, Pittsburgh, Wilkes-Barre (Pennsylvania), Baltimore, Shenandoah, and Salem (Massachusetts). James Morris insists, "There is evidence, meager to be sure, that some unionists considered these and other labor colleges to be 'subsidiaries of the Brookwood College.' "[8]

Some labor leaders noted Brookwood's high visibility in these struggles. For example, Jacob S. Potofsky, ACWA president, praised the efforts of Brookwood graduates in the massive 1933 Shirt Campaign that covered many states. In 1936, he recalled:

> Those were unforgettable days; picket lines, investigations, trucks
> filled with singing girls, arrests, and hearings crowded every hour.
> The shirt makers marched as a victorious army, from Allentown
> to Shamokin, from Pottsville to Pottstown, Hazleton, Reading,
> Myerstown. . . . The campaign was by no means confined to Penn-
> sylvania. New Jersey and Connecticut were in it practically from
> the start. New centers have come under its protection in an ever
> widening circle: Troy, Albany, Kingston, in upper New York State;
> Reading, Lebanon, Elizabethton, Pennsylvania; Knoxville and
> Cincinnati, Providence and Morgantown.[9]

In their efforts to smash shirt industry sweatshops, union officials "enlisted" the services of former Brookwooders such as Josephine Kaczor in Shamokin, Pennsylvania; Mike Demchack in Mount Carmel, Pennsylvania; Philomene Reinsch in both Scranton and Wilkes-Barre; and Larry Heimbach in Allentown, Pennsylvania. Leo Sitko, Johnny Coveleski, Elizabeth "Zilla" Hawes, Griselda Kuhlman, Mike Schulman, and Rose Greenstein served on the field staff as well. "When we went to Providence to organize a shirt factory," Potofsky remembered, "our only contact was a Brookwood student. The Providence mill was organized, and along with it other shops in Fall River and New Bedford. Here another Brookwooder, Tom Flavell, did a fine piece of work." Potofsky concluded his remarks by encouraging Brookwood to continue to "turn out such able and efficient people" for the cause of labor.

The Labor Colleges' Impact on the Labor Movement

Clearly, the labor colleges produced many graduates who assumed active roles in the union movement. But it is equally clear that the labor colleges did not achieve their larger dream of broad social change. A new social order, as they—and the noncommunist left—envisioned it, did not come into being. Nonetheless, many labor college graduates successfully altered the structure of the American labor movement. Many Work People's College graduates became organizers and leaders of the CIO. While it stood for industrial unionism, the CIO departed profoundly from the IWW brand of industrial unionism because it concentrated solely on organizing unskilled and semiskilled workers and largely ignored fundamental social reform. Nevertheless, in spite of the Wobbly ideology prevalent at the Work People's College and the school's ideological differences with the CIO, these graduates felt that the CIO adopted some of the basic premises of the industrial-union movement.

Still, of the three colleges here discussed, it was Brookwood that fielded the most numerous and prominent CIO activists. "Brookwood," Thomas B. Brooks writes, "trained an impressive number of people who played a leading role in the founding of the Congress of Industrial Organizations and have since filled many positions of leadership in the unions."[10] Among them were Julius Hochman, an ILGWU vice-president; Rose Pesotta, an ILGWU organizer active in the Akron sit-down strikes by rubber workers; and Clinton Golden, who, with other Brookwood graduates, was active in founding the Steelworkers' Union. Many less-renowned graduates became involved in the CIO movement also. One former Brookwooder, Kenneth Koch, received a severe clubbing by a "hatchet gang" hired by the Wierton Steel Company for his organizing activities among its employees. However, Katherine Pollak, qualifies the generalization of labor historians like Brooks and others: "While various people from Brookwood played a role in the CIO . . . the [CIO] movement was so much bigger than anything Brookwood could have promoted." [11] Brookwood did not single-handedly create the CIO, but it did train a great many key organizers and leaders for it.

THE 1929 SOUTHERN TEXTILE WORKERS' STRIKE

The exploits of Alfred Hoffman, an organizer in the 1929–30 southern textile strikes, clearly illustrate the uncharted, and often dangerous, waters that former Brookwooders plied in their organizing and strike campaigns. By the late 1920s, the southern Appalachian region and the Piedmont plains represented the predominant textile-producing area of the United States, particularly in rayon and cotton fibers and fabrics. Some 300,000 workers were employed in textiles, with 100,000 in North Carolina, 69,000 in South Carolina, and 25,000 in Tennessee. Building mills in the South enabled the textile industry to escape northern unionism and concomitant high labor costs. Moreover, labor was plentiful. The mill owners had at their disposal an oversupply of mill workers, which further depressed wages. With blacks generally barred from mill work, workers were either poor white tenant farmers or mountain people. They were largely of Anglo-Saxon heritage, longtime southerners who had previously eked out a living largely through subsistence farming. Imbued with a deep sense of individualism, they were fiercely independent. The mill owners, meanwhile, maintained absolute control over their mill villages, replicating, in many ways, the position of power formerly accorded to the ante-bellum plantation owners. [12] These differences were the source of serious labor conflict in the South.

Local walkouts dotted the whole Piedmont area, from Greenville, in eastern North Carolina, to Elizabethton, Tennessee, during the spring and summer of 1929. In the fall of 1930, as the nation was slipping deeper into the Depression, textile workers in Danville, Virginia, initiated a similar strike action. The workers protested against night work for women and children, company housing, long hours, low wages, company stores, and the stretch-out (speed-up) system. Approximately 18,000 workers participated in the walkouts, which local law enforcement officers were often hard-pressed to quell. This caused the state militias of North Carolina, South Carolina, Tennessee, and Virginia to enter the strike areas to crush the protests. This massive strike action, and the accompanying violence, can be likened only to the Great Steel Strike of 1919.

The Elizabethton strike, the first and the largest of the 1929 strikes, erupted suddenly on March 12. Before the strike was a week old, the town bristled with armed National Guardsmen. Brookwood graduate Alfred Hoffman, on the staff of the American Federation of Full-Fashioned Hosiery Workers in Durham, North Carolina, rushed in to organize a United Textile Workers (UTW) local, an affiliate of the AFL and the parent union of the Hosiery Workers. He found the task daunting. Working directly with the UTW, a small and weak union that preferred union-management cooperation rather than confrontation, proved to be frustrating. Although other contributions came from the AFL and the Emergency Committee for Strikers' Relief, a New York organization headed by Norman Thomas, the meagerness of the UTW's war chest especially hampered his efforts. But more serious impediments came from goons hired by the mill owners. Shortly after Hoffman's arrival in Elizabethton, a group of these "vigilantes" kidnapped him at gunpoint, blindfolded him, shoved him into a car, drove him across the state line into North Carolina, and threatened his life if he returned. Hoffman ignored those threats, arriving the following day, with an armed escort of workers, to resume his organizing activities. After several long months of tedious negotiations, picketing, and menacing militia patrols, the company finally crushed the union and blacklisted the strikers.

The early, heady strike news from Elizabethton, as well as from another strike in Gastonia, North Carolina, inspired textile workers in nearby Marion to organize a union. Representatives of the Marion mill workers traveled to Elizabethton to seek Hoffman's advice on organizing matters. On their return, the Marion workers held their first union meeting in mid-June, with Hoffman in attendance. The mill owners reacted to these unionizing efforts by discharging twenty-two of the most active union sympathizers. This precipitated a walkout on July 11, 1929. Hoffman had returned in the meantime to Elizabethton. Responding to a plea from Lawrence Hogan, a Marion leader, Hoffman tore himself away from the Tennessee conflict to rush to the assistance of the Marion workers. He found defiant strikers holding union meetings night and day. The assemblies took on the character of revivalist gatherings, with the singing of church hymns that were later transformed into strike songs; thousands of workers, singing in unison, paraded through the streets. An injunction was issued, which the workers disobeyed.

Yet, for all their zeal, the workers lacked practical strike experience. Hoffman wrote the press releases, organized picket lines, arranged mass meetings, made speeches, marched in parades, collected money, and distributed relief. In short, Hoffman had on his hands a difficult strike that he had not called himself. To make matters worse, the AFL offered little aid. A frustrated Hoffman returned to Durham to raise strike funds. Most of the money and assistance came from outside sources—namely, the Emergency Committee for Strikers' Relief, the Federal Council of Churches, the Quakers, the League for Industrial Democracy (LID), the Young Women's Christian Association, the Conference for Progressive Labor Action, and Brookwood Labor College.

Despite mass picketing, the mills reopened on August 19, and the governor of North Carolina ordered troops into Marion to protect the mills. The eviction of a striker and his family from their home on August 28 prompted the workers to protest by moving the furniture back into the house. Arriving quickly on the scene, the police arrested Hoffman and 148 other protestors on the charges of insurrection, rioting, and resisting arrest. By early September, the Marion strike had been quashed, and the workers were forced back into the mills.

Another skirmish, this time with fatalities, erupted on October 2 when workers staged a spontaneous strike outside the mill. When they refused to disperse, the sheriff fired tear gas into the crowd and the deputies opened fire. Three strikers were killed outright, three were mortally wounded, and twenty-five were seriously hurt. Witnesses claimed that no shots were fired by the strikers. The Marion strike was finally over. Yet the episode still had one final ignominious moment: on November 30, Hoffman was convicted of rioting, sentenced to thirty days in jail, and fined $1,000.

THE 1936 AUTO WORKERS' STRIKE

The General Motors sit-down of 1936, in Flint, Michigan, provides a case study of how some Brookwood graduates used their labor college training to serve the CIO movement.[13] Specifically, the Reuther brothers and Merlin D. Bishop, as leaders of the striking workers, illustrate the often direct connection between training at, or association with, the labor colleges and the cause of unionization and workers' rights.

By the 1930s, General Motors had grown to a corporation of colossal proportions, with sixty-nine automotive plants in thirty-five cities and fourteen states. Its total assets exceeded $1.5 billion. Its 171,711 hourly workers labored an average 40.5 hours per week for a wage of just over seventy-five cents an hour. On the surface, it appeared that the corporation treated its employees well, because this wage rate dwarfed the average hourly rate of fifty-five cents paid to production workers in all other manufacturing industries. Further, GM management, vehemently antiunion, had instituted, during the 1920s, an elaborate corporate welfare program, including subsidized housing, investment programs, insurance plans, and recreational activities, in an effort to nurture employee loyalty and discourage unionism. With the advent of the New Deal and prounion federal legislation, the corporation resorted to company unionism. Management infiltrated the plants with labor spies in an effort to resist independent unionization. These measures, particularly the complex espionage system, drove union organizing activities underground. Corporate efforts to thwart unionization appeared to be successful, because by early 1936 union membership in GM's Flint plants amounted to a paltry 120 members.

Worker dissatisfaction did exist, however. The speed of production, perhaps the major cause of the sit-down strike, exacted a horrible toll of amputated fingers, serious burns, nervous disorders, and countless other injuries. Irregular employment further disillusioned workers. For instance, from September 1933 to September 1934, almost 40 percent of GM's hourly employees worked less than twenty-nine weeks. Thus, the well-publicized high hourly wages of GM workers seldom translated into equally high annual earnings. Generally speaking, this lack of security profoundly undermined workers' allegiance to the company.

Brookwood Labor College graduates and ideals played important roles in the development of the United Auto Workers (UAW). Progressives in the union succeeded in supplanting AFL sympathizers at the UAW's second convention, held in April 1936, and immediately formulated an organizing agenda reflecting their outlook. Merlin Bishop, member of Brookwood's extension staff, joined the union in June as an educational director. Shortly thereafter, the UAW formally launched its organizing drive. When CIO and UAW leaders met in Pittsburgh in November and decided to intensify the organizing effort, they listed the following demands, which mirrored the objectives of the progressive element in the labor movement: the immediate establishment of collective bargaining, a seniority system, an eight-hour day, a forty-hour week, an annual salary, and the elimination of the speed-up. The organizing campaign, pushed by mass meetings, solicitation at factory games, home visits, and some successful sit-down or "quickie" strikes in November and December, experienced steady gains, amounting to 63,000 members by late December. A confrontation appeared imminent. [14]

Roy Reuther, Roy's older brother, Walter, and his younger brother, Victor, played significant roles; they were literally the offspring of the labor movement. Their father, a German immigrant, had served as an organizer for the United Brewery Workers and as president of the Ohio Valley Trades and Labor Assembly in Wheeling, West Virginia. The elder Reuther was also well acquainted with Eugene Debs and in 1919 visited him regularly during his incarceration at the Moundsville penitentiary, just south of Wheeling. The Reuther boys followed in their father's footsteps. They departed for Detroit in the late 1920s, found jobs in the auto industry, attended Wayne State University on a part-time basis, participated in socialist activities, and assisted Briggs strikers in early 1933. During the course of the strike, Walter and Victor cavalierly embarked on a bicycle tour of the world. Their travels included the Soviet Union, where they worked for sixteen months in a Gorki auto plant. While his brothers were touring Europe and the Soviet Union, Roy attended Brookwood Labor College and later enrolled in workers' education classes at the University of Wisconsin. In 1934, he conducted workers' education programs, first in Detroit and then in Flint.

All three brothers were eventually reunited at Brookwood Labor College. Walter and Victor found themselves unemployed when they returned to Detroit in the early fall of 1935. They undertook a lecture tour, under LID auspices, and then joined Roy at Brookwood. By that time, Roy was on the Brookwood staff. Walter and Victor, in addition to giving lectures about their Soviet experiences at the school, spent their time rekindling their friendship with Tucker Smith, then Brookwood's director. As Victor recalls, "We had known him through the peace movement and the LID, and I was very interested when he broached the possibility of my working with him on a Quaker project to establish a labor division within the Emergency Peace Campaign. This was an effort being made by many groups, including churches, to arouse the country to the dangers of war—an issue of enormous importance to me, and one with deep family and ideological roots." [15] Using Brookwood as his base of operations, Victor traveled across the country giving countless speeches. During the summer of 1936, he addressed the Southern Anti-War School held at Commonwealth College. Walter, meanwhile, continued to lecture at Brookwood and was even invited to join the school's instructional staff, but relinquished this opportunity for increased involvement with the organizing activities of the automotive union. He returned to Detroit and was elected to the General Executive Board of the UAW.

By November 1936, all three Reuthers were together, once again, and deeply involved in organizing efforts for the UAW. Walter concentrated his organizing activities in Detroit while Roy left Brookwood to join the campaign in Flint. His intimate knowledge of Flint (because of his previous workers' education experience in the city) and of working conditions in the auto assembly plants there persuaded the UAW leadership to call him back as an organizer. Yet Roy's best asset proved to be oratory, and his primary task consisted of delivering speeches to large crowds of auto workers. Both Walter and Roy sent a telegram to Victor, who was in Philadelphia; he abandoned his speaking tour, literally leaving his wife to pack, joined Walter in Detroit for a briefing, and eventually settled in Flint to assist Roy. Their efforts and skills soon bore fruit. Because of astute organizing techniques and the expulsion of labor spies from the Flint local, the union by the end of the year claimed 4,500 members, some 10 percent of the total GM work force in Flint.[16] The workers were primed and ready.

The actual sit-down strike in Flint began after Cleveland auto workers sparked a spontaneous sit-down on December 26, 1936. At 7:00 A.M. on December 30, approximately fifty workers on the body line in Fisher Body No. 2 in Flint sat down in the plant, causing production to grind to a halt. Workers closed Fisher Body No. 1 with similar tactics three hours later. The local UAW leadership—and Bob Travis and Roy Reuther in particular—made all of the day-to-day decisions regarding the strike. Outside the plants, a network of committees was improvised to coordinate picketing, welfare, education, defense, sound cars, food distribution, entertainment, and publicity.

Brookwooders played key roles in organizing and sustaining the strike. Len De Caux, a former Brookwooder and the editor of the CIO's *Union News Service*, arrived early in January to handle strike publicity for the CIO. Frank Winn, based in Detroit, and still another product of Brookwood, served as the UAW's publicity director. The CIO fully backed the UAW and sent, among others, Rose Pesotta, a former Brookwooder and organizer for the Ladies' Garment Workers.

What unfolded at Flint assumed all of the characteristics of a textbook version of a strike as taught at the labor colleges. As Sidney Fine points out, the success of the strike "depended not only on what transpired outside of the occupied plants but, also, on whether the strikers on the inside, who had never before engaged in such a venture, could organize their activities with sufficient effectiveness to be able to live within the walls of a factory until a settlement of the strike could be reached."[17] This was particularly critical, since the first day of the strike was chaotic. From all accounts, strike leaders, particularly former Brookwooder Bishop, quickly organized the strikers into "communities" within the plants in which they sat. This feeling of solidarity fostered cooperation. In Fisher No. 1, a strike committee of fourteen members was selected to represent the various departments of the plants. It met daily and functioned democratically. The meetings, as the workers agreed, opened and closed with a verse of "Solidarity," the strikers favorite song. The committee banned liquor from the plants and appointed a special patrol to ward off employer intrusions and to discourage individual acts of worker sabotage. A variety of committees, such as food, recreation, education, postal services, and sanitation, were similarly designated.

After the first few hectic days, life in the occupied plants became routinized and monotonous, and the strikers required entertainment as well as other activities. Some of the subsequent entertainment was conceived purely for recreational purposes, while other efforts combined entertainment with strike-oriented issues. The former was manifested through a variety of games—cards, checkers, chess, dominoes, ping-pong, and volleyball—that the workers played. The latter area was addressed through labor plays, songs, and education. The Contemporary Theatre of Detroit, a workers' group, put on the two-act play *Virtue Rewarded* in both the No. 1 and No. 2 plants. The players adapted the skit especially for the sit-downers from a Brookwood play and presented it in a burlesque, melodramatic style. Bishop, as the union's educational director, also encouraged singing, for he had learned the lesson well at Brookwood; that is, music could play an important part in building a union. Thus, the strikers composed crude verses which they set to popular tunes. For instance, one strike song was sung to a current tune, "Goody, Goody":

We Union men are out to win today,
  Goody, Goody
General Motors hasn't even got a chance,
  Goody, Goody. [18]

Seemingly borrowing background and tool courses directly from the Brookwood curriculum, Bishop further conducted classes inside the plants in the history of the labor movement, parliamentary procedure, public speaking, collective bargaining, and the duties of a shop steward.

Former Brookwooders were equally busy outside the plants, with the Reuthers proving their mettle as aggressive and inspirational leaders. GM management attempted to break the stalemate on January 11, 1937, when the legendary "Battle of Bull's Run" erupted. Victor Reuther raced to the scene in a union sound car, playing martial music to hearten the workers, and frantically directed them to stand firm. Fourteen strikers were wounded in the melée with the police, yet they retained control of the plants. In another incident, Bob Travis and Roy Reuther devised a "battle plan" to secure Chevrolet No. 4, a key plant. On February 1, workers in Chevrolet No. 9 decoyed security guards by staging a supposedly impromptu sit-down strike. A large group of picketers and a union sound car with Roy Reuther inside quickly assembled, according to plan, outside the newly struck plant. The company fell for the ruse. While GM management and company police focused their attention on Chevrolet No. 9, leaving Chevrolet No. 4 unguarded, the strikers, directed by Bishop in yet another sound car, along with Walter Reuther, who led a large contingent of Detroit auto workers, rushed into Chevrolet No. 4 and seized control. A brilliantly executed strategy had thwarted GM and broken the stalemate.

The strike, for all intents and purposes, was over. Negotiations resumed on February 3. Representatives for UAW and GM, with pressure from Washington, hammered out an agreement that they signed on February 11. The strikers approved the contract, poured out of the GM plants, and jubilantly paraded through the streets. Later, Victor Reuther reflected about the Flint strike and the workers who

endured what seemed an unending nightmare; they suffered terror, broken heads, their families' hunger, and extreme risk, not just for another nickel an hour, but for dignity and individuality denied them by an arrogant corporation. They won a richer life for millions of industrial workers in other towns and cities. They exhibited the most selfless quality men can possess; the ability to sacrifice immediate material security for desirable . . . goals for humankind. They were the real heroes; it was our privilege to help them chart the narrow passage between defeat and victory. [19]

The history of the labor colleges is replete with ironic twists that reflected the complex, and often contradictory, actions of working people, and their institutions, in shaping historical events. First, the schools strived for industrial unionism. Yet, while industrial unionism was on the ascent, the colleges were on the descent. *Time* magazine, noting the passing of Brookwood, best articulated this experience for all of the labor colleges: "Having survived Labor's poverty, Brookwood was closed by Labor's prosperity." The New Deal legitimated unionization and concurrently stimulated organization, causing workers and labor leaders, as Muste recalled, to be "preoccupied with the daily struggle" instead of being attentive to the fate of the schools. [20]

Second, while conservatives pointed to the labor colleges as dens of "red" iniquity, leftists chose to point fingers at one another rather than presenting a sustained united front. Socialists first tolerated and then denounced Communists; Wobblies rejected liberals and Socialists, then Communists; Communists castigated Socialists, quarreled with Wobblies, and blasted liberals. This Punch-and-Judy show would have been comical if it had not contributed to the destruction of the labor colleges. "I think it's terribly important to realize that you need broad support," Brookwood's Katherine Pollak later reflected, "that splinter groups keep splintering, or have in the past kept splintering; and that considerable experience shows that they defeat themselves by so much infighting with other groups that are not very different, rather than paying attention to the great majority of workers or other people they are trying to reach." [21]

Third, even if the factionalism of the left had been resolved, the result would have been the same. Generalizing from Nick Salvatoré's incisive analysis of the early socialist movement, neither it nor the labor colleges failed. That they were not successful in achieving their larger goal of transforming society is evident. But "failure" assumes the possibility of "success," and that was never a serious prospect for either the socialist movement or the labor colleges. If the left had been able to maintain some unity, the effects would have been indeed important in strengthening the tenuous relations between the left and the broader spectrum of American workers. Yet it would not have signaled a prelude to revolution, because, as so many Americans learned during the First World War and in subsequent red scares, their society was not a tolerant one.[22] As Gramsci reminds us, bourgeois society expects ideological conformity and views nonconformists with suspicion, if not outright hostility. And the power of state coercion serves as the ultimate mechanism to ensure compliance with bourgeois hegemony. Thus the labor colleges, like the radical working-class movement, confronted a largely unfriendly context at the state and local levels, provoking unrelenting harassment from the very beginning, as we have seen.

Fourth, the independent nature of the schools proved to be an enigma. While independence represented their most distinctive quality, it also contributed to their demise. Challenges from various groups within the labor movement, such as the AFL, the CPLA, and the Communists, constantly forced the labor colleges to face the gut-wrenching exercise of re-evaluating their social and educational goals and activities. This process often triggered internecine battles that weakened the colleges. Further, independence produced an ironical twist because it did not necessarily presuppose tolerance. Work People's College, the least independent of the schools, maintained only two loose political affiliations, Socialist and Wobbly. That college's steadfast allegiance to a declining organization dictated its fate. Brookwood, repeatedly reaffirming its independence and nonsectarianism, became increasingly anticommunist, thus narrowing its political base. Commonwealth, perhaps the most independent of the labor colleges, only gradually evolved to a position of playing host to all factions of the left. Still, serious tensions remained, leading, in one case, to some Commoners calling on the local sheriff to evict striking communist students and, in another case, to an assassination attempt against socialist H. L. Mitchell on campus. Finally, independence produced financial vulnerability, which eventually led to its antithesis, institutional affiliation. Because of dire financial problems, both Brookwood and Commonwealth contravened their earlier policy of institutional and concomitant political independence, and instead sought institutional support in order to survive. Brookwood flirted with an alliance with the CIO and then with the ILGWU, while the Commoners' plan to link up with the New Theatre League was short-circuited.

Finally, it is difficult—if not impossible—to gauge, in any precise fashion, the impact of the labor colleges. The data and documentation, to a large degree, are not extant. More importantly, that simply has not been the task of this study. What is significant is that American workers saw a need for these schools and, with liberal support, created and sustained them. Still, it appears, with few exceptions, that labor college graduates assumed active roles in cooperative movements, workers' education classes and schools, the labor press, and union-organizing activities. How may this tendency be explained? More specifically, was it due to their labor college training? James Morris once assessed labor colleges, such as Brookwood, as follows: "The contribution made by Brookwood, so far as classroom training is concerned, was not . . . that the college increased the number of progressives in the labor movement, but rather that it brought together promising members of the ILGWU, UTW, Hat and Cap Workers, and other organizations and equipped them for better union service."[23] His conclusions were essentially correct. Their labor college training culminated in conflicts like the unsuccessful textile workers' strikes in the Piedmont region and the victorious auto worker sit-downs in the Flint plants. Theoretical and practical courses, as well as a pedagogy based on cooperation and solidarity, prepared labor college students for the rigors of the labor campaigns that awaited them. Employers often reacted to these confrontations with violence, arrests, and litigation. Led by labor college graduates, the workers responded with mass picketing, relief committees, songs, labor dramas, prounion propaganda, and sound trucks.

Katherine Pollak sees the accomplishments of the labor colleges in even more abstract, but nobler, terms. In addition to training workers to become active unionists, the labor colleges struggled to sustain workers' dreams during a decidedly antiunion era: A "lesson I learned from that period was that it is a good idea to keep ideas alive in periods when you can't make much actual progress, but that substantial social progress comes when the conditions are right. The mass movement and the success of the CIO certainly demonstrated this."[24] Thus, to some extent, Gramsci's educational strategy of the "war of position" was served. In the face of almost unsurmountable odds, the labor colleges symbolized the hopes of many workers while at the same time preparing them for labor service. When the New Deal dawned and the CIO emerged, trained labor leaders and activists were ready to assume their roles. Ironically, while 1937 represented a banner year for the UAW and the CIO, it was also the same year that Brookwood closed its doors. Work People's College and Commonwealth College soon experienced the same fate.

Nevertheless, while the outcome was disappointing, the cause was not. The labor colleges' contribution to the labor movement may not be readily apparent to those who measure the colleges' limited achievements against the lofty dreams of early socialists, or in light of the small proportion of American workers who took an active role in protesting their grievances and struggled to improve the lot of their comrades. These activists were in the minority; many workers passively submitted to their plight, while others pragmatically responded in whatever ways benefited them, but without the vision of a larger, more abstract social goal. This study has been about that "militant" minority which made the crucial difference, which persevered against formidable odds to seek radical solutions to economic injustice.[25] The students may have arrived at the doorsteps of the schools with baggage and ideals in hand, but it was the labor colleges that provided them with the training and instilled them with the confidence to actuate that commitment, serving the cognitive domain of human agency. Thus the colleges' role in orienting workers towards the most practical application of their energies cannot be overestimated. An insightful observation by an imprisoned Wobbly in 1917 epitomized the labor colleges' reason for existence: "The end in view is well worth striving for, but in the struggle itself lies the happiness of the fighter."[26] The courage, passion, and persistence exemplified by the founders, teachers, students, and supporters of the labor colleges remain indelible.

Notes, Bibliography, and Index

Notes

INTRODUCTION

1. For a discussion of the concept of the "cognitive dimension" in human agency, see Paula Allman, "Gramsci, Freire, and Illich: Their Contributions to Education for Socialism," in *Radical Approaches to Adult Education: A Reader*, ed. Tom Lovett (London: Routledge, 1988), 85–113; and Martin Carnoy, "Education, Economy, and the State," in *Cultural and Economic Reproduction in Education: Essays on Class, Ideology, and the State*, ed. Michael W. Apple (Boston: Routledge & Kegan Paul, 1982), 79–126. Also see Kenneth N. Teitelbaum, "Schooling for 'Good Rebels': Socialist Education for Children in the United States, 1900–1920" (Ph.D. diss., University of Wisconsin, 1985), 33–45. Gloria Garrett Samson, "Toward a New Social Order—The American Fund for Public Service: Clearinghouse for Radicalism in the 1920s" (Ph.D. diss., University of Rochester, 1987), 8, illustrates how radicals "anticipated" Gramsci's theory of hegemony.

2. Antonio Gramsci, *The Modern Prince and Other Writings* (New York: International Publishers, 1978), 74; Lynne Lawner, ed., *Antonio Gramsci: Letters from Prison* (New York: Harper & Row, 1973).

3. Gramsci, *Modern Prince*, 124.

4. Leon Fink et al., "A Round Table: Labor, Historical Pessimism, and Hegemony," *Journal of American History* 75 (June 1988): 115–62; Gramsci, *Modern Prince*, 77, 99; Carnoy, "Education, Economy, and the State," 87.

5. Ibid., 89.

6. T. J. Jackson Lears, "The Concept of Cultural Hegemony: Problems and Possibilities," *American Historical Review* 90 (1985): 567–93.

7. Carnoy, "Education, Economy, and the State," 90. Original emphasis.

8. Ibid., 88; Gramsci, *Modern Prince*, 73.

9. Carnoy, "Education, Economy, and the State," 88.

10. Ibid., 91. Original emphasis.

11. Harold Entwistle, *Antonio Gramsci: Conservative Schooling for Radical Politics* (London: Routledge & Kegan Paul, 1979), 118.

12. Quinton Hoare and Goeffrey Nowell Smith, eds., *Selections from the*

271

Prison Notebooks of Antonio Gramsci (New York: International Publishers, 1971), 397.

13. Entwistle, *Antonio Gramsci*, 124–27.

14. Ibid., 111–12.

15. Ibid., 147–48. Lawrence Goodwyn, *The Populist Movement: A Short History of the Agrarian Revolt in America* (New York: Oxford University Press, 1978), provides a similar, but non-Marxist, perspective. His fine introduction explains "social constraint" as a variation of "mass deference," which is "pervasive and subtle." Such "cultural presumptions" make protest seem pathological. Given this reality, how does protest occur? Goodwyn describes his sequential process as "movement forming," "movement recruiting," "movement educating," and "movement politicized," ultimately serving a "movement culture."

16. Len De Caux, *Labor Radical: From the Wobblies to the CIO* (Boston: Beacon Press, 1970), 103.

17. See the following articles by David Montgomery, "The Conventional Wisdom," *Labor History* 13 (Winter 1972): 107–36; "To Study the People: The American Working Class," *Labor History* 21 (Fall 1980): 485–512; and "Trends in Working-Class History," *Labour/Le Travail* 19 (Spring 1987): 13–22. Also see David Brody, "The Old Labor History and the New: In Search of an American Working Class," *Labor History* 20 (Winter 1979): 111–26; and Robert Ozanne, "Trends in American Labor History," *Labor History* 21 (Fall 1980): 513–21. For a more in-depth discussion of social history, refer to James B. Gardiner, ed., *Ordinary People and Everyday Life: Perspectives on the New Social History* (Nashville, Tenn.: American Association of State and Local History, 1983).

18. Lawrence A. Cremin, *Traditions of American Education* (New York: Basic Books, 1977), viii. Cremin's broad approach to the history of education elaborates a theme first proposed by Bernard Bailyn, *Education in the Forming of American Society* (Chapel Hill: University of North Carolina Press, 1960).

19. Herbert G. Gutman, "Observations on Selected Trends in American Working-Class Historiography," manuscript. I appreciate Professor David Tyack's generosity in sharing this highly valuable manuscript with me.

20. Rolland G. Paulston, *Nonformal Education: An Annotated International Bibliography* (New York: Praeger, 1972), ix. Also see, by Rolland G. Paulston, *Folk Schools in Social Change: A Partisan Guide to the International Literature* (Pittsburgh, Pa.: University of Pittsburgh Center for International Studies, 1974); *Conflicting Theories of Social and Educational Change: A Typological Review* (Pittsburgh, Pa.: University of Pittsburgh Center for International Studies, 1976); and *Other Dreams, Other Schools: Folk Colleges in Social and Ethnic Movements* (Pittsburgh, Pa.: University of Pittsburgh Center for International Studies, 1980).

21. For some illustrative examples of these views see, for consensus history, Paul F. Peterson, *The Politics of Urban School Reform* (Chicago: University

of Chicago Press, 1985); and Rush Welter, *Popular Education and Democratic Thought in America* (New York: Columbia University Press, 1962). Ira Katznelson and Margaret Weir, in their *Schooling for All: Class, Race, and the Decline of the Democratic Ideal* (New York: Basic Books, 1985), 29, see a "broad consensus." For reproduction and social control studies, refer to Samuel Bowles and Herbert Gintis, *Schooling in Capitalist America: Educational Reform and the Contradictions of Economic Life* (New York: Basic Books, 1976); Joel Spring, *Education and the Rise of the Corporate State* (Boston: Beacon Press, 1972); Clarence J. Karier, *Shaping the American Educational State* (New York: Free Press, 1975); and Paul C. Violas, *The Training of the Urban Working Class* (Chicago: Rand McNally, 1978). Also refer to Frank Tracy Carlton, *Economic Influences on Educational Progress in the United States, 1820–1850* (New York: Teachers College Press, Columbia University, 1965); Jay M. Pawa, "Workingmen and Free Schools in the Nineteenth Century: A Comment on the Labor-Education Thesis," *History of Education Quarterly* 11 (Fall 1971): 287–302; Richard J. Altenbaugh, " 'Our Children Are Being Trained Like Dogs and Ponies': Schooling, Social Control, and the Working Class," *History of Education Quarterly* 21 (Summer 1981): 223–39; E. P. Thompson, *The Making of the English Working Class* (New York: Vintage Books, 1963); and David Montgomery, "History As Human Agency," *Monthly Review* 33 (October 1981): 42–48. For the Buhles, see Fink et al., "A Round Table," 151.

22. William J. Reese, *Power and the Promise of School Reform: Grass-Roots Movements during the Progressive Era* (Boston: Routledge & Kegan Paul, 1986), xix–xx.

23. David P. Hogan, *Class and Reform: School and Society in Chicago, 1880–1930* (Philadelphia: University of Pennsylvania Press, 1985), 231.

24. James R. Barrett, "Class Formation and Social Reform in Chicago during the Progressive Era," *Educational Theory* 37 (Winter 1987): 81–88. David Montgomery alludes to the role of workers' education in "Thinking about American Workers in the 1920s," *International Labor and Working-Class History* 32 (Fall 1987): 4–24.

25. Teitelbaum, "Schooling for 'Good Rebels,' " 6.

26. David Montgomery, *The Fall of the House of Labor: The Workplace, the State, and American Labor Activism, 1865–1925* (New York: Cambridge University Press, 1987), 2. Also refer to Richard Johnson, "Three Problematics: Elements of a Theory of Working-Class Culture," in *Working-Class Culture: Studies in History and Theory,* ed. Joan Clarke, Charles Critcher, and Richard Johnson (London: Hutchinson, 1979): 201–37.

27. Barbara Mayer Wertheimer, ed., *Labor Education for Women Workers* (Philadelphia: Temple University Press, 1981).

28. Joyce L. Kornbluh and Mary Frederickson, eds., *Sisterhood and Solidarity: Workers' Education for Women, 1914–1984* (Philadelphia: Temple University Press, 1984).

29. See, for example, Douglas J. Ollila, Jr., "The Work People's College: Immigrant Education for Adjustment and Solidarity," in *For the Common Good: Finnish Immigrants and the Radical Response to Industrial America*, ed. Michael G. Karni et al. (Superior, Wis.: Tyomies Society, 1977); Charles F. Howlett, "Brookwood Labor College and Worker Commitment to Social Reform," *Mid-America* 61 (January 1979): 47–66; William H. Cobb, "Commonwealth College Comes to Arkansas, 1923–25," *Arkansas Historical Quarterly* 23 (Summer 1964): 99–122; and Raymond Koch and Charlotte Koch, *Educational Commune: The Story of Commonwealth College* (New York: Schocken Books, 1972).

30. David Gordon, Richard Edwards, and Michael Reich, *Segmented Work, Divided Workers: The Historical Transformation of Labor in the United States* (New York: Cambridge University Press, 1982), 243.

CHAPTER 1

Workers' Education

1. Margaret Byington, *Homestead: The Households of a Mill Town* (1910; reprint, Pittsburgh, Pa.: University of Pittsburgh Center for International Studies, 1974); Helen Todd, "Why Children Work: The Children's Answer," *McClure's Magazine* 40 (November 1912–April 1913): 68–79. Helen Todd was a factory inspector when she conducted her survey of Chicago factory children in 1911. Herbert G. Gutman, "Class, Status, and the Gilded Age Radical: A Reconsideration," in *Many Pasts: Readings in American Social History, 1865–Present*, ed. Herbert G. Gutman and Gregory S. Kealey (Englewood Cliffs, N.J.: Prentice-Hall, 1973), provides accounts of child labor by another factory inspector, Lawrence Fell. See *Report of the Committee of the Senate upon the Relations between Labor and Capital*, vols. 1 and 2 (Washington, D.C.: GPO, 1885); U.S. Department of Labor, Bureau of Labor Statistics, *Report on the Condition of Women and Child Wage Earners in the United States* (Washington, D.C.: GPO, 1911); and U.S. Department of Labor, Bureau of Labor Statistics, *Summary of the Report on Conditions of Women and Child Wage Earners in the United States*, bulletin no. 175 (Washington, D.C.: GPO, 1916). Also, see the many fine documents in Robert H. Bremner, ed., *Children and Youth in America: A Documentary History, 1866–1932*, vols. 1 and 2 (Cambridge, Mass.: Harvard University Press, 1971).

2. Alexander Fichlander, "Workers' Education: Why and What?" *Labor Age* 10 (1921): 49–50. Emphasis is mine. Also refer to "Workers' Schools," *Elementary School Journal* 26 (1926): 571–72; and Gloria Garrett Samson, "Toward a New Social Order—The American Fund for Public Service: Clearinghouse for Radicalism in the 1920s" (Ph.D. diss., University of Rochester, 1987), 351.

3. E. P. Thompson, "Time, Work-Discipline, and Industrial Capitalism," *Past and Present* 38 (1967): 56–97; Herbert G. Gutman, "Work, Culture, and

Society in Industrializing America, 1815–1919," *American Historical Review* 78 (1973): 531–88.

4. Horace Mann, *Annual Reports of the Secretary of the Board of Education of Massachusetts for Years 1845–1848* (Boston: Lee and Shepard, 1981), 93–96; Kathleen Edgerton Kendall, "Education as 'The Balance Wheel of Social Machinery': Horace Mann's Arguments and Proofs," *Quarterly Journal of Speech* 54 (February 1968): 13–21. See also Henry J. Perkinson's assessment of Mann's view of society in *Two Hundred Years of American Educational Thought* (New York: David McKay, 1976), 61.

5. Maris A. Vinovskis, "Horace Mann on the Economic Productivity of Education," *New England Quarterly* 43 (December 1970): 550–71.

6. Todd, "Why Children Work," 75–76.

7. Michael B. Katz, *Class, Bureaucracy, and Schools: The Illusion of Educational Change in America* (New York: Praeger, 1975), pp. 149–50; Michael B. Katz, "The Origins of Public Education: A Reassessment," *History of Education Quarterly* 16 (Winter 1976): 381–407. Also see David J. Hogan's fine critique of schooling as social control in chapter 1 of *Class and Reform: School and Society in Chicago, 1880–1930* (Philadelphia: University of Pennsylvania Press, 1985).

8. Jean Y. Tussey, *Eugene V. Debs Speaks* (New York: Pathfinder Press, 1972), 56.

9. Berger is quoted in William J. Reese, *Power and the Promise of School Reform: Grass-Roots Movements during the Progressive Era* (Boston: Routledge & Kegan Paul, 1986), xix.

10. Ibid.; William J. Reese, "Partisans of the Proletariat: The Socialist Working Class and the Milwaukee Schools, 1890–1920," *History of Education Quarterly* 21 (Summer 1980): 3–50. Also refer to George S. Counts, *The Social Composition of Boards of Education: A Study of the Social Control of Public Education* (1927; reprint, New York: Arno Press, 1969).

11. Richard W. Hogue, "The Value of Our Own Education," *Labor Age* 13 (May 1924): 12. This article represented Hogue's address as director of the Workers' Education Department of the Pennsylvania Federation of Labor, at a miners' convention. Also see J. B. S. Hardman, "Workers' Education," *Forum* 75 (March 1926): 450; and Richard J. Altenbaugh, " 'Our Children Are Being Trained Like Dogs and Ponies': Schooling, Social Control, and the Working Class," *History of Education Quarterly* 21 (Summer 1981): 213–22.

12. Bruce Sinclair, *Philadelphia's Philosopher Mechanics: A History of the Franklin Institute, 1824–1865* (Baltimore: Johns Hopkins University Press, 1976), 3–4; Kenneth Schlicter, "Mechanics' Institutes in America, 1820–1860" (master's research paper, Northern Illinois University, 1974); C. Hartley Gratten, *In Quest of Knowledge: A Historical Perspective of Adult Education* (New York: Association Press, 1955), 83–89; Lawrence A. Cremin, *American Education: The National Experience, 1783–1876* (New York: Harper & Row, 1980), 298, 303–18, 344–52.

13. Edward Pessen, *Most Uncommon Jacksonians: The Radical Leaders of the*

Early Labor Movement (Albany: State University of New York Press, 1967), 18–20, 55.

14. Gratten, *In Quest of Knowledge*, 241; Bruce C. Nelson, *Beyond the Martyrs: A Social History of Chicago's Anarchists, 1870–1900* (New Brunswick, N.J.: Rutgers University Press, 1988), 127–52.

15. Nelson, *Beyond the Martyrs*, 115, 120–21.

16. J. F. C. Harrison, *Learning and Living, 1790–1960: A Study in the History of the English Adult Education Movement* (Toronto: University of Toronto Press, 1961), 294; Marius Hansome, *World Workers' Educational Movements: Their Social Significance* (1931; reprint, New York: AMS Press, 1968), 283–86, 314–33; Margaret Hodgen, *Workers' Education in England and the United States* (London: Kegan Paul, 1925). Also refer to Richard E. Dwyer, "Workers' Education, Labor Education, Labor Studies: An Historical Delineation," *Review of Educational Research* 47 (Winter 1977): 179–207; or Richard E. Dwyer, *Labor Education in the United States: An Annotated Bibliography* (Metuchen, N.J.: Scarecrow Press, 1977).

17. Henry de Man, "Labor's Challenge to Education," *New Republic* 2 (March 1921): 16–18; Dagmar Schultz, "The Changing Political Nature of Workers' Education: A Case Study of the Wisconsin School for Workers" (Ph.D. diss., University of Wisconsin, 1972), 1–2.

18. Nancy Schrom Dye, "Creating a Feminist Alliance: Sisterhood and Class Conflict in the New York Women's Trade Union League, 1903–1914," in *Our American Sisters: Women in American Life and Thought*, ed. Jean E. Friedman and William G. Shade (Lexington, Mass.: D. C. Heath, 1982); Robin Miller Jacoby, "The Women's Trade Union League Training School for Women Organizers, 1914–1926," in *Sisterhood and Solidarity: Workers' Education for Women, 1914–1984*, ed. Joyce L. Kornbluh and Mary Frederickson (Philadelphia: Temple University Press, 1984); Elizabeth Anne Payne, *Reform, Labor, and Feminism: Margaret Dreier Robins and the Women's Trade Union League* (Urbana: University of Illinois Press, 1988); Joyce L. Kornbluh and Lyn Goldfarb, "Labor Education and Women Workers: An Historical Perspective," in *Labor Education for Women Workers*, ed. Barbara Mayer Wertheimer (Philadelphia: Temple University Press, 1981); Amy Hewes, "Early Experiments in Workers' Education," *Adult Education* 6 (Summer 1956): 211–20; Elsie Gluck, "The Educational Work of the New York Women's Trade Union League," in *Brookwood Labor College Fifteenth Anniversary Review* (Katonah, N.Y.: Brookwood Labor College, 1936), 46–47 (this document can be found in the Carnegie Library in Pittsburgh, Pa.). Gluck served as educational director at the time she wrote the article.

19. James Weinstein, *The Decline of American Socialism in America, 1912–1925* (New York: Monthly Review Press, 1967), 84–85; Ira Kipnis, *The American Socialist Movement, 1897–1912* (New York: Columbia University Press, 1952), 246–47; George Cotkin, "The Socialist Popularization of Science in America, 1901 to the First World War," *History of Education Quarterly* 24 (Summer 1984): 201–14.

20. Elliot Shore, *Talkin' Socialism: J. A. Wayland and the Role of the Press in American Radicalism, 1890–1912* (Lawrence: University Press of Kansas, 1988), 4–5, 106, 163, 187.

21. Ibid., 168.

22. Ibid., 215, 221.

23. Allen Ruff, " 'We Called Each Other Comrade!' Charles Kerr and the Charles H. Kerr & Company, Publishers, 1886–1928" (Ph.D. diss., University of Wisconsin, 1987), iv, 252. Kerr is quoted on 243–44.

24. Ibid., 219, 223, 266, 417, 419–20, 431.

25. Ibid., 470, 506, 517–18.

26. William J. Reese and Kenneth N. Teitelbaum, "American Socialist Pedagogy and Experimentation in the Progressive Era: The Socialist Sunday School," *History of Education Quarterly* 23 (Winter 1983): 429–54; Kenneth N. Teitelbaum, "Schooling for 'Good Rebels': Socialist Education for Children in the United States, 1900–1920" (Ph.D. diss., University of Wisconsin, 1985).

27. Hansome, *Educational Movements*, 299–311. Also see Kipnis, *American Social Movement*, 257; David A. Shannon, *The Socialist Party in America: A History* (New York: Macmillan, 1955), 9.

28. Philip S. Foner, *History of the Labor Movement in the United States: The Industrial Workers of the World, 1905–1917* (New York: International Publishers, 1973), vol. 4: 147–51. According to Joseph Conlin, *Bread and Roses Too: Studies of the Wobblies* (Westport, Conn.: Greenwood Press, 1974), 80, some leaders wanted the IWW to become technocratic: that is "to transform the union into something of a research bureau." Also, refer to Joseph Conlin, ed., *The American Radical Press, 1880–1960* (Westport, Conn.: Greenwood Press, 1974), for background on IWW and socialist publications.

29. J. B. S. Hardman, *American Labor Dynamics: In the Light of Post-War Developments* (1928; reprint, New York: Arno Press, 1969).

30. Warren R. Van Tine, *The Making of the Labor Bureaucrat: Union Leadership in the United States, 1870–1920* (Amherst: University of Massachusetts Press, 1973).

31. Nora Levin, *While Messiah Tarried: Jewish Socialist Movements, 1871–1917* (New York: Schocken Books, 1977), 93–95; John H. M. Laslett, *Labor and the Left: A Study of Socialist and Radical Influences in the American Labor Movement, 1881–1924* (New York: Basic Books, 1970).

32. I have relied on Gratten's categorization of workers' education in *In Quest of Knowledge*, 247, which closely parallels that of Schultz in "Changing Political Nature," 47, and K. Lindsay's in "Workers' Education That Works," *Survey* 50 (September 15, 1923): 623–34. For other categorizations and goals of workers' education, see Arthur Gleason, *Workers' Education: American Experiments with a Few Foreign Examples* (New York: Bureau of Industrial Research, 1921); and Mark Starr, *Workers' Education Today* (New York: League for Industrial Democracy, 1941). Also see "Recent Developments in Adult Workers' Education in the United States," *Monthly Labor Review* 23 (July 1926): 91–100;

and Marius Hansome, "The Development of Workers' Education," in *Workers' Education in the United States*, ed. Theodore Brameld (New York: John Dewey Society, 1941).

33. Robert J. Schaefer, "Educational Activities of the Garment Unions, 1890–1948: A Study in Workers' Education in the International Ladies' Garment Workers' Union and the Amalgamated Clothing Workers of America in New York City" (Ph.D. diss., Columbia University, 1951), 48, 70–71.

34. Alice Kessler-Harris, "Organizing the Unorganizable: Three Jewish Women and Their Union," *Labor History* 17 (Winter 1976): 5–23; Schaefer, "Educational Activities," 71–72.

35. Laslett, *Labor and the Left*, 119, 122–23, 129. Laslett devotes an insightful chapter, "Jewish Socialism and the Ladies' Garment Workers of New York," to this topic.

36. Susan Stone Wong, "From Soul to Strawberries: The International Ladies' Garment Workers' Union and Workers' Education, 1914–1950," in *Sisterhood and Solidarity*, ed. Kornbluh and Frederickson; Henry de Man, "Labor's Challenge," 16–18; and Louis (Levine) Lorwin, *The Women's Garment Workers* (1924; reprint, New York: Arno Press, 1969), 483, also point to the strong socialist roots of the ILGWU and to its educational efforts.

37. Wong, "From Soul to Strawberries," 42.

38. Quoted in Gleason, *Workers' Education*, 20, and Schaefer, "Educational Activities," 68–69.

39. Wong, "From Soul to Strawberries," 42. Also refer to Schaefer, "Educational Activities," 90–97.

40. Alexander Fichlander, "Labor Education," *Survey* 45 (January 1921); 542–43; Lorwin, *Women's Garment Workers*, 487–92; Schaefer, "Educational Activities," 71–73, 87–89; Gleason, *Workers' Education*, 21–22, 27; Hansome, *Educational Movements*, 225–29.

41. American Federation of Labor [hereafter AFL], *Proceedings of the Thirty-Eighth Annual Convention of the American Federation of Labor* (Washington, D.C.: Law Reporter Printing, 1918), 322; AFL, *Proceedings of the Thirty-Ninth Annual Convention of the American Federation of Labor* (Washington, D.C.: Law Reporter Printing, 1919), 144. Henry Sterling, "Labor's Attitude Toward Education," *School and Society* 10 (August 2, 1919): 128–32.

42. Workers' Education Bureau, *Proceedings of the First National Conference on Workers' Education in the United States* (New York: WEB, 1921), 6, 142–44. Gompers wrote the introduction that was used in the *Proceedings*. See Hansome, *Educational Movements*, 229–41; and David Montgomery, "New Tendencies in Union Struggles and Strategies in Europe and the United States, 1916–1922," in *Work, Community, and Power: The Experience of Labor in Europe and America, 1900–1925*, ed. James E. Cronin and Carmen Sirianni (Philadelphia: Temple University Press, 1983), 88–116.

43. Wong, "From Soul to Strawberries," 48.

44. AFL, *Proceedings of the Forty-Second Annual Convention of the American Federation of Labor* (Washington, D.C.: Law Register Printing, 1922), 357–58. Spencer Miller, Jr., "Workers' Education," *Survey* 48 (May 6, 1922): 221–22.

45. James O. Morris, *Conflict within the AFL: A Study of Craft versus Industrial Unionism, 1901–1938* (Ithaca, N.Y.: Cornell University Press, 1958), 87.

46. Leo Wolman, "Economic Conditions and Union Policy," in *American Labor Dynamics*, ed. Hardman, 38, 40. Irving Bernstein, *The Lean Years: A History of the American Worker, 1920–1933* (Boston: Houghton Mifflin, 1960), 87–89. Also see Leo Wolman, *The Growth of American Trade Unions, 1880–1925* (1924; reprint, New York: Arno Press, 1975); and Richard W. Hogue, "The Status of Workers' Education," *Survey* 53 (December 15, 1924): 343; and Schaefer, "Educational Activities," 114.

47. Laslett, *Labor and the Left*, 127.

48. Schaefer, "Educational Activities," 124, 127; Lorwin, *The Women's Garment Workers*, 354–57; Bernstein, *Lean Years*, 136–38.

49. Bernstein, *Lean Years*, 85, 138–41.

50. Laslett, *Labor and the Left*, 129.

51. Bernstein, *Lean Years*, 141; Laslett, *Labor and the Left*, 128; Richard O. Boyer and Herbert M. Morais, *Labor's Untold Story* (New York: United Electrical, Radio and Machine Workers of America, 1955), 245.

52. Wong, "From Soul to Strawberries," 50–51.

53. Schaefer, "Educational Activities," iv–v, 137–38. This theme represents Schaefer's conceptual framework. Also refer to Alice S. Cheyney, "Workers' Education in the United States," *International Labour Review* 32 (July 1935): 44–45, where she states: "A small number of determined communists were trying to win the workers to revolutionary measures; the nature of their activities and the threat which they constituted to labor solidarity, impelled many leaders to attempt to nip in the bud any leanings toward 'radicalism.'"

54. Schaefer, "Educational Activities," 139–47, 158, 166, 168–69; Lorwin, *Women's Garment Workers*, 500; Theresa Wolfson, "The Recent Social Climate," in *Workers' Education in the United States*, ed. Brameld, 75.

55. Schaefer, "Educational Activities," iv, 178–90; Starr, *Workers' Education Today*, 17–18.

56. Rita Heller, "Blue Collars and Bluestockings: The Bryn Mawr School for Women Workers, 1921–1938," in *Sisterhood and Solidarity*, ed. Kornbluh and Frederickson.

57. Gratten, *In Quest of Knowledge*, 249; Hewes, "Early Experiments," 213–14; Schultz, "Political Nature," 19, 38; and Hilda W. Smith, "Old Trails for New Explorers," *Survey* (March 15, 1929): 802–04.

58. Quoted in Gleason, *Workers' Education*, 58–59. See Hilda W. Smith, *Workers at the Bryn Mawr Summer School* (New York: Affiliated Summer Schools for Women Workers, 1929), 7, for the profound change in the political tone of the school's objectives by 1923: "The aim of the School is to offer young

women in industry opportunities to study liberal subjects and to train themselves in clear thinking; to stimulate an active and continued interest in the problems of our economic order; to develop a desire for study as a means of understanding and of enjoyment in life. The School is not committed to any theory or dogma."

59. Hansome, *Educational Movements*, 70; Gleason, *Workers' Education*, 58–59; Susan M. Kingsbury, "The Worker at School," *Survey* 53 (February 15, 1925): 600–603.

60. Schultz, "Political Nature," 2–3, 62. Emphasis added. Irvine L. H. Kerrison, *Workers' Education at the University Level* (New Brunswick, N.J.: Rutgers University Press, 1951), likewise sees similar problems facing college- and university-sponsored workers' education. See chapter 2, "Problems Facing College and University Workers' Education."

61. Mary Frederickson, "Citizens for Democracy: The Industrial Programs of the YWCA," in *Sisterhood and Solidarity*, ed. Kornbluh and Frederickson.

62. Schultz, "Political Nature," 181–94.

63. I draw heavily here on Dagmar Schultz's fine study, "Political Nature." However, please also refer to Ernest E. Schwarztrauber, *Workers' Education: A Wisconsin Experiment* (Madison: University of Wisconsin Press, 1942); Caroline F. Ware, *Labor Education in Universities: A Study of University Programs* (New York: American Labor Education Service, 1946); "Summer Schools for Working Women," *School and Society* 26 (September 1927): 326–27; "Three Summer Schools," *Monthly Labor Review* 33 (December 1931): 1403–5; and Mark Starr, "The Current Panorama," in *Workers' Education in the United States*, ed. Brameld.

CHAPTER 2

A Culture in Overalls and Workmarked Hands

1. Dagmar Schultz, "The Changing Political Nature of Workers' Education: A Case Study of the Wisconsin School for Workers" (Ph.D. diss., University of Wisconsin, 1972), 53.

2. Marius Hansome, *World Workers' Educational Movements: Their Social Significance* (1931; reprint, New York: AMS Press, 1968), 95.

3. "Labor Union Colleges," *Educational Review* 6 (May 1921): 446–49.

4. Carl Ross, *The Finn Factor in American Labor, Culture, and Society* (New York Mills, Minn.: Parta Printers, 1977), 48–75; A. William Hoglund, *Finnish Immigrants in America: 1880–1920* (Madison: University of Wisconsin Press, 1960); Stephen Thernstrom, ed., *Harvard Encyclopedia of American Ethnic Groups* (Cambridge: Harvard University Press, 1980), s.v. "Finns." Parts of this section have appeared in Richard J. Altenbaugh and Rolland G. Paulston, "Work People's College: A Finnish Folk High School in the American Labor College

Movement," *Paedagogica Historica* 18, no. 2 (1978): 237–56; and in Rolland G. Paulston, ed., *Other Dreams, Other Schools: Folk Colleges in Social and Ethnic Movements* (Pittsburgh, Pa.: University of Pittsburgh Center for International Studies, 1979). See also Matti Kaups, "The Finns in the Copper and Iron Mines of the Western Great Lakes Region, 1864–1905: Some Preliminary Observations," in *The Finnish Experience in the Western Great Lakes Region: New Perspectives,* ed. Michael G. Karni, Matti Kaups, and Douglas J. Ollila, Jr. (Turku, Finland: Institute for Migration, 1975), 55–88.

5. Peter Kivisto, *Immigrant Socialists in the United States: The Case of Finns and the Left* (Rutherford, N.J.: Farleigh Dickinson University Press, 1984), 37.

6. John H. M. Laslett, *Labor and the Left: A Study of Socialist and Radical Influences in the American Labor Movement, 1881–1924* (New York: Basic Books, 1970), emphasizes the interaction of immigrant radicalism and severe exploitation and low wages for immigrant workers as the reasons for socialist activities among the German brewery workers and the Jewish garment workers. For the Finnish experience, see Douglas J. Ollila, Jr., "From Socialism to Industrial Unionism (IWW): Social Factors in the Emergence of the Left-Labor Radicalism among Finnish Workers on the Mesabi, 1911–1919," in *The Finnish Experience,* ed. Karni, Kaups, and Ollila, 161; Michael Passi, "Finnish Immigrants and the Radical Response to Industrial America," in *For the Common Good: Finnish Immigrants and the Radical Response to Industrial America,* ed. Michael G. Karni et al. (Superior, Wis.: Tyomies Society, 1977), 9–22; Michael G. Karni, "The Founding of the Finnish Socialist Federation and the Minnesota Strike of 1907," in *For the Common Good,* ed. Karn, et al., 65–87; U. S. Congress, Senate, *Reports of the Immigration Commission: Immigrants in Industry, Copper Mining, and Smelting* (Washington, D.C.: GPO, 1911), 25–26, 39, 42–53, 228–29, 244; and Ross, *Finn Factor,* 109–11.

7. Karni, "Founding," 75, 78, 82; Ross, *Finn Factor,* 113–14. Ollila, "IWW," 158, states: "Those Finns who had been active organizers and members of the union were blacklisted, and many were forced to flee into the surrounding countryside to try their hand at farming. Some Finns who had no part in the strike at all were victims of discriminatory hiring practices since it was often assumed that all Finns were Socialists."

8. Passi, "Finnish Immigrants," 12; David A. Shannon, *The Socialist Party in America: A History* (New York: Macmillan, 1955), 44; Ollila, "IWW," 156; Arne Halonen, "The Role of Finnish-Americans in the Political Labor Movement" (master's thesis, University of Minnesota, 1945), 51; John I. Kolehmainen, "The Inimitable Marxists: The Finnish Immigrant Socialists," *Michigan History* 36 (December 1952): 395–405.

9. Douglas J. Ollila, Jr., "The Work People's College: Immigrant Education for Adjustment and Solidarity," in *For the Common Good,* ed. Karni et al., 90; Kivisto, *Immigrant Socialists,* 107–9.

10. Quoted in Ollila, "Work People's College," 97.

11. Guss Aakula, "Short Sketches of the Features of Työväen Opisto, Work People's College, Duluth, Minnesota," unpublished and undated MS. trans. Eva Lahonen and ed. Linda Hoshal (obtained from the Duluth Campus Library, University of Minnesota). The Immigration History Research Center (hereafter IHRC), University of Minnesota, also has a copy in its archives. Aakula attended Work People's College as a student and later served as a teacher and an administrator. Also see *Articles of Incorporation and By-Laws of the Work People's College* (Duluth, Minn.: 1929), 1, housed at IHRC; and John Wiita, "Työväen Opisto—Working People's College," unpublished and undated MS., IHRC. Like Aakula, Wiita had intimate connections with the school as a student and later became a member of the Board, assistant instructor, managing director of the correspondence school, and dean of the faculty (or principal) in 1915. Biographical information is in John Wiita, personal letter to author, December 24, 1978.

12. Ollila, "Work People's College," 101.

13. Ollila, "Work People's College," 87–88; Kivisto, *Immigrant Socialists*, 107.

14. Kivisto, *Immigrant Socialists*, 154.

15. Halonen, "Finnish-Americans," 65; Ollila, "Work People's College," 102, 106; Wiita, "Työväen," 1–2.

16. Quoted in Halonen, "Finnish-Americans," 65.

17. Ibid., 54.

18. Ollila, "IWW," 159–61, 162–63, 169.

19. Quoted in Halonen, "Finnish-Americans," 69.

20. Ibid., 71–73; Ollila, "IWW," 163–64.

21. Middle District Committee of the National Finnish Socialist Organization of the United States, *The Controversy within the Finnish Socialist Organization of United States, Its Issues and Reasons* (Superior, Wis., 1914).

22. Wiita, "Työväen," 8–9; Industrial Workers of the World Collection, box 137, folder 1, Archives of Labor and Urban Affairs, Wayne State University (hereafter WSU); Ollila, "Work People's College," 103, 111; Kivisto, *Immigrant Socialists*, 139–41.

23. Elizabeth Gurley Flynn, *The Rebel Girl: An Autobiography* (New York: International Publishers, 1973), 135–36.

24. William D. Haywood, *The Autobiography of Big Bill Haywood* (New York: International Publishers, 1976), 264.

25. Ibid., 282; Work People's College Collection, folder 26, Stock Register, Alphabetical List, IHRC.

26. *Work People's College Announcement of Courses, 1923–24* (Duluth, Minn.: Work People's College, 1923), 2.

27. T. Kekkonen, "Education as a Social and Mass Problem," *Industrial Pioneer* 2 (November 1924): 42; "The Need for Workers' Education: The Work People's College and Its Courses," *Industrial Pioneer* 1 (October 1923): 37–38.

Both of these documents served as advertisements for the school. Also see Kristen Svanum "The Work People's College: Where Industrial Unionists Are Efficiently Educated," *Industrial Pioneer* 2 (February 1925): 47–48.

28. Steve Golin, "Defeat Becomes Disaster: The Paterson Strike of 1913 and the Decline of the IWW," *Labor History* 24 (Spring 1983): 223–48; Ollila, "IWW," 168; Melvyn Dubofsky, *We Shall Be All: A History of the IWW* (New York: Quadrangle, 1969), 457–62, 475–77; Len De Caux, *Labor Radical: From the Wobblies to the CIO* (Boston: Beacon Press, 1970), 88–89.

29. William M. Fincke, "How Brookwood Began," in *Brookwood Labor College Fifteenth Anniversary Review* (Katonah, N.Y.: Brookwood Labor College, 1936), 14–16, in the Carnegie Library of Pittsburgh. This article was written by the son of William W. Fincke, one of the founders of Brookwood. Charles F. Howlett, "Brookwood Labor College and Worker Commitment to Social Reform," *Mid-America* 61 (1979): 47–66. Mark and Helen Starr Oral History, November 15, 1974, Labor Archives, Pennsylvania State University (hereafter PSU); Nellie M. Seeds, "William W. Fincke: The Founder of Brookwood and Manumit," *Labor Age* 16 (August 1927): 10–11; Jo Ann Ooiman Robinson, *Abraham Went Out: A Biography of A. J. Muste* (Philadelphia: Temple University Press, 1981), 32; "Plan Workers' College," *New York Times*, April 1, 1921, p. 18, col. 3.

30. "Plan Workers' College," *New York Times*, April 1, 1921, p. 8, col. 3; A. J. Muste, *The Essays of A. J. Muste*, ed. Nat Hentoff (New York: Simon & Schuster, 1967), 92; Graduation, 1923–1937: Correspondence, Lists, Miscellaneous, Programs, Brookwood Labor College Collection, box 95, folder 7, Archives of Labor and Urban Affairs (WSU). Jonathan D. Bloom, "Brookwood Labor College, 1921–1933: Training Ground for Union Organizers" (master's thesis, Rutgers University, 1978). Bloom covers the Muste years at Brookwood in great detail. Also see James O. Morris, *Conflict within the AFL: A Study of Craft versus Industrial Unionism, 1901–1938* (Ithaca, N.Y.: Cornell University Press, 1958), 90–93.

31. Morris, *Conflict*, 86; David Montgomery, "Thinking about American Workers in the 1920s," *International Labor and Working-Class History* 32 (Fall 1987): 4–24; Muste, *Essays*, 43; Robinson, *Abraham Went Out*, 8–14.

32. Muste, *Essays*, 43; Robinson, *Abraham Went Out*, 15.

33. Muste, *Essays*, 43; Robinson, *Abraham Went Out*, 16.

34. Muste, *Essays*, 97; Robinson, *Abraham Went Out*, 25–32. Also refer to Muste's oral history, "The Reminiscences of A. J. Muste" (New York: Columbia University Oral History Office, 1965), as well as "Socialist Movement Project: A. J. Muste (1962), Columbia University Oral History Collection. See p. 5 concerning Brookwood as a "radical socialist" institution. (I thank the Columbia Oral History Office for permission to examine this document.) Also see "Who Is This A. J. Muste?" *World Tomorrow* 12 (June 1929): 250–54; and Bloom, "Brookwood Labor College," 18.

35. Muste, *Essays*, 92–93.

36. James H. Maurer, *It Can Be Done: The Autobiography of James Hudson Maurer* (New York: Rand School Press, 1938), 87–88, 100, 108–12, 115, 133–36, 139, 143, 158; Gloria Garrett Samson, "Toward a New Social Order—The American Fund for Public Service: Clearinghouse for Radicalism in the 1920s" (Ph.D. diss., University of Rochester, 1987), 363–65.

37. Maurer, *It Can Be Done*, 36. James H. Maurer, "Labor's Demand for Its Own Schools," *Nation* 111 (September 1922): 276–78.

38. From an address delivered by Maurer as presiding officer at the Fifth Annual Conference of the Workers' Education Bureau, held in Boston April 22, 1927; a copy of this speech is included in Maurer's autobiography, *It Can Be Done*, 367–70. Maurer, "Labor's Demand," 277; Muste, *Essays*, 93–94.

39. Schultz, "Political Nature," 30.

40. Robinson, *Abraham Went Out*, 32; Muste, *Essays*, 96; Bloom, "Brookwood Labor College," 1, 8.

41. See "Plan Workers' College," *New York Times*; "Academic Freedom in Labor College," *New York Times*, April 2, 1921, p. 8, col. 3. Also refer to Muste, *Essays*, 98; Bloom, "Brookwood Labor College," 38–39; and Spencer Miller, Jr., "Fifteen Years of the Workers' Education Bureau of America," in *Brookwood Labor College Fifteenth Anniversary Review*.

42. "Aims of Workers' College," *New York Times*, June 16, 1921, 8, col. 1.

43. *Brookwood Bulletin and Announcement of Courses for 1932–33* (Katonah, N.Y.: Brookwood Labor College, 1932), 3. Curiously, Brookwood's objectives, as outlined in its Articles of Incorporation, appear tame: "To conduct an educational institution seeking primarily to provide an education to men and women in the labor and farmer movements; to teach students right methods of approach to their problems, namely: respect for facts, willingness to face facts, ability to determine relevant facts to solve problems and to make generalizations on the basis of such facts. Furthermore, to assist such persons with the ability and training for progressively shaping policies with regard to any issues confronting organized workers and further, to offer and give training in the technique of labor union administration and to prepare students for activities such as public speaking, writing, organizing and teaching in which such students may be called upon to engage." See Certificate of Incorporation of Brookwood, April 10, 1925, Brookwood Labor College Collection, box 10, folder 3, WSU. Tamiment Institute also houses several different years of the *Brookwood Bulletin*.

44. Howlett, "Brookwood Labor College," 50. For background on the Manumit School, consult Devere Allen, "A School for Workers' Children," *Nation* 119 (October 15, 1924): 417–18; and "A New Community School," *Survey* 53 (October 1924): 91–92. Robinson, *Abraham Went Out*, 33. The "romantic affair" view was expressed by Mark and Helen Starr, Labor Archives, PSU.

45. Evelyn Preston, "Brookwood Carries On," in *Brookwood Fifteenth Anniversary Review*, 50–51; Brookwood Collection, box 1, folder 22, WSU.

46. Philip S. Foner and Sally M. Miller, *Kate Richards O'Hare: Selected Writings and Speeches* (Baton Rouge: Louisiana State University Press, 1982), 13. Also see Raymond Koch and Charlotte Koch, *Educational Commune: The Story of Commonwealth College* (New York: Schocken Books, 1972), 12–13. This autobiography reviews the Koches' experiences at Commonwealth as students, teachers, and administrators.

47. Neil K. Basen, "Kate Richards O'Hare: The 'First Lady' of American Socialism, 1901–1917," *Labor History* 21 (Spring 1980): 165–99; Foner and Miller, *Kate Richards O'Hare*, 5; Sally M. Miller, "Other Socialists: Native-Born and Immigrant Women in the Socialist Party of America, 1901–1917," *Labor History* 24 (Winter 1983): 84–102; James R. Green, *Grass-Roots Socialism: Radical Movements in the Southwest, 1895–1943* (Baton Rouge: Louisiana State University Press, 1978).

48. Basen, "Kate Richards O'Hare," 198; James Weinstein, *The Decline of Socialism in America, 1912–1925* (New York: Monthly Review Press, 1967), 56. For a more detailed perspective of O'Hare's views, see her writing and speeches in Foner and Miller, *Kate Richards O'Hare*. Also see "Kate Richards O'Hare," *World Tomorrow* 9 (February 1926): 55–56. For information about Ruskin College, refer to Hansome, *Educational Movements*, 299, 442.

49. "Zeuch Tells Students of Pioneer Years," *Commonwealth College Fortnightly* [hereafter *Fortnightly*], March 1, 1927, 1.

50. For Commonwealth's early history, I relied heavily on Commonwealth College papers, Microfilm no. 356, 3 reels, University of Arkansas, Fayetteville. Also see William H. Cobb, "Commonwealth College Comes to Arkansas, 1923–1925," *Arkansas Historical Quarterly* 23 (Summer 1964): 99–122, and his master's thesis, "Commonwealth College: A History" (University of Arkansas, 1960), 27–29, 39, 41–44, 49, 52, 68–72. Also see Bill Murrah, "Llano Cooperative Colony, Louisiana," *Southern Exposure* 1, nos. 3–4 (Winter 1974): 88–105. Likewise refer to Koch and Koch, *Educational Commune*, 15–16, 21.

51. Baldwin is quoted in Samson, "New Social Order," 37, and Samson's comment is on 39.

52. Ibid., 356.

53. American Fund for Public Service, Brookwood Collection, box 22, folders 10, 11, WSU; Raymond and Charlotte Koch Collection, box 1, folder 26, and box 3, folder 1, and the Arthur W. Calhoun Collection, box 8, folder 3, both collections in Archives of Labor and Urban Affairs, WSU.

54. Commonwealth College Papers, microfilm no. 356, reel 1, University of Arkansas, Fayetteville; "Kate Richards O'Hare Outlines Commonwealth Aims at Opening Exercises," *Fortnightly*, November 1, 1925, 1.

55. "Commonwealth Enters Its Second Year," *Brookwood Review*, December

1924, 4; "Clinton S. Golden Visits Commonwealth," *Fortnightly*, December 1, 1925, 1.

56. See "What Commonwealth College Means to the Workers," in Foner and Miller, *Kate Richards O'Hare*, 344–51. Likewise consult "Workers' Education Will Save Society," *Fortnightly*, October 15, 1927, 1, 3.

57. William E. Zeuch, "Progressive Workers' Education," *Fortnightly*, April 1, 1929, 2. Also see Harold Coy, "A New Experiment for Workers," *Monthly Labor Review* 20 (1925): 1120–221. Coy served as an English teacher at Commonwealth.

58. Commonwealth College Papers, microfilm no. 356, reel 1, University of Arkansas, Fayetteville; "The Commonwealth Idea," *Fortnightly*, March 1, 1927, 2; "Why Commonwealth?" *Fortnightly*, September 1, 1927, 2; "It Is Different at Commonwealth," *Fortnightly*, May 15, 1927, 1; "Why Workers' Education?" *Fortnightly*, August 15, 1926, 2.

59. Koch and Koch, *Educational Commune*, 9–10.

60. Arthur W. Calhoun, "The Place of the Scientific Spirit in the Workers' Education Movement," *Fortnightly*, May 15, 1926, 2.

CHAPTER 3

Knowledge Is Power

1. Lucien Koch, "Commonwealth College," *Progressive Education* 11 (April–May 1934): 301–2; William H. Cobb, "Commonwealth College: A History" (master's thesis, University of Arkansas, 1960), 113–14.

2. Helen G. Norton, "Brookwood—A Cross Section of the Labor Movement," *Brookwood Review*, August 1926, 2. Emphasis added. Rolland G. Paulston, ed., *Other Dreams, Other Schools: Folk Colleges in Social and Ethnic Movements* (Pittsburgh, Pa.: University of Pittsburgh Center for International Studies, 1980), 261–64, discusses the concept of ideological-confrontational pedagogy.

3. "Workers Study: How To Do It," *Brookwood Review*, February 1932, 4.

4. *Brookwood Bulletin and Announcement of Courses for 1932–33* (Katonah, N.Y.: Brookwood Labor College, 1932), 7; James H. Maurer, "Labor's Demand for Its Own Schools," *Nation* 111 (September 1922): 276–78; Jonathan D. Bloom, "Brookwood Labor College, 1921–1933: Training Ground for Union Organizers" (master's thesis, Rutgers University, 1978), 67–68, 130; James O. Morris, *Conflict within the AFL: A Study of Craft versus Industrial Unionism, 1901–1938* (Ithaca, N.Y.: Cornell University Press, 1958), 98–99.

5. Brookwood Labor College Collection, box 5, folder 1, Curricula, Archives of Labor and Urban Affairs, Wayne State University (hereafter WSU).

6. David J. Saposs, *Left Wing Unionism* (New York: International Publishers, 1926), 6.

7. "Vassar–Brookwood Students Debate," *Brookwood Review*, March 1926,

1. Also see Bloom's account of the debate in "Brookwood Labor College," 87–88, *Brookwood Bulletin* (1932–33), 9; "Workers' College at Katonah, N.Y.," *Monthly Labor Review* 14 (May 1922): 1084; "Training of Labor Leaders in the United States," *International Labour Review* 8 (July 1923): 138–39; Brookwood Collection, box 5, folder 1, Curricula, WSU; Gloria Garrett Samson, "Toward a New Social Order—the American Fund for Public Service: Clearinghouse for Radicalism in the 1920s" (Ph.D. diss., University of Rochester, 1987), 342.

8. *Brookwood Bulletin* (1932–33), 9–10; Brookwood Collection, box 1, folder 2, and box 5, folder 1, Curricula, WSU. Consult Brookwood Collection, folder 1, Tamiment Institute, New York University. Jo Ann Ooiman Robinson, *Abraham Went Out: A Biography of A. J. Muste* (Philadelphia: Temple University Press, 1981), 35.

9. *Brookwood Bulletin* (1932–33), 10–11. The series of *Brookwood Bulletins* at the Tamiment Institute clearly reveal the evolution of the second-year course of study at Brookwood from 1924–25 to 1932–33. Also see Bloom, "Brookwood Labor College," 78.

10. "Brookwood," *New Republic* 43 (August 1925): 287–89; *Brookwood Bulletin* (1932–33), 8–9; Marius Hansome, *World Workers' Educational Movements: Their Social Significance* (1931; reprint, New York: AMS Press, 1968), 203–04.

11. Guss Aakula, "Short Sketches of the Features of Työväen Opisto, Work People's College, Duluth, Minnesota," unpublished and undated MS, trans. Eva Lahonen and ed. Linda Hoshal (obtained from the Duluth Campus Library, University of Minnesota), 2; John Wiita, "Työväen Opisto—Working People's College," unpublished and undated MS, Immigration History Research Center (hereafter IHRC), University of Minnesota, 2–3; Douglas J. Ollila, Jr., "The Work People's College: Immigrant Education for Adjustment and Solidarity," in *For the Common Good: Finnish Immigrants and the Radical Response to Industrial America*, ed. Michael G. Karni et al. (Superior, Wis.: Tyomies Society, 1977), 104–13; Hans R. Wasastjerna, *History of the Finns in Minnesota* (New York Mills, Minn.: Northwestern Publishing 1957), 228.

12. Ollila, "Work People's College," 106; Wiita, "Työväen," 2–3; George Sirola, "The Finnish Working People's College," *International Socialist Review* 14 (August 1913): 102–4.

13. Wiita, "Työväen," 4; Ollila, "Work People's College," 102.

14. Aakula, "Short Sketches," 3; Wiita, "Työväen," 4; Wasastjerna, *History of the Finns*, 228; Ollila, "Work People's College," 107; Allen Ruff, " 'We Called Each Other Comrade!' Charles Kerr and the Charles H. Kerr & Company, Publishers, 1886–1928" (Ph.D. diss., University of Wisconsin, 1987), 369–74.

15. Wasastjerna, *History of the Finns*, 230; Ollila, "Work People's College," 105.

16. John Olli, personal letter to author December 30, 1978; Ollila, "Work People's College," 107.

17. Fred W. Thompson, personal letter to author, February 4, 1983.

18. Peter Kivisto. *Immigrant Socialists in the United States: The Case of Finns and the Left* (Rutherford, N.J.: Farleigh Dickinson University Press, 1984), 151–52.

19. "Work People's College: A Residential School for Rebellious Workers," undated pamphlet from Work People's College, obtained from the Minnesota Historical Society, Duluth. Fred W. Thompson, letter, December 1, 1929, on school letterhead, obtained from Minnesota Historical Society.

20. *Work People's College Announcement of Courses, 1923–24* (Duluth, Minn.: Work People's College, 1923), 3–5; Rosa Knutti, "The Work People's College," *Industrial Pioneer* 1 (October 1921): 59–61; *Articles of Incorporation and By-Laws of the Work People's College* (Duluth, Minn.: 1929), 9–10; "The Need for Workers' Education: The Work People's College and Its Courses," *Industrial Pioneer* 1 (October 1923): 37–38; quotation is from Ruff, " 'We Called Each Other Comrade!' " 236.

21. *Work People's College Announcement of Courses, 1923–24*, 6. Emphasis added.

22. Industrial Workers of the World Collection, box 137, folders 13 and 14, Archives of Labor and Urban Affairs, WSU; *Work People's College Announcement of Courses, 1923–24*, 6–7; Hansome, *Educational Movements*, 210–11; Sulo Peltola, personal letter to author, April 9, 1983. Peltola was a student at Work People's College. Also see Vera Smith, "Work Peoples," *One Big Union Monthly* 2 (April 1938): 14–15. The entire issue of *One Big Union Monthly* for April 1938 is devoted to Work People's College.

23. "Education for Workers: Commonwealth College, 1927–28," *Commonwealth College Fortnightly Supplement*, December 1, 1927, 5–8.

24. "Fundamental Changes in Course of Study," *Commonwealth College Fortnightly* [hereafter *Fortnightly*], June 15, 1928, 1.

25. "Quarterly System Adopted by Faculty," *Fortnightly*, October 1, 1928, 1, 3.

26. "Courses of Study and Entrance Requirements," *Fortnightly*, January 1, 1930, 2.

27. Ibid.; "Fortnightly Issued at Commonwealth," *Fortnightly*, March 15, 1932, 1.

28. "Announcement of Commonwealth College: School for Workers," *Fortnightly*, July 1, 1933, 2; Raymond Koch and Charlotte Koch, *Educational Commune: The Story of Commonwealth College* (New York: Schocken Books, 1972), 98–101; "Zeuch to Research Abroad," *Fortnightly*, May 1, 1931, 1; Cobb, "From Education to Agitation," chapter 5 in "Commonwealth College," perhaps overstates the transition and argues, 164, that after Zeuch's departure, "the formal curriculum of the Zeuch years virtually disappeared as actual participation in labor organization became the order." What remained were courses "oriented exclusively toward labor organization." Refer to William H. Cobb, "From Utopian Isolation to Radical Activism: Commonwealth College, 1925–1935," *Arkansas Historical Quarterly* 32 (Summer 1973): 132–47.

29. "Courses of Study," *Fortnightly*; "Commonwealth College: Suggested Three-Year Course of Study," *Fortnightly*, December 1, 1931, 3; "Twelve Courses to be Given Next Term," *Fortnightly*, December 15, 1932, 1, 4; "Courses for Spring Picked by Faculty," *Fortnightly*, March 15, 1932, 1, 3.

30. Carol J. Poore, *German-American Socialist Literature, 1865–1900* (Bern: Peter Lang, 1982), 100–06; Bruce C. Nelson, *Beyond the Martyrs: A Social History of Chicago's Anarchists, 1870–1900* (New Brunswick, N.J.: Rutgers University Press, 1988), 131–34; Bruce A. McConachie and Daniel Friedman, eds., *Theatre for Working-Class Audiences in the United States, 1830–1980* (Westport, Conn.: Greenwood Press, 1985), 11; Jay Williams, *Stage Left* (New York: Charles Scribner's Sons, 1974), 7; Karen Malpede Taylor, *People's Theatre in Amerika* (New York: Drama Book Specialists, 1972), 5–9, 102; Gerald Rabkin, *Drama and Commitment: Politics in the American Theatre of the Thirties* (Bloomington: Indiana University Press, 1964), 32.

31. Mordecai Gorelik, "Theatre Is a Weapon," *Theatre Arts Monthly* 18 (June 1934): 420–33; *The Illustrated Encyclopedia of World Theatre* (London: Thames & Hudson, 1977), 12, reveals that the "Agitprop Theatre" had a profound influence on professional theater and on directors like Meyerhold, Brecht, and Piscator. Parts of this section on the labor drama appeared in Richard J. Altenbaugh, "Proletarian Drama: An Educational Tool of the American Labor College Movement," *Theatre Journal* 34 (May 1982): 197–210.

32. Gorelik, "Theatre," 423; Malcolm Goldstein, *The Political Stage: American Drama and Theatre of the Great Depression* (New York: Oxford University Press, 1974), 28–34; Taylor, *People's Theatre*, 32, 139 (see, for example, the play *Vote Communist*, 32–36); Williams, *Stage Left*, 36; and Rabkin, *Drama*, 46–47.

33. Goldstein, *Political Stage*, 32. Later, 51–52, Goldstein remarks that Clifford Odets's *Waiting for Lefty* represented the most popular of all agitprop pieces. For Goldstein, "the play is . . . put together in the usual agitprop fashion, with scenes centering on the underdogs followed by passages of dialogue exposing members of the exploiting class and an ending in which the underdogs become organized and militant." Also see Rabkin, *Drama*, 46–47, 57, where he explains agitprop as follows: "A variety of dramaturgical devices were employed, many of them stemming from the theatrical experimentation of the twenties: choral recitation, episodic structure, satiric caricature, theatrical stylization."

34. Williams, *Stage Left*, 36.

35. "Brookwood Labor College," *School and Society* 22 (November 7, 1925): 585.

36. "Presto! Old Barn Becomes Theatre," *Brookwood Review*, November 1931, 3; "Student–Workers Give Japanese Play," *Fortnightly*, March 15, 1926, 1; "School Stages Russian Play in Final Dramatic Program," *Fortnightly*, May 1, 1926, 1; quotation is from "Ready for 1927–28 at Commonwealth," *Fortnightly*, August 15, 1927, 1; "Irish Play Features Monthly Theatrical," *Fortnightly*, June 15, 1928, 1; "Seminar Opened by Greek Drama Talk," *Fortnightly*, February 1,

1929, 1; "Program for 1929–30 at Commonwealth," *Fortnightly*, April 1, 1929, 1; "Twelve Courses to Be Given Next Term," *Fortnightly*, December 15, 1932, 1; "Labor Drama Is Now Full-Time Part of the Curriculum," *Fortnightly*, October 15, 1935, 1.

37. "Commoners Tableau Sorrows of Masses," *Fortnightly*, January 1, 1928, 1. Also see "Commoners Celebrate Soviet Anniversary," *Fortnightly*, December 1, 1930, 1.

38. C. Hittenrauch, "Commonwealth College," in *The College Writer: An Anthology of Student Prose Edited for College Composition Classes*, ed. Warren Bower (New York: Norton, 1935). Hittenrauch once attended Commonwealth as a student and later went to Highlander Folk School in Tennessee. Quotation is from "Experimental Theatre Group Presents Mass Poem-Play," *Fortnightly*, September 1, 1935, 4; and *Work People's College Announcement of Courses, 1923–24*.

39. "Dramas of Toil Are Staged at Brookwood Labor College," *New York Times*, March 7, 1926, sec. 9; Helen G. Norton, "Drama at Brookwood," *Labor Age* 15 (May 1926): 18–19.

40. Jesse Slaughter, "Does Drama Belong?" *Brookwood Review*, December 1927–January 1928, 3; "To Dramatize Workers' Lives," *Brookwood Review*, December 1925, 1; A. J. Muste, "Dramatizing the Labor Movement," *Brookwood Review*, December 1925, 2; Cobb, "Commonwealth College," 161–62.

41. "Presto!" *Brookwood Review*; Norton, "Drama at Brookwood," 18–19; Koch and Koch, *Educational Commune*, 106.

42. Rosa Knutti, "The Workers' Play," *Industrial Pioneer* 3 (November 1925): 26–27.

43. "Dramas," *New York Times*; Rosa Knutti, "The 'Rain' of Colton and Randolph," *Industrial Pioneer* 3 (December 1925): 26–27; Rosa Knutti, "Knocking the 'el Out of 'Glory,'" *Industrial Pioneer* 3 (February 1926): 22–23.

44. This study does not attempt to provide an exhaustive examination of the various themes of the labor dramas used by the labor colleges but illustrates representative themes. Joseph K. Hart, "Framed," *Survey* 55 (January 1926): 469–70; David Pinski, *Ten Plays* (New York: Huebsch, 1920); Susan Glaspell, *Plays* (Boston: Small, Maynard, 1920); Harold Williamson, *Peggy, Carolina Folk-Plays*, ed. Frederick H. Koch (New York: Henry Holt, 1941). Also see "Brookwood Players Appear in New York," *Brookwood Review*, April 1926, 4; Norton, "Brookwood," 18–19; Bloom, "Brookwood Labor College," 76–77.

45. Norton, "Brookwood," 18–19; Bloom, "Brookwood Labor College," 77.

46. Quoted in Rudolph Johnson, "Work People's College," *North Country Anvil* 19 (July–August 1976): 17; Norton, "Brookwood," 18–19; Koch and Koch, *Educational Commune*, 106. A copy of *Risen from the Ranks* appears in *Fortnightly*, December 1, 1932, 2–3.

47. Brookwood Labor College, *The Tailor Shop* (Katonah, N.Y., 1926). Lyrics quoted with the permission of the Archives of Labor and Urban Affairs, Wayne State University.

48. Koch and Koch, *Educational Commune*, 106; Cobb, "Commonwealth College," 161–62; Rachel France, ed., *A Century of Plays by American Women* (New York: Richards-Posen Press, 1979); "Dramatics Club Rehearsing John Reed Play, 'Freedom,'" *Fortnightly*, January 15, 1935, 1; "New Dramatics Director," *Fortnightly*, March 15, 1936, 1.

49. Commonwealth Labor College, *Get Goin' George* (Mena, Ark., 1938).

50. Quotation from Commonwealth Labor College, *We Are Not Alone* (Mena, Ark., 1938). For general information about racism as an impediment to unionization, see Philip S. Foner, *Organized Labor and the Black Worker, 1619–1973* (New York: International Publishers, 1976). Also, for background material concerning racism and the unionization of southern tenant farmers, see Donald H. Grubbs, *Cry from the Cotton: The Southern Tenant Farmers' Union and the New Deal* (Chapel Hill: University of North Carolina Press, 1971); H. L. Mitchell, *Mean Things Happening in This Land: The Life and Times of H. L. Mitchell, Cofounder of the Southern Tenant Farmers' Union* (Montclair, N.J.: Allanheld, Osmun, 1979).

51. Cobb, "Commonwealth College," 161; Slaughter, "Does Drama Belong?" 3; Bloom, "Brookwood Labor College," pp. 77–78; United Mine Workers, Illinois Sub-district no. 5, *What Price Coal?* (1926).

52. Fred W. Thompson, personal letter to author, February 4, 1983. The play Thompson refers to, *The Economic Tragedy of Mr. Peel*, may be found in IWW Collection, box 137, WSU. Sulo Peltola, personal letter to author, April 9, 1983. Play Library, List of Rentals, 1933–35, folder 35, and Play Library, List of Plays Available, folder 39, Work People's College Collection, IHRC; Wasastjerna, *History of the Finns*, 230; "Labor Skits," *Fortnightly*, March 1, 1933, 2; Bloom, "Brookwood Labor College," 77.

53. Slaughter, "Does Drama Belong?" 3; "Students Do Tippett Play," *Brookwood Review*, February 1932, 1; Williams, *Stage Left*, 111. Tippett's words are quoted in Bloom, "Brookwood Labor College," pp. 142–43.

54. "Workers' Education on Wheels," *Brookwood Review*, June 1934, 1; "Crowds Like Labor Drama," *Brookwood Review*, May 1932, 1; Alice S. Cheyney, "Workers' Education in the United States," *International Labour Review* 32 (July 1935): 39–59.

55. "The Chautauqua Grows," *Brookwood Review*, November 1935, 1.

56. Laurence Spitz, "Let Freedom Ring," *New Theatre* 3 (November 1936): 24–25.

57. Koch and Koch, *Educational Commune*, 106; "Big Crowd Comes to Tenth Opening," *Fortnightly*, November 1, 1932, 1. *Until the Mortgage Is Due* appears in *Fortnightly*, November 1, 1932, 2–3. Also see Claire Sifton and Paul Sifton, *1931: A Play* (New York: Farrar & Rinehart, 1931).

58. "Dramas," *New York Times*; Koch and Koch, *Educational Commune*, 106.

59. Norton, "Brookwood," 18–19. Also consult "Our Miners Like Education," *New York Times*, September 10, 1932, p. 20, col. 4.

60. "Former Students Active in Movement" and "Chicago Group Active,"

Fortnightly, November 15, 1932, 1, 4. Williams, *Stage Left*, 84. Also refer to "The Forgotten Man," *Fortnightly*, May 15, 1932, 2–4.

61. *Brookwood Labor College Twelfth Anniversary Review* (Katonah, N.Y.: Brookwood Labor College, 1933), 5; "Field Work and Political Action Courses Are Added to Curriculum," *Brookwood Review*, February 1931, 1. See Bloom's discussion of labor action in "Brookwood Labor College," 132–39.

62. *Brookwood Bulletin* (1932–33), 10.

63. Knutti, "Work People's College," 60.

64. Brookwood Students Out on Strike—But Not against Brookwood," *Brookwood Review*, April 1923, 3; "Students Help Win New Garment Strike," *Brookwood Review*, March 1926, 1; "Sacco and Vanzetti," *Brookwood Review*, September 1927, 1–2; "Brookwood Helps in Miners' Relief," *Brookwood Review*, December 1927–January 1928, 1. Brookwooders participated in other similar fund-raising activities for miners. See "Students Give up Desserts to Help Evicted Miners," *New York Times*, January 22, 1923, p. 21, col. 2. "What Price Coal?" *Brookwood Review*, December 1927 to January 1928, p. 3; Melvyn Dubofsky and Warren Van Tine, *John L. Lewis: A Biography* (New York: Quadrangle, 1977), 127–28; Robinson, *Abraham Went Out*, 37–38; Charles F. Howlett, "Brookwood Labor College and Worker Commitment to Social Reform," *Mid-America* 61 (January 1979): 47–66.

65. A. J. Muste, *The Essays of A. J. Muste*, ed. Nat Hentoff (New York: Simon & Schuster, 1967), 146; Bloom, "Brookwood Labor College," 126; "Brookwooders Active in Marion, N.C., Strike," *Brookwood Review*, October–November 1929, 1.

66. Tom Tippett, *When Southern Labor Stirs* (New York: Jonathan Cape & Harrison Smith, 1931), viii.

67. Ibid., 48–51.

68. "Trial Postponed," *Fortnightly*, November 1, 1932, 1; "Kentuckians Eject Party of Students," *New York Times*, April 11, 1932, p. 3, col. 5; "Students Identify Deputy As Beater," *New York Times*, April 12, 1932, p. 5, col. 6; Koch and Koch, *Educational Commune*, 99–101.

69. "Off to Illinois," and "Extra," *Fortnightly*, April 15, 1932, 1; "Announcement of Commonwealth College," *Fortnightly*; Edward J. Falkowski Collection, box 5, folder 22, Archives of Labor and Urban Affairs, WSU.

70. IWW Collection, box 137, folders 10, 12, WSU; Sulo Peltola, personal letter to author, April 9, 1983; Johnson, "Work People's College," 17; Wasastjerna, *History of the Finns*, 228.

71. Fred Thompson, "School Days at Work People's College," *One Big Union Monthly* 2 (September 1937): 18–20. The special issue was *One Big Union Monthly* 2 (April 1938).

72. Brookwood Collection, box 10, folders 11, 12, 13, 15, 16, and box 22, folder 22 WSU; A. J. Muste, "Brookwood Labor Institute," *American Federationist*, October 1925, 939–41; *Brookwood Bulletin* (1932–33), 11; "Brookwood

Summer School," *Brookwood Review*, December 1924, 1; A. J. Muste, "Labor Vacation and Summer Schooling," *Survey* 54 (September 15, 1925): 633–35; Helen G. Norton, "Brookwood's Summer Institutes, 1927," *Survey* 59 (October 15, 1927): 95–96; Morris, *Conflict*, 99–103; Bloom, "Brookwood Labor College," 61–62.

73. "Rest and Recreation for the Work Worn," *Fortnightly*, April 1, 1927, 1; "Quarterly System," *Fortnightly*; "Summer Session Is Past History," *Fortnightly*, May 1, 1931, 1. Commonwealth continued its youth summer camps during its regular summer sessions. See "Youth Camp Begins and Summer School Opens," *Fortnightly*, July 1, 1931, 1; and "Commonwealth Summer Camp," *Fortnightly*, April 15, 1933, 2.

74. Brookwood Collection, box 13, folder 1, WSU; Arthur W. Calhoun Collection, box 27, folder 4; Raymond and Charlotte Koch Collection, box 3, folders 25, 26, both in Archives of Labor History and Urban Affairs, WSU. "Onward Brothers" is reprinted with the permission of the Archives of Labor and Urban Affairs, Wayne State University.

75. Helen G. Norton, "Strike Relief," pamphlet (Katonah, N.Y.: Brookwood Labor College, 1933). A copy of this pamphlet is at the Carnegie Public Library of Pittsburgh.

76. Bill Stencil, *Handbook of Mimeograph Technique* (Mena, Ark.: Commonwealth Labor College, 1937), n.p.; housed at the New York City Public Library. Also consult Elizabeth Schlosser Cousins, *Labor Journalism Handbook* (Mena, Ark.: Commonwealth Labor College, 1940).

77. Aakula, "Short Sketches," 10; Wasastjerna, *History of the Finns*, 228; Johnson, "Work People's College," 17.

78. *Labor Pamphlets* (Katonah, N.Y.: Brookwood, 1932). A series of six of these pamphlets exists now at Carnegie Public Library of Pittsburgh. Also see "Come to Brookwood by Correspondence," *Brookwood Review*, October–November 1929, 2; "Correspondence Courses," *Brookwood Review*, February 1930, 24. Katherine H. Pollak, *Our Labor Movement Today* (Katonah, N.Y.: Brookwood Labor College, 1932), 22–26, 104–10.

79. Oral history, Katherine Pollak Ellickson Collection, Archives of Labor and Urban Affairs, WSU.

80. Herbert G. Gutman, "*Labor Age*, 1921–1933," in *The American Radical Press, 1880–1960*, ed. Joseph R. Conlin (Westport, Conn.: Greenwood Press, 1974), 191–97; Robinson, *Abraham Went Out*, 37. Also see *Labor Age*, January 1926–December 1928. Each issue contains the feature "Brookwood's Pages."

81. Gutman, "*Labor Age*," 191–97.

82. *Brookwood Bulletin* (1932–33), 12; Bloom, "Brookwood Labor College," 96–97; "Extension Courses Given by Faculty," *Brookwood Review*, January 1926, 4; "J. C. Kennedy to Join Brookwood Faculty" and "Extension Courses Are Well Launched," *Brookwood Review*, October–November 1928, 4; Curricula, Brookwood Collection, box 5, folder 1, and box 56, folder 5, WEVD, WSU.

83. "Advance Announcement of the First Museum of Capitalistic Decay in America" (Mena, Ark.: Commonwealth Labor College, 1934), n.p., New York City Public Library. "Commonwealth: New Museum Shows 'Collapse of Capitalism,' " *Newsweek*, February 16, 1935, 27.

84. Published at Commonwealth in 1936, 1938, and 1939, respectively.

CHAPTER 4

Teachers and Students

1. Gramsci is quoted by Harold Entwistle, *Antonio Gramsci: Conservative Schooling for Radical Politics* (London: Routledge & Kegan Paul, 1979), 48; Paulo Freire, *Pedagogy of the Oppressed* (New York: Seabury Press, 1970), 67. Original emphasis. Although Freire is a contemporary educational theorist, his analysis of radical education is appropriate here. For other radical critiques of education, refer to Leo Huberman, "How to Spread the Word"; Bruce M. Rappaport, "Toward a Marxist Theory and Practice of Teaching"; and Jean Bethke Elshtain, "The Social Relations of the Classroom: A Moral and Political Perspective," all in *Studies in Socialist Pedagogy*, ed. Theodore Mills Norton and Bertell Ollman (New York: Monthly Review Press, 1978). Samuel Bowles and Herbert Gintis, *Schooling in Capitalist America: Educational Reform and the Contradictions of Economic Life* (New York: Basic Books, 1976), also address the social relationships between classroom and work. See, especially, 131–33.

2. Anarchist educators maintained a similar pedagogy. See Paul Avrich, *The Modern School Movement: Anarchism and Education in the United States* (Princeton, N.J.: Princeton University Press, 1980); and Jo Ann Ooiman Robinson, *Abraham Went Out: A Biography of A. J. Muste* (Philadelphia: Temple University Press, 1981), 35.

3. Mark and Helen Starr Oral History, November 15, 1974, Labor Archives, Pennsylvania State University (hereafter PSU).

4. Raymond Koch and Charlotte Koch, *Educational Commune: The Story of Commonwealth College* (New York: Schocken Books, 1972), p. 37; Robinson, *Abraham Went Out*, 35; "Commonwealth, Workers' School, Completes Third Academic Year," *Commonwealth College Fortnightly* [hereafter *Fortnightly*], April 15, 1926, 2; "Are Commonwealth Teachers 'Good' Teachers?" *Fortnightly*, July 1, 1932, 2.

5. Quoted in Robinson, *Abraham Went Out*, 36. Also, refer to "Commonwealth," *Fortnightly*; William H. Cobb, "Commonwealth College: A History" (master's thesis, University of Arkansas, 1960), 121; and Clifford B. Ellis, "What Life Means to a Worker: The Story of the Past Winter at the Work People's College," *Industrial Pioneer* 4 (May 1926): 14–18.

6. Correspondence, Brookwood Labor College Collection, box 22, folder 3, Archives of Labor and Urban Affairs, Wayne State University (hereafter WSU), Lucien Koch, "Commonwealth College," *Progressive Education* 11 (April–May

1934): 301–2; "Life Here Demands Three Adjustments," *Fortnightly*, December 1, 1932, 1; Ellis, "What Life Means," 15; Edward J. Falkowski Collection, box 5, series 1 and 2, Archives of Labor and Urban Affairs, WSU. Falkowski's wry account of Friedrich is also cited in Jonathan D. Bloom, "Brookwood Labor College, 1921–1933: Training Ground for Union Organizers" (master's thesis, Rutgers University, 1978), 79; and in Cobb, "Commonwealth College," 120–21.

7. Fred W. Thompson, interview with author, October 20, 1984.

8. A. J. Muste, "What's It All About?" *Labor Age* 13 (April 1924): 1–4. Original emphasis.

9. Tucker P. Smith, "Workers Prepare for Power," *Progressive Education* 11 (April–May 1934): 303–6; "Studies in Curriculum," *Brookwood Review*, April 1923, 2.

10. Falkowski Collection, box 5, folder 10, WSU.

11. William Cunningham, "Commonwealth College: An Educational Mutant," *World Tomorrow* 12 (December 1929): 503–5.

12. Ellis, "What Life Means," 15; "Law Class Learns through Mock Trial," *Fortnightly*, December 15, 1926, 1, 3.

13. Allen Ruff, " 'We Called Each Other Comrade!' Charles Kerr and the Charles H. Kerr & Company, Publishers, 1886–1928," (Ph.D. diss., University of Wisconsin, 1987), 334–35.

14. Guss Aakula, "Short Sketches of the Features of Työväen Opisto, Work People's College, Duluth, Minnesota," unpublished and undated MS, trans. Eva Lahonen and ed. Linda Hoshal (obtained from Duluth Campus Library, University of Minnesota); John Wiita, "Työväen Opisto—Working People's College," unpublished and undated MS, Immigration History Research Center (hereafter IHRC), University of Minnesota; Douglas J. Ollila, Jr., "The Work People's College: Immigrant Education for Adjustment and Solidarity," in *For the Common Good: Finnish Immigrants and the Radical Response to Industrial America*, ed. Michael G. Karni et al. (Superior, Wis.: Tyomies Society, 1977).

15. Brookwood Collection, box 1, folder 1, WSU; A. J. Muste, *The Essays of A. J. Muste*, ed. Nat Hentoff (New York: Simon & Schuster, 1967), 102; Len De Caux, *Labor Radical: From the Wobblies to the CIO* (Boston: Beacon Press, 1970), 97–98; Ellis, "What Life Means," 15; Rudolph Johnson, "Work People's College," *North County Anvil* 19 (July–August 1976): 17; Marius Hansome, *World Workers' Educational Movements: Their Social Significance* (1931; reprint, New York: AMS Press, 1968), 203–4, 445–46.

16. Sarah N. Cleghorn, *Threescore: The Autobiography of Sarah N. Cleghorn* (1936; reprint, New York: Arno Press, 1980), 60, 226, 230, 242, 253; Robinson, *Abraham Went Out*, 35–36; Bloom, "Brookwood Labor College," 86.

17. *Work People's College Announcement of Courses, 1923–24* (Duluth, Minn.: Work People's College, 1923), 8; *Articles of Incorporation and By-Laws of the Work People's College* (Duluth, Minn.: Work People's College, 1929), 13–15.

18. Hansome, *Educational Movements*, 212.

19. *Brookwood Bulletin and Announcement of Courses for 1932–33* (Katonah, N.Y.: Brookwood Labor College, 1932), 13; Hansome, *Educational Movements*, 203; Executive Board Minutes, 1922–1923, Brookwood Collection, box 6, folder 1, and box 7, folder 1, WSU; Starr Oral History, PSU, p. 27.

20. "Education for Workers: Commonwealth College," *Fortnightly Supplement*, December 1, 1927, 2; Raymond and Charlotte Koch Collection, box 1, folder 1, Archives of Labor and Urban Affairs, WSU.

21. Ellis, "What Life Means," 14–18.

22. Lee B. Stanley Oral History, April 13, 1972, Labor Archives, PSU; "New Students Come From 16 Industries," *Brookwood Review*, October–November 1928, 1; "Workers Flock to School's 10th Year," *Brookwood Review*, September 1930, 1; "A Motley Gang at Brookwood," *Brookwood Review*, December 1932, 4; Bloom, "Brookwood Labor College," 21–24, 81–83; Tom Tippett, *When Southern Labor Stirs* (New York: Jonathan Cape & Harrison Smith, 1931), 164–65; Brookwood Collection, box 22, folder 3, WSU; Lawrence Rogin, interview with author, March 18, 1984.

23. Falkowski Collection, box 5, folder 10, WSU.

24. De Caux, *Labor Radical*, 95–96.

25. Hansome, *Educational Movements*, 209; C. Mauritz Erkkila, personal letter to author, March 3, 1983.

26. "Meet New Commoners!" *Fortnightly*, November 1, 1926, 1; "Here's a Peek at New Student Group," *Fortnightly*, November 15, 1926, 1; "Wobbly, Cabby, Electrician, Wind Up New Student List," *Fortnightly*, December 1, 1926, 3; "Cosmopolitan Group at Commonwealth," *Fortnightly*, November 1, 1927, 1.

27. "Growth of Brookwood," *Brookwood Review*, December 1924, 8; "Gunnar," *Brookwood Review*, February 1926, 3; "Brookwood Opens for Seventh Year," *Brookwood Review*, October–November 1927, 1; Bloom, "Brookwood Labor College," 23; "Commonwealth, Workers' School," *Fortnightly*; "Meet New Commoners!" *Fortnightly*; "Education for Workers," *Fortnightly Supplement*, 1–2; "Society Notes: Cuba," *Fortnightly*, September 1, 1929, 3; "Cubans Welcomed," *Fortnightly*, October 1, 1929, 3; "Students Hike to College," *New York Times*, October 12, 1923, p. 27, col. 1; Koch and Koch, *Educational Commune*, 22–30; Ellis, "What Life Means," 15; Hansome, *Educational Movements*, 445–46.

28. Fred W. Thompson, letter, December 1, 1929, on school letterhead, obtained from Minnesota Historical Society.

29. Sulo Peltola, personal letter to the author, April 9, 1983.

30. *Brookwood Labor College Twelfth Anniversary Review* (Katonah, N.Y.: Brookwood Labor College, 1933), 10. Also see Starr Oral History, PSU. "Meet New Commoners!" *Fortnightly*.

31. Stanley Oral History, PSU; Brookwood Collection, box 13, folders 7, 8, 18, WSU. *Brookwood Twelfth Anniversary Review* contains many photographs

of graduation classes attesting to the diverse nature of the school's students. Ben Thomas, "The Negro Problem," *Brookwood Review*, May 1925, 2; "Negroes Can Organize Is Conference Feature," *Brookwood Review*, June–July 1927, 1; "Negro Students Tell of Race's Problems," *Brookwood Review*, October–November 1927, 4; "Negro Workers' Problems, Conference Subject," *Brookwood Review*, February 1931, 2; "Drive Planned to Aid Negroes in Industry," *New York Times*, January 2, 1931, p. 6, col. 7; Charles F. Howlett, "Brookwood Labor College: Voice of Support for Black Workers," *Negro History Bulletin* 45 (April–June 1982): 38–39; Bloom, "Brookwood Labor College," 60, 83–84; Robinson, *Abraham Went Out*, 37.

32. Koch and Koch, *Educational Commune*, 42; "United Front Formed at Commonwealth," *Fortnightly*, February 15, 1935, 1; "Sharecroppers' Union Greets Commonwealth," *Fortnightly*, January 15, 1936; "Butler, President of the STFU, Joins Commonwealth College Faculty," *Fortnightly*, February 1, 1936, 1. The relationship between the STFU and Commonwealth is somewhat contested. See, for example, Sue Thrasher, "Radical Education in the 30s," *Southern Exposure* 1 (Winter 1974): 204–210. Reed's recollection is quoted from H. L. Mitchell, *Mean Things Happening in This Land: The Life and Times of H. L. Mitchell, Cofounder of the Southern Tenant Farmers' Union* (Montclair, N.J.: Allanheld, Osmun, 1979), 63.

33. Katherine Pollak Ellickson Oral History, 1974, Archives of Labor and Urban Affairs, WSU. Also refer to Hansome, *Educational Movements*, p. 447; "Education for Workers," *Fortnightly Supplement*, 6; "Kirkpatricks Coming to Commonwealth," *Fortnightly*, December 1, 1929, 1; "F. M. Goodhue," *Fortnightly*, July 1, 1926, 2; "Wilbur Clarke Benton," *Fortnightly*, September 1, 1926, 2; "Two Jayhawkers Join Faculty," *Fortnightly*, June 15, 1927, 1; "Ready for 1927–28 at Commonwealth," *Fortnightly*, August 15, 1927, 1; "Your Opportunity: Enter the Subscription Contest," *Fortnightly*, September 15, 1936, 1.

34. "On the Job," *Work People's College Bulletin*, December 15, 1923, 2; Hansome, *Educational Movements*, 209–10; *Articles of Incorporation and By-Laws of the Work People's College*, 10–11.

35. Wiita, "Työväen Opisto," 6–10.

36. Douglas J. Ollila, "Work People's College," 105; John Wiita, personal letter to author, December 24, 1983; C. Mauritz Erkkila, personal letter to author, March 3, 1983; Archie Brown, personal letter to author March 29, 1983.

37. Fred W. Thompson, interview with author, October 20, 1984; Studs Terkel, *Hard Times: An Oral History of the Great Depression* (New York: Washington Square Books, 1970), 353–58.

38. Arthur W. Calhoun Collection, box 1, folder 1, Archives of Labor and Urban Affairs, WSU; Correspondence, American Fund for Public Service, Brookwood Collection, box 22, folder 3, WSU.

39. Curricula, Brookwood Collection, box 5, folder 1, WSU; Correspondence, American Fund for Public Service, Brookwood Collection, WSU;

Bloom, "Brookwood Labor College," 27; Bertha Saposs, interview with author, March 18, 1984.

40. Cleghorn, *Threescore*, 239–52.

41. Falkowski Collection, box 5, folder 10, WSU; Robinson, *Abraham Went Out*, 33, 35; Bloom, "Brookwood Labor College," 29–30; "Four Teachers Added to Faculty," *Brookwood Review*, October 1934, 4; Muste, *Essays*, 104.

42. Clinton Golden Papers, box 7, file 15, Labor Archives, PSU; "Faculty and Staff," *Brookwood Review*, April–May 1928, 26; Golden is quoted in Gloria Garrett Samson, "Toward a New Social Order—the American Fund for Public Service: Clearinghouse for Radicalism in the 1920s" (Ph.D. diss., University of Rochester, 1987), 333–34.

43. Starr Oral History, PSU; Martin Lawn, "Mark Starr: Socialist Educator," and Ronda Hawben, "A Pioneer in Workers' Education: Mark Starr and Workers' Education in Great Britain," both in *Llafur: The Journal of the Society for the Study of Welsh Labour History* 4, no. 2 (1985): 91–100.

44. Lawrence Rogin, interview with author, March 18, 1984.

45. Covington Hall, *Dreams and Dynamite: Selected Poems*, ed. Dave Roediger (Chicago: Charles Kerr, 1985), 6; Hall, "Revolt of the Brotherhood," *One Big Union Monthly* 2 (April 1938): 18–22; "Labor Lethargic, Says Cov," *Fortnightly*, November 1, 1926, 1; Melvyn Dubofsky, *We Shall Be All: A History of the IWW* (New York: Quadrangle, 1969), 212, 216; Koch and Koch, *Educational Commune*, 65–66; Covington Hall, "The Strike," *Southern Exposure* 1 (Winter 1974): 101; Commonwealth College Papers, microfilm no. 356, 3 reels, University of Arkansas, Fayetteville. "The Strike" is reprinted with the permission of *Southern Exposure*, a quarterly journal of Southern politics and culture, available for $16 a year by writing to P.O. Box 531, Durham, NC 27702.

46. Koch and Koch, *Educational Commune*, 22–30; Lucien Koch Collection, box 1, folder 1, and Raymond and Charlotte Koch Collection, box 1, folder 1, both in Archives of Labor and Urban Affairs, WSU.

47. "Brookwood," *American Teacher* 15 (February 1931): 12; "Brookwood Local 189," *American Teacher* 16 (October 1931): 28–29; "Brookwood Local 189," *American Teacher* 19 (November–December 1934): 28; "Commonwealth Local 194," *American Teacher* 16 (October 1931): 28–29; "Commonwealth College Local 194," *American Teacher* 18 (October 1934): 28; Koch and Koch, *Educational Commune*, 71; Brookwood Collection, box 22, folder 14, WSU; "Teachers Take Stock of Labor Education," *Brookwood Review*, February–March 1928, 1; "Teachers Review Decade of Workers' Education," *Brookwood Review*, May 1931, 2; "Record Crowd at Conference," *Brookwood Review*, February 1932, 1; Hansome, *Educational Movements*, 205; "To Gather School Data," *New York Times*, March 1, 1931, p. 6, col. 1; Helen G. Norton, "Workers' Education Teachers Meet," *Labor Age* 20 (April 1931): 20, 29; Helen G. Norton, "Workers' Education Conferences," *Labor Age* 21–22 (March 1932): 11; Bloom, "Brookwood Labor College," 37–38; quoted matter from William Cunningham, "Commonwealth College, Learning and Earning," *AAUP Bulletin* 15 (February 1929): 158.

48. Brookwood Collection, box 13, folder 6, WSU; Bertha Saposs, interview with author, March 18, 1984; Starr Oral History, PSU; "Faculty and Staff Members Added," *Brookwood Review*, October–November 1926, 4; "Negroes Can Organize Is Conference Feature," *Brookwood Review*, June–July 1927, 1; "Brookwood Opens for Seventh Year," *Brookwood Review*, October–November 1927, 1; "Prof. Schlicter Sees Co-Op Plan Future," *Brookwood Review*, February–March 1928, 4; "Sinclair Lewis Sees Unionism Urgent Need" and "Ameringer Undaunted by Life's Knockouts," *Brookwood Review*, September 1930, 1, 4; "37 Enroll in Brookwood," *New York Times*, October 12, 1929, p. 40, col. 3. The *Fortnightly* carried numerous accounts of guest speakers. See, for example, "Russelite and Ex-Wobbly Address College Luncheons," December 15, 1926, 1; and "Lecture and Discussion Courses," April 15, 1933, 3. General Correspondence, Dec. 2, 1912–Oct. 7, 1949, box 1, folder 7, and Posters and Broadsides, folder 60, Work People's College Collection, IHRC.

49. Brookwood Collection, box 5, folder 1, WSU.

50. *Work People's College Announcement of Courses, 1923–24*; Hans R. Wasastjerna, *History of the Finns in Minnesota* (New York Mills, Minn.: Northwestern Publishing Co., 1957), 227; Wiita, "Työväen Opisto," 6. *Articles of Incorporation and By-Laws of the Work People's College*, 13–15; "A Diversity of Action," *Work People's College Bulletin*, January 1, 1924, 3; Hansome, *Educational Movements*, 211–12; *Brookwood Bulletin* (1932–33), 15; Executive Board Minutes, 4 Apr. 1925, Brookwood Collection, box 1, folders 6, , 13; box 6, folder 14; and box 7, folder 1; Correspondence, box 11, folder 2, and box 22, folder 3, WSU; Bloom, "Brookwood Labor College," 85–87; "Students Elect Council; Many States Represented," *Fortnightly*, February 15, 1926, 1; "Student Council Includes Urbanites and Ruralites," *Fortnightly*, November 15, 1926, 1; "Jersey Wins Election," *Fortnightly*, March 15, 1927, 1; "Students Admitted to Governing Body," *Fortnightly*, October 15, 1928, 1; "The Seat of Power at Commonwealth," *Fortnightly*, November 15, 1929, 1; "Students Admitted to Governing Body," *Fortnightly*, February 1, 1933, 1; "Five New Members Admitted to College Association," *Fortnightly*, May 15, 1933, 1.

51. "Durability and Service Form Clothes Criteria," *Fortnightly*, April 15, 1926, 1; "Commonwealth, Workers' School," *Fortnightly*; "Teachers Employ Informal Methods," *Fortnightly*, December 1, 1931, 1; "Are Commonwealth Teachers 'Good Teachers'?" *Fortnightly*.

52. Robinson, *Abraham Went Out*, 34; "All Are Workers at Commonwealth," *Fortnightly*, January 1, 1930, 2; Alice Hanson, "New Teacher Outlines View of Commonwealth," *Fortnightly*, February 1, 1926, 4; "Friends of Commonwealth Purchase Founders' Bonds," *Fortnightly*, February 15, 1926, 1; "Educational Pioneering," *Fortnightly Supplement*, December 1, 1927, 4; "Brookwood's Seventh Year Begins Oct. 17," *Brookwood Review*, September 1927, 1, 6; Archie Brown, personal letter to author, March 29, 1983. Lawrence Rogin, interview with author, March 18, 1984.

53. *Brookwood Bulletin* (1932–33), 14–15, also assumed that all students

would work. "Brookwooders Have Easy Time Now," *Brookwood Review*, December 1927–January 1928, 2; Bloom, "Brookwood Labor College," 68–69. Starr Oral History, 6, PSU; "New Industrial Plan," *Fortnightly*, June 15, 1930, 1; "Hectic Days Harass Happy Commoners," *Fortnightly*, January 15, 1927, 1–3; Lucien Koch Collection, box 1, folder 2, WSU.

54. Ellis, "What Life Means," 16; C. Mauritz Erkkila, personal letter to author, March 3, 1983; Sulo Peltola, personal letter to author, April 9, 1983; IWW Collection, box 137, folders 13, 29, WSU. Eli Hill's poem is reprinted with the permission of the Archives of Labor and Urban Affairs, Wayne State University.

55. Starr Oral History, PSU; "Brookwood Opens for Seventh Year," *Brookwood Review*, October–November 1927, 1. Also refer to "Student Participation Big Factor in Brookwood Community Life," *Brookwood Review*, December 1930, 3; and *Brookwood Bulletin* (1932–33), 5. "Student Is Elected General Manager," *Fortnightly*, April 1, 1926, 1. Ernest's brother received a similar appointment in 1929. See "Koch Appointed Personnel Manager," *Fortnightly*, November 1, 1929, 3.

56. Bertha Saposs, interview with author, March 18, 1984; Starr Oral History, PSU; "Stone House Built by Student Workmen," *Brookwood Review*, October–November 1926, 4; "New Garage Built by Students This Summer," *Brookwood Review*, October–November 1927, 2; "No More Dry Washes for Cabin Inhabitants," *Brookwood Review*, October–November 1928, 3; *Brookwood Twelfth Anniversary Review*, 9.

57. "Students and Teachers Plow to Feed College Next Term," *Fortnightly*, March 15, 1926, 1; "Canning Goes On," *Fortnightly*, April 1, 1926, 1; "Commonwealth Cheese," *Fortnightly*, July 1, 1927, 1; "Commoners Fatten on Two Bits a Day," *Fortnightly*, September 1, 1930, 1; "Students Initiate Fruit Farm Program," *Fortnightly*, February 15, 1926, 1; "Our Struggle for Existence," *Fortnightly*, September 1, 1930, 1; "College Buns and Onions Take Prize in Arkansas," *Fortnightly*, October 1, 1926, 1; "Cane, Peanuts, Spuds Scurry from Frost," *Fortnightly*, November 1, 1926, 1.

58. "Store and Office Appear on Campus," *Fortnightly*, April 15, 1926, 1; "New Crops Include Peanuts and Cotton," *Fortnightly*, May 15, 1926, 1; "School Nears Stage of Village Economy," *Fortnightly*, June 1, 1926, 1; "Crops All Planted: College Builds Now," *Fortnightly*, July 1, 1926, 1; "Lumber Abounds as Fund Extends Aid," *Fortnightly*, July 15, 1926, 1; "New Dorm Appears: Spud Crop Exhumed," *Fortnightly*, August 15, 1926, 1; "New Labor and Cottages Swell Building Total," *Fortnightly*, September 15, 1926, 1; "College Improvement," *Fortnightly*, November 1, 1929, 1; Lucien Koch Collection, box 1, folder 2, WSU.

59. "Operating Expenses $6,281.35 for Year," *Fortnightly*, February 1, 1933, 1, 4; Koch and Koch, *Educational Commune*, 10.

60. Falkowski Collection, box 5, folder 11, WSU.

61. *Fortnightly*, January 1, 1930; Brookwooders made a similar, although less detailed, evaluation in the *Brookwood Twelfth Anniversary Review*, 9.

62. Aakula, "Short Sketches," 4–5.

63. *Brookwood Twelfth Anniversary Review*, 10. See Smith, "Workers Prepare," 303, for an elaboration of the working-class lifestyle.

64. Koch and Koch, *Educational Commune*, 39; Lawrence Rogin, interview with author, March 18, 1984.

65. Devere Allen, "A School for Workers' Children," *Nation* 119 (October 15, 1924): 417–18; Cleghorn, *Threescore*, 253.

66. Quoted in "A New Community School," *Survey* 53 (October 1924): 91–92.

67. Graduation, 1923–27, Brookwood Collection, box 95, folder 1, WSU.

68. George S. Counts, *The Social Composition of Boards of Education: A Study of the Social Control of Public Education* (1927; reprint, New York: Arno Press, 1969), 87. Also refer to George S. Counts, *Dare the School Build a New Social Order?* (1932; reprint, New York: Arno Press, 1969); John Dewey, "Internal Social Reorganization After the War," *Journal of Race Development* (*Journal of International Relations*) 8 (April 1918): 385–400; and John Dewey, *Education and the Social Order* (New York: League for Industrial Democracy, 1934).

CHAPTER 5

Harassment

1. Carl Ross, *The Finn Factor in American Labor, Culture, and Society* (New York Mills, Minn.: Parta Printers, 1977), insightfully analyzes the tensions between radical and conservative Finns. See, in particular, 73–74, 115–18, 135, 146–47, 151. William D. Haywood, *The Autobiography of Big Bill Haywood* (1929; reprint, New York: International Publishers, 1976), 367; Peter Kivisto, *Immigrant Socialists in the United States: The Case of the Finns and the Left* (Rutherford, N.J.: Fairleigh Dickinson University Press, 1984), 156.

2. "Plan Bolshevism Meeting," *New York Times*, May 3, 1919, p. 3, col. 3; "Bolshevist Inquiry June 1," *New York Times*, May 25, 1919, sec. 2, II, p. 14, col. 1; "Says Bolshevism Is Growing Fast Here," *New York Times*, June 4, 1919, p. 3, col. 4; "Extra Court Term for Radical Cases," *New York Times*, July 10, 1919, p. 1, col. 7; "The Lusk Investigation," *New York Times*, July 11, 1919, p. 10, col. 4; "Government Joins 'Red' Investigation," *New York Times*, July 25, 1919, p. 6, col. 1.

3. "Hear Bolsheviki Plan a Test Here," *New York Times*, May 7, 1919, p. 7, col. 2; "New York Office of the Bolsheviki Raided by State," *New York Times*, June 13, 1919, p. 1, col. 1; "Find Soviet Envoy Aided Socialists and IWW Here," *New York Times*, June 19, 1919, p. 1, col. 1; "Raid Rand School, 'Left Wing,'

and IWW Offices," *New York Times,* June 22, 1919, sec. 1, p. 1, col. 1; "Rand School Safe Under Close Guard," *New York Times,* June 23, 1919, p. 15, col. 4.

4. "Moves to Close the Rand School," *New York Times,* June 28, 1919, p. 1, col. 2; "Attacks Charter of Rand School," *New York Times,* July 9, 1919, p. 17, col. 1; "Rand School Wins Temporary Writ," *New York Times,* July 17, 1919, p. 17, col. 4; "Rand School Loses Plea for Papers," *New York Times,* August 1, 1919, p. 13, col. 1; "Says 300,000 Finns in U.S. Are 'Reds,'" *New York Times,* December 28, 1919, sec. 1, p. 7, col. 1; Ross, *Finn Factor,* 160.

5. New York Joint Legislative Committee Investigating Seditious Activities, *Revolutionary Radicalism: Its History, Purpose, and Tactics with an Exposition and Discussion of the Steps Being Taken and Required to Curb It* (Albany, N.Y.: J. B. Lyon, 1920), Pt. 1, vol. 1, 1112–21; pt. 2, vol. 3, 2292.

6. Ross, *Finn Factor,* 160–61; Arnold Alanen, "The Development and Distribution of Finnish Consumers' Cooperatives in Michigan, Minnesota, and Wisconsin, 1903–1973," in *The Finnish Experience in the Western Great Lakes Region: New Perspectives,* ed. Michael G. Karni, Matti Kaups, and Douglas J. Ollila, Jr. (Turku, Finland: Institute for Migration, 1975), 103–29. Alanen primarily focuses on the CCE. Also see David A. Shannon, *The Socialist Party in America: A History* (New York: Macmillan, 1955), 121, 128, 163.

7. Arne Halonen, "The Role of Finnish-Americans in the Political Labor Movement" (master's thesis, University of Minnesota, 1945), 75–77, 97; Auvo Kostiainen, "The Finns and the Crisis Over 'Bolshevization' in the Workers' Party, 1924–25," in *The Finnish Experience,* ed. Karni, Kaups, and Ollila, *Finn Factor,* 171–85; Ross, 163–64; Michael G. Karni, "Struggle on the Cooperative Front: The Separation of Central Cooperative Wholesale from Communism, 1929–30," in *The Finnish Experience,* ed. Karni, Kaups, and Ollila, 186–201.

8. Halonen, "Finnish-Americans," 97, 100, 102.

9. Douglas J. Ollila, Jr., "The Work People's College: Immigrant Education for Adjustment and Solidarity," in *For the Common Good: Finnish Immigrants and the Radical Response to Industrial America,* ed. Michael G. Karni et al. (Superior, Wis.: Tyomies Society, 1977), 87–118.

10. Brookwood Labor College Collection, box 1, folder 9, Archives of Labor and Urban Affairs, Wayne State University (hereafter WSU); "Labor College to Expand," *New York Times,* May 2, 1926, sec. 2, p. 19, col. 4; "Labor College Seeks $2,000,000," *New York Times,* February 2, 1928, p. 16, col. 6; "Endowment Campaign Generously Endorsed," *Brookwood Review,* October–November 1926, 1; "$50,000 for Building and Endowment Fund in Sight," *Brookwood Review,* February–March 1928, 1; Jonathan D. Bloom, "Brookwood Labor College, 1921–1933: Training Ground for Union Organizers" (master's thesis, Rutgers University, 1978), 97–99; Jo Ann Ooiman Robinson, *Abraham Went Out: A Biography of A. J. Muste* (Philadelphia: Temple University Press, 1981), 33–34; "Teachers Take Stock of Labor Education," *Brookwood Review,* February–March 1928, 1.

11. Herbert G. Gutman, "*Labor Age,* 1921–1933," in *The American Radical*

Press, 1880–1960, ed. Joseph R. Conlin (Westport, Conn.: Greenwood Press, 1974), 191–97; Robinson, *Abraham Went Out*, 37; Solon DeLeon, *American Labor Who's Who* (New York: Hauford Press, 1925), 31.

12. Irving Bernstein, *The Lean Years: A History of the American Worker, 1920–1933* (Boston: Houghton Mifflin, 1960), 97–106; A. J. Muste, *The Essays of A. J. Muste*, ed. Nat Hentoff (New York: Simon & Schuster, 1967), 124–31; Robert J. Schaefer, "Educational Activities of the Garment Unions, 1890–1948: A Study in Workers' Education in the International Ladies' Garment Workers' Union and the Amalgamated Clothing Workers of America in New York City" (Ph.D. diss., Columbia University, 1951), 124; Bloom, "Brookwood Labor College," 88–91, 93–96; Evelyn Preston, "Brookwood Carries On," *Brookwood Labor College Fifteenth Anniversary Review* (Katonah, N.Y.: Brookwood Labor College, 1935), 50–51. The NCF quotation is from James Weinstein, *The Decline of Socialism in America, 1912–1925* (New York: Monthly Review Press, 1967), 235.

13. Brookwood Labor College Collection, box 6, folder 1, WSU; Preston, "Brookwood Carries On," 50–51.

14. Robinson, *Abraham Went Out*, 38–39.

15. John Brophy, *A Miner's Life* (Madison: University of Wisconsin Press, 1964), 214–16.

16. Melvyn Dubofsky and Warren Van Tine, *John L. Lewis: A Biography* (New York: Quadrangle, 1977), 127–28.

17. James O. Morris, *Conflict within the AFL: A Study of Craft versus Industrial Unionism, 1901–1938* (Ithaca, N.Y.: Cornell University Press, 1958), provides a thoroughly researched analysis of the AFL–Brookwood conflict; See chapter 5, "The Split with the Progressives." Robinson's description of the controversy in *Abraham Went Out*, 38–39, is largely based on Morris. Also see Bloom, "Brookwood Labor College," 91–93, 111–15, for another fine, but similar, analysis.

18. Morris, *Conflict*, 113–14; Robinson, *Abraham Went Out*, 38. The report has never been made public.

19. "Brookwood Denies A. F. of L.'s Charges," *New York Times*, August 9, 1928, p. 8, col. 1.

20. Executive Board Minutes, Brookwood Collection, box 7, folder 2, WSU. On September 10, 1928, the Executive Board discussed plans to prepare for a public hearing. Also see "Friends Rally to Brookwood: A. F. of L. Postpones Action," *Labor Age* 17 (October 1928): 21; "What Brookwood Means," *Nation* 127 (September 1928): 241; and "Labor Heeds Protest," *New York Times*, August 29, 1928, p. 11, col. 6.

21. William E. Zeuch, "The A. F. of L. on Trial," *Commonwealth College Fortnightly* [hereafter *Fortnightly*], October 1, 1928, 2.

22. Arthur W. Calhoun Collection, box 28, folder 1, Archives of Labor and Urban Affairs, WSU.

23. "Red Activity Here to be Investigated," *New York Times*, September 21, 1928, p. 49, col. 3.

24. Calhoun Collection, box 28, folder 2, WSU.

25. "Labor Withdraws Support of College," *New York Times,* October 31, 1928, p. 33, col. 4. Emphasis mine. Also refer to Gene Grabiner, "Conservative Labor Leaders Clean House: The Case of Brookwood Labor College," *Educational Theory* 29 (Summer 1979): 195–209. Calhoun was not the only Brookwood instructor perceived as "red." Tom Tippett spoke at the University of Pittsburgh in 1928, and the faculty member who sponsored him, Albert S. Whitely, was censured by university administrators. See Raymond F. Howes, *Low Point at Pitt: A Study of the Loss of Academic Freedom* (Riverside, Calif.: n.p., 1972), 14–15.

26. "Labor College Side Not Heard, He Says," *New York Times,* November 1, 1928, p. 9, col. 1.

27. Quoted in "Brookwood Drafts Appeal to AFL," *New York Times,* November 5, 1928, p. 28, col. 2; *The Injunction Against Brookwood* (Katonah, N.Y.: Brookwood Labor College, 1928); "Brookwood Carries On: Condemned by Council without Hearing," *Labor Age* 17 (November 1928): 3.

28. Quoted in "New York Teachers Protest AFL Action," *Brookwood Review,* October–November 1928, 4. Dewey asked Muste to examine a draft of his speech to the New York City Teachers Union. A draft of that speech, and correspondence between Dewey and Muste, appear in AFL Correspondence, 1928–29, Brookwood Collection, box 17, folder 16, WSU.

29. Quoted in "Denounces Action on Brookwood School," *New York Times,* November 10, 1928, p. 7, col. 2.

30. Quoted in "New York Teachers," *Brookwood Review.*

31. Muste, *Essays,* 129. Also refer to Robinson, *Abraham Went Out,* 38; A. J. Muste, "Mitten Management and Union: Some Straightforward Questions," *Labor Age* 17 (May 1928): 4–6.

32. American Federation of Labor, *Proceedings of the Forty-Eighth Annual Convention of the American Federation of Labor* (Washington, D.C.: Law Register Printing, 1928), 314–17, 319–20, 323 (emphasis in Green's remarks is added), 324–25, 327–29. Muste points out that Woll's report was neither published nor, to this date, open to public scrutiny. Muste, *Essays,* 127. Also see Morris, *Conflict,* 115, 130; Calhoun Collection, box 28, folder 4, WSU. "Delegates Clash on Labor College," *New York Times,* November 28, 1928, p. 11, col. 1; "Brookwood Victim of Convention Lynching," *Brookwood Review,* October–November 1928, 1. Anti-intellectualism was apparently a tradition among Federation leaders. See Lyle W. Cooper, "The American Federation of Labor and the Intellectuals," *Political Science Quarterly* 43 (September 1928): 388–407.

33. Mark and Helen Starr Oral History, November 15, 1974, Labor Archives, Pennsylvania State University (hereafter PSU); Katherine Pollak Ellickson Oral History, 1974, Archives of Labor and Urban Affairs, WSU; Brookwood Collection, box 12, folder 1, WSU; Muste, *Essays,* 131; Morris, *Conflict,* 117–20; Robinson, *Abraham Went Out,* 37–38.

34. Morris, *Conflict*, 121, 124.

35. "Commoners Will Attend A. F. of L. Convention," *Fortnightly*, November 15, 1928, 4; "The Gospel According to Matthew," and "Words, Words, Words," *Fortnightly*, December 15, 1928, 2; Morris, *Conflict*, 114–15.

36. "Teachers' Federation Stands by Brookwood," *Brookwood Review*, October–November 1928, 4; "Green's 'Irrefutable' Charges Answered," "An Open Letter to President Green," and "Supporters Send Money and Encouraging Words," *Brookwood Review*, December–January 1928, 1–3.

37. Carl Haessler, "A. F. of L. Convention High Lights: Aggressiveness and Militancy Missing," *Labor Age* 18 (January 1929): 3–4; "Labor Expunges Tribute to Dewey," *New York Times*, November 29, 1928, p. 12, col. 1.

38. Dewey allowed Muste to read a draft of the *New Republic* article. AFL Controversy, 1928–29, Brookwood Collection, box 17, folder 17, and box 12, folder 7, WSU. Muste informed Dewey, in this correspondence, that "Ralph Easley definitely stated that the National Civic Federation was out to 'get him' [Dewey] and that Woll's reference to yourself at the A. F. of L. convention was therefore by no means an accident, but part of a carefully planned campaign." Also see John Dewey, "Labor Politics and Labor Education," *New Republic* 57 (January 9, 1929): 211–14. A condensed version appeared in "Quotations: Brookwood Labor College and the American Federation of Labor," *School and Society* 29 (January 1929): 92–93.

39. "Urges Overthrow of A. F. of L. Chiefs," *New York Times*, February 23, 1929, p. 9, col. 4. At Brookwood's annual workers' education conference, supporters and teachers of workers' education severely criticized the action of the AFL. See "Brookwood Alumni Protest to Green," *New York Times*, February 14, 1929, p. 11, col. 2.

40. A. J. Muste, "Shall Workers' Education Perish?" *Labor Age* 18 (January 1929): 5–6; A. J. Muste, "The Why of Workers' Education," *World Tomorrow* 12 (January 1929): 28–30. Also see Brookwood Collection, box 7, folder 3, WSU. Brookwooders anticipated the attack on the WEB and prepared for it.

41. "Jim Maurer's Warning," *Labor Age* 18 (May 1929): 3–4; "Brookwood Group Bolts Labor Parley," *New York Times*, April 7, 1929, sec. 1, p. 21, col. 1; Calhoun Collection, box 28, folder 10, WSU.

42. Morris, *Conflict*, 123–24; David Saposs, "Which Way Workers' Education?" *Survey* 62 (May 1929): 250–51; Muste, *Essays*, 139; John R. Commons, "Workers' Education and the Universities," *American Federationist* 34 (April 1927): 424–26, also expressed some early misgivings over the usefulness of university-sponsored workers' education: "One difficulty with our colleges and universities is that they tend to educate workers away from the labor movement. . . . State universities are controlled by the taxpayers and they will not give the courses that workers want unless workers are in an independent position to go ahead on their own hook."

43. Calhoun Collection, box 28, folder 3, WSU.

44. Commonwealth College Papers, microfilm no. 356, 3 reels, University of Arkansas, Fayetteville; "Legion Loses Sleep Over Commonwealth," *Fortnightly*, September 15, 1926, 1; "Labor, Press, and Townsfolk Scout Legion 'Red Gold' Tale," *Fortnightly*, October 1, 1926, 1; "Department of Justice Denies Any Report on Commonwealth," *Fortnightly*, October 15, 1926, 1; "Legion Falls Down on School Inquiry," *Fortnightly*, November 1, 1926, 1; Raymond Koch and Charlotte Koch, *Educational Commune: The Story of Commonwealth College* (New York: Schocken Books, 1972), 72–74.

45. William H. Cobb, "Commonwealth College: A History" (master's thesis, University of Arkansas, 1960), 94, 135–36; "Thanks, Your Honor," *Fortnightly*, June 1, 1927, 1; "Thanks Friends," *Fortnightly*, March 15, 1928, 2; "Campaign Results," *Fortnightly*, April 15, 1928, 3; "Commonwealth Is Honored by DAR," *Fortnightly*, May 15, 1928, 1; "Commonwealth Aids Are Now Harassed," *Fortnightly*, October 1, 1930, 1; "Thanks Friends," *fortnightly*, December 1, 1932, 1.

46. "Supplement: Commonwealth to Be Investigated," *Fortnightly*, February 15, 1935; " 'Red' Inquiry at College Urged," *New York Times*, February 4, 1935, p. 6, col. 2.

47. The entire text of testimony for all witnesses is in the Commonwealth College Papers, microfilm no. 356, reel 1, University of Arkansas, Fayetteville. For a transcript of the hearing, see Raymond and Charlotte Koch Collection, box 1, folder 29, Archives of Labor and Urban Affairs, WSU. Parts of it also appear in Koch and Koch, *Educational Commune*, 162–63.

48. Cobb, "Commonwealth College," 186, 188–89; "Push Inquiry on 'Reds' in Arkansas College," *New York Times*, February 17, 1935, p. 20, col. 2.

49. Cobb, "Commonwealth College," 191–92; "The Arkansas Legislature Shows Good Sense," *Christian Century* 52 (April 1935): 501–2. See whole issue of *Fortnightly*, March 15, 1935; "Legislature Kills Suppressive Bills" and "Sentiment of Nation against Fascist Bills," *Fortnightly*, April 1, 1935, 1–2.

50. Quoted in Cobb, "Commonwealth College," 192.

51. Lucien Koch Collection, box 1, folder 2, Archives of Labor and Urban Affairs, WSU; "College Visited by Brookwood Chief," *Fortnightly*, March 15, 1936, 1; "Prominent Leaders Join Advisory Board," *Fortnightly*, November 1, 1936, 1; "Einstein Aids College" and "Unions Send Donations," *Fortnightly*, November 15, 1936, 1.

52. Raymond and Charlotte Koch Collection, box 1, folder 13, WSU; "Liberty Exposes Commonwealth After Two-Hour Investigation," *Fortnightly*, December 15, 1936, 1; "Commonwealth Requests Civil Liberties Investigation as Answer to Liberty," *Fortnightly*, January 1, 1937, 2; "Attack on Commonwealth College Renewed," *American Teacher* 21 (January–February 1937): 28–29; "Another Attack on Commonwealth," *Christian Century* 54 (January 1937): 83–84; Koch and Koch, *Educational Commune*, 191–92; "Denounces Critics of Labor College," *New York Times*, December 28, 1936, p. 19, col. 6; "Arkansas War on Labor School," *New York Times*, December 27, 1936, sec. 5, p. 2, col. 5.

53. "Drafts Bill for Oath Test," *New York Times*, December 27, 1936, sec. 1; "Red Brains: Left-Wing College Raises Storm-Clouds over Arkansas Ozarks," *Literary Digest* 123 (January 1937): 4–5; Koch and Koch, *Educational Commune*, 193; Cobb, "Commonwealth College," 211–14; "Protest!" *Fortnightly*, February 1, 1937, 1; "Nationwide Ire at Sedition Bill Wins Many Liberal Solons," *Fortnightly*, February 15, 1937, 1; "Liberal Solons Smash Gag Bill 46–19 as Protests Pave Victory," *Fortnightly*, March 1, 1937, 1.

54. David Montgomery, "New Tendencies in Union Struggles and Strategies in Europe and the United States, 1916–1922," in *Work, Community, and Power in Europe and America, 1900–1925*, ed. James E. Cronin and Carmen Sirianni (Philadelphia: Temple University Press, 1983), 88–116.

CHAPTER 6

Fratricide

1. Gloria Garrett Samson, "Toward a New Social Order—The American Fund for Public Service: Clearinghouse for Radicalism in the 1920s," (Ph.D. diss., University of Rochester, 1987), 6–7; Lillian Symes, "V. F. Calverton, Socialist," *Modern Quarterly* 12 (Fall 1940): 20–24.

2. A. J. Muste, *The Essays of A. J. Muste*, ed. Nat Hentoff (New York: Simon & Schuster, 1967), 149.

3. Mark and Helen Starr Oral History, November 15, 1974, Labor Archives, Pennsylvania State University (hereafter PSU); Muste, *Essays*, 140–42; "A. J. Muste Heads Labor Militants," *New York Times*, June 7, 1929, p. 13, col. 4; "Wide Reform Urged in A. F. of L. Policies," *"New York Times*, June 9, 1929, sec. 2, p. 1, col. 7. The CPLA also received other support. See "Progressive Labor's Institute: C.P.L.A.'s Educational Conference at Brookwood," *Labor Age* 18 (September 1929): 17–18; James O. Morris, *Conflict within the AFL: A Study of Craft versus Industrial Unionism, 1901–1938* (Ithaca, N.Y.: Cornell University Press, 1958), 127–35.

4. Arthur W. Calhoun Collection, box 28, folder 8, Archives of Labor and Urban Affairs, Wayne State University (hereafter WSU).

5. Calhoun Collection, box 5, folders 12, 13, WSU; Jo Ann Ooiman Robinson, *Abraham Went Out: A Biography of A. J. Muste* (Philadelphia: Temple University Press, 1981), 41–43.

6. "Katonah Faculty Opposes Calhoun" and "Denies Communist Membership," *New York Times*, June 4, 1929, p. 2, col. 3; Jonathan D. Bloom, "Brookwood Labor College, 1921–1933: Training Ground for Union Organizers" (master's thesis, Rutgers University, 1978), 115–20; Brookwood Labor College Collection, box 12, folder 8, Archives of Labor and Urban Affairs, WSU.

7. Brookwood Collection, box 1, folder 11, WSU; Calhoun Collection, box 28, folder 15, WSU; "Dr. Calhoun Quoted by Labor College," *New York Times*,

June 10, 1929, p. 27, col. 7; "Dr. Calhoun at Brookwood," *New York Times*, June 17, 1929, p. 22, col. 7; "Dr. Calhoun Replies," *New York Times*, June 20, 1929, p. 24, col. 6; Bloom, "Brookwood Labor College," 121–26; Robinson, *Abraham Went Out*, 43–44.

8. Brookwood Collection, box 36, folder 1, WSU; William E. Zeuch, "The Apostasy of Brookwood," *Commonwealth College Fortnightly* [hereafter *Fortnightly*], October 1, 1929, 2; "Correspondence: Dr. Calhoun and Brookwood," *New Republic* 59 (August 7, 1929): 314–15.

9. "Muste, In Protest over Norris, Quits," *New York Times*, December 30, 1930, p. 3, col. 3; Robinson, *Abraham Went Out*, 40–41.

10. Brookwood Collection, box 1, folder 19, and box 23, folder 20, WSU; "Help for Brookwood," *Nation* 135 (December 1932): 592. Also see A. J. Muste, "Help Brookwood to Help Workers," *Brookwood Review*, December 1932, 4. George S. Counts appeared as a guest speaker at a Workers' Education symposium in New York City: "Luncheon Symposium on Workers' Education," *Brookwood Review*, October 1933, 4. Also see "Back Brookwood!" *World Tomorrow* 15 (December 1932): 558.

11. Robinson, *Abraham Went Out*, 42.

12. Ibid., 44–45; "Socialist Movement Project: A. J. Muste" (1967), Columbia University Oral History Collection.

13. "Report on Political Organization," *Labor Age* 20 (August 1931): 4–6; Katherine Pollack Ellickson Collection, box 3, folders 8, 25, Archives of Labor and Urban Affairs, WSU.

14. A. J. Muste, "The Meaning of the Convention," *Labor Age* 21–22 (September 1932): 3–5; Ellickson Collection, box 3, folder 6, WSU.

15. Muste, *Essays*, 148.

16. Ellickson Collection, box 3, folder 14, WSU; Brookwood Collection, box 23, folder 12, WSU.

17. Ellickson Collection, box 3, folder 24, WSU.

18. Ibid., folder 18; Brookwood Collection, box 23, folder 12, WSU; Clinton Golden Collection, Labor Archives, PSU; Morris, *Conflict*, 125–35; Muste, *Essays*, 150; Bloom, "Brookwood Labor College," 146–47, 149; Robinson, *Abraham Went Out*, 45.

19. Brookwood Collection, box 7, folder 16, WSU; Ellickson Collection, box 3, folder 18, WSU; Golden Collection, PSU; Muste, *Essays*, 150.

20. Ellickson Collection, box 3, folder 17, WSU.

21. Brookwood Collection, box 7, folder 17, WSU.

22. Ibid.

23. Ellickson Collection, box 3, folder 24, WSU.

24. Ibid., folder 7.

25. Muste, *Essays*, 150.

26. Ibid.

27. Ellickson Collection, box 3, folder 25, WSU.

28. Muste, *Essays*, 151; Colby is quoted in Robinson, *Abraham Went Out*, 46.

29. Quoted in "Dean Heads Bolt at Labor College," *New York Times,* March 8, 1933, p. 15, col. 1. Also see "Whither Brookwood," *Labor Age* 21–22 (February–March 1933): 14–17; Brookwood Collection, box 1, folder 3, WSU.

30. "Muste Quits in Rift over CPLA," *Brookwood Review,* May 1933, 1.

31. "New Program for Labor College," *New York Times,* June 5, 1933, p. 4, col. 4; "Tucker Smith Heads Brookwood," *World Tomorrow* 16 (July 1933): 441; "Tucker Smith Appointed Director," *Brookwood Review,* May 1933, 1; "Brookwood to Continue," *New York Times,* March 9, 1933, p. 14, col. 5; "Brookwood Splits," *Survey* 69 (April 1933): 165; Starr Oral History, PSU.

32. Muste, *Essays,* 152–53.

33. "Brookwood Schism," *World Tomorrow* 16 (March 1933): 220; Muste, *Essays,* 135; Morris, *Conflict,* 135. Also see "The Call of the Left: From 'Progressive Labor Action' to Trotskyism," chapter 4 in Robinson, *Abraham Went Out,* 49–61.

34. "Correspondence: Students on Strike," *Nation* 136 (January 1933): 19; "The Commonwealth Strike," *Nation* 136 (1933): 476. These articles included letters written by the various parties involved in the strike. "Strike Over, School Goes on with Work," *Fortnightly,* December 15, 1932, 1; Cobb, "Commonwealth College," 167–69; Raymond Koch and Charlotte Koch, *Educational Commune: The Story of Commonwealth College* (New York: Schocken Books, 1972), 114–15.

CHAPTER 7

The End of the Labor Colleges

1. Arthur Gleason, "Workers' Education," *New Republic* 26 (April 20, 1921): 235–37.

2. Florence H. Schneider, *Patterns of Workers' Education: The Story of the Bryn Mawr Summer School* (Washington, D.C.: American Council on Public Affairs, 1941), 9. Also see Frank Fernbach Oral History, Labor Archives, Pennsylvania State University (hereafter PSU). Fernbach taught at Brookwood during its final year, 1936–37.

3. "Hail Brookwood's Fifteenth Year," *Brookwood Review,* March 1936, 1; "Workers' School Has Anniversary," *New York Times,* January 19, 1936, sec. 1, p. 23, col. 3.

4. *Brookwood Labor College Fifteenth Anniversary Review* (Katonah, N.Y.: Brookwood Labor College, 1936), 19; "Union Meetings Vote Brookwood Support," *Brookwood Review,* July 1936, 1.

5. "Hochman Chosen Board Chairman," *Brookwood Review,* July 1936, 5.

6. Brookwood Labor College Collection, box 1, folders 21, 22, 24, and box 12, folder 14, Archives of Labor and Urban Affairs, Wayne State University (hereafter WSU); Lawrence Rogin, interview with author, March 18, 1984.

7. Executive Board Committee, Correspondence, 1932–37, Brookwood

Collection, box 7, folder 4, WSU. See, in particular, document dated September 29, 1936. Also see A. J. Muste, *The Essays of A. J. Muste*, ed. Nat Hentoff (New York: Simon & Schuster, 1967), 148; Mark and Helen Starr Oral History, November 15, 1974, Labor Archives, PSU; Roger Baldwin, "Brookwood and the Garland Fund," *Brookwood Fifteenth Anniversary Review*, 39–41.

8. American Fund for Public Service, Brookwood Collection, box 8, WSU.

9. Ibid., boxes 22, 23; Lawrence Rogin, interview with author, March 18, 1984.

10. Brookwood Collection, box 1, folder 4, WSU.

11. Ibid., box 9, folder 17. Emphasis original.

12. Cohn's comment is quoted in the Fernbach Oral History, PSU; "Brookwood Graduates 19," *New York Times*, March 2, 1937, sec. 2, p. 3, col. 8.

13. "Blame Labor Split in College Closing: Brookwood Directors Point to CIO and AFL Conflict as Major Cause for Action," *New York Times*, November 21, 1937, sec. 2, p. 6, col. 2; Executive Board Committee, Correspondence, 1932–37, Brookwood Collection, box 7, folder 4, WSU; Muste, *Essays*, 152; Robert J. Schaefer, "Educational Activities of the Garment Unions, 1890–1948: A Study in Workers' Education in the International Ladies' Garment Workers' Union and the Amalgamated Clothing Workers of America in New York City" (Ph.D. diss., Columbia University, 1951), 213–14.

14. Workers' Education Local 189 Collection, Archives of Labor and Urban Affairs, WSU.

15. Gloria Garrett Samson, "Toward a New Social Order—The American Fund for Public Service: Clearinghouse for Radicalism in the 1920s" (Ph.D. diss., University of Rochester, 1987), 371, 374. "Subsidizing Red Radicalism," *National Republic* 18 (November 1930): 26–27; this article also claimed that Brookwood, another "red" institution, received some $74,000 and Manumit School received $11,000 from the Fund. John Dewey was also alluded to as a "red." William H. Cobb, "Commonwealth College: A History" (master's thesis, University of Arkansas, 1960), 151–53, 177–79; Commonwealth College Papers, microfilm no. 356, 3 reels, University of Arkansas, Fayetteville; "Commonwealth Must Have $2,500 If It Is to Operate Next Year," *Commonwealth College Fortnightly* [hereafter *Fortnightly*], May 1, 1933, 1; "School Finances Are Still in Bad Shape," *Fortnightly*, June 15, 1933, 1; "Will Commonwealth Go On?" *Fortnightly*, April 15–May 1, 1934, 1; "Financial Aid Urgent: Response Is Slow," *Fortnightly*, November 1, 1936, 1.

16. Donald H. Grubbs, *Cry from the Cotton: The Southern Tenant Farmers' Union and the New Deal* (Chapel Hill: University of North Carolina Press, 1971), 9–10, 12, 22–23. Hall's poem is quoted in H. L. Mitchell, *Mean Things Happening in This Land: The Life and Times of H. L. Mitchell, Cofounder of the Southern Tenant Farmers' Union* (Montclair, N.J.: Allanheld, Osnum, 1979), 20. It is reprinted here with the permission of Rowman & Littlefield Publishers, Savage, Md.

17. Cobb, "Commonwealth College," 179–80; William H. Cobb and Don-

ald H. Grubbs, "Arkansas' Commonwealth College and the Southern Tenant Farmers' Union," *Arkansas Historical Quarterly* 25 (Winter 1966): 293–311; "Wave Explains Plan of Radical Farmers," *Fortnightly*, October 1, 1932, 1; "Expropriation of the Small Farmer," *Fortnightly*, February 1, 1933, 3.

18. David A. Shannon, *The Socialist Party in America: A History* (New York: Macmillan, 1955), 106–9; James Weinstein, *The Decline of Socialism in America, 1912–1925* (New York: Monthly Review Press, 1967), 139–40, 182; Mitchell, *Mean Things*, 28–29, 33–36, 43; Wilma Dykeman and James Stokely, *Seeds of Southern Change: The Life of Will Alexander* (New York: Norton, 1962), 209; Michael Honey, "Labor and Civil Rights in the South: The Industrial Labor Movement and Black Workers in Memphis, 1929–1945" (Ph.D. diss., Northern Illinois University, 1986), 246; James R. Green, *Grass-Roots Socialism: Radical Movements in the Southwest, 1895–1943* (Baton Rouge: Louisiana State University Press, 1978).

19. Sue Thrasher and Leah Wise, "The Southern Tenant Farmers' Union," *Southern Exposure* 1, nos. 3–4 (Winter 1974): 9–32; Cobb and Grubbs, "Arkansas' Commonwealth College," 296; Dykeman and Stokely, *Seeds*, 209.

20. Honey, "Labor," 246–48.

21. Mitchell, *Mean Things*, 74; Honey, "Labor," 244–45.

22. Cobb and Grubbs, "Arkansas' Commonwealth College," 297; Raymond Koch and Charlotte Koch, *Educational Commune: The Story of Commonwealth College* (New York: Schocken Books, 1972), 151–60; Mitchell, *Mean Things*, 62–64.

23. Samson, "New Social Order," 199–200; Mitchell, *Mean Things*, 82; Grubbs, *Cry From the Cotton*, 86.

24. "Sharecroppers' Union Greets Commonwealth," *Fortnightly*, January 1, 1936, 1; Cobb and Grubbs, "Arkansas' Commonwealth College," 299; Cobb, "Commonwealth College," 197.

25. "Butler, President of the STFU, Joins Commonwealth College Faculty," *Fortnightly*, February 1, 1936, 1; "Sharecroppers Arrive to Get Training," *Fortnightly*, April 15, 1936, 1; "Mena Local of STFU Organized," *Fortnightly*, May 1, 1936, 2; "C. Williams and J. R. Butler Nominated by Socialists," *Fortnightly*, August 15, 1936, 3; Cobb, "Commonwealth College," 200–202.

26. Mitchell, *Mean Things*, 48–49, 95, 97; Cobb and Grubbs, "Arkansas' Commonwealth College," 299–300; Grubbs, "Cry from the Cotton," 114.

27. "Dick Whitten Resigns as Commonwealth Director: Statement Urges Aid for School," *Fortnightly*, October 1, 1936, 1; Sue Thrasher, "Radical Education in the Thirties," *Southern Exposure* 1, nos. 3 and 4 (Winter 1974): 204–10.

28. Mitchell, *Mean Things*, 64–65.

29. Claude C. Williams Collection, series 1, box 17, folder 21, Archives of Labor and Urban Affairs, WSU; Cobb and Grubbs, "Arkansas' Commonwealth College," 302–3.

30. Williams Collection, series 1, box 1, WSU; Mark Nelson, "Claude and

Joyce Williams: Pilgrims of Justice," *Southern Exposure* 1, nos. 3 and 4 (Winter 1974): 38–50; Cedric Belfrage, *Let My People Go* (London: Gollancz, 1940), 254, 267–73.

31. "Commonwealth Changes," *Time*, August 23, 1937, 30–31; "Announces Reorganization," *Fortnightly*, August 15, 1937, 1; "Reorganization Plan Hailed Nationally," *Fortnightly*, September 1, 1937, 1; Claude Williams, "The Program of Commonwealth College," *Fortnightly*, November 15, 1937, 1.

32. "Commonwealth Begins Fall Quarter as Training School for Labor Leaders" and "College Gives Extension Course at Muskogee," *Fortnightly*, October 15, 1937, 1; "Commonwealth Association Meeting Plans Extensive Program for School" and "College Lecturers Visit STFU Locals," *Fortnightly*, December 15, 1937, 1; "Farm Unions Plan Session at College," *Fortnightly*, January 15, 1938, 1. Mitchell, *Mean Things*, 158, reports that the card-brandishing incident occurred in July 1937, but see Cobb, "Commonwealth College," 220–22.

33. Williams Collection, series 1, box 17, folder 26, WSU.

34. "Southern Tenant Farmers' Union Purges Ranks," *Commoner*, September 1938, 1; Cobb, "Commonwealth College," 225–31; and Cobb and Grubbs, "Arkansas' Commonwealth College," 306–7.

35. Grubbs, *Cry from the Cotton*, 163–64, 173–75, 190–91.

36. Koch and Koch, *Educational Commune*, 184–85.

37. "STFU Purges CIO," *Commoner*, March 1939, 3; Grubbs, *Cry from the Cotton*, 162–92.

38. Koch and Koch, *Educational Commune*, 197–98.

39. Williams Collection, series 1, box 17, folder 21, WSU; "Williams on Tour," *Commoner*, April 1938, 1.

40. Grubbs, *Cry from the Cotton*, 191; Raymond and Charlotte Koch Collection, box 3, folder 18, Archives of Labor and Urban Affairs, WSU; Williams Collection, series 1, box 17, folder 21, WSU.

41. The announcement had no title; see *Commoner*, July 1940, 1; Cobb, "Commonwealth College," 223–31.

42. Cobb, "Commonwealth College," 233–36; "Commonwealth College Ends Stormy Career," *Christian Century* 57 (July 1940): 934; "College Is Fined $2,500," *New York Times*, September 25, 1940, p. 24, col. 4; Koch and Koch, *Educational Commune*, 206–8; and Cobb, "Commonwealth College," 236–43.

43. Aakula is quoted in Hans R. Wasastjerna, *History of the Finns in Minnesota* (New York Mills, Minn.: Northwestern Publishing, 1957), 230; Douglas J. Ollila, Jr., "The Work People's College: Immigrant Education for Adjustment and Solidarity," in *For the Common Good: Finnish Immigrants and the Radical Response to Industrial America*, ed. Michael G. Karni et al. (Superior, Wis.: Tyomies Society, 1977), 110; "Time Passes Duluthian College," *Duluth Herald*, March 8, 1967.

44. Melvyn Dubofsky, *We Shall Be All: A History of the IWW* (New York: Quadrangle, 1969), 462–63, 477–78.

45. Ollila, "Work People's College," 111–12; Arne Halonen, "The Role of Finnish-Americans in the Political Labor Movement" (master's thesis, University of Minnesota, 1945), 114.

46. Correspondence, General, December 22, 1912–October 7, 1949; folder 7, and Correspondence, General, July 13, 1950–May 2, 1959, folder 8, Work People's College Collection, Immigration History Research Center, University of Minnesota; Ollila, "Work People's College," 112–13; Wasastjerna, *History of the Finns*, 229–31.

CHAPTER 8

Achievements of the Labor Colleges

1. For a clear delineation of the expectations of a "typical" labor college student, see Jack Lever, "Labor Student," *Brookwood Review*, October 1925, 12.

2. Joseph Ozanic Collection, series 2, folder 1, Brookwood Labor College Notebook, Labor Archives, West Virginia University. I have taken the liberty of inserting some punctuation. Otherwise, the comments cited are Ozanic's verbatim notes. Also, Brookwood Labor College Collection, box 1, folder 14, Archives of Labor and Urban Affairs, Wayne State University (hereafter WSU).

3. For background on the Progressive Mine Workers, consult Melvyn Dubofsky and Warren Van Tine, *John L. Lewis: A Biography* (New York: Quadrangle, 1977), 169–70.

4. C. Mauritz Erkkila, personal letter to author, March 3, 1983; Sulo Peltola, personal letter to author, November 30, 1982; Fred W. Thompson, personal letter to author, February 4, 1983; Fred W. Thompson, interview with author, October 20, 1984; Archie Brown, personal letter to author, March 29, 1983; Kristen Svanum, "The Work People's College: Where Industrial Unionists Are Efficiently Educated," *Industrial Pioneer* 3 (October 1925): 16; Douglas J. Ollila, Jr., "The Work People's College: Immigrant Education for Adjustment and Solidarity," in *For the Common Good: Finnish Immigrants and the Radical Response to Industrial America*, ed. Michael G. Karni et al. (Superior, Wis.: Tyomies Society, 1977), 107. For information about *Socialisti* and *Tyomies*, refer to George Hummasti, " 'The Working Man's Daily Bread: Finnish-American Working-Class Newspapers, 1900–1921," in *For the Common Good*, ed. Karni et al., 167–94.

5. "Former Students Active in Movement," *Commonwealth College Fortnightly* [hereafter *Fortnightly*], November 15, 1932, 1; Raymond and Charlotte Koch Collection, box 1, folder 2, and box 3, folder 18, Archives of Labor and Urban Affairs, WSU; John M. Glen, *Highlander: No Ordinary School, 1932–1962* (Lexington: University Press of Kentucky, 1988), 48.

6. "Two Commoners Take Positions," *Fortnightly*, July 1, 1931, 1. Other Commoners also attended graduate school. Refer to "Commoner Is Graduate Student at Wisconsin," *Fortnightly*, March 1, 1929, 1; "Degree for Commoner,"

Fortnightly, June 15, 1930, 3; "Barbara Gibbon," *Fortnightly*, September 1, 1930, 3; "Workers' Education Receives Approval," *Fortnightly*, December 1, 1927, 1–3.

7. Marius Hansome, *World Workers' Educational Movements: Their Social Significance* (1931; reprint, New York: AMS Press, 1968), 204; Marius Hansome, "The Development of Workers' Education," in *Workers' Education in the United States*, ed. Theodore Brameld (New York: John Dewey Society, 1941), 60; *Brookwood Labor College Fifteenth Anniversary Review* (Katonah, N.Y.: Brookwood Labor College, 1936), 27–28.

8. James O. Morris, *Conflict within the AFL: A Study of Craft versus Industrial Unionism, 1901–1938* (Ithaca, N.Y.: Cornell University Press, 1958), 106; "Bob Roberts in Prison" and "Southern Grads Framed Then Freed," *Brookwood Review*, October 1933, 2–3; "Students Teach West Virginia Classes," *Brookwood Review*, December 1932, 4; Elizabeth D. Hawes, "The Highlander Folk School," in *Brookwood Fifteenth Anniversary Review*, 40; Len De Caux, *Labor Radical: From the Wobblies to the CIO* (Boston: Beacon Press, 1970), 100–105; Glen, *Highlander*, 26.

9. Jacob S. Potofsky, "Chasing Sweatshops," in *Brookwood Fifteenth Anniversary Review*, 37–38; "Grads Help Union," *Brookwood Review*, May 1933, 1.

10. Thomas B. Brooks, *Toil and Trouble: A History of American Labor* (New York: Dell, 1964), 154; "Women Witnesses Accuse Weir Man: Sisters at NLRB Hearing Say They Were Badly Hurt in Attack on CIO Escort," *New York Times*, August 21, 1937, p. 30, col. 1. Also consult Frank Cormier and William J. Eaton, *Reuther* (Englewood Cliffs, N.J.: Prentice-Hall, 1970), 58, which notes that Brookwood was "financed by wealthy liberals and the more progressive AFL unions that formed the nucleus of the newborn CIO."

11. Katherine Pollack Ellickson Oral History, 1974, Archives of Labor and Urban Affairs, WSU.

12. Tom Tippett, *When Southern Labor Stirs* (New York: Jonathan Cape & Harrison Smith, 1931), covers the specific details of the strikes and Hoffman's role in them. See especially 54–75, 109–55, 157. Also refer to the fine analysis of Irving Bernstein, *The Lean Years: A History of the American Worker, 1920–1933* (Boston: Houghton Mifflin, 1960), 1–43.

13. Rose Pesotta, *Bread upon the Waters* (New York: Dodd, Mead, 1945), 16, 242–43. Pesotta's account of the Akron strike is carried in the *Brookwood Review*, March 1936, 2.

14. Many of the details for this section were derived from Sidney Fine's solid historical account of the strike, *Sit-Down: The General Motors Strike of 1936–1937* (Ann Arbor: University of Michigan Press, 1969), 99.

15. Victor G. Reuther, *The Brothers Reuther and the Story of the UAW* (Boston: Houghton Mifflin, 1976), pp. 125–26; "Reuther, Peace Organizer, Worked in Soviet Union," *Fortnightly*, September 15, 1936, 3.

16. Reuther, *Brothers Reuther*, 133. Also refer to Jean Gould and Lorena

Hickok, *Walter Reuther: Labor's Rugged Individual* (New York: Dodd, Mead, 1972), 100, 101, 112, 148; Cormier and Eaton, *Reuther*, 58–59, 243; Wyndham Mortimer, *Organize: My Life as a Union Man* (Boston: Beacon Press, 1971), 123–41.

17. Fine, *Sit-Down*, 156.

18. Quoted ibid., 164; reprinted with the permission of the Archives of Labor and Urban Affairs, Wayne State University.

19. Reuther, *Brothers Reuther*, 131–32, 143–72, 196–97.

20. "Academic Labor," *Time*, November 29, 1937, 66–67; A. J. Muste, *The Essays of A. J. Muste*, ed. Nat Hentoff (New York: Simon & Schuster, 1967), 152.

21. Ellickson Oral History, WSU.

22. Nick Salvatoré, *Eugene Debs: Citizen and Socialist* (Urbana: University of Illinois Press, 1982), 271.

23. Morris, *Conflict*, 99.

24. Ellickson Oral History, WSU.

25. David Montgomery, *The Fall of the House of Labor: The Workplace, the State, and American Labor Activism, 1865–1925* (New York: Cambridge University Press, 1987), 2.

26. This latter statement is quoted in Dubofsky, *We Shall*, 484, as his closing comment on the IWW.

Bibliography

MANUSCRIPT SOURCES

Brookwood Labor College. Tamiment Institute, Bobst Library, New York University, New York.

Brookwood Labor College Collection. Archives of Labor and Urban Affairs, Wayne State University, Detroit, Michigan.

Calhoun, Arthur W., Collection. Archives of Labor and Urban Affairs, Wayne State University, Detroit, Michigan.

Carnegie Library, Pittsburgh, Pennsylvania.

Commonwealth College Papers. University of Arkansas, Fayetteville.

Ellickson, Katherine Pollak, Collection. Archives of Labor and Urban Affairs, Wayne State University, Detroit, Michigan.

Falkowski, Edward J., Collection. Archives of Labor and Urban Affairs, Wayne State University, Detroit, Michigan.

Golden, Clinton, Papers. Labor Archives, Pennsylvania State University, State College, Pennsylvania.

Industrial Workers of the World Collection. Archives of Labor and Urban Affairs, Wayne State University, Detroit, Michigan.

Koch, Lucien, Collection. Archives of Labor and Urban Affairs, Wayne State University, Detroit, Michigan.

Koch, Raymond and Charlotte, Collection. Archives of Labor and Urban Affairs, Wayne State University, Detroit, Michigan.

New York City Public Library, New York.

Ozanic, Joseph, Collection. West Virginia University, Morgantown, West Virginia.

Williams, Claude C., Collection. Archives of Labor and Urban Affairs, Wayne State University, Detroit, Michigan.

Workers' Education Local 189 Collection. Archives of Labor and Urban Affairs, Wayne State University, Detroit, Michigan.

Work People's College Collection. Immigration History Research Center, University of Minnesota, Saint Paul, Minnesota.

ORAL HISTORIES AND INTERVIEWS

Ellickson, Katherine Pollack. Oral History. Archives of Labor and Urban Affairs, Wayne State University, Detroit, Michigan.

Fernbach, Frank. Oral History. Labor Archives, Pennsylvania State University, State College, Pennsylvania.

Hauben, Ronda. "A Pioneer in Workers' Education: Mark Starr and Workers' Education in Great Britain." *Llafar: The Journal of the Society for the Study of Welsh Labour History* 4, no. 2 (1985): 96–100.

Lawn, Martin. "Mark Starr: Socialist Educator." *Llafur: The Journal of the Society for the Study of Welsh Labour History* 4, no. 2 (1985): 91–96.

"Reminiscences of A. J. Muste." New York: Columbia University Oral History Office, 1965.

Rogin, Lawrence. Interview with author, March 18, 1984.

Saposs, Bertha. Interview with author, March 18, 1984.

"Socialist Movement Project: A. J. Muste." New York: Columbia University Oral History Office, 1967.

Stanley, Lee B. Oral History. Labor Archives, Pennsylvania State University, State College, Pennsylvania.

Starr, Mark, and Helen. Oral History. November 15, 1974, Labor Archives, Pennsylvania State University, State College, Pennsylvania.

Terkel, Studs. *Hard Times: An Oral History of the Great Depression.* New York: Washington Square Books, 1970.

Thompson, Fred W. Interview with author, October 20, 1984.

GOVERNMENT DOCUMENTS

New York Joint Legislative Committee Investigating Seditious Activities. *Revolutionary Radicalism: Its History, Purpose, and Tactics with an Exposition and Discussion of the Steps Being Taken and Required to Curb It.* Albany, N.Y.: J. B. Lyon, 1920.

U.S. Congress, Senate. *Report of the Committee of the Senate upon the Relations between Labor and Capital.* 2 vols. Washington, D.C.: GPO, 1885.

U.S. Congress, Senate. *Reports of the Immigration Commission: Immigrants in Industry, Copper Mining, and Smelting.* Washington, D.C.: GPO, 1911.

U.S. Department of Labor. Bureau of Labor Statistics. *Report on the Condition of Women and Child Wage Earners in the United States.* Washington, D.C.: GPO, 1911.

———. *Summary of the Report on Conditions of Women and Child Wage Earners in the United States.* Bulletin no. 175. Washington, D.C.: GPO, 1916.

REPORTS AND PROCEEDINGS

American Federation of Labor. *Proceedings of the Thirty-Eighth Annual Convention of the American Federation of Labor.* Washington, D.C.: Law Reporter Printing Co., 1918.

———. *Proceedings of the Thirty-Ninth Annual Convention of the American Federation of Labor*. Washington, D.C.: Law Reporter Printing Co., 1919.

———. *Proceedings of the Forty-Second Annual Convention of the American Federation of Labor*. Washington, D.C.: Law Register Printing Co., 1922.

———. *Proceedings of the Forty-Eighth Annual Convention of the American Federation of Labor*. Washington, D.C.: Law Register Printing Co., 1928.

Mann, Horace. *Annual Reports of the Secretary of the Board of Education of Massachusetts for Years 1845–1848*. Boston: Lee and Shepard, 1981.

Workers' Education Bureau. *Proceedings of the First National Conference on Workers' Education in the United States*. New York: WEB, 1921.

UNPUBLISHED THESES AND DISSERTATIONS

Bloom, Jonathan D. "Brookwood Labor College, 1921–1933: Training Ground for Union Organizers." Master's thesis, Rutgers University, 1978.

Cobb, William H. "Commonwealth College: A History." Master's thesis, University of Arkansas, 1960.

Halonen, Arne. "The Role of Finnish-Americans in the Political Labor Movement." Master's thesis, University of Minnesota, 1945.

Honey, Michael. "Labor and Civil Rights in the South: The Industrial Labor Movement and Black Workers in Memphis, 1929–1945." Ph.D. diss., Northern Illinois University, 1986.

Ruff, Allen. " 'We Called Each Other Comrade!': Charles Kerr and the Charles H. Kerr & Company, Publishers, 1886–1928." Ph.D. diss., University of Wisconsin, 1987.

Samson, Gloria Garrett. "Toward a New Social Order—The American Fund for Public Service: Clearinghouse for Radicalism in the 1920s." Ph.D. diss., University of Rochester, 1987.

Schaefer, Robert J. "Educational Activities of the Garment Unions, 1890–1948: A Study in Workers' Education in the International Ladies' Garment Workers' Union and the Amalgamated Clothing Workers of America in New York City." Ph.D. diss., Columbia University, 1951.

Schlicter, Kenneth. "Mechanics' Institutes in America, 1820–1860." Master's research paper, Northern Illinois University, 1974.

Schultz, Dagmar. "The Changing Political Nature of Workers' Education: A Case Study of the Wisconsin School for Workers." Ph.D. diss., University of Wisconsin, 1972.

Teitelbaum, Kenneth N. "Schooling for 'Good Rebels': Socialist Education for Children in the United States, 1900–1920." Ph.D. diss., University of Wisconsin, 1985.

AUTOBIOGRAPHIES AND BIOGRAPHIES

Basen, Neil K. "Kate Richards O'Hare: The 'First Lady' of American Socialism, 1901–1917." *Labor History* 21 (Spring 1980): 165–99.

Belfrage, Cedric. *Let My People Go*. London: Gollancz, 1940.

Brophy, John. *A Miner's Life*. Madison, Wis.: University of Wisconsin Press, 1964.

Cleghorn, Sarah N. *Threescore: The Autobiography of Sarah N. Cleghorn*. 1936. Reprint. New York: Arno Press, 1980.

Cormier, Frank, and William J. Eaton. *Reuther*. Englewood Cliffs, N.J.: Prentice-Hall, 1970.

De Caux, Len. *Labor Radical: From the Wobblies to the CIO*. Boston: Beacon Press, 1970.

DeLeon, Solon. *American Labor Who's Who*. New York: Hauford Press, 1925.

Dubofsky, Melvyn, and Warren Van Tine. *John L. Lewis: A Biography*. New York: Quadrangle, 1977.

Fine, Sidney. *Sit-Down: The General Motors Strike of 1936–37*. Ann Arbor: University of Michigan Press, 1969.

Flynn, Elizabeth Gurley. *The Rebel Girl: An Autobiography*. New York: International Publishers, 1973.

Foner, Philip S., and Sally M. Miller. *Kate Richards O'Hare: Selected Writings and Speeches*. Baton Rouge: Louisiana State University Press, 1982.

Gould, Jean, and Lorena Hickok. *Walter Reuther: Labor's Rugged Individual*. New York: Dodd, Mead, 1972.

Haywood, William D. *The Autobiography of Big Bill Haywood*. New York: International Publishers, 1976.

"Kate Richards O'Hare." *World Tomorrow* 9 (February 1926): 55–56.

Kessler-Harris, Alice. "Organizing the Unorganizable: Three Jewish Women and Their Union." *Labor History* 17 (Winter 1976): 5–23.

Koch, Raymond, and Charlotte Koch. *Educational Commune: The Story of Commonwealth College*. New York: Schocken Books, 1972.

Maurer, James H. *It Can Be Done: The Autobiography of James Hudson Maurer*. New York: Rand School Press, 1938.

Miller, Sally M. "Other Socialists: Native-Born and Immigrant Women in the Socialist Party of America, 1901–1917." *Labor History* 24 (Winter 1983): 84–102.

Mitchell, H. L. *Mean Things Happening in This Land: The Life and Times of H. L. Mitchell, Cofounder of the Southern Tenant Farmers' Union*. Montclair, N.J.: Allanheld, Osmun, 1979.

Mortimer, Wyndham. *Organize: My Life As a Union Man*. Boston: Beacon Press, 1971.

Muste, A. J. *The Essays of A. J. Muste*. Edited by Nat Hentoff. New York: Simon & Schuster, 1967.

Nelson, Mark. "Claude and Joyce Williams: Pilgrims of Justice." *Southern Exposure* 1, no. 3–4 (Winter 1974): 38–50.

Pesotta, Rose. *Bread upon the Waters*. New York: Dodd, Mead, 1945.

Reuther, Victor G. *The Brothers Reuther and the Story of the UAW*. Boston: Houghton Mifflin, 1976.

Robinson, Jo Ann Ooiman. *Abraham Went Out: A Biography of A. J. Muste*. Philadelphia: Temple University Press, 1981.

Salvatoré, Nick. *Eugene Debs: Citizen and Socialist*. Urbana: University of Illinois Press, 1982.

Symes, Lillian. "V. F. Calverton, Socialist." *Modern Quarterly* 12 (Fall 1940): 20–24.

"Who Is This A. J. Muste?" *World Tomorrow* 12 (June 1929): 250–54.

BOOKS

Avrich, Paul. *The Modern School Movement: Anarchism and Education in the United States*. Princeton, N.J.: Princeton University Press, 1980.

Bailyn, Bernard. *Education in the Forming of American Society*. Chapel Hill: University of North Carolina Press, 1960.

Bernstein, Irving. *The Lean Years: A History of the American Worker, 1920–1933*. Boston: Houghton Mifflin, 1960.

Bowles, Samuel, and Herbert Gintis. *Schooling in Capitalist America: Educational Reform and the Contradictions of Economic Life*. New York: Basic Books, 1976.

Boyer, Richard O., and Herbert M. Morais. *Labor's Untold Story*. New York: United Electrical, Radio and Machine Workers of America, 1955.

Brameld, Theodore, ed. *Workers' Education in the United States*. New York: John Dewey Society, 1941.

Bremner, Robert H., ed. *Children and Youth in America: A Documentary History, 1866–1932*. 2 vols. Cambridge, Mass.: Harvard University Press, 1971.

Brooks, Thomas R. *Toil and Trouble: A History of American Labor*. New York: Dell, 1964.

Byington, Margaret. *Homestead: The Households of a Mill Town*. 1910. Reprint. Pittsburgh, Pa.: University of Pittsburgh, Center for International Studies, 1974.

Carlton, Frank Tracy. *Economic Influences on Educational Progress in the United States, 1820–1850*. New York: Teachers College Press, Columbia University, 1965.

Conlin, Joseph. *Bread and Roses Too: Studies of the Wobblies*. Westport, Conn.: Greenwood Press, 1974.

———, ed. *The American Radical Press, 1880–1960*. Westport, Conn.: Greenwood Press, 1974.

Counts, George S. *The Social Composition of Boards of Education: A Study of the Social Control of Public Education*. 1927. Reprint. New York: Arno Press, 1969.

———. *Dare the School Build a New Social Order?* 1932. Reprint. New York: Arno Press, 1969.

Cremin, Lawrence A. *Traditions of American Education*. New York: Basic Books, 1977.

———. *American Education: The National Experience, 1783–1876*. New York: Harper & Row, 1980.

Dewey, John. *Education and the Social Order*. New York: League for Industrial Democracy, 1934.

Dubofsky, Melvyn. *We Shall Be All: A History of the IWW*. New York: Quadrangle, 1969.

Dwyer, Richard E. *Labor Education in the United States: An Annotated Bibliography*. Metuchen, N.J.: Scarecrow Press, 1977.

Entwistle, Harold. *Antonio Gramsci: Conservative Schooling for Radical Politics*. London: Routledge & Kegan Paul, 1979.

Foner, Philip S. *History of the Labor Movement in the United States: The Industrial Workers of the World, 1905–1917*. New York: International Publishers, 1973.

———. *Organized Labor and the Black Worker, 1619–1973*. New York: International Publishers, 1976.

France, Rachel, ed. *A Century of Plays by American Women*. New York: Richards-Posen, 1979.

Freire, Paulo. *Pedagogy of the Oppressed*. New York: Seabury Press, 1970.

Gardiner, James B., ed. *Ordinary People and Everyday Life: Perspectives on the New Social History*. Nashville, Tenn.: American Association of State and Local History, 1983.

Glaspell, Susan. *Plays*. Boston: Small, Maynard, 1920.

Gleason, Arthur. *Workers' Education: American Experiments with a Few Foreign Examples*. New York: Bureau of Industrial Research, 1921.

Glen, John M. *Highlander: No Ordinary School, 1932–1962*. Lexington: University Press of Kentucky, 1988.

Goldstein, Malcolm. *The Political Stage: American Drama and Theatre of the Great Depression*. New York: Oxford University Press, 1974.

Goodwyn, Lawrence. *The Populist Movement: A Short History of the Agrarian Revolt in America*. New York: Oxford University Press, 1978.

Gordon, David, Richard Edwards, and Michael Reich. *Segmented Work, Divided Workers: The Historical Transformation of Labor in the United States*. New York: Cambridge University Press, 1982.

Gramsci, Antonio. *The Modern Prince and Other Writings*. New York: International Publishers, 1978.

Gratten, C. Hartley. *In Quest of Knowledge: A Historical Perspective of Adult Education*. New York: Association Press, 1955.

Green, James R. *Grass-Roots Socialism: Radical Movements in the Southwest, 1895–1943*. Baton Rouge: Louisiana State University Press, 1978.

Grubbs, Donald H. *Cry from the Cotton: The Southern Tenant Farmers' Union and the New Deal*. Chapel Hill: University of North Carolina Press, 1971.

Hall, Covington. *Dreams and Dynamite: Selected Poems*. Edited by David Roediger. Chicago: Charles Kerr, 1985.

Hansome, Marius. *World Workers' Educational Movements: Their Social Significance*. 1931. Reprint. New York: AMS Press, 1968.

Hardman, J. B. S. *American Labor Dynamics: In the Light of Post-War Developments*. 1928. Reprint. New York: Arno Press, 1969.

Harrison, J. F. C. *Learning and Living, 1790–1960: A Study in the History of the English Adult Education Movement*. Toronto: University of Toronto Press, 1961.

Hoare, Quinton, and Geoffrey Nowell Smith. *Selections from the Prison Notebooks of Antonio Gramsci*. New York: International Publishers, 1971.

Hodgen, Margaret. *Workers' Education in England and the United States*. London: Kegan Paul, 1925.

Hogan, David J. *Class and Reform: School and Society in Chicago, 1880–1930*. Philadelphia: University of Pennsylvania Press, 1985.

Hoglund, A. William. *Finnish Immigrants in America, 1880–1920*. Madison: University of Wisconsin Press, 1960.

Karier, Clarence J. *Shaping the American Educational State*. New York: Free Press, 1975.

Karni, Michael G., Matti Kaups, and Douglas J. Ollila, Jr. *The Finnish Experience in the Western Great Lakes Region: New Perspectives*. Turku, Finland: Institute for Migration, 1975.

Karni, Michael G., et al. *For the Common Good: Finnish Immigrants and the Radical Response to Industrial America*. Superior, Wis.: Tyomies Society, 1977.

Katz, Michael B. *Class, Bureaucracy, and Schools: The Illusion of Educational Change in America*. New York: Praeger, 1975.

Katznelson, Ira, and Margaret Weir. *Schooling for All: Class, Race, and the Decline of the Democratic Ideal*. New York: Basic Books, 1985.

Kerrison, Irvine L. H. *Workers' Education at the University Level*. New Brunswick, N.J.: Rutgers University Press, 1951.

Kipnis, Ira. *The American Socialist Movement, 1897–1912*. New York: Columbia University Press, 1952.

Kivisto, Peter. *Immigrant Socialists in the United States: The Case of Finns and the Left*. Rutherford, N.J.: Farleigh Dickinson University Press, 1984.

Kornbluh, Joyce L., and Mary Frederickson, eds. *Sisterhood and Solidarity: Workers' Education for Women, 1914–1984*. Philadelphia: Temple University Press, 1984.

Laslett, John H. M. *Labor and the Left: A Study of Socialist and Radical Influences in the American Labor Movement, 1881–1924*. New York: Basic Books, 1970.

Lawner, Lynne, ed. *Antonio Gramsci: Letters from Prison*. New York: Harper & Row, 1973.

Levin, Nora. *While Messiah Tarried: Jewish Socialist Movements, 1871–1917*. New York: Schocken Books, 1977.

Lorwin, Louis (Levine). *The Women's Garment Workers*. 1924. Reprint. New York: Arno Press, 1969.

McConachie, Bruce A., and Daniel Friedman, eds. *Theatre for Working-Class Audiences in the United States, 1830–1980*. Westport, Conn.: Greenwood Press, 1985.

Montgomery, David. *The Fall of the House of Labor: The Workplace, the State, and American Labor Activism, 1865–1925*. New York: Cambridge University Press, 1987.

Morris, James O. *Conflict within the AFL: A Study of Craft versus Industrial Union-ism, 1901–1938*. Ithaca, N.Y.: Cornell University Press, 1958.

Nelson, Bruce C. *Beyond the Martyrs: A Social History of Chicago's Anarchists, 1870–1900*. New Brunswick, N.J.: Rutgers University Press, 1988.

Norton, Theodore N., and Bertell Ollman, eds. *Studies in Socialist Pedagogy*. New York: Monthly Review Press, 1978.

Paulston, Rolland G. *Nonformal Education: An Annotated International Bibliogra-phy*. New York: Praeger, 1972.

———. *Folk Schools in Social Change: A Partisan Guide to the International Lit-erature*. Pittsburgh, Pa.: University of Pittsburgh Center for International Studies, 1974.

———. *Conflicting Theories of Social and Educational Change: A Typological Review*. Pittsburgh, Pa.: University of Pittsburgh Center for International Studies, 1976.

———, ed. *Other Dreams, Other Schools: Folk Colleges in Social and Ethnic Move-ments*. Pittsburgh, Pa.: University of Pittsburgh Center for International Studies, 1980.

Payne, Elizabeth Anne. *Reform, Labor, and Feminism: Margaret Dreier Robins and the Women's Trade Union League*. Urbana: University of Illinois Press, 1988.

Perkinson, Henry J. *Two Hundred Years of American Educational Thought*. New York: David McKay, 1976.

Pessen, Edward. *Most Uncommon Jacksonians: The Radical Leaders of the Early Labor Movement*. Albany: State University of New York Press, 1967.

Peterson, Paul F. *The Politics of Urban School Reform*. Chicago: University of Chicago Press, 1985.

Pinski, David. *Ten Plays*. New York: Huebsch, 1920.

Poore, Carol J. *German-American Socialist Literature, 1865–1900*. Bern: Peter Lang, 1982.

Rabkin, Gerald. *Drama and Commitment: Politics in the American Theatre of the Thirties*. Bloomington: Indiana University Press, 1964.

Reese, William J. *Power and the Promise of School Reform: Grass-Roots Movements during the Progressive Era*. Boston: Routledge & Kegan Paul, 1986.

Ross, Carl. *The Finn Factor in American Labor, Culture, and Society*. New York Mills, Minn.: Parta Printers, 1977.

Saposs, David J. *Left Wing Unionism*. New York: International Publishers, 1926.

Schneider, Florence H. *Patterns of Workers' Education: The Story of the Bryn Mawr Summer School*. Washington, D.C.: American Council on Public Affairs, 1941.

Schwarztrauber, Ernest E. *Workers' Education: A Wisconsin Experiment*. Madi-son: University of Wisconsin Press, 1942.

Shannon, David A. *The Socialist Party in America: A History*. New York: Macmil-lan, 1955.

Shore, Elliot. *Talkin' Socialism: J. A. Wayland and the Role of the Press in American Radicalism*. Lawrence: University Press of Kansas, 1988.

Sifton, Claire, and Paul Sifton. *1931: A Play*. New York: Farrar & Rinehart, 1931.

Sinclair, Bruce. *Philadelphia's Philosopher Mechanics: A History of the Franklin Institute, 1824–1865*. Baltimore: Johns Hopkins University Press, 1976.

Smith, Hilda W. *Workers at the Bryn Mawr Summer School*. New York: Affiliated Summer Schools for Women Workers, 1929.

Spring, Joel. *Education and the Rise of the Corporate State*. Boston: Beacon Press, 1972.

Starr, Mark. *Workers' Education Today*. New York: League for Industrial Democracy, 1941.

Taylor, Karen M. *People's Theatre in Amerika*. New York: Drama Book Specialists, 1972.

Thernstrom, Stephen, ed. *Harvard Encyclopedia of American Ethnic Groups*. Cambridge: Harvard University Press, 1980.

Thompson, E. P. *The Making of the English Working Class*. New York: Vintage Books, 1963.

Tippett, Tom. *When Southern Labor Stirs*. New York: Jonathan Cape & Harrison Smith, 1931.

Tussey, Jean Y. *Eugene V. Debs Speaks*. New York: Pathfinder Press, 1972.

Van Tine, Warren R. *The Making of the Labor Bureaucrat: Union Leadership in the United States, 1870–1920*. Amherst: University of Massachusetts Press, 1973.

Violas, Paul C. *The Training of the Urban Working Class*. Chicago: Rand McNally, 1978.

Ware, Caroline F. *Labor Education in Universities: A Study of University Programs*. New York: American Labor Education Service, 1946.

Wasastjerna, Hans R. *History of the Finns in Minnesota*. New York Mills, Minn.: Northwestern Publishing Co., 1957.

Weinstein, James. *The Decline of American Socialism in America, 1912–1925*. New York: Monthly Review Press, 1967.

Welter, Rush. *Popular Education and Democratic Thought in America*. New York: Columbia University Press, 1962.

Wertheimer, Barbara Mayer, ed. *Labor Education for Women Workers*. Philadelphia: Temple University Press, 1981.

Williams, Jay. *Stage Left*. New York: Charles Scribner's Sons, 1974.

Williamson, Harold. *Peggy, Carolina Folk-Plays*. Edited by Frederick H. Koch. New York: Henry Holt, 1941.

Wolman, Leo. *The Growth of American Trade Unions, 1880–1925*. 1924. Reprint. New York: Arno Press, 1975.

ARTICLES

Allen, Devere. "A School for Workers' Children." *Nation* 119 (October 15, 1924): 417–18.

Allman, Paula. "Gramsci, Freire, and Illich: Their Contributions to Education for Socialism." In *Radical Approaches to Adult Education: A Reader*, edited by Tom Lovett. London: Routledge, 1988.

Altenbaugh, Richard J. "'Our Children Are Being Trained Like Dogs and Ponies': Schooling, Social Control, and the Working Class." *History of Education Quarterly* 21 (Summer 1981): 213–22.

———. "Proletarian Drama: An Educational Tool of the American Labor College Movement." *Theatre Journal* 34 (May 1982): 197–210.

"Another Attack on Commonwealth." *Christian Century* 54 (January 1937): 83–84.

"The Arkansas Legislature Shows Good Sense." *Christian Century* 52 (April 1935): 501–2.

"Attack on Commonwealth College Renewed." *American Teacher* 21 (January–February 1937): 28–29.

"Back Brookwood!" *World Tomorrow* 15 (December 14, 1932): 558.

Barrett, James R. "Class Formation and Social Reform in Chicago during the Progressive Era." *Educational Theory* 37 (Winter 1987): 81–88.

Brody, David. "The Old Labor History and the New: In Search of an American Working Class." *Labor History* 20 (Winter 1979): 111–26.

"Brookwood." *New Republic* 43 (August 1925): 287–89.

"Brookwood." *American Teacher* 15 (February 1931): 12.

"Brookwood Carries On: Condemned by Council without Hearing." *Labor Age* 17 (November 1928): 3.

"Brookwood Labor College." *School and Society* 22 (November 1925): 585.

"Brookwood Local 189." *American Teacher* 16 (October 1931): 28–29.

"Brookwood Local 189." *American Teacher* 19 (November–December 1934): 28.

"Brookwood Schism." *World Tomorrow* 16 (March 1933): 220.

"Brookwood Splits." *Survey* 69 (April 1933): 165.

Carnoy, Martin. "Education, Economy, and the State." In *Cultural and Economic Reproduction in Education: Essays on Class, Ideology, and the State*, edited by Michael W. Apple. Boston: Routledge & Kegan Paul, 1982.

Cheyney, Alice S. "Workers' Education in the United States." *International Labour Review* 32 (July 1935): 39–59.

Cobb, William H. "Commonwealth College Comes to Arkansas, 1923–25." *Arkansas Historical Quarterly* 23 (Summer 1964): 99–122.

———. "From Utopian Isolation to Radical Activism: Commonwealth College, 1925–1935." *Arkansas Historical Quarterly* 32 (Summer 1973): 132–47.

Cobb, William H., and Donald H. Grubbs. "Arkansas' Commonwealth College and the Southern Tenant Farmers' Union." *Arkansas Historical Quarterly* 25 (Winter 1966): 293–311.

Commons, John R. "Workers' Education and the Universities." *American Federationist* 34 (April 1927): 424–26.

"Commonwealth College Ends Stormy Career." *Christian Century* 57 (July 1940): 934.

"Commonwealth College Local 194." *American Teacher* 18 (October 1934): 28.

"Commonwealth Local 194." *American Teacher* 16 (October 1931): 28–29.

"Commonwealth: New Museum Shows 'Collapse of Capitalism.'" *Newsweek*, February 16, 1935, 27.

"Commonwealth Strike." *Nation* 136 (April 1933): 476.

Cooper, Lyle W. "The American Federation of Labor and the Intellectuals." *Political Science Quarterly* 43 (September 1928): 388–407.

"Correspondence: Dr. Calhoun and Brookwood." *New Republic* 59 (August 1929): 314–15.

"Correspondence: Students on Strike." *Nation* 136 (January 1933): 19.

Cotkin, George. "The Socialist Popularization of Science in America, 1901 to the First World War." *History of Education Quarterly* 24 (Summer 1984): 201–14.

Coy, Harold. "A New Experiment for Workers." *Monthly Labor Review* 20 (June 1925): 10–11.

Cunningham, William. "Commonwealth College: An Educational Mutant." *World Tomorrow* 12 (December 1929): 503–5.

———. "Commonwealth College, Learning and Earning." *AAUP Bulletin* 15 (February 1929): 158.

de Man, Henry. "Labor's Challenge to Education." *New Republic* 2 (March 1921): 16–18.

Dewey, John. "Internal Social Reorganization After the War." *Journal of Race Development (Journal of International Relations)* 8 (April 1918): 385–400.

———. "Labor Politics and Labor Education." *New Republic* 57 (January 9, 1929): 211–14.

Dwyer, Richard E. "Workers' Education, Labor Education, Labor Studies: An Historical Delineation." *Review of Educational Research* 47 (Winter 1977): 179–207.

Dye, Nancy Schrom. "Creating a Feminist Alliance: Sisterhood and Class Conflict in the New York Women's Trade Union League, 1903–1914." In *Our American Sisters: Women in American Life and Thought*, edited by Jean E. Friedman and William G. Shade. Lexington, Mass.: D. C. Heath, 1982.

Ellis, Clifford B. "What Life Means to a Worker: The Story of the Past Winter at the Work People's College." *Industrial Pioneer* 4 (May 1926): 14–18.

Fichlander, Alexander. "Labor Education." *Survey* 45 (January 1921): 542–43.

———. "Workers' Education: Why and What?" *Labor Age* 10 (1921): 49–50.

Fink, Leon, et al. "A Round Table: Labor, Historical Pessimism, and Hegemony." *Journal of American History* 75 (June 1988): 115–62.

"Friends Rally to Brookwood: A. F. of L. Postpones Action." *Labor Age* 17 (October 1928): 21.

Gleason, Arthur. "Workers' Education." *New Republic* 26 (April 1921): 235–37.

Golin, Steve. "Defeat Becomes Disaster: The Paterson Strike of 1913 and the Decline of the IWW." *Labor History* 24 (Spring 1983): 223–48.

Gorelik, Mordecai. "Theatre Is a Weapon." *Theatre Arts Monthly* 18 (June 1934): 420–33.

Grabiner, Gene. "Conservative Labor Leaders Clean House: The Case of Brookwood Labor College." *Educational Theory* 29 (Summer 1979): 195–209.

Gutman, Herbert G. "Class, Status, and the Gilded Age Radical: A Reconsideration." In *Many Pasts: Readings in American Social History, 1865–Present,* edited by Herbert G. Gutman and Gregory S. Kealey. Englewood Cliffs, N.J.: Prentice-Hall, 1973.

———. "Work, Culture, and Society in Industrializing America, 1815–1919." *American Historical Review* 78 (1973): 531–88.

———. "*Labor Age,* 1921–1933." In *The American Radical Press, 1880–1960,* edited by Joseph R. Conlin. Westport, Conn.: Greenwood Press, 1974.

———. "Observations on Selected Trends in American Working-Class Historiography." Manuscript.

Haessler, Carl. "A. F. of L. Convention High Lights: Aggressiveness and Militancy Missing." *Labor Age* 18 (January 1929): 3–4.

Hall, Covington. "Revolt of the Brotherhood." *One Big Union Monthly* 2 (April 1938): 18–22.

Hardman, J. B. S. "Workers' Education." *Forum* 75 (March 1926): 450.

Hart, Joseph K. "Framed." *Survey* 55 (January 1926): 469–70.

"Help for Brookwood." *Nation* 135 (1932): 592.

Hewes, Amy. "Early Experiments in Workers' Education." *Adult Education* 6 (Summer 1956): 211–20.

Hittenrauch, C. "Commonwealth College." In *The College Writer: An Anthology of Student Prose Edited for College Composition Classes,* edited by Warren Bower. New York: Norton, 1935.

Hogue, Richard W. "The Value of Our Own Education." *Labor Age* 13 (May 1924): 12.

———. "The Status of Workers' Education." *Survey* 53 (December 15, 1924): 343.

Howlett, Charles F. "Brookwood Labor College and Worker Commitment to Social Reform." *Mid-America* 61 (January 1979): 47–66.

———. "Brookwood Labor College: Voice of Support for Black Workers." *Negro History Bulletin* 45 (April–June 1982): 38–39.

Johnson, Richard. "Three Problematics: Elements of a Theory of Working-Class Culture." In *Working-Class Culture: Studies in History and Theory,* edited by Joan Clarke, Charles Critcher, and Richard Johnson. London: Hutchinson, 1979.

Katz, Michael B. "The Origins of Public Education: A Reassessment." *History of Education Quarterly* 16 (Winter 1976): 381–407.

Kekkonen, T. "Education as a Social and Mass Problem." *Industrial Pioneer* 2 (November 1924): 42.

Kendall, Kathleen Edgerton. "Education as 'The Balance Wheel of Social

Machinery': Horace Mann's Arguments and Proofs." *Quarterly Journal of Speech* 54 (February 1968): 13–21.

Kingsbury, Susan M. "The Worker at School." *Survey* 53 (February 15, 1925): 600–603.

Knutti, Rosa. "The Work People's College." *Industrial Pioneer* 1 (October 21): 59–61.

———. "The Workers' Play." *Industrial Pioneer* 3 (November 1925): 26–27.

———. "The 'Rain' of Colton and Randolph." *Industrial Pioneer* 3 (December 1925): 26–27.

———. "Knocking the 'el Out of 'Glory.'" *Industrial Pioneer* 3 (February 1926): 22–23.

Koch, Lucien. "Commonwealth College." *Progressive Education* 11 (April–May 1934): 301–2.

Kolehmainen, John I. "The Inimitable Marxists: The Finnish Immigrant Socialists." *Michigan History* 36 (December 1952): 395–405.

"Labor Union Colleges." *Educational Review* 6 (May 1921): 446–49.

Lears, T. J. Jackson. "The Concept of Cultural Hegemony: Problems and Possibilities." *American Historical Review* 90 (1985): 567–93.

Lindsay, M. "Workers' Education That Works." *Survey* 50 (September 25, 1923): 623–34.

Maurer, James H. "Labor's Demand for Its Own Schools." *Nation* 111 (September 1922): 276–78.

"Maurer's Warning." *Labor Age* 18 (May 1929): 3–4.

Miller, Spencer, Jr. "Workers' Education." *Survey* 48 (May 6, 1922): 221–22.

Montgomery, David. "The Conventional Wisdom." *Labor History* 13 (Winter 1972): 107–36.

———. "History As Human Agency." *Monthly Review* 33 (October 1981): 42–48.

———. "New Tendencies in Union Struggles and Strategies in Europe and the United States, 1916–1922." In *Work, Community, and Power: The Experience of Labor in Europe and America, 1900–1925*, edited by James E. Cronin and Carmen Sirianni. Philadelphia: Temple University Press, 1983.

———. "To Study the People: The American Working Class." *Labor History* 2 (Fall 1980): 485–512.

———. "Trends in Working-Class History." *Labour/Le Travail* 19 (Spring 1987): 13–22.

———. "Thinking about American Workers in the 1920s." *International Labor and Working-Class History* 32 (Fall 1987): 4–24.

Murrah, Bill. "Llano Cooperative Colony, Louisiana." *Southern Exposure* 1, nos. 3–4 (Winter 1974): 88–105.

Muste, A. J. "What's It All About?" *Labor Age* 13 (April 1924): 1–4.

———. "Brookwood Labor Institute." *American Federationist* (October 1925): 939–41.

———. "Labor Vacation and Summer Schooling." *Survey* 54 (September 15, 1925): 633–35.

———. "Mitten Management and Union: Some Straightforward Questions." *Labor Age* 17 (May 1928): 4–6.

———. "Shall Workers' Education Perish?" *Labor Age* 18 (January 1929): 5–6.

———. "The Why of Workers' Education." *World Tomorrow* 12 (January 1929): 28–30.

"The Need for Workers' Education: The Work People's College and Its Courses." *Industrial Pioneer* 1 (October 1923): 37–38.

"A New Community School." *Survey* 53 (October 1924): 91–92.

Norton, Helen G. "Drama at Brookwood." *Labor Age* 15 (May 1926): 18–19.

———. "Brookwood's Summer Institutes, 1927." *Survey* 59 (October 15, 1927): 95–96.

———. "Workers' Education Teachers Meet." *Labor Age* 20 (April 1931): 20, 29.

———. "Workers' Education Conferences." *Labor Age* 21–22 (March 1932): 11.

Ozanne, Robert. "Trends in American Labor History." *Labor History* 21 (Fall 1980): 513–21.

Pawa, Jay M. "Workingmen and Free Schools in the Nineteenth Century: A Comment on the Labor-Education Thesis." *History of Education Quarterly* 11 (Fall 1971): 287–302.

"Progressive Labor's Institute: C.P.L.A.'s Educational Conference at Brookwood." *Labor Age* 18 (September 1929): 17–18.

"Recent Developments in Adult Workers' Education in the United States." *Monthly Labor Review* 23 (July 1926): 91–100.

"Red Brains: Left-Wing College Raises Storm-Clouds over Arkansas Ozarks." *Literary Digest* 123 (January 1937): 4–5.

Reese, William J. "Partisans of the Proletariat: The Socialist Working Class and the Milwaukee Schools, 1890–1920." *History of Education Quarterly* 21 (Summer 1980): 3–50.

Reese, William J., and Kenneth N. Teitelbaum. "American Socialist Pedagogy and Experimentation in the Progressive Era: The Socialist Sunday School." *History of Education Quarterly* 23 (Winter 1983): 429–54.

"Report on Political Organization." *Labor Age* 20 (August 1931): 4–6.

Saposs, David J. "Which Way Workers' Education?" *Survey* 62 (May 15, 1929): 250–51.

Seeds, Nellie M. "William W. Fincke: The Founder of Brookwood and Manumit." *Labor Age* 16 (August 1927): 10–11.

Sirola, George. "The Finnish Working People's College." *International Socialist Review* 14 (August 1913): 102–4.

Smith, Hilda W. "Old Trails for New Explorers." *Survey* (March 15, 1929): 802–4.

Smith, Tucker. "Workers Prepare for Power." *Progressive Education* 11 (April–May 1934): 303–6.

Spitz, Laurence. "Let Freedom Ring." *New Theatre* 3 (November 1936): 24–25.

Sterling, Henry. "Labor's Attitude Toward Education." *School and Society* 10 (August 2, 1919): 128–32.

"Subsidizing Red Radicalism." *National Republic* 18 (November 1930): 26–27.

"Summer Schools for Working Women." *School and Society* 26 (September 1927): 326–27.

Svanum, Kristen. "The Work People's College: Where Industrial Unionists Are Efficiently Educated." *Industrial Pioneer* 2 (February 1925): 47–48.

———. "Work People's College." *Industrial Pioneer* 3 (October 1925): 16.

Thompson, E. P. "Time, Work-Discipline, and Industrial Capitalism." *Past and Present* 38 (1967): 56–97.

Thompson, Fred W. "School Days at Work People's College." *One Big Union Monthly* 2 (September 1937): 18–20.

Thrasher, Sue. "Radical Education in the Thirties." *Southern Exposure* 1, nos. 3–4 (Winter 1974): 204–10.

Thrasher, Sue, and Leah Wise. "The Southern Tenant Farmers' Union." *Southern Exposure* 1, nos. 3–4 (Winter 1974): 5–8.

Todd, Helen. "Why Children Work: The Children's Answer." *McClure's Magazine* 40 (November 1912–April 1913): 68–79.

"Training of Labor Leaders in the United States." *International Labour Review* 8 (July 1923): 138–139.

"Tucker Smith Heads Brookwood." *World Tomorrow* 16 (July 1933): 441.

Vinovskis, Maris A. "Horace Mann on the Economic Productivity of Education." *New England Quarterly* 43 (1970): 550–71.

"What Brookwood Means." *Nation* 127 (September 1928): 241.

"Whither Brookwood." *Labor Age* 21–22 (February–March 1933): 14–17.

"Work People's College." *Industrial Pioneer* 1 (October 1921): 59–61.

"Work People's College." *One Big Union Monthly* 2 (April 1938): 14–15.

"Workers' College at Katonah, N.Y." *Monthly Labor Review* 14 (May 1922): 1084.

"Workers' Education and Training." *Monthly Labor Review* 33 (1931): 1403–5.

"Workers' Schools." *Elementary School Journal* 26 (1926): 571–72.

Index